HOLISTIC BIOETHICS

Holistic Bioethics

JUDE THADDAEUS BUYONDO

WIPF & STOCK · Eugene, Oregon

HOLISTIC BIOETHICS

Copyright © 2024 Jude Thaddaeus Buyondo. All rights reserved. Except for brief quotations in critical publications or reviews, no part of this book may be reproduced in any manner without prior written permission from the publisher. Write: Permissions, Wipf and Stock Publishers, 199 W. 8th Ave., Suite 3, Eugene, OR 97401.

Wipf & Stock
An Imprint of Wipf and Stock Publishers
199 W. 8th Ave., Suite 3
Eugene, OR 97401

www.wipfandstock.com

PAPERBACK ISBN: 979-8-3852-1747-2
HARDCOVER ISBN: 979-8-3852-1748-9
EBOOK ISBN: 979-8-3852-1749-6

10/29/24

Dear Dad, it is over a year since you eternally joined that anamnetic holistic solidarity with our beloved ancestors! Salutations from your adorable family, especially Mum, little Jude, Caroline, and my charming twin!

An ethics sympathetically respecting nonhuman animals,
an ethics of anamnetic solidarity,
a eco-theological bioethics founded on the relational Other
as its theological heart
is our solemn pursuit today.

Contents

Preface | ix

Acknowledgments | xi

List of Abbreviations and Acronyms | xii

1   In Search of a Holistic Bioethics | 1

PART I   From Ethics of Nonhuman Animals to Complementing Bioethical Principlism with an African Approach of Solidarity | 5

2   Solidarity in Bioethical Principlism | 7

3   An African Approach to Holistic Bioethics | 63

PART II   Holistic Solidarity, the Relational Other, and Eco-theological Bioethics | 125

4   Towards Holistic Solidarity | 127

5   Conclusion | 213

Bibliography | 217

Preface

Considering several criticisms from numerous scholars on bioethical inequalities, from an African relational social reality of looking at the whole life as a unity, a life that incorporates the three-dimensional community and all life forces surrounding it, the book before you uniquely proposes an African normative approach of "holistic bioethics." The proffered holistic bioethics is a *modest contribution* towards integral interconnected local-global bioethics, which not only goes beyond some African scholarship that emphasizes the local significance of African approaches to bioethical interventions, nor simply emphasizes the nonconformity to Western cultural academic discourses, but also goes further than the principlistic common morality of Beauchamp and Childress, as well as other Western principle-based approaches. In a further practical attempt to answer how principlistic approaches can be complemented, both locally and globally, I tender a holistic approach. Although the fundamental holistic approach I propose appreciates cultural commonalties across sub-Sarahan Africa (SSA), it appreciates them not as abstractly self-validating in themselves, but rather validated by reference to their relational augmentation of life, that is, the extent to which they practically promote holistic solidarity.

The African moral thought, therefore, of the interconnectedness of all beings, which translates into the normative attitude of holistic solidarity, suggests already that a holistic sense of life would be a unifying bioethical approach that could function as a penetrative bridge between universalized principlism and the bioethical discourse in Africa. The holistic African imperative of solidarity penetrates not only the anthropocentric sense (interpersonal and humanistic solidarity), but also the structural-universal sense (solidarity between global institutions, generations, and communities of nations) and the cosmic-religious sense (which includes the biocentric sense within the community of living things—"ecological solidarity"—and the community of nonliving things). Therefore, a holistic solidarity extends to the community of institutions and nations, biodiversity and ecology, the created living and nonliving entities, the living, the living dead, those not yet born, the victims of the present, the victimized of the past, etc. In this regard, holistic bioethics is far broader than the anthropocentric limitations depicted in most principlistic biomedical approaches.

Vienna, July 8, 2024
Mag. Dr. Jude Thaddaeus Buyondo
Department of Systematic Theology and Ethics
Faculty of Catholic Theology, University of Vienna

Acknowledgments

From my heart, I am profoundly thankful to my friends: Maxmillian Mittmansgruber, Sebastian Harwardt, Thomas Schenk—indeed, I am indebted to you all and those I have not mentioned here.

I am extremely thankful to Gerfried-Werner-Hunold Stiftung for generously funding my research stays in Europe, Africa, and USA, and the eventual realization of this publication.

Mag. Dr. Jude Thaddaeus Buyondo

List of Abbreviations and Acronyms

AIDS	acquired immunodeficiency syndrome
AD	Anno Domini (in the year of the Lord)
BCE	Before Christian Era (a year before the birth of Jesus Christ), before Common Era, or before Current Era
BC	Before Christ
ca.	Circa, around, or approximately
DNA	Deoxyribonucleic acid, the biological uniqueness of each species
ECMO	Extracorporeal membrane oxygenation
EEA	European Economic Area
ET	Embryo transfer
EU	European Union
FAO	Food and Agriculture Organization of the United Nations
FGM	Female genital mutilation/cutting
FT	"*Fratelli Tutti*: On Fraternity and Social Friendship." By Pope Francis. Vatican, Oct. 3, 2020. https://www.vatican.va/content/francesco/en/encyclicals/documents/papa-francesco_20201003_enciclica-fratelli-tutti.html
H3Africa	Human Heredity and Health in Africa
HIV	Human immunodeficiency virus
HRE	Health research ethics
HvTSt	*Hervormde teologiese studies*

LIST OF ABBREVIATIONS AND ACRONYMS

IAB		International Association of Bioethics
IBC		International Bioethics Committee (of UNESCO)
Int		*Interpretation*
IUCN		International Union for Conservation of Nature
IVF		In vitro fertilization
LCL		Loeb Classical Library
LS		"*Laudato Si'*: On Care for Our Common Home." By Pope Francis. Vatican, May 24, 2015. https://www.vatican.va/content/francesco/en/encyclicals/documents/papa-francesco_20150524_enciclica-laudato-si.html
PBE		*Principles of Biomedical Ethics.* By Tom L. Beauchamp and James F. Childress. 8th ed. New York: Oxford University Press, 2019
POP		Persistent organic pollutant
RECs		Research ethics committees
SMC		Safe male circumcision
SOPs		Standard operating procedures
TRC		Truth and Reconciliation Commission
TS		*Theological Studies*
UDBHR		*Universal Declaration on Bioethics and Human Rights.* By UNESCO. Paris, UNESCO, 2006. http://unesdoc.unesco.org/images/0014/001461/146180e.pdf
UNAIDS		Joint United Nations Programme on HIV/AIDS
UNEP		United Nations Environment Programme
UNESCO		United Nations Educational, Scientific and Cultural Organization
VS		"*Veritatis Splendor.*" By Pope John Paul II. Vatican, Aug. 6, 1993. https://www.vatican.va/content/john-paul-ii/en/encyclicals/documents/hf_jp-ii_enc_06081993_veritatis-splendor.html
WHO		World Health Organization
WMA		World Medical Association
WWF		World Wildlife Fund

1

In Search of a Holistic Bioethics

HOLISTIC BIOETHICS AS RESPECTFUL SYMPATHETIC LOVE TOWARD THE RELATIONAL OTHER

The study bilaterally aims at finding out more about how the universalized bioethical principles (Western moral thought) could be more solidarily adapted through local approaches (African religious moral thought), on the one side; while on the other side, the universalized approach to bioethics can also be more informed by local values, so that, bioethics would be more inclusively and comprehensively applied to the academia, the contemporary world, the global community, and ameliorate the flourishing of the cosmic[1] (ecological)-religious life at large.

Consequently, in this whole investigation, I ask and attempt to answer *how bioethical principlism can be complemented so that we could unite the African (religious) approach to bioethics from a universally oriented principlism*. In trying to answer this question partly, African scholars wonder whether we cannot additionally appeal to an African *modest* contribution to mitigate global bioethical inequalities. The broad question is whether we cannot welcome an all-inclusive African relational approach to life, which could be modernly translatable into the virtue of holistic solidarity, i.e., extending respectful sympathy to all creation and life forces. This is because we all share, inclusive of all entities, an equal vulnerability to bioethical challenges, whereby solidarity can become either a normative harnessing principle or one of the additional approaches to the traditional Western approach to bioethics.[2] This work aims at investigating to which extent an

---

1. By cosmic, I refer to the natural ecological life of the universe.
2. See Tangwa et al., "Global health inequalities," 242. The work keeps in mind the

ethics that builds on the African holistic understanding could develop into holistic bioethics and enable a genuine dialogue between African and Western bioethical thoughts.

Developing holistic bioethics is to promote an integral life in the understanding of black Africans. This means, it would be a moral cost if the vital energy within every creature isn't tapped as we work towards "promoting life," since for black Africans, nothing is known to be lifeless. And since all creation shares in the life principle—and on condition that this hierarchical participation of all phenomena aims at (conversion to) harmony—then we can say that life across all creation and systems of collaboration can be abundantly or fully promoted, first of all, by human beings. Thusly, the life principle as envisaged by the African relational moral thought includes, not only the living things, but rather everyone and everything wholly. So, for an African, we can reliably infer, that human survival is implicated in the survival of all entities and functioning systems across the life principle. Furthermore, this confirms the interdependence of all cosmic beings, besides human beings collaborating with all universal partners. It means we cannot do bioethics less of this "holistic" tone. As a consequence, African social reality is characterized with a *holistic cosmic-ecological-religious outlook*, which appreciates a harmonious relationship with the whole natural world as a functioning cooperation (unity).[3] However the challenge to which some Western and African scholarships are exposed remains—given the holistic nature of the African attitude of the interconnectedness of life—an African concept of bioethics needs neither to be restricted to the local realities only (over-stressing the Africanness of bioethics), nor to the community of the living only, nor simply the natural world only, but rather also embrace and share in the holistic anamnetic solidarity of the invisible community—think of the victimized ancestors of the historical past—moreover, not only with the local but also with the universal communal partners. The sense of *anamnetic poiēsis* (reestablishing) is part of the life of Black Africans in which they call to mind the real presence of their ancestors and the unborn as they practically live out their contemporary life of solidarity.[4]

I proffer a holistic African understanding of solidarity, extending respectful sympathy and friendliness to the broader communities of all

---

four principle-approach developed by Tom L. Beauchamp and James F. Childress in their *magnum opus, Principles of Biomedical Ethics* (PBE).

3. Mkhize, "Ubuntu-Botho Approach to Ethics," 33–40; Sindima, *Ethics in Africa*, 169, 171; Bujo, *An African Ethic*, 103, 167–174; Kelbessa, "Environmental Philosophy," 323; Behrens, *Environmental Ethics*; Ilogu, *Interaction of Christianity and Ibo Culture*, 26, 128.

4. Bujo, *An African Ethic*, 34–36; Bujo, *Differentiations in African Ethics*, 433.

entities. My approach is *in dialogue with* but gets beyond challenges not only from principlism itself, but also from some elements of numerous conclusive evidence from evolutionary science, scientific experiments by cognitive ethologists as well as from results of neuroscience. With the help of scientific findings, evidence confirms a shared heritage and affinity, shared cognitive capacities— atleast all pointing to a minimal and decent shared moral system, making nonhuman entities to deserve *sympathetic respectful love* from our human community systems.[5]

In confirming this shared heritage and affinity, I strongly appreciate this metaphysical interconnectedness as presented in the African religious moral thought. Besides, I argue for holistic bioethics understood by appreciating the *theological heart of the Other* as the core substance of theological bioethics. I argue not only in conversation with an African anthropocentric understanding of solidarity—my humanity is co-substantively bestowed upon the other and me—but also remain in dialogue with Emmanuel Levinas' "ethics of the other," the stranger, and the encyclical *Fratelli tutti* that opens our ethical eyes in the recent Covid-19 pandemic to the failure in interstate human fraternities and the urgent need to cultivate an ethics of fraternal global solidarity that would ground a realizable theological heart of bioethics of the *other* as my an inevitable neighbor. Here the African moral thought re-echoes once again that the theological heart of theological bioethics cannot simply be limited to my human neighbor but rather broadly incorporates the *holistic Other*.

METHOD AND PROCEDURE OF THE INVESTIGATION

The investigation makes use of systematic and hermeneutical methods to re-appraise scientific scholarships in its effort to propose a holistic approach to bioethics.

In grounding holistic bioethics, the book initially explores ethics of nonhuman animals at length. Evidence shows that nonhuman animals deserve our moral concern in our holistic search for functional bioethics. Establishing the status and standing of nonhuman entities in our pursuit of holistic bioethics essentially demands an approach that never precludes any creature or life force.

Though with challenges from bioethical principlism and some elements of principle based evolutionary science, cognitive ethologists, and neuroscience, the book suggests further an African approach to a holistic

---

5. See Bradie, "The Moral Life of Animals," 554, 558–59, 570–71.

solidarity of respectful sympathy towards all other communities of nonhuman entities.

The book assumes that the solutions to global religious-cosmic-ecological inequalities require a holistic dialogue with all moral approaches as equal partners, and all created nature, supporting a normative translation from the African understanding of the interconnectedness of life to a broader holistic approach of inclusive solidarity.

I further demonstrate how the African understanding of solidarity can be expressed with the help of Levinas' account of responsibility to the stranger as well the encyclical letter *Fratelli Tutti*'s emphasis of the *other* as my neighbor. Without excluding everything and every life force, the theological heart as the broader "Other," is further understood essentially by Black Africans to include all the triad-community members not forgetting the ancestors and victimized of history with whom we necessarily need to reconcile our present life, in order to achieve a holistic healing and all-encompassing solidarity. Lastly, I write off my conclusive recommendations.

PART I

From Ethics of Nonhuman Animals to Complementing Bioethical Principlism with an African approach of Solidarity

ABSTRACT OF PART I

In response to the critique of bioethical principlism in an African context, to which diverse disordered exploitations of the Other are predominant, in this chapter, I suggest *holistic bioethics* as a response to these various exploitations of the Other. Holistic bioethics goes further than stressing the Africanness of African bioethics. It is mutually informed by the true lived social reality of Black Africans (*African moral thought*) as well as obvious elements of scientific conclusive evidence from evolutionary science, scientific experiments by cognitive ethologists as well as the results from neuroscience. Relying on the African approach to moral thought, where no creation is lifeless, we can scarcely talk of holistic bioethics without granting a status to all created entities in their *hierarchies* (hierarchy of forces) as we endeavor to establish a more inclusive functional bioethics. It is the reason *part I* primarily discusses the position of other nonhuman entities, their moral status or moral standing in relation to their human siblings.

Further, on the one hand, *part I* suggests that the main approach to universalized principlism, broadly stemming from Western cultural approaches, can be complemented (think of a roundtable) with the normative idea of holistic solidarity (moving from local contexts to general globalized inclusive principles) arising from the relational social realities of Black Africans, understood as the African moral thought. On the other hand, *part I* proposes that principlism can *richly inform contextual realities* so that domestication, integration, indigenization, and contextualization of bioethical principlism is more ably effective within the host cultures (from generalized approaches to local approaches). One important issue is to blend and adapt principlism to the host culture, by letting it be consistent with the social-religious realities, incorporate and balance it with different cultural values against imperialism or any cultural superiority. As the chapter partly reacts to the exploited relationships (the *Other*), it assumes that the solutions to global bioethical inequalities require a holistic approach to bioethics, an approach that does not seek support from but rather remains in *a dynamic conversational palaver constitutive of a genuine dialogue* between bioethical principlism, international declarations, other sciences, and the cultural worlds of the both the Western and African moral thoughts. For that reason, in *part I*, I tellingly discuss rich contributions of principlism and other sciences in awarding moral status to nonhuman entities and later on answer how bioethical principlism can be complemented through the African idea of solidarity, both locally and globally. I will begin with the general understanding of solidarity.

2

Solidarity in Bioethical Principlism

PRINCIPLISTIC SOLIDARITY

Universalized Understanding of Solidarity

I will begin by explaining how solidarity is generally universally understood in more principle-based declarations. In 2005, UNESCO accepted the universal bioethical principle and human rights of Article 13 and 24 (solidarity) of the Universal Declaration of Bioethics and Human Rights (UDBHR).[1] For the first time in the history of international declarations in bioethics, solidarity gained the status of a universal ethical principle. The UDBHR was accepted unanimously by all member states (without any notated dissentient vote, reserve or qualification),[2] making it the only one to which almost all the governments in the world wholly committed themselves.[3] Just like in bioethical principlism, the "Foreword" of the UDBHR described its content as "universal principles based on shared ethical values" (UNESCO 2006)—also known as "common morality."[4] Though common morality was emphasized, there seems to be an impression of similar mistakes as already discussed pertaining to the Universal Declaration of Human Rights of 1948 whose approach to human rights didn't fit non-Western cultures. Likewise, the drafting process of UDBHR between 2003–2005 was not a common agreement neither, since it registered some shortcomings, for example, of

---

1. UNESCO, *Universal declaration on bioethics and human rights*.
2. IBC, *Report of the IBC*; Henk and Jean, "Introduction," 17.
3. Rheeder, "Solidarity as a global bioethical principle," 1; UNESCO, *Records of the general conference*, 3–21.
4. Rheeder, "Solidarity as a global bioethical principle," 2; UNESCO declaration on bioethics 2005.

religiously upheld universal ideas. Studies note one short meeting, which was granted to religions (Islam, Confucianism, Buddhism, Hinduism, Roman Catholicism and Judaism) in order to make an official contribution. Given the short time, two years before the draft was presented before the General Assembly for approval, some relevant actors like the Protestant tradition were not consulted, while others did not feel represented by the experts involved.[5] If we are to *found* a universal approach to bioethical principles on *shared values*,[6] it cannot be some specific way of life, but rather a contribution of ethical values from multiple customary moralities. For instance, if the African holistic approach to solidarity is not part of the shareable minimum values, would the ultimate declared common morality be commonly binding to them or locally be well received? To give a quick answer, if local approaches fail, from their own moral point of view, to successfully contribute to the shared bioethical values, that alone would disharmoniously break apart their originally well-ordered local sociality.

Another moral challenge with the universalized sense of solidarity is the strong emphasis of anthropocentrism similar to the understanding in bioethical principlism. The official UNESCO education guide, *The Bioethics Core Curriculum 1*, defines solidarity as a moral value oriented towards collective care of the vulnerable members of the community to allow them to experience a mutual sense of belonging. Solidarity in this sense is humanitarian.[7] So a humanitarian solidarity is quite limited in its audience and implies a strong anthropocentrism as spread throughout Article 13 of the UNESCO declaration on bioethics 2005: "Solidarity among human beings and international cooperation towards that end are to be encouraged." Beyond humanitarian relationships, solidarity is extended to cooperation within structural systems like towards states, as elaborated in Article 24, clause 3 of the UNESCO declaration on bioethics 2005: "States should respect and promote solidarity between and among States, as well as individuals, families, groups and communities, with special regard for those rendered vulnerable by disease or disability or other personal, societal or environmental conditions and those with the most limited resources." Two aspects

5. Henk and Jean, "Introduction," 31; Tham, "Introduction: The principle of vulnerability, 1–7, 2–3; IBC, *Eleventh session (of the) IBC*, 2–4. Gallagher, "Human vulnerability in healthcare and research," 135–41; Ten Have, *Global bioethics*, 102; Rheeder, "Solidarity as a global bioethical principle," 1.

6. John Rawls acknowledges pluralism as a permanent historical reality, where each human has a view of God and life, right and wrong, good and bad. Diverse ethical traditions or groups can support shared values, but each from its own point of view, confirmed by one's own moral grounds, as part of their own moral system. Rawls, *Political liberalism*, 134–44; Rheeder, "Solidarity as a global bioethical principle," 2.

7. UNESCO, *Bioethics core curriculum: Section 1*, 45.

of solidarity are emphasized, one *towards humans* and the other towards *international networks*. In UDBHR, human dignity, in Article 3 and Article 2(c), is emphasized, while in reference to Articles 13 and 24 as cited above, as well as in *The Bioethics Core Curriculum*, solidarity is situated "among and between" human beings, given that humans not only reciprocally share collective identity, but they are also objects of vulnerability.[8] In relation to these two aspects, solidarity in the UDBHR further implies health which is also basically oriented to human relationships and their broader networks. The IBC of UNESCO discusses Article 14, "Social responsibility and health," of the UDBHR in relation to Article 13 on "solidarity and co-operation," emphasizing that solidarity has to promote qualitative human health.[9] In addition to *The Bioethics Core Curriculum 1*, solidarity and cooperation are understood as intrinsic values concerned with the well-being of the vulnerable humans.[10] Moreover studies show that cooperation along solidarity is used together for the first time as a universal principle in the UNESCO declaration. It is clear in both Articles 13 and 24, which connect solidarity and (international) active cooperation, though seemingly limited to the wellbeing of humans, they are atleast toward a common end of individuals, groups and countries.[11] Consequently, from the UDBHR (Articles 13 and 24) and the UNESCO Bioethics Core Curriculum 1, one can atleast deduce three categories of existence: The individual existence, collective existence (states, groups, communities), and one large international/universal community/collectivity (international cooperation or global community).[12] The moral challenge is to repeatedly associate existence, health, international cooperation with only human vulnerability and benefit, which limits the broad theme of solidarity to a few species and systems that benefit humans. Moreover, in article 3(2), the UNESCO declaration on bioethics 2005 emphasizes how "the interests and welfare of the individual should have priority over the sole interest of science or society." Besides, throughout the declaration, for instance articles 5-9, the mightiness of an autonomous individual

---

8. Rheeder, "Solidarity as a global bioethical principle," 3-4. Ten Have, *Global bioethics*, 216-18.

9. Rheeder, "Solidarity as a global bioethical principle," 5; UNESCO declaration on bioethics 2005; IBC, *On social responsibility and health*; IBC, *On the principle of the sharing of benefits*, 7.

10. Rheeder, "Solidarity as a global bioethical principle," 5-6; Ten Have, *Global bioethics*, 218-20; UNESCO, *Bioethics core curriculum: Section 1*, 54.

11. Rheeder, "Solidarity as a global bioethical principle," 5; Ten Have, *Global bioethics*, 217-18; see also UNESCO, *Bioethics core curriculum: Section 1*; UNESCO Chair in Bioethics, *Bioethics for judges* (Israel); IBC, *On the principle of the sharing of benefits*, 7.

12. Rheeder, "Solidarity as a global bioethical principle," 3.

legitimates what ethical choices are which is in contrast to the African social reality of the community palaver. In its indispensable pursuance of life, the African palaver does neither mean that the individual must blindly or passively follow the community, nor must the individual surrender her identity, creativity, freedom, and conscience to be crushed by the community. Such a cluster of limitations (over emphasis of individual determinations) in the globalized approach to solidarity seem no different to what is assembled in the universalized bioethical principlism. Taken from the face value, what is underemphasized in universalized principlism, is overemphasized in the contextual richness of other cultural moralities, such as the African moral thought in contrast to bioethical principlism as I will show below.

Is the African Approach more a Bottom-up approach? While Bioethical Principlism a Top-down approach?

Majorly, bioethics works deductively or inductively, making us to standardly talk about top-down models and bottom-up models respectively. I would generally categorize bioethical principlism as a top-down model, since it works deductively via structures of general normative codes, just like mathematicians, to formulate theories, moral standards, principles, healthy policies, rules, etc. In my earlier book, *The Critique of Bioethical Principlism in Contrast to an African Approach to Bioethics*, I noted how some critics such as Clouser and Gert[13] look at bioethical principles as too abstract, too general, too vague, too indeterminate, and unsystematically related to each other in guiding moral action, i.e., in circumstances when confronted with bioethical conflicts. Surely different scholarships have tried restructuring this top-down model of principlism. For example, Henry Richardson proposed replacing bioethical principlism (deductive subsumption and balancing) with specification just like in pragmatism.[14] For Richardson, the two dominant theories in bioethics—principlism, put forward by Beauchamp and Childress in PBE, and common morality, put forward by Gert, Culver and Clouser in *Bioethics: A Return to Fundamentals*—are deficient because they employ balancing rather than specification to resolve conflicting disputes between principles or rules. In Bernard Gert et al's article: "Common Morality versus Specified Principlism: Reply to Richardson," they show that the major problem with principlism, or the specified principlism of Richardson, is that it conceives of morality as being composed of free-standing principles, rather than as common morality conceives it, as

---

13. Clouser and Gert, "A Critique of Principlism," 219–36.
14. See Richardson, "Bioethical principles," 285–307.

being a complete public system, composed of rules, ideals, morally relevant features, and a procedure for determining when a rule can be justifiably contravened. It is why Bernard Gert et al., just like Thomas Hobbes, believe that "truth arises more easily from error than from confusion" that is inherent in principlism.[15] To cater for critics and refine their approach, Childress and Beauchamp buttress principlism by the method of reflective equilibrium. Building from John Rawls's theory of reflective equilibrium—bringing considered judgements, principles, and background theories into a state of equilibrium or harmony—Beauchamp and Childress try emphasizing coherence as an exiting strategy from confusion, or rather from the war zone. Though they aim at achieving a reflective equilibrium and an overall coherence amidst contingent conflicts, specifications and so on,[16] their approach actually creates more methodological upheavals and *confusions* in the war zone.[17] To loosen these confusions and achieve practical coherence, principlism supplements the model of specification alongside the model of balancing with an intention of reducing on bulkiness and unwieldiness of the normative system—that would have included millions of rules. Nevertheless, indeterminacy remains despite specification and balancing, given that one moral group (principlists) may be justified in reaching a conclusion that another group (customary moralists) is justified in rejecting.[18] Even when a customary community holds onto certain substantive beliefs that are incorrect to some, their cultural position may have all good reasons to be sustained on their substantive beliefs as accurately understood by them. The

15. Gert et al., "Common Morality versus Specified Principlism," 308–22.

16. See Beauchamp and Childress, PBE, 440, 443–44, 457–58; wide reflective equilibrium is not a satisfactory approach for justifying moral beliefs and propositions, given that it is the most prominent version of coherentism. Strong, "Reflective equilibrium in bioethics," 123–40.

17. "Recently, when I was a Fellow in the Program in Ethics and the Professions at Harvard, I was quite astounded to learn from other Fellows that the field of bioethics was in a state of methodological upheaval, fractured along many fault lines . . . . They portrayed an intellectual war zone, reminiscent of evolutionary theory or paleontology, where there are many bones to pick. When I expressed my surprise, I was chided. How 'out of it' could I be? Had I not heard that 'principlism' (a position held by Beauchamp and Childress) had been routed 'from above,' by advocates of 'theory' (like Clouser and Gert and Green) and, more effectively, ambushed 'from below,' by contextualists (like Hoffmaster) and their allies, the casuists (like Jonsen and Toulmin)? Had I not heard that 'theory' was out, that 'deductivism' and other 'top–down' approaches were defeated in favour of 'bottom up' ones? The battle was so advanced that new rescue efforts for old fortifications had already been mounted, like Richardson's 'specifying norms' or DeGrazia's 'specified principlism.' I was abashed. I had not noticed that I was working in a war zone and that defending or applying a moral principle put me at risk of taking a sniper's bullet." Daniels, "Wide Reflective Equilibrium," 96–114.

18. See Beauchamp and Childress, PBE, 22–25.

open question however is how far can the reflective equilibrium coherently bring the widely considered pluralistic substantive beliefs in cooperation? How can abstract theoretical coherence necessarily yield into practical coherence? Aren't historical immoral incoherencies from exploitive biomedical interventions in Africa, slavery, racism, partition of Africa, colonialism stemming from the said coherence?

In contrast to principlism, the African approach to bioethics works largely inductively, majorly as a bottom-up model, or to put it differently, this model works from contextual cases, cultural substantive beliefs, particular judgements, analogies and so on. This is evident in African scholarships, since in their interpretation of the African moral thought, while grounding a more holistic African approach to biomedical ethics, they derive content from cultural, epistemological, relational ontology, and community contextual social realities. Africanists believe, it is one way we can successfully contextualize bioethical principles in different cultural settings without the fear of hegemonic domination, top-bottom exploitation, marginalization, enslavement, etc.[19] When Black Africans think inductively by being context-sensitive, some may think, it is on the whole no different from *casuistry* that is not only case (*casus*) based, but consistently recommends argument by analogy from paradigm cases.[20] But the African thought is uniquely more inclusively comprehensive than casuistry since it handles contextual cases in relatedness to their interactive triad-community life, which hardly has chances of being contextually overridden as it is in casuistry. Albert Jonsen and Stephen Toulmin, the other rivals of principlism as well as the main proponents of casuistry maintain that moral judgements are frequently made with no appeal to principles, similar to the discussed African ethical approach. To give an example, in practical paradigmatic cases of the African community palaver as it reconciles moral conflicts between community members, it must be understood that in the process of enactment of proverbs as raw materials and compendia of varied indigenous moral knowledge, the relatedness of the three-community dimension in form of a unionized vitalistic energy is relationally promoted. In partial dialogue with the African ethic, the casuists insist that moral certitude resides not at

---

19. See Tangwa and Henk, "Colony of Genes," 1041–42.

20. Casuistry focuses on the circumstances of particular cases rather than on the application of ethical theories and principles. Jonsen, "Casuistry," 237–51, especially 237, 250; We may find something resembling the *phronesis* that alone can render reasonable and prudent decisions about particular moral perplexities (appreciate circumstances). Jonsen, "Problem for Casuistry," 37–49, especially 37, 47–48; Casuistry in medical ethics has been criticized too. Strong, "Critiques of Casuistry," 395–411; Cudney, "Casuistry from principlism," 205–29.

the top in theoretical principles; but at the bottom, in consensually shared perceptions about precedent cases, eventually facilitating analogy from paradigm cases.[21] However in order to save the life of biomedical ethics and its questions from being too abstract and general,[22] the African approach to bioethics inductively proceeds relationally from concrete practical cases but it *doesn't end there.*

Given that we do not have one kind of bioethical problem but many kinds, a division of ethical labor is practical to parallelly tap various contributions as many as they are pluralistic approaches in bioethics. Otherwise sticking to one cultural approach would simply be a contemporary rehearsal of an ancient unsolved problematic. It is because most ethical problem solving can neither be top down nor bottom up but must be multifaceted and responsive to both context and the generalized principlism (common morality). Indeed, our beautiful differences should never be a source of our moral disagreements in our unified moral goal in the deep future. Of course disagreements are not a sign of irrationality, they are not only healthy given that we have no infallible approach to moral truths, but also progress in bioethics depends on our respect for the sources of our disagreements.[23] Respecting our sources, such as substantive beliefs, lived authentic realities, contextual values and so on, will awaken us to appreciate the need for agreement at least on some elements that bring us together towards an integral approach. For instance, in policy making, some bioethics commissions and committees have indicated the need only for agreement on a set of basic action-guides other than an agreement on their theoretical foundations.[24] In many instances of disagreements that come our way in bioethical theories are several dichotomies. This is where Africanists like Tangwa believe that we have been misinformed by bioethical principlism that ethics is about balancing various opposing dual interests and systematically calculating consequences, thereby running "a grave risk of facilitating the possibility of nicely dressing up self-interest or exploitation in the robes of moral acceptability or even those of altruism and philanthropy."[25] Even amidst dualistic clashes

---

21. Though analogies may sometimes fail. If one gets better after using a certain medicine, she may feel comfortable recommending it further, but it doesn't mean that her friends will feel better after using the recommended medicine. Beauchamp and Childress, PBE, 434–435, 438; Tangwa and Henk, "Colony of Genes," 1041–42.

22. See Toulmin, "Medicine Saved the Life of Ethics," 736–50; Bioethics is dominated by universalist and particularist impulses. Callahan, "Universalism and Particularism," 37–44.

23. See Daniels, "Wide Reflective Equilibrium," 96–114.

24. See Beauchamp and Childress, PBE, 417–18.

25. Tangwa, "Medical research in developing countries," 48–49.

or disagreements based on theoretical moral convictions or substantive beliefs emphasized as persuasive or derivative from either moral approaches, neither principlism nor the African moral thought should be prioritized. So, a holistic thinking should go beyond both approaches by launching a genuine dialogue between both while getting beyond them. To ground a holistic approach with the help of the African approach to solidarity (later on in the discussion), we proceed by disregarding anthropocentric theoretical standards, standards that disrespect the *hierarchy of life forces* inclusive of *other created entities* as one of the chief characteristics of the African moral thought. *In dialogue with* different sciences and principle-based studies along their honest approach to moral affinities between human and nonhuman entities, in upholding holistic bioethics, I argue for a minimum moral status for other nonhuman entities.

MORAL STANDING AND MORAL STATUS: PRINCIPLE BASED AFFINITY BETWEEN ENTITIES BUILT ON EVOLUTIONARY, NEUROLOGICAL, COGNITIVE ETHOLOGICAL EVIDENCE

I presuppose solidary relationships to ground a holistic approach. When the question of the status of nonhuman entities is determined, granting a solidary relationship between creation, our initial question of investigation, i.e., pursuing a holistic approach to bioethics, will be much more well-defined. Here *moral standing* entails the special status that we and other entities have. On principle-based approaches, scholars like Christopher Morris argue that an entity can have instrumental or extrinsic value if it is valuable to something else; while an entity has intrinsic value if it is valuable. Even-though some entities have both intrinsic and instrumental value,[26] e.g., fellowship of *muntu* in the community, the easiest argument to qualify any entity as having moral standing is by virtue of its intrinsic value. Although we may agree that not all animals are humans, we cannot refute that humans are animals. This is predicated on the reality that we are certainly one among the animals. So invariantly, we *could* initially deduce that human cognitive capacities are one among the cognitive capacities of animals, while human moral systems are one among the moral systems of animals.[27] Though we seem to *easily* attribute intrinsic values to almost all animals (human animals and nonhuman animals or other animals), instrumental and extrinsic

---

26. See Morris, "Moral Standing," 256, 258–59.
27. See Bradie, "The Moral Life of Animals," 554, and 570–71.

values *aren't easily* attributed to nonhuman animals since it is claimed for instance, that they cannot self-govern or self-value themselves. My understanding here will get clearer later in the course of this section, but primarily, let me briefly clarify why nonhuman animals are said not to be moral.

We should categorically note that while human animals are moral, nonhuman animals are said not to be moral. Proto-morality argues that although some nonhuman animal species possess the rudimentary features that manifest themselves in human systems, they cannot be said to be truly moral for some reasons. Firstly, they do not possess language, which is necessary for forming the propositional attitudes that are fundamental to the expression of moral sentiments. Secondly, although some nonhuman animals may be able to communicate with each other, they are not conscious, and as such, lack the inner life necessary to be subjects of moral concern.[28] Thirdly, even if nonhuman animals were conscious, they do not have the requisite complex brain capacities needed to reflect on their behavior in relationship to the behavior of others.[29] Further—this may make us to atleast *presume* that though not every entity has moral standing as it is unbeknownst to some, every entity may have some *moral status*. Different studies understand moral status in general as whatever status an entity might morally have. For instance, moral standing is basically a kind of moral status.[30] For the case of human animals, atleast there are a great many theories why they are decorated with moral status while the same moral status is not conferred on many nonhuman animals. These postulations are commonly founded on "human properties," "cognitive and moral properties" and properties of "sentience," but which properties we can positively employ to conform homologous forms to all animals (human animals and nonhuman animals) in the subsequent subsections.

Human properties

In the first instance and the commonest, in conferring moral status to human animals, some postulations are *founded on human properties* (*homo sapiens*), viz., if and only if that individual is conceived by human parents and has a human genetic code even when an infant has irreversible abnormalities like a permanent loss of consciousness or a persistent vegetative state.[31]

---

28. See Bradie, "The Moral Life of Animals," 569–71.
29. Bradie, "The Moral Life of Animals," 569–70.
30. See Morris, "Moral Standing," 256.
31. See Beauchamp and Childress, PBE, 68.

In this typical category, nonhuman entities will be outrightly excluded since they are not like us.

Cognitive and Moral properties

In conferring moral status in the second instance, some other postulations are instituted on *cognitive and moral properties*. In PBE, it is mostly a competent human adult considered to have access to cognitive processes of awareness such as perception, memory, understanding, and thinking. Properties of these cognitive processes include self-consciousness of oneself over time; freedom to act and the capacity to engage in purposeful actions; ability to give and appreciate reasons for acting in some specific way and not the other; capacity for substantive beliefs, desires, and thoughts; capacity to communicate with other persons using some language; capacity for rationality and higher order volitions. In a broader sense, the exercise of cognitive properties gives birth to moral properties, whereby an entity is a moral agent if it is not only capable of making moral judgments about the rightness and wrongness of actions, but also necessarily has motives that can be judged morally.[32] Holding such moral criterion gives an impression of attributing full moral status only to rational moral agents,[33] excluding for instance, not only nonhuman animals, but also human animals that have permanently lost consciousness, and so cannot use their actual capacity—a consequence that revivifies the potential-actual problem in moral debates. Scholars like Mary Anne Warren, in her interpretation of Kant, explores a similar position since some entities are not capable of acting on general moral principles of ethics.[34] Relying exclusively on such Kantian ethics—which seemingly excludes nonhuman entities because only human beings are understood to act according to the moral law—the value intrinsic in the access to cognitive processes (moral agency, axiological or deontological sense) sounds adequate for a moral status on the one hand, but not actually necessarily sufficient a condition for a moral status on the other hand. Studies expressly defend this intrinsic value of cognitive processes, for instance, those principle-based studies of Raymond Frey seem to suggest, we can

---

32. See Beauchamp and Childress, PBE, 72–75.

33. Principlists, and more specifically Patzig, understand Kant to mean: "Only reasonable beings can have duties, and duties can only be towards other reasonable beings. Therefore, the supposed duties of the human person towards animals are actually just duties of the human person towards oneself." Quoted from Bujo, *The Ethical Dimension of Community*, 222.

34. See Warren, *Moral Status*, 101–2.

base intrinsic value on the quality of an entity's life (valuationism) since "the intrinsic value of a life is a function of its quality."[35] But this postulation fails in various circumstances. Take an example of arguments from "marginal cases" which maintain that every major cognitive criterion of moral status (intelligence, agency, self-consciousness, etc.) excludes some human animals (e.g., in a permanent loss of consciousness), whose cases are akin to some nonhuman animals, and therefore to exclude or include these nonhuman animals is also to exclude or include comparably human animals.[36] Therefore, prioritizing the valuationist's postulation on intrinsic value is unsuccessful in the sense that some lives of some healthy nonhuman animals in our everyday social realities have a higher qualitative value than some lives of human animals.

Even if we were to generally emphasize actual use of cognitive properties (in an axiological or deontological sense) as prerequisites for moral agency, we would actually qualify moral subjects as only those entities with moral standing (having both intrinsic and extrinsic values), to be exact, human animals. In spite of the fact that it *may* still largely be unorthodox to actually claim that nonhuman animals can be moral subjects or objects (on the claim they lack moral standing), it is reasonably orthodox to consider them, at least, as objects of moral concern (think of them as moral patients),[37] which objects can either be direct or indirect. Even if they were mere indirect moral objects, whereby we only had duties *regarding* them without having duties *to* them (presumably like cultural historical sites, museums, some or all nonhuman animals),[38] it still remains reasonably

---

35. Frey, "Moral Standing," 197. On axiological or deontological sense of value, see Tooley, "Are Nonhuman Animals Persons," 337.

36. This position precludes a high level of moral status for many weak, vulnerable, and incapacitated humans. A nonhuman animal can overtake a human animal in moral status once the human animal loses a measure of mental abilities after a cataclysmic event or a decline of capacity. PBE gives an example: Once a primate training in a language laboratory exceeds a deteriorating Alzeheimer's patient on the relevant scale of cognitive capacities, the primate would attain a higher moral status. Beauchamp and Childress, PBE, 72–74; Frey, "Moral Standing," 198; Copp, "Fundamental Moral Standing," 287.

37. See Rowlands, "Animals that Act for Moral Reasons," 521, 543, footnote 2. For defence of the idea that our obligations to animals are both direct and indirect, see Regan, *Animal Rights*, 243–48; and Rowlands, "Contractarianism and Animal Rights," 235–47; and Singer, *Animal Liberation*; Rowlands, *Animal Rights*; and Sapontzis, *Morals, Reason, and Animals*; Rowlands, *Animals Like Us*.

38. Akin to the discussed significance of cognitive processes in Kantian ethics, Aquinas seems to be no different. Both believe that nonhuman animals lack moral standing since they don't exercise cognitive properties like human animals do. Precisely, for Aquinas, the rational creatures are governed for their own sakes, while others

satisfactory to consider some entities as having a standing if they are owed duties, where some are duties to them while others are duties regarding them.[39] Complexities become apparent that even if we were to owe nonhuman animals duties, given their limited moral agency, it would still be difficult to enter into the required day-to-day truth-based moral contracts as equal partners who know exactly what we/they want, how to get it and know what we/they shall subsequently benefit. This thesis is backed by contractualists or contractarians, according to whom moral truths are largely rational constructions entered into and maintained between moral agents. For them, "morality is a sort of agreement among rational, independent, self-interested persons, persons who have something to gain from entering into such an agreement."[40] The accurate complexity here is literally twofold. On the one hand, nonhuman animals are not capable either of entering into contracts or managing them. On the other hand, human animals seem to gain nothing from the very contracts which go ahead to additionally create restrictions on how nonhuman animals are to be treated.[41] Such a double complexity exhibited in contractarianism makes us to further deduce, first, that nonhuman animals cannot be potential contractors even when given some time, or to put it differently, nonhuman animals as rational agents will find it not only difficult to manage normative rules and their consequences; but also, they will not appreciate the emotional energy necessary to maintain these contracts.[42] Second, just like we have stressed above, likewise Singer argues in the same line, that contractarianism cannot consistently deny moral standing to nonhuman animals without similarly withholding it, for example, from human infants or even human animals with a permanent loss of consciousness.[43] Consequently, it is my view that many human animals and nonhuman animals without access to *actual use* of cognitive processes, like those who have permanently lost consciousness and those nonhuman animal subjects in biomedical research, shouldn't be held as lacking moral status. And in view of some scholarships, indeed wide-ranging moral challenges remain that biomedical research generally attaches moral weight to how *fortunate* an entity can exercise its capacities

---

are governed in subordination to them (*Quod creaturae rationales gubernantur propter seipsas, aliae vero in ordine ad eas.*) Aquinas, *The Summa Contra Gentiles*, 112.

39. See Morris, "Moral Standing," 261–262.
40. Narveson, "Meat Eating," 192–194.
41. See Tooley, "Are Nonhuman Animals Persons," 349.
42. See Carruthers, "Animal Mentality," 390.
43. See Singer, *Practical Ethics*. Cited from Carruthers, "Animal Mentality," 387, 404.

and enjoy a set of rights than another.[44] But since some entities are excluded from this classification, it is for this reason different scholarships such as those of Evelyn Pluhar argue, that certain other capacities are required for moral agency, including capacities for emotion, memory, and goal-directed behavior.[45] Evidence indicates that both human and nonhuman entities are indeed capable of other admissible similarities that we would call "moral" or "virtuous" behavior, which similarities are among the properties of cognitive processes that found moral status: e.g., evidence shows that nonhuman entities have cognitive properties and are capable of essential intuitions, intentional plans, social life, practicing interactive morality as moral subjects, and so on and so forth.

Among such evidence of cognitive properties is the *evolutionary* principle-based position, which supplies one of the scientific pieces of evidence that establishes affinity between entities. Though we experienced a brink of annihilation or extinction or an ecological shadow of our genealogy, thanks to the fortuity of our evolution,[46] entities owe their existence to an unbroken providential chain of environmental reproduction that began with the beginning of life some 3.5 billion years ago. About 600 million years ago, some of the homeostatic living things on this planet became aware of their surroundings—continued to maintain themselves through nutrition and replaced their fragile materials, among them being nonhuman animals with complex, multicellular organisms that feed on other life forms to-date. Others are human animals that historically evolved approximately two hundred thousand years ago in Africa from the other great apes.[47] Indeed the Darwinian evolutionary conception of the nineteenth century supports the thesis that animals (human animals and the nonhuman animals) have a shared evolutionary history. Supporting arguments are in the publication of Darwin's *Origin of Species* of 1859, his *Descent of Man* of 1871, and *The*

---

44. Chan and Harris, "Human Animals and Nonhuman Persons," 308.

45. See Pluhar, *Beyond Prejudice*, 2.

46. "Rejoicing in the fortuity of our genealogy, however, can obscure an equally salient but far less auspicious pattern in the history of life—namely, the extinction of nearly every species that has ever existed. There have been geological moments, and one in particular about 250 million years ago, when complex life itself teetered on the brink of annihilation. Yet the fragility of animal life per se pales in comparison to that of individual taxa. The mean duration of species is around four million years—an incomprehensibly vast interval to the human mind, but a mere pittance geologically speaking. And as we will see, species do not seem to get any better over time at not going extinct. What is more, if it were not for the most recent mass extinction, mammals might still be relegated to a small, nocturnal existence in the ecological shadow of dinosuaria." Powell, "Nature of Species," 603.

47. Korsgaard, "Interacting with Animals," 91–92.

Expression of Emotions in Man and Animals of 1872. In *Descent of Man*, Darwin argues that differences in the mental and moral capacities between nonhuman animals are largely differences of degree, evidenced in shared senses of sight, touch, smell, hearing, and taste, which indicate shared fundamental intuitions. Given our common descent, atleast the biological basis of moral behavior is shared with our close evolutionary relatives. Besides, nonhuman animals experience pleasure and pain, happiness and misery, and emotions. Although Darwin thought that the roots of mind and morality were to be found in nonhuman animals too, a true moral sense required a capacity for self-reflection that was only possessed by human beings.[48] Studies after Darwin likewise demonstrate multifarious additional biological similarities between human animals and nonhuman animals such as "the skeletal structure of humans will resemble that of chimpanzees; the blood of humans and rats will circulate in similar ways; the mechanisms whereby rabbits and humans exchange gases with the air will be comparable; and the reactions of humans and guinea pigs to toxic substances will be akin."[49] Such findings necessitate no emphasis of any special status for human animals. And it is the reason the Darwinian anthropocentric claim can never go unchallenged since it sets human standards as the criteria for the moral status of all animals, in a milieu where human animals are merely one among numerous entities, and in which same milieu nonhuman animals are constrained by normative systems appropriate and set by their fellow animals (humans).[50] One may say that human animals are discriminatory to their relatives, and to put in a different voice, for human animals to disparage this evolutionary "common ground is a bit like arriving at the top of a tower only to declare that the rest of the building is irrelevant."[51] Holding such a standpoint may lead us to construe that letting human standards to set the criteria of what is commonly good and bad for all is like to embrace human superiority on grounds that we are subject to normative standards, while the other animals are unfortunately not subject to the same standards,[52] a perspective that seems to divert us further from our correlative shared evolutionary affinity.

---

48. Bradie, "The Moral Life of Animals," 549–51, 561; Darwin, *Descent of Man*, 36–48; *The Origin of Species; Emotions in Man and Animals*; In 1880s, Romanes George, drew partly on Darwin's work on animal intelligence for his two studies cited below. In reference to Darwin's theory of common descent, he came up with a comparative psychology. He is also known for the theory of mental evolution. *Animal Intelligence*, and *Mental Evolution in Animals*.

49. Lafollette, "Animal Experimentation," 800.

50. See Bradie, "The Moral Life of Animals," 568–69.

51. De Waal, *Good Natured*, 7.

52. See Korsgaard, "Interacting with Animals," 115, footnote 37.

Among other properties of cognitive processes that found moral status, there is the capacity to engage in purposeful intentioned actions, that is traceable in nonhuman entities. Our discussion above has to an extent distanced us from nonhuman entities insinuating that they have no intentions beyond instincts. Comparable to human beings, we vividly know primates have opposable fingered hands. Moreover, like we can open closet cabinets, closed doors, shut shelves or drawers, screw, and unscrew lids or tops, unlock doors or windows, turn on or off water taps, etc., primates are able too. Besides primates, crows act with novelty in their demonstration of behavior through tool use, that is beyond instincts and conditioning, to achieve an objectively desirable circumstantial problem-solving outcome.

> A remarkable demonstration of behavior that cannot be explained by instinct alone is the example of a crow who, without trial and error or other conditioning-type learning, bent a straight tool to produce a hook when such a tool was required. Crows natively use sticks and other straight tools in the wild and can learn to use hooked tools. The use of naturally occurring tools in wild crows is thought to be partly inherited and partly learnt. However, the ability to fashion entirely new tools in response to new circumstances, can be explained by neither.[53]

Beyond such an appropriate contingent problem-solving skill common in crows, behaviorally great apes appear to make self-references—self-awareness or self-recognition—and some nonhuman animals learn from the past and use their mastery to forge intentional social plans of action for hunting, stocking, reserve foods, and constructing dwellings. In social life, numerous nonhuman animals understand assigned functions and either follow designated roles or decide for themselves what roles to play.[54] And if some nonhumans take on assigned functions, they seem to fulfil planned actions in ways that some human animals, who have permanently lost their consciousness, cannot. And on any reasonable appreciation of moral agency, it is one of the reasons different studies defend nonhuman animals as moral subjects (moral agents). For instance, DeGrazia supports "the attribution of moral agency—specially, actions manifesting virtues—in cases in which the actions are not plausibly interpreted as instinctive or conditioned."[55]

53. Chan and Harris, "Human Animals and Nonhuman Persons," 319. On whether nonhuman animals share in the capacity for intention, see more on crows in Chappell, "Avian Cognition," R244–R245 (*originally numbered thus*); Chappell and Kacelnik, "Tool Selectivity," 71–78; Emery and Clayton, "The Mentality of Crows," 1903–7; Kenward et al., "Behavioral Ecology," 121; Weir et al., "Shaping of Hooks," 317–34.

54. See Beauchamp and Childress, PBE, 74–75.

55. DeGrazia, *Taking Animals Seriously*, 203.

And if nonhuman animals fulfill assigned functions or act without being conditioned, it means nonhuman animals plan far better than some of their human animal counterparts. Given that fulfilling an assigned function or a plan is one of the properties of cognitive processes that morally founds moral status, it would be morally inapt not to award an elevated moral status to nonhuman animals while awarding it to human animals who lack the relevant capacities for planning or fulfilling assignments. The question is whether this wouldn't be suggesting that some nonhuman animals may equally be moral agents as some human animals?

Over and above that, another principle based scientific approach that establishes affinity between entities, is the growing body of evidence from *cognitive ethologists* who support the view that animal social behavior is permeated by norms and values.[56] In *Wild Justice*, cognitive ethologists Marc Bekoff and Jessica Pierce show that some nonhuman animals share the property of being moral subjects just like human animals through a broad repertoire of behavior that can correctly be regarded as moral. Examples include being fair, showing empathy, exhibiting trust, and acting reciprocally, which behaviors are the causal result of a complex range of emotions.[57] In their same book *Wild Justice*, given that for them morality entails interrelated other-regarding behaviors that cultivate and regulate complex interactive social groups, they confer morality to nonhuman animals since their behaviors manifest empathy, cooperation, and a sense of fairness akin to human animals. As an illustration, *neurological* evidence suggests homogenous spindle cells associated with the production of empathy, emotional reactions, and a sensitivity of the feelings of others in both apes and human animals that lead to similar experience under similar circumstances—and precisely current research shows that whales have spindle cells three times as many as human animals. Even-though these behaviors may not constitute morality in themselves owing to the fact that a certain level of cognitive and emotional sophistication is required, scholarships like those of Bekoff and Pierce emphasize the importance of studying nonhuman animals in their natural habitats and not merely in the confines of laboratories where they perform in accordance with the interests of their behaviorists, which may not necessarily reflect their own interests. Moreover, to overcome the Darwinian limited human standards of morality as we argued earlier on, what constitutes morality for Bekoff and Pierce has to be understood as *species specific*—how morality is manifested differently in their own world (nonhuman animals) of empathy, cooperation, and sense of fairness. And

---

56. See Bradie, "The Moral Life of Animals," 549–50.
57. See Rowlands, "Animals that Act for Moral Reasons," 522, 544 footnote 9.

since human animals are proto-typical moral agents, we may expand and attune our moral understanding to include all characteristic features of other species themselves (conspecifics).[58] Beyond this, Bekoff and Pierce emphasize another illustration that shows how morality is manifested differently in the world of nonhuman animals if viewed along their conspecifics, which is evident in De Waal's critical research designed to determine whether apes, for instance, have a "theory of mind," that is, the capacity to anticipate and understand what a conspecific (or any other nonhuman animal) is thinking or experiencing. According to De Waal, problems may arise if interactions between human animals and chimps face a species barrier. To the apes, we appear as "all-knowing gods." Experiments designed to discover whether apes have theories of mind, that is, whether apes are capable of attributing intentions and expectations to fellow apes (conspecifics), he argues, often only yield results about an ape's ability to fathom the intentions and expectations of human experimenters. The presence of human experimenters and the design of experiments to elicit answers to questions posed by human experimenters and guided by human interests are likely to yield answers that may not reflect the true nature of the interest and motivations of nonhuman animals, who have their own interests and motivations. When we remove human experimenters from the experiments and focus on conspecifics, De Waal argues, we get positive results that apes do have a suitably relativized theory of mind. This neurological evidence suggests similar brain structures that animals have inner experiences similar to those that humans experience under similar circumstances.[59] Cognitive ethologists therefore suggest that agency is *species-specific* (conspecific),[60] besides, human animals are proto-typical moral agents since they can flexibly familiarize themselves with other organisms without separating them from their own habitats. Although exhibiting empathy, emotional reactions, and a sensitivity of the feelings of others are among some properties of cognitive processes that award moral status to entities, the moral question remains how to handle cross-species interactions since each community (*inter alia*, apes, chimpanzees, whales, humans) may have a dissimilar moral code? Would each community have an obligation to non-conspecifics? And since we are flexible proto-typical moral agents, don't other organisms indeed deserve our sympathetic respect in various biomedical interventions?

58. See Bekoff and Pierce, *Wild Justice*, 1, 7, 30, 114. Summarized by Bradie, "The Moral Life of Animals," 555–58.

59. See De Waal, *Primates and Philosophers*, 61–67, 70. Summarized by Bradie, "The Moral Life of Animals," 554–55, 562.

60. See Bekoff and Pierce, *Wild Justice*, 144.

Properties of Sentience

In conferring moral status in the third instance, beyond human, cognitive and moral properties, other postulations are founded on *sentience*, i.e., the capacity among human animals and nonhuman animals for consciousness experienced in a range of affective and emotional responses (feelings and sensations). Being able to experience pain and suffering is almost certainly sufficient to confer some measure of moral status, and biomedical ethics finds it reasonable to reduce or limit pain and suffering as well as accompany those pathetic cases of suffering and pain: "What matters, with respect to pain, is not species membership or the complexity of intellectual or moral capacities. It is the pain . . . . The reason to use animals in research is that they are so similar to humans, and the reason not to use animals in research is that they are so similar to humans in their experience of pain and suffering."[61] Though the terms pain and suffering are frequently interchangeable, I take suffering to require more cognitive ability than the mere experience of pain.[62] In relying on studies done—for instance, by Daniel C. Dennett, Michael Tye and others—Sahar Akhtar strikes a difference between the ability to suffer and the ability to feel pain and thus concludes that, one's ability to suffer would only apply to sophisticated beings, whereas the ability to feel pain, would be pertinent to both sophisticated and unsophisticated beings. And moreover, Tye associates the sophisticated demands of suffering to cognitive awareness of our experience of pain.[63] Here pain is a bodily sensation, while suffering is the cognitive account of that very bodily pain. It further means that entities who suffer necessitate being aware, capable of anticipating and remembering pain, recognizing that their desires and goals will be frustrated by pain in the due course. Thus, suffering requires

---

61. Beauchamp and Childress, PBE, 76.

62. Upper limits of risk of pain, suffering, and distress are uncommon in animal research. A revised European Directive 2010/63/EU on the Protection of Animals Used for Scientific Purposes and accompanying instruments could have a substantial influence on the ethics of animal research worldwide, especially in the development of morally sound legal frameworks. Beauchamp and Morton, "Pain and Suffering in Animal Research," 431–47.

63. In Michael Tye's example, one who gets a bad headache and is distracted for a moment does not simultaneously suffer. The headache continues, though briefly not noticing it does not eliminate it, without any cognitive awareness of pain and hence no suffering. Akhtar, "Animal Pain and Welfare," 508, also footnote 1, 511; see Dennett's works, *Brainchildren*, and *Kinds of Minds*. In *Kinds of Minds*, Dennett demonstrates beings capable of experiencing pain without suffering. He attributes moral significance to suffering than to pain (163–64). For him, it is not the brain but the creature's life to be studied if we are to understand suffering (p. 167); Tye, *Consciousness, Color, and Content*, 182.

awareness of *self* and *time* (cognitive sophistication),[64] which sophistication many nonhuman animals are said to lack.

Among examples of cognitive sophistications, human animals are said to positively choose pain for spiritual or bodily gains, e.g., mortifications of the body during the Lenten period or spiritual retreats and pilgrimages among Christians. Courageous devotees walk on hot coals as a rite passage in Hinduism ("Theemithi" or "firewalking") in exchange for blessings of their faith, a practice dating back from Iron Age India c. 1200 BCE.[65] In other sophisticated examples among high-level beings, to achieve *higher order* or *longer term*[66] and complex interests, professional sportspersons are too capable of discounting pain. By contrast, it is claimed nonhuman animals can barely discount pain since they cannot see themselves as existing over time, cannot reflect on the value or meaning of their life taken entirely, cannot form interests for life taken as a whole, and cannot formulate lifelong objectives. Akhtar argues that a given measure of pain might sometimes be worse for nonhuman animals than it is for human animals, since with only a basic or rudimentary sense of time and of self, a nonhuman animal may be at the greatest disadvantage from pain.[67] But even though nonhuman animals can scarcely discount pain, given their rudimentary sense of time and self, it does not mean they *cannot entirely* feel a range of painful bodily sensations, which is almost unquestionably sufficient for human animals to bestow on nonhuman animals some measure of moral status. To this extent, that nonhuman animals are capable of discounting some pain, they might qualify as moral patients who deserve not to be ill-treated despite the fact that they cannot be held accountable for their conduct. And it is

---

64. Akhtar, "Animal Pain and Welfare," 498–99.

65. See Pankratz, "Fire Walking," 291–98.

66. "Imagine that you are sitting at your desk reading a book and your friend comes up beside you, inserts that tip of a three-inch needle in a vein in your arm, holds it there for few seconds, and then removes it. Now, imagine that you are at a doctor's office and the doctor inserts the tip of a needle of the same length, in the same spot, withdraws blood, and then removes it. It is not hard to imagine that the pain in the first scenario would be more intense than in the second scenario. Knowing that there would be a good reason for having the needle inserted in the second scenario—that there is a long-term or higher order interest in health, for instance—would likely lessen the intensity of the pain felt from the stick of the needle." Akhtar, "Animal Pain and Welfare," 506.

67. See Akhtar, "Animal Pain and Welfare," 504–5, 509–510; Referencing to Akhtar, in addition to cognitive ethological and biological studies, other scientific studies likewise deny many animals self-and time-awareness necessary for the exercise of intertemporal decision making in relation to humans. See Roberts, "Are Animals Stuck in Time?" 473–89; Ramseyer A et al., "Reciprocity in brown capuchin monkeys," 179–184 and Ainslie, "Impulse Control in Pigeons," 485–89; and Bateson and Kacelnik, "The Foraging Starling," 341–52.

in this sense they can be subsequently granted moral standing given their moral patient-hood, which implicitly grants them moral agency, or even both.[68] And if nonhuman animals are likewise understood as *homologous* moral agents and moral patients, there arises no or limited moral questions of obligations "to" (direct obligation) or "regarding" them (indirect obligation)—atleast obligations to protect them from suffering.

In support of these homologous forms, neuroscientist findings in the latter part of the twentieth century revealed that the brain structures and neural networks that underlie the human capacity for moral behavior exist in homologous structures, that is, have a common ancestral course, across a wide range of nonhuman organisms.[69] Paul MacLean's "triune brain" hypothesis in 1990 defends deep homologies emerging from a shared evolutionary lineage between the brains of all animals. Neurological evidence points to deep structural similarities, particularly, the basic qualitative feels or affects. The structures in the human animal brain are activated by basic emotional and affective responses which are also found in related nonhuman animals. Just as these activations in human animals are correlated with experiences of pain, fear, anger, and the like, in a similar fashion, we could comparably be convinced that these activations of the homologous circuits in nonhuman animals are correlated with similar experiences.[70] The convictions that the homologous activations along all animals are correlated with similar experiences is almost certainly sufficient to confer atleast some measure of moral status not only as far as properties of sentience are concerned; but also, as far as human, cognitive and moral properties. It is one reason; in building up a holistic approach, I subsequently argue out a moral status in favor of *nonhuman entities*. I demonstrate concretely in the next seven classifications how *cognitive* and *moral properties* as well as *properties of sentience* are rightly observable in nonhuman entities since time immemorial.

Moral Status of Nonhuman Animals in the Antiquity

In conferring moral status to human animals and nonhuman animals, numerous properties of cognitive processes that award moral status like, cleverness, intelligence, sentience, speech, have been appreciated since the time of Greeks. An earlier Platonist, Plutarch of Chaeronea (A.D. 46–122), who "wrote on the relative cleverness of land and sea creatures, on the eating of

---

68. See Bradie, "The Moral Life of Animals," 564.

69. See Bradie, "The Moral Life of Animals," 549–50.

70. Bradie, "The Moral Life of Animals," 553–55, 561–62; MacLean, *The Triune Brain*.

flesh, and the dialogue Gryllus, in which a talking pig explains why animals are far superior to humans,"[71] and the pagan Neoplatonist author Porphyry (A. D. 234–305), have been the original sources of many later arguments about the intelligence of animals, and whether we are justly entitled to make use of them.[72] Plutarch mentions yet another unique nonhuman animal cognitive property, i.e., superiority in intelligence and properties of sentience, as in, feeling of pain and sorrow. "It is extraordinary that (those who deny any intelligence in animals) obviously fail to notice many things that animals do and many of their movements that show anger or fear or, help me, envy or jealousy. They themselves punish dogs and horse that make mistakes, not idly but to discipline them; they are creating in them through pain a feeling of sorrow, which we call repentance."[73] Plutarch seems to be suggesting a single unbroken interaction between nonhuman and human animals since they all have homologous activations of properties correlated with related experiences which is practically adequate to confer some measure of moral status, *atleast to all animals*. Comparably, the same conviction seems to be picked up by Porphyry who insists that since nonhuman animals can speak and actually do communicate with each other as well as with human animals, these are parallel processes and properties that may still suggest an uninterrupted flux of life: "I myself reared (he writes) at Carthage, a tame partridge which flew to me, and as time went on and habit made it very tame, I observed it not only making up to me and being attentive and playing, but even speaking in response to my speech and, so far as was possible, replying, differently from the way that partridges call to each. It did not speak when I was silent; it only responded when I spoke."[74]

Even when we have had such life realities before us, of how we relate to some creatures through communication and speech, unfortunately our historical relationships toward attaining an uninterrupted flux of life have neither been wholly just nor conferred a befitting moral status to nonhuman animals. Indeed in the antiquity, the most notable text of Porphyry (the vegetarian) is *On Abstinence from Killing Animals*, which gives evidence that the Hellenistic schools of Stoics and Epicureans understood justice in a strong anthropocentric sense (terms based on human standards): "We cannot act unjustly towards creatures which cannot act justly towards us."[75] Such unjust relationships depict some stoics as largely adamant to accept

71. Plutarch, "Beasts are Rational," 492–31. Cited from Clark, "Animals," 37–38.
72. See Clark, "Animals," 37–38.
73. Plutarch, "The Cleverness of Animals," 333.
74. Porphyry, *On Abstinence from Killing Animals*, 82.
75. Porphyry, *On Abstinence from Killing Animals*, 32.

nonhuman animals as possessing properties of cognitive processes, like talking or thinking or feeling, which confer moral status. However, they eventually suggest that some nonhuman animals could reason syllogistically like human animals. For example, in pursuit of a scent, a dog, on approaching a parting in the road would take a scent down one path.[76] Besides, stoics conceive our affectivity as similar to emotional attachments in nonhuman animals. If "love of one's offspring is the very foundation of our social life and administration of justice and observe that animals possess such love in every marked degree,"[77] then nonhuman animals possess atleast some affective properties necessary to grant them moral status. This affective life to offsprings is implanted holistically in homologous forms across nature:

> For just as in uncultivated plants, such as wild vines and figs and olives, Nature has implanted the principles, though crude and imperfect, of cultivated fruits, so on irrational animals she has bestowed a love of offspring, though imperfect and insufficient as regards the sense of justice and one which does not advance beyond utility; but in the case of man, a rational and social animal, Nature, by introducing him to a conception of justice and law and to the worship of the gods and to the founding of cities and to human kindness, has furnished noble and beautiful and fruitful seeds of all these in the joy we have in our children and our love for them, emotions which accompany their first beginnings; and these qualities are found in the very constitution of their bodies.[78]

Plutarch is convinced of a rich single unbroken life across nature (creatures), correlated with similar experiences which are practically adequate to confer some measure of moral status, atleast to all. Comparably, Porphyry's emphasis of the Pythagorean way of life is against treating not only nonhuman animals merely as things meant for our use[79]—but also all animate things, whereby one should be "content with simple things, so he will not seek to feed on animate creatures as if inanimate foods were not enough for him."[80] In this particular state, it seems life for the Greeks cuts continuously across the horizon of creatures, from humans to nonhumans and then nature. Moreover, the Pythagorean way of life, believed in metempsychosis (μετεμψύχωσις), viz., the supposed migration of the soul of a human animal

---

76. See Porphyry, *On Abstinence from Killing Animals*, 51.
77. Plutarch, "The Cleverness of Animals," 337.
78. Plutarch, "On Affection for Offspring," 343–45.
79. See Clark, "Animals," 38.
80. Porphyry, *On Abstinence from Killing Animals*, 54.

or a nonhuman animal into the same new body after death (reincarnation). Even if this metempsychotic thesis may be successfully challenged, the cosmic multiplicity of beauty is in an uninterrupted flux with no single form holding forever. In appreciation of this cosmic multiplicity, "we can locate the anecdote about Pythagoras (ca. 580–ca. 490 B.C.), that he rebuked a man who was beating a dog, with the words 'That's a friend of mine—I knew him by his voice.'"[81] The functioning flux between these creatures (Pythagoras and the dog) seems unbroken and uninterrupted since the age of the classical period in Ancient Greece "as Plato remarks, to divide the world into the human and nonhuman is as silly as diving it into cranes and non-cranes."[82] Moreover in the fourth century B.C., the hedonistic and materialistic Epicurus similarly understood the human animal as an entirely material entity without distinguishing between the body (*sarx*) and mind (*psyché*) as different ontological substances (as Descartes did), but simply made up of different kinds of atoms. In upholding a non-dichotomized way of thinking, for Epicurus, *sarx* and *psyché* were two parts of a single, whole organism, and the mind couldn't exist without the body. This non-dualistic distinction, according to Noelia Bueno-Gómez, parallels with the Epicurean distinction between the "pains of the body" (*ponos*) and the "sufferings of the soul" (*lype*). Their parallel opposites are *aponía* (absence of physical pain) and *ataraxía* (absence of spiritual suffering), suggesting that total happiness (*eudaimonía*) was only possible if one enjoyed both *aponía* and *ataraxic*.[83] This is in contrast to other accounts that show how "'the Greeks' were dualists, dividing souls from bodies and Heaven from Earth, and that it is this heritage—assisted by the supposed Hebraic dictate that we have dominion over all the earth—that has blighted Western attitudes to animals and the wider biological environment."[84] If we are to uphold further such dichotomies in the various interventions of biomedical ethics, we would be unsuccessful in contributing to a holistic thinking that accords moral status to every creature. The Greeks, Plutarch and Porphyry seem in a way to be suggesting an unbroken way of thinking that appreciates a beautiful cosmic

---

81. According to Xenophanes (Diogenes Laertius 8.36). Kirk et al., *Presocratic Philosophers*, 219. Cited from Clark, "Animals," 50–51.

82. Plato, *Platonis Opera*, 263d: "τὸ δέ γε, ὦ πάντων ἀνδρειότατε, τάχ᾽ ἄν, εἴ που φρόνιμόν ἐστί τι ζῷον ἕτερον, οἷον δοκεῖ τὸ τῶν γεράνων, ἤ τι τοιοῦτον ἄλλο, ὃ κατὰ ταὐτὰ ἴσως διονομάζει καθάπερ καὶ σύ, γεράνους μὲν ἓν γένος ἀντιτιθὲν τοῖς ἄλλοις ζῴοις καὶ σεμνῦνον αὐτὸ ἑαυτό, τὰ δὲ ἄλλα μετὰ τῶν ἀνθρώπων συλλαβὸν εἰς ταὐτὸ οὐδὲν ἄλλο πλὴν ἴσως θηρία προσείποι." The quoted English version (Plato, *Statesman*, 263d) is cited by Clark, "Animals," 52.

83. Bueno-Gómez, "Conceptualizing suffering and pain," footnote 3.

84. Clark, "Animals," 36.

multiplicity of life that apportions some moral status atleast to numerous creatures based on properties of sentience, cognitive and moral properties. As a dialogue partner, Black African social reality along its interventions in bioethics is not dichotomized, but conveys a non-dualistic thinking, i.e., it conceives entities not as dualities, but rather as a single unity encompassing the totality of life.

Moral Status Based on Sentience and Humanly Dispositions in Nonhuman Animals

Though sentience generally remains not only an adequate but a sufficient condition of some significant level of moral standing, it may be argued, it is not a necessary requirement for moral status. However in favor of nonhuman animal moral status, principlistic utilitarians have for 150 years identified with Jeremy Bentham's sentiency criterion that pain and suffering (pain as bodily sensation, whilst suffering as the cognitive account of the bodily pain) are sufficient conditions of moral standing.[85] Making reference to the limited legal protection provided at that time to slaves in the French West Indies by the Code Noir, Bentham unearthed some inadequate treatment toward nonhuman animals: "The question is not, Can they *reason*? nor, Can they *talk*? But, can they *suffer*?"[86] For Bentham, nonhuman animals like human animals deserve moral protection since they have relevant similarities, the chief being the capacity of sentience, viz., the capacity to experience pleasure, pain, and suffering.[87] If we rely on these relevant similarities, we can hardly fail to agree with Hume that the reasoning capacity of human

---

85. Bentham, "Principles of Morals and Legislation," Chapter 4. See the interpretation in Frey, "Utilitarianism and Animals," 174–75.

86. "The day has been, I am sad to say in many places it is not yet past, in which the greater part of the species, under the denomination of slaves, have been treated by the law exactly upon the same footing, as, in England for example, the inferior races of animals are still. The day may come when the rest of the animal creation may acquire those rights which never could have been witholden from them but by the hand of tyranny. The French have already discovered that the blackness of the skin is no reason a human being should be abandoned without redress to the caprice of a tormentor. It may one day come to be recognized that the number of the legs, the villosity of the skin, or the termination of the os sacrum are reasons equally insufficient for abandoning a sensitive being to the same fate. What else is it that should trace the insuperable line? Is it the faculty of reason or perhaps the faculty of discourse? But a full-grown horse or dog, is beyond comparison a more rational, as well as a more conversable animal, than an infant of a day or a week or even a month, old. But suppose the case were otherwise, what would it avail? The question is not, Can they *reason*? nor, Can they *talk*? but, Can they *suffer*?" Bentham, "Penal Branch of Jurisprudence," 307–35, 309.

87. Frey, "Utilitarianism and Animals," 173.

animals is not superior to nonhuman animals since nature is the *parent of all through her unerring precepts*. And given that nature indeed nurtures natural sentimentalism unerringly,[88] we are moved not only to learn about our nature through other natural life, but we are explicitly or implicitly compelled to likewise extend *human exceptionalism* (moral standing) to nonhuman animals. This thesis is in dialogue with the earlier emphasis on the property of sentience—that *the reason to use animals in research is that they are so similar to humans, and the reason not to use animals in research is that they are so similar to humans in their experience of pain and suffering*. The dialogue continues with Julia Driver's account, "A Humean Account of The Status and Character of Animals," in which she is of the view that we typically emulate Hume whenever we learn about our own nature by looking at nonhuman animals on the one hand, yet on the other hand we learn about nonhuman animals by looking at ourselves, suggesting that nature is not radically bifurcated into dichotomies of human animals and nonhuman animals. And if but only if, given the network of non-bifurcation, in consideration of atleast non-sophisticated cognitive abilities like non-demonstrative reasoning, Driver holds that nonhuman animal capacities are on a continuum with human animals, viz., the way human animals learn about the natural world is the same way nonhuman animals do—*nature* remaining equally *the parent of all* through its *unerring precepts*. And since non-demonstrative reason involves the sort of inference that yields probability rather than certainty (demonstrative reason), moreover based on features of past experience, it qualifies nature to engage in *cause-and-effect reasoning*.[89] So clearly, we have no other way to interpret Hume other than

---

88. "There is this obvious and material difference in the conduct of nature, with regard to man and other animals, that, having endowed the former with a sublime celestial spirit, and having given him an affinity with superior beings, she allows not such noble faculties to lie lethargic or idle; but urges him, by necessity, to employ, on every emergence, his utmost art and industry. Brute-creatures have many of their necessities supplied by *nature*, being cloathed and armed by this beneficent *parent of all* things: And where their own industry is requisite on any occasion, *nature*, by implanting instincts, still supplies them with the art, and guides them to their good, by her *unerring precepts*. But man, exposed naked and indigent to the rude elements, rises slowly from that helpless state, by the care and vigilance of his parents . . . ." Hume, "The Stoic," 23. *Emphasis is mine*; *Nature* nurtures natural sentimentalism: "A father knows it to be a duty to take care of his children: But he has also a natural inclination to it. And if no human creature had that inclination, no one cou'd lie under any such obligation" "And when we omit that duty, the immorality of the omission arises from its being a proof, that we want the natural sentiments of humanity," Fate and Norton, *A Treatise of Human Nature*, 3.2.5.6.

89. "Reason is nothing but a wonderful and unintelligible instinct in our souls, which carries us along a certain train of ideas, and endows them with particular qualities, according to their particular situations and relations. This instinct 'tis true, arises

understanding him to have believed that nonhuman animals, just like their human counterparts, engage in *cause-and-effect reasoning*. In catering for this natural sentimentalism (*nature* remaining equally *the parent of all* through its *unerring precepts*), it is yet another reason why Hume positively extends human exceptionalism to the moral status of nonhuman animals:

> Tis from the resemblance of the external actions of animals to those we ourselves perform, that we judge their internal likewise to resemble ours; and the same principle of reasoning, carry'd one step farther, will make us conclude that because our internal actions resemble each other, the causes, from which they are deriv'd, must also be resembling. When any hypothesis, therefore, is advanc'd to explain a mental operation, which is common to men and beasts, we must apply the same hypothesis to both....[90]

And since nature nurtures natural sentimentalism faultlessly, considering a balanced diet of evidence, it is harmless to suppose that nonhuman animals have atleast some virtuous dispositions, an example being the gratifying mental qualities. Nonhuman animals are observed in daily realities engaging in behaviors that we can anthropomorphically refer to as virtuous or superior for them, as they risk their lives to dutifully treat well or furiously defend their offsprings (drawing from my own experience of free grazing in my natal village where we see freely moving poultry defending its young ones on a daily basis) from any threatening danger just like our dutiful parents always did during our infancy or pubertal juvenile stages. Ofcourse one will still wonder whether nonhuman animals are virtuous! If understood atleast in an artificial sense, given that for Hume justice is an artificial virtue, its usefulness is doubtlessly understood in conventional terms—that is, justice is beneficial for us to live in sociality not solely due to our humanity. To this, Humeans like Julia Driver reliably note that one can possess a virtue itself, not only through moral agency, but also through a natural ability. Even-though the dispositions to act in a certain way may not be necessarily voluntarily acquired, it does not plausibly follow that the dispositions in accordance with the virtue are not, themselves, voluntary.[91] A

---

from past observation and experience; but can anyone give the ultimate reason, why past experience and observation produces such an effect, any more than why nature alone shou'd produce it? Nature may certainly produce whatever can arise from habit: Nay, habit is nothing but one of the principles of nature and derives all its force from that origin." Fate and Norton, *A Treatise of Human Nature*, 1.3.16.9; See an interpretation in Driver, "Status and Character of Animals," 167 footnote 4, 146, 149–50.

90. Fate and Norton, *A Treatise of Human Nature*, 1.3.16.3.

91. See Driver, "Status and Character of Animals," 156–57, 159, 164.

naturally tenderhearted human animal will still freely schedule sympathetic engagements, which could correspondingly apply to dispositions manifested in nonhuman animals. Even when nonhuman animals don't decently manifest moral excellences in their dispositions as they passionately defend their offsprings akin to human animals, it does not equal to misconstruing their dispositions out of the sphere of virtuous dispositions or some sort of voluntary actions. If we still maintain atleast an artificial sense of virtues, whereby we don't restrict sociality or virtuous dispositions simply to entities that are regarded as empowered to exercise moral agency, then the exercise of reason can't be held as solely determinant for practical morality as we shall stress in the African moral logic—that an actively lived practical moral life of Bantu cannot be simply founded on the absoluteness of reason. Likewise, Hume's—one of the members of Scottish "moral sense school," the other being Hutcheson—practical moral sentimentalism does not ground morally ethical decisions on reason: "Morals excite passions and produce or prevent actions. Reason itself is utterly impotent in this particular. The rules of morality, therefore, are not conclusions of our reason."[92] Meaning "'tis in vain to pretend, that morality is discover'd only by a deduction of reason. An active principle can never be founded on an inactive."[93] So, for Hume, morality is practically active while reason is inactive. The question is how inactivity can coherently produce active practicality. Other scholars like Peter Singer agree with Hume's thesis that we should never pretend that morality is unearthed only by deductions of an inactive reason since practical morality cannot have a rational basis alone. And since morality is essentially practical, for Hutcheson, reason can simply show us how best to achieve our ends, but it cannot determine what those ends should be since it is incapable of moving one to action except in accordance with some prior

92. According to the moral sense school well known in the works of two Scottish philosophers, Francis Hutcheson (1694–1746) and David Hume (1711–1776), morality is essentially practical. "Since morals, therefore, have an influence on the actions and affections, it follows, that they cannot be deriv'd from reason; and that because reason alone, as we have already prov'd, can never have any such influence. *Morals excite passions, and produce or prevent actions. Reason of itself is utterly impotent in this particular. The rules of morality, therefore, are not conclusions of our reason.*" Hume, *Method of Reasoning*, 458, especially T 3.1.1.6. Italics mine.

93. "No one, I believe, will deny the justness of this inference; nor is there any other means of evading it, than by denying that principle, on which it is founded. As long as it is allow'd, that reason has no influence on our passions and actions, *'tis in vain to pretend, that morality is discover'd only by a deduction of reason. An active principle can never be founded on an inactive; and if reason be inactive* in itself, it must remain so in all its shapes and appearances, whether it exerts itself in natural or moral subjects, whether it considers the powers of external bodies, or the actions of rational beings. Hume, *Method of Reasoning*, 458, especially T 3.1.1.7. Italics mine

want or desire.[94] Even-though nonhuman entities may not be understood as moral agents or even moral subjects, in the least sense of interpreting natural sentimentalism and its accent of artificial virtues as well as the moral sense school that discredits reason as inactive, nonhuman animals are moral patients. To put it differently, they are objects of social moral consideration to whom we can neither restrict sociality nor discredit their virtuous dispositions, making nonhuman entities to qualify for moral status.

Social Cognition, Spatial Thinking in Eusocial insects, Primates, Mammals

Some nonhuman entities have a complex social life akin to human animals. From extensive studies of Cythia Moss, Katy Payne, Martha Nussbaum, creatures with larger bodies (e.g., elephants) have *slower life spans*, in which stages unfold more gradually and last longer. Slow life span is highly correlated with the ability to develop and exhibit complex forms of intelligence, and elephants are among the most long-lived of the nonhuman mammals, often living to sixty years or so. In the elephants' complex forms of social organization, child-rearing tasks are amicably shared among a group of cooperative older females, who help younger females familiarize themselves with raising a young elephant child. The eldest as the matriarch takes the lead in moving the group from place to place, and also in initiating complicated communication about movement and food. In analyzing a wide range of elephant calls, it is now factually known that these calls are a highly complex long-distance communication system, based on low-frequency sound, that not only enables each group, to stay together though widely dispersed for foraging, but also enables males and females to locate one another for mating. Besides, elephants appear to have an understanding of death, and have rituals of mourning when a member of the group dies, and appear to feel grief.[95] More specifically, in Amboseli National Park within the sub-Saharan

---

94. Hutcheson was concerned with showing, against the intuitionists, that moral judgment cannot be based on reason and therefore must be a matter of whether an action is "amiable or disagreeable" to one's moral sense. Hume, like Hutcheson, held that reason cannot be the basis of morality. For Hume "'Tis not contrary to reason to choose my total ruin, to prevent the least uneasiness of an Indian or person wholly unknown to me." To have these preferences is to have certain desires or feelings; they are not matters of reason at all. Morality is determined by sentiment, so moral judgments are based on a feeling. The question is whether this feeling is common to all individuals? Singer, "Climax of moral sense theory."

95. Nussbaum, "Capabilities Approach and Animal Entitlements," 229, 233–34. Nussbaum makes use of the elephant discussions found in Moss, *Elephant Memories*, 73, and Payne, "Social Complexity in Three Elephant Species," 57–86.

African country of Kenya (formerly Maasai Amboseli Game Reserve), Moss and Nussbaum describe succinctly the grief of other elephants to the death of a young female elephant killed by a poacher's bullet:

> Teresia and Trista became frantic and knelt down and tried to lift her up. They worked their tusks under her back and under her head. At one point they succeeded in lifting her into a sitting position but her body flopped back down. Her family tried everything to rouse her, kicking and tusking her, and Tallulah even went off and collected a trunkful of grass and tried to stuff into her mouth.[96] . . . . The elephants then sprinkled earth over the corpse, eventually covering it completely before moving off. When elephants come upon the bones of elephants, even bones old and dry, they examine them carefully, something they don't do with the bones of other species, as if they are trying to recognize the individual who has inhabited them.[97]

Purposefully engaging in a highly complex communication system, and in a network of social organization which spans from cognitive cooperative values of sharing child-rearing tasks to understanding of death and burying one's loved ones, all proves how elephants use their properties to impact cognitive processes, which atleast concertedly confers some moral status on them. Beyond elephants living in an intricate social organization, monkeys use rocks to crack open nuts, a wide range of other creatures experience emotions, use cognitive maps for navigation, while others use tools which may include crows, vultures, and apes. I have seen chimpanzees in my home area either instilling social values by disciplining their younger ones when they do wrong or when squeezing plant leaves to apply on their injured bodies. According to the complexity of the social environment, we can quickly identify a few systems among nonhuman social creatures. First, tools are not only used for food, think of monkeys that are highly flexible in identifying the potential usefulness of tool-like objects placed in their environment or caused by nature—think of dried tree branches rolled down by wind—which objects they causally connect ("causal thinking") to some tasks beneficial to them, but they also use them in their own social contexts, like for grooming, e.g., apes groom one another's teeth using a range of tools. Second, dolphins and chimpanzees are capable of "perspectival thinking" —distinguishing between the way they see situations and the way another person on the scene will see them. Third, coupled with social cognition through various interactions, chimpanzees are able to read and use *spatial*

---

96. Moss, *Elephant Memories*, 73.
97. Nussbaum, "Capabilities Approach and Animal Entitlements," 234.

models made by human animals. With "spatial thinking," nonhuman entities find their way by navigating through vast environmental complexities that even human animals can scarcely attempt.[98] Besides primates, spatial thinking is observable in other nonhuman animals such as rats, birds, and insects that form cognitive maps.

Among these are eusocial insects like honeybees, to which we can grant a special advanced level of social status given their perspective, belief, desire, abridged in a cognitive architecture of spatial thinking. In Peter Carruthers' extensive scientific account, "Animal Mentality: Its Character, Extent, and Moral Significance," he likens honeybees to many other insects and invertebrates in their use of various navigation systems, think of their cognitive architecture of spatial thinking, that is aided by *dead reckoning*. Dead reckoning involves integrating a succession of directions of motion with the distance travelled in each direction, to yield a representation of the honeybee's current location in relation to the place of origin. First of all, to succeed with spatial thinking, honeybees have to learn the likely location of the sun at any given time of day, as measured by an internal clock of some sort, a mechanism that permits them to navigate from distant or local landmarks. Secondly, some research shows that bees will also construct crude mental maps to navigate their surroundings or environment. Notwithstanding the maps being crude because of the poor resolution of honeybee eyesight, they contain the relative locations of principal landmarks such as big freestanding trees, a forest edge, or a lake shore. Thirdly, spatial thinking requires learning from the dances of other bees about the spatial relationships between the hive and various desired substances and objects (including nectar, pollen, water, and potential new nest sites).[99] This learning helps honeybees encode not only differences but also similarities,[100] new memories, and discrimination between different colors[101] as well as help in signaling and detecting threat.[102] To this end, the essential details in the cognitive architecture of the honeybee, are provided through the "waggle

---

98. Nussbaum, "Capabilities Approach and Animal Entitlements," 232–33.

99. Carruthers, "Animal Mentality," 380–82; Additional in-depth studies include Menzel et al., "Map-Like Spatial Memory," 3040–45; Seeley, *The Wisdom of the Hive*; More on honeybees' capacity to transmit the distance and direction, Gould and Gould, *The Honey Bee*, and, Von Frisch, *Dance Language and Orientation of Bees*.

100. See Menzel and Giurfa, "'Difference' in an insect," 930–33; Menzel and Giurfa, "Cognition in an Insect," 24–40.

101. See Gallistel, *The Organisation of Learning*; Gould, "Map of Honey Bees," 861–63; Menzel and Giurfa, "Cognition in an Insect," 26; Menzel, "Memory Trace," 53–62; Zhang et al., "Learning by Honeybees," 267–82.

102. See Igns and Chittka, "Bee Responses to Cryptic Predators," 1520–24; Menzel et al., "Reward Expectations in Honey bees," 491–96.

dance" that indeed necessarily conveys details about the interval, route and how excellent the desired source of substance is:

> When a high-quality food source is found near the hive, honeybee scouts use a "round" dance that informs the other bees that they should search for the odor associated with the scout upon leaving the hive. However, for more distant food sources a more elaborate "waggle dance" is used to convey information about the direction, distance, and quality of the food source. Direction is indicated by the angle of the movements of the abdomen across the center of a figure eight (which represents the angle from the position of the sun); distance is indicated by the duration of the dance (and sounds); and quality is indicated by the vivacity of the dance.[103]

The difference in the vivacity of the dance is, when the employed honeybee foragers return to the hive from visiting the desirable worksites, they dance longer and more vivaciously than bees who have visited less desirable foraging sites. Decisions, like deploying foragers, exhibit collective mental states of eusocial insects, what similarly compels Bryce Huebner's study, "Minimal Minds," to interpret Thomas Seeley's perspective of honeybee colonies as a collective unified system that relies on the iconic representations of the waggle dance to disseminate details in a way that allows the colony to respond collectively. Centrally, all specializations of functions take place at the level of the colony, i.e., propagated only between the members of a colony with very differently specified tasks of complex representations, but cannot be carried out by any of the individual bees. Examples include, monitoring and evaluation of the quality of a foraging site, location of a nest site or richness of food sources as far as 10 km away. It is the reason Seeley is of the view that *even* the comparative judgements (inclusive of cognitive states and processes) carried out by distributed computational architecture are only realized by the coordinated choice and facts of the colony as a whole (in collectivity).[104] Such collective decision-making mechanisms

---

103. Huebner, "Minimal Minds," 455; For a thorough representation of landmarks, predators, location and the internal states displayed in the communicative activity within the waggle dance of honeybees, see Carruthers, *Architecture of The Mind*, 74.

104. Huebner, "Minimal Minds," 459, 461. Reference is made to Thomas Seeley's extensive studies, *The Wisdom of the Hive*; "Social Foraging by Honeybees," 343–54; "Tremble Dance of the Honey Bee," 375–83; "Honey Bee Colonies," 22–41; "Division of Labour," 253–59; "Selection in Honey Bee," 417–24. See also Seeley et al., "Nectar Foraging," 737–38; "Collective Decision-Making in Honey Bees," 277–90; "Scouts Guide a Honeybee Swarm," 161–71. See also Seeley and Towne, "Dance Choice in Honey Bees," 59–69; Seeley and Passino, "Selection by Honey Swarms," 427–42; Seeley and Buhrman, "Nest-Site Selection," 416–27; Seeley and Visscher, "Scouts in Honey Bee

are observable in building of nests in some specific sites rather than others. The same collectivity can be observed in allocation of more resources in the field of collecting or storing nectar, depending on where more numbers are most needed. These collective mental states or collective coordinations of choice give reasonable corroboration of a rich social-communal existence of eusocial insects, atleast among honeybees.

The question of whether these coordinated representations (collective mental states and processes) operative in honeybee colonies are decisions or judgements become apparent, since they seem not to be aggregated out of cognitive sophisticated representations, like beliefs, proper to human animals or what could confer both moral standing and moral status in anthropocentric terms. Honeybee minimum minds can be defended in different studies, like those of Huebner, given that representational structures of honeybees "share much in common with the perceptual-motor and attentional structure in a human brain. While waggle and tremble dances, as well as search times, can stand in for features of the environment (specifically the location of a food source and the rate or consumption by the system), they do so only when the system is immediately presented with raw data about the natural environment."[105] On the one hand, the collective mind of honeybee colonies may appear weak in relation to the structure in a human brain, and even if we were to homogeneously transmit their framework to the general collective-sociality of life, it does not necessitate us presuming that colonies are similar to some of the properties of cognitive processes like the capacity for beliefs, desires, ambitions and so on, which are important for conferring moral status in humanistic terms. On the other hand, in-spite of the fact that the collective mind of colonies seems impoverished since their system is only presented with raw data making the honeybee motivations to be innately fixed, in the mind of Peter Carruthers, the goals that are activated on specific occasions—such as whether or not to move from one foraging patch to another, whether to finish foraging and return to the hive, and whether or not to dance on reaching it—appear to be variedly influenced. Even-though we have to take into cognizant the seemingly inflexible behavioral systems as well as the numerous things that bees cannot do such as linguistic representations akin to human animals; such doesn't encompass their complex navigation system. From the above and much other balanced diet of scientific data, we reliably come to know that not only do bees have distinct information and goal-oriented states, but their states interact

---

Swarm," 511–20.

105. Huebner, "Minimal Minds," 463.

collectively in the determination of behavioral systems.[106] With Carruthers, along several consulted scientific studies, we can deduce that the bee case exemplifies a realistic perception/belief/desire cognitive architecture as a simple form of collective practical reasoning. Even-when there are mental states that we cannot yet scientifically explain in reference to anthropocentric standards, for instance, whether they have inferential capacities for *transitive inferences* akin to representations in language users,[107] they are all reasons to accord them atleast a minimum collective mind. Transitive inference is the capacity to use basic logic or previous knowledge to check omissions before discerning something anew. To cite a popular example, it is only older children who can infer that if John is taller than Mary, and Mary is taller than Sue, then John is taller than Sue. Transitive inferences are kindred forms of reasoning to *class inclusion*, the capacity to hierarchically classify objects into two or more categories at the same time. For instance, it is older children who understand that a grocery store will contain more fruit than apples.[108] However, in reference to eusocial insects, this maybe an unsuccessful argument in awarding moral status to them, since this logic is significantly absent in human infants before five years, but they neither lack their moral status nor moral standing. Summarily, the various coordinated social interactions grant some nonhuman entities (eusocial insects, primates, mammals, etc.) not only "social cognition" but also properties of "causal thinking," "spatial thinking," "perspectival thinking" granting them access to some of the properties of cognitive processes conferring moral status to some, while moral standing to others.

Primates Approximate Human Language: Language not a Prerequisite for Internal logic

For nonhuman entities to carry out mental processes akin to robust linguistic capacities in *Homo Sapiens* animals and thereby be honored with minimal minds, it is claimed it would require their properties to use linguistic representations. This is because linguistic capacities increase the flexibility to access sophisticated cognitive processes necessary for remembering the

---

106. Carruthers, "Animal Mentality," 380–81; Carruther explicates honeybee perception/belief/desire cognitive architecture in reference to Collett and Collett, "Insect Visual Navigation," 542–52; Bermúdez, *Thinking Without Words*, 288; more on honeybee representational mental states, see also Dyer and Seeley, "Foraging Range," 227–34; and Evans, *Varieties of Reference*, 101, 104; and Carruthers, *Architecture of The Mind*, 78–81.

107. Menzel and Giurfa, "Cognition in an Insect," 36.

108. Phillips et al., "Transitive inference."

past, coordinating the future along present beliefs and desires. It is why it is claimed that nonlinguistic minds are unlikely to have representations that can be completely decoupled from their environmental triggers.[109] Eventhough human animals are uniquely endowed with a fully developed linguistic mind that easily communicates cognitive details, emotional states, imperatives, norms, approvals and disapprovals not conditioned on their environmental triggers; they are not privileged because even *higher primates may approximate bits of that language*.[110] Meaning, simply stressing the issue of linguistic minds may not entirely be satisfactory in granting human animals a unique moral status.

Neurological evidence reveals that the distinctive moral capacity that human animals have, and other animals lack, is a function of *neocortical activity* that grounds the possibility of human language and enables human animals, to not only have beliefs and desires, but to reflect on what they do and think, as well as form judgements of approval and regret.[111] The neocortex is a complex brain network that is in control of the neuronal computations, such as attention, awareness, perception, memory, emotions, cognition and thought.[112] This neurological evidence rhythms with what Descartes noted: "The reason why animals do not speak as we do is not that they lack the organs but that they have no thoughts."[113] Contra Descartes, there are numerous examples of animals who can understand and use language as human animals do, atleast to some extent, such as dolphins, parrots, gorillas, chimpanzees. Chimpanzees have been taught to communicate using sign language and have proven able to use language in a manner parallel to basic human neuronal computations. In addition to Chimpanzees, there is stronger evidence presented in the case of gorillas, who understand spoken English and respond appropriately using sign. Gorillas have demonstrated abilities to use sign language to communicate, most importantly, their understanding of self (*inter alia*, elephants, dolphins, Gorillas and chimpanzees).[114] Over and above, there is an exceptional chimpanzee

---

109. Huebner, "Minimal Minds," 443–44, 453, 458; Huebner references Zawidzki, "Folk Psychology," 193–210; More on the role of language in the human cognitive system, see Carruthers, *Architecture of The Mind*; "Our Own Minds," 121–38; Bermúdez, *Thinking Without Words*.

110. Bradie, "The Moral Life of Animals," 568–69.

111. See Bradie, "The Moral Life of Animals," 553–54, 561–62.

112. Kalebic et al., "Neocortical expansion," 7; Lei Xing et al., "Increased memory flexibility."

113. Descartes, "Animals are Machines," 64.

114. Gardner et al., "Cross-fostered Chimpanzees," 27–57; Gardner et al., *Sign Language to Chimpanzees*. For more on the mirror self-recognition trials of elephants,

species, "namely, bonobos (or pygmy chimpanzees). This species of primate is, of extant species, the one most closely related to humans, and two bonobos, Kanzi and Panbanisha, have learned to understand spoken language . . . and more recently it has claimed that Kanzi understands about three thousand spoken English words."[115] The question is whether the said used language can formulate atleast futuristic (or antiquated) thoughts and fulfil the necessary conditions for having any external expression of psychological properties such as the concept of self, affection, just like human animals do. From their study, "Human Animals and Nonhuman Persons," Sarah Chan and John Harris note:

Of course nonhuman animals who have acquired the tool of human language and can thus communicate directly with us, at least some have demonstrated a concept of self, an understanding of death and an ability to hold preferences about their future selves, indicating to us that these animals at least can be persons. The absence of language, however, need not by itself signify a corresponding lack of self-awareness. "Language," at least . . . is not a prerequisite for the exercise of logic and reasoning, of which animals have been shown to be capable . . . . A real possibility exists that some animals may be self-ware even in the absence of language, and that their awareness of self extend to a capacity to value their continued lives.[116]

The logical error premised on anthropocentric standards, which Chan and Harris are trying to correct, is to equate the external life of nonhuman entities with their internal states as parallels. Moreover, already philosophers and psychologists "warn us away from giving linguist behavior too much of a privileged position . . . . If one does not yet have external language, one cannot be thinking in language—unless external language is not necessary for thinking in language, and in that case there would be no reason to exclude animals from the class of thinkers."[117] For psychologists, to emphasize the necessity of language for various psychological properties is logically unsuccessful and so comparably flawed. Relying on different scholarships, psychological research with prelinguistic human infants due

---

dolphins, Gorillas and chimpanzees, see Patterson and Gordon, "Personhood of Gorillas," 58–77; Gallup, "Chimpanzees: Self-Recognition," 86–87; Reiss and Marino, "Self-Recognition in the Bottlenose Dolphins," 5937–42; Plotnik, De Waal and Reiss, "Self-Recognition in Asian Elephant," 17053–57. Referenced in Chan and Harris, "Human Animals and Nonhuman Persons," 311–313.

115. Savage-Rumbaug and Lewin, *Kanzi*; and Raffaele, "Speaking Bonobo." Cited from Tooley, "Are Nonhuman Animals Persons," 358, 369.

116. Chan and Harris, "Human Animals and Nonhuman Persons," 312–313; Reference is made to Watanabe and Huber, "Animal Logics," 235–45.

117. Andrews, "Beyond Anthropomorphism," 475–76.

to adultomorphic concerns, i.e., ascribing adult psychological properties to children, more specifically in the works of Kristin Andrews, having language cannot be a necessary condition for having any psychological properties. Even-though the child is a potential language-user, a scientist is not sufficiently justified in ascribing psychological traits to her simply because she will ultimately use language in the future. This is because *not all infants gain language use in the future*, and using language is only one kind of a behavioral trait.[118] Remaining in dialogue with Chan and Harris' findings and the above sciences, we can infer that the absence or *lack of external language is not a corresponding prerequisite of internal logic or reasoning*. As noted above, we should neither error in assuming that an external spoken, written, or gestural language as mostly observable in adults is a necessary precondition to having an internal language of thought, nor erringly presuming that there are no alternative internal representational vehicles other than an externally used language. We may therefore not disregard conscious thoughts of nonhuman entities based on language anymore, since some do even approximate bits of human language. Like we already stressed, analogously it is one reason the African moral thought employs a nonverbal palaver. And since a nonverbal communication validly passes on moral treasures, at least making use of nonverbal thinking in nonhuman animals is defensible. The question is no longer whether they have thoughts, but only if they truly have a concept of self and can approve or disapprove their mental states as well as the mental states of others, and thereby make judgements of approval and disapproval to qualify as moral subjects.

Metacognition, Mind-reading, Propositional Attitudes in Nonhuman Entities

We have advocated for mental states amongst eusocial insects, primates, mammals as well as the view that nature engages in *cause-and-effect reasoning*, what conveys the impression of *gratifying mental states*. The challenge, here and now, is whether such mental states suffice for the kind of reflective properties necessary for moral evaluations, namely, atleast thoughts about

---

118. Andrews, "Beyond Anthropomorphism," 472. Andrews' proof for arguments against representationalism from cognitive sciences include Brooks, "Intelligence without Representation," 139–59; Thelen and Smith, *A Dynamic Systems Approach*; Philosophical arguments against representationalism include Clark and Toribio, "Doing without Representing," 401–31; Van Gelder, "What Might Cognition Be," 345–81. For arguments in favor of cartographical representationalism, see Camp, "Thinking with Maps," 145–82; Braddon-Mitchell and Jackson, *Mind and Cognition*; Rescorla, "Cognitive Maps," 377–407.

the entity's mental states (metacognition). Since it is claimed that nonhuman entities are incapable of metacognitive capacities—what some schools like the Humeans would regard as majorly important to confer moral agency and moral standing— it remains only human animals that have been awarded a pronounced moral standing, in that, they have been decorated with a better "meta-affect."[119] In Driver's studies, the most famous experiments on nonhuman animal metacognition have dwelt on attitude of uncertainty amongst dolphins and macaque monkeys, with results matching the results for human animals—whereby monkeys selectively and correctly declined discrimination errors (Uncertainty Response), dolphins, like human animals, reported similar conscious uncertainty—leading the experimenters to conclude that there is strong cross-species isomorphism, explaining some of the closest existing human animal – nonhuman animal performance correspondences. These metacognitive studies give highly suggestive evidence that some higher animals, such as monkeys and dolphins, do have beliefs about their own mental states.[120] This is to suggest that to be able to have beliefs about one's mental states (metacognitive capacities) is significant enough for self-regulation and suggestive of reflective properties.

In other strong cross-species isomorphism, viz., human animal – nonhuman animal performance correspondences are found in recent empirical nonhuman animal psychology findings about certain nonhuman animal personality traits that prove meta-effects. Among them, Samuel Gosling and Oliver John note that "Extraversion, Neuroticism, and Agreeableness showed the strongest cross-species generality, followed by Openness; as separate Conscientiousness dimension appeared only in chimpanzees, humans' closest relatives."[121] Although the empirical study included dogs, hyenas, rats, donkeys, cats, pigs, different monkeys, guppies, octopi (octopods), chimpanzees displayed conscientious behaviors that are isomorphically associated with moral awareness and agency in human animals, including: "deliberation, self-discipline, dutifulness, order."[122] Being morally aware of the *self* seems discernable in both nonhuman and human animals. In defense of the view that nonhuman animals are self-conscious, one understands why Tomasello and Call argue that "primates know a good bit about their bodies. Some parts they know visually, and probably all parts they know tactually and/or proprioceptively . . . . Mirror self-recognition

119. Driver, "Status and Character of Animals," 152.

120. See Driver, "Status and Character of Animals," 153; For some contemporary experiments on animals (including humans) metacognition with a focus of the attitude of uncertainty, see Smith, "Animal Metacognition," 389–90.

121. Gosling and Oliver, "Personality Dimensions in Nonhuman Animals," 69–75.

122. Gosling and Oliver, "Personality Dimensions in Nonhuman Animals," 70.

is thus about perception of the body, which all primates are likely skillful at with no special training or experiences."[123] And being in touch with the one*self*, one's mental states, is not only limited to primates, but also among non-primates with exception of guppies and octopi. Notwithstanding, "remarkable commonalities across such a wide range of *taxa* suggest that general biological mechanism are likely responsible."[124] And given that nonhuman animals are in touch with their mental states (metacognition), the arising challenge is whether they have thoughts about the mental states of other entities (mind-reading), a kind of reflective property essential for moral evaluations. Can they scrutinize the dispositions of other entities, or do they have some *thoughts about the thoughts* of other entities?

Mind-reading has been widely used in cognitive science, developmental psychology, and comparative psychology to signify the ability to understand the mental states of others. Mind-reading is often taken to be an example of second-order representation or meta–representation—a description of what goes on in representing a representation, for example, we draw animations or cartoons as representations of something in our minds—which occurs when a thinker takes another thinker's representation of a state of affairs (thoughts), i.e., *thoughts about the thoughts of another entity*. It may be argued that morally plausible mind-reading skills that require sensitivity to another subject's emotional states, desires, and needs are not the same as "mind-blind" social coordinations[125] that are common amongst nonhuman animals; for example, in natural parks, amongst pastoralists or nomads, and those creatures domesticated. Such mind-blind social coordinations (team works) include *flocking* or *stampeding* behaviors among cattles, lions, elephant herds, buffaloes, zebras, sheep, goats, horses, colonies of ants, swarms of honeybees, colonies of beavers, waddles of penguins, wild dogs and so on. But some examples show emotional states beyond mind-blinding, which include the smartness exhibited in the mechanisms of earthworms. In Darwin's final book, "The Formation of Vegetable Mould through the Actions of Worms with Observations on Their Habits," he ethologically observes earthworms' smartness as intelligent. This derives

---

123. Tomasello and Call, *Primate Cognition*, 337.

124. Gosling and Oliver, "Personality Dimensions in Nonhuman Animals," 70. *Emphasis is mine*; "A 'taxon' (plural: 'taxa') refers to a taxonomic category or grouping used in biological classification, typically reflecting phylogenetic (revolutionary) relationships and character traits and distinguish it from other such units. A taxon may or may not be given a formal rank in the nested biological hierarchy, which includes populations of organisms, species, genera, families, orders, classes, phyla, and kingdoms, in ascending order of inclusiveness." Powell, "Nature of Species," 621, footnote 1.

125. See Bermúdez, "Mindreading," 407, 410–11, 418.

from the fact that earthworms can variedly pull leaves in similarly human manner without discriminating any shapes: "If worms have the power of acquiring some notion, however rude, of the shape of an object and of their burrows, as seems to be the case, they deserve to be called intelligent; for they can act in a manner as would a man under similar conditions."[126] For Darwin, we can say earthworms are smartly intelligent because they adapt, just like humans, according to novel features of given new environments.

Some of the said forms of social coordination in creatures may succeed in proving mind-reading but not "representing what philosophers standardly term propositional attitudes (psychological states such as belief, desire, hope and fear)," as in the thought of José Luis Bermúdez. For him, the difference is that, "mindreading involves representing another creature as perceiving, say, that the food is under the tree, while proposition attitude mind-reading represents another creature as believing that the food is under the tree," in that regard, "propositional attitudes are standardly interpreted in terms of two components—a propositional content and a thinker's attitude toward that content."[127] These two components are apparent whenever we articulate propositional attitudes with verbs like believe, desire, hope, fear, intend, know. I believe/desire/hope/fear/intend to see snow at Christmas. Knowledge in this sense is a propositional attitude, meaning, to know something (snow at Christmas) is to stand in an attitude to a proposition.[128] As regard to standing in an attitude to a proposition, evidence seems clear that the chimpanzees and bonobos tested do not have the level of understanding of false belief manifested in the young children tested concurrently. What is more complex, this conclusion is entirely consistent with the fact that propositional attitude mind-reading is restricted to language-using creatures, as in, propositional attitude mind-reading requires linguistic abilities of a kind, a similar perspective emphasized by Michael Tomasello et al. in their study, "Do Chimpanzees know what Conspecifics Know?."[129] At this stage we are again challenged with the claim that nonhuman animals cannot be propositional attitude mind-readers given the fact that propositional attitude mind-reading necessarily requires meta-representations which are strictly language based.[130] Excluding nonhuman animals from propositional attitude mind-readers, not only excludes them from the creaturely world of

---

126. Darwin, *Actions of Worms*, 93.
127. Bermúdez, "Mindreading," 415–16.
128. See Bermúdez, "Mindreading," 428.
129. Bermúdez, "Mindreading," 422, 428–32; Tomasello et al., "Do Chimpanzees *know* what Conspecifics *Know*?" 139–51.
130. See Bradie, "The Moral Life of Animals," 562.

moral patient-hood, but also hinges on the claim whether they have atleast beliefs, intentions and desires since these are indispensable propositional attitudes for elaborating and evaluating moral propositions with the use of linguistic channels. But this claim seems still not to succeed.

Among concrete examples of moral evaluations in ethological and social-biological studies, chimpanzee communities practice fairness, award punishment of negative actions and understand underlying goals: "I once saw an adolescent female interrupt a quarrel between two youngsters over a leafy branch. She took the branch away from them, broke it in two, then handed each one a part."[131] Here the adolescent female can be decorated as a propositional attitude mind-reader since she knew how to handle the case and succeeded in disapproving or rather evaluating the youngsters' moral behavior. Nonhuman animals, such as Chimpanzees, display isomorphic representations of understanding associated with human animals: "We believe that there is only one reasonable conclusion to be drawn for the ten studies reviewed here: Chimpanzees, like humans, understand the actions of others not just in terms of surface behaviors but also in terms of the underlying goals, and possibly intentions, involved."[132] To this end, we may safely argue that it is not only understanding but also appreciating the underlying goals and intentions depict propositional attitude mind-reading associated with meta-representations of moral awareness and agency prevalent in human animals.

Given that chimpanzees are conscientious, understand actions and the underlying goals before deliberating, they are autonomous propositional attitude mind-readers, to which bioethical principlists agree. Among them are Tom Beauchamp and Victoria Wobber who note that even-though chimpanzees' psychological mechanisms differ from those of human animals, chimpanzees satisfy the two basic conditions of autonomy: (1) liberty (the absence of controlling influences) and (2) agency (self-initiated intentional action), each of which is specified in terms of conditions of understanding, intention, and self-control. In this account, chimpanzees make knowledge-based choices that reflect a richly information-based and socially sophisticated understanding of the world.[133] This means nonhuman animals are not

---

131. De Waal and Luttrell, "Social Reciprocity in Three Primate Species" 101–18; and De Waal, *The Age of Empathy*. Cited from Andrews, "Beyond Anthropomorphism," 492.

132. Call and Tomasello, "Chimpanzee Have a Theory of Mind? 189.

133. Two major theories of autonomy (Kantian theory and two-level theory) are rejected as too narrow. Beauchamp and Wobber, "Autonomy in chimpanzees," 117–32; Defending animal consciousness in the philosophy of mind and the philosophy of science is criticized. Collin, "Assessing animal cognition," 42–47.

only autonomous and conscious propositional attitude mind-readers, but they are also intelligent and correspondingly have moral rights in the mind of cognitive ethologists.[134] But when we qualify nonhuman animals as intelligent and autonomous moral agents, it does not necessarily imply language use. Like we already argued, emphasis of an external use of language is not a necessary requirement to have internal reflective properties for propositional attitude mind-readers. The inner thoughts could have alternative mechanisms of meta-representation beyond the verbal linguistic minds in order to enrich the entity's social sophistication. The fact that they have intentions, beliefs, desires, can approve or disapprove the moral actions of their community members. This presupposes an adequate ground for reflective properties necessary for moral evaluations, namely, inclusive of their mental states as well as the mental states of others, something that earns them both moral status and moral standing. As mind-readers, nonhuman animals stand in multifarious attitudes to numerous propositions which may not standardly be on an equal footing with those of human animals.

The biggest failure in biomedical interventions has been to use strong anthropocentric standards to study nonhuman entities. Strong anthropocentrism is already implicitly challenged by Darwin, when he observes earthworms' smartness as their intelligence. He thinks that his notion may "strike everyone as improbable; but it may be doubted *whether we know enough about the nervous system of the lower animals to justify our natural distrust of such a conclusion.*"[135] It is still the same pronounced strong anthropocentrism that influences numerous human biomedical ethicists to claim that chimpanzees, for instance, do not have a sense of fairness simply because they fail tests based on human norms of sharing. To embrace such an approach is to fail establishing whether a species-normal behavior of the chimpanzees naturally involves a norm about sharing. But there is scarcely any norm about sharing food resources as part of the chimpanzee natural interactions. Analogously, sharing of spouses in olden days was a sign of human hospitality in some African communities, which gesture cannot contemporarily indicate hospitable sharing anymore. If sharing one's spouse was to be studied in today's biomedical ethics, I believe several humans would be labelled inhospitable and far distanced from the spirit of sharing. To test chimpanzees' fairness by examining whether they share food is akin to testing us outside our norms, viz., if we conventionally share our spouses, what actually doesn't accommodate the *folk expert understanding*

---

134. See Bekoff and Jamieson, "Cognitive ethology," 156–59.
135. Darwin, *Actions of Worms*, 97. *Emphasis is mine.*

of the human species.[136] Such limitations in the folk expert opinion (knowledge about the species) are also visible not only in the early gorilla mirror-recognition studies,[137] but also typically visible in daily interactions between human animals and nonhuman animals where genuine communication is linguistically limited. Given our anthropocentric standards, on the one hand, it is primarily the language barrier that prevents us from sitting down as fellow conspecifics with nonhuman animals, say in some African tropical Savannah, and asking them what they are thinking and feeling, while on the other hand, we too remain largely handicapped to honestly interactively experience what it is like to be nonhuman animals, as nonhuman animals are likewise handicapped in asking us what it is like to be human animals.[138] Whenever we find ourselves in such helplessness to interactively experience what our actual relationships with them would be, such failures qualify nonhuman animals as having none of our mental states, because we generally rate their mechanisms analogous to ours and ultimately suppose their abilities. To prevail over these suppositions, there is need to develop *folk expertise* that goes beyond our own experience, taxon[139] and conspecifics.

Even-though we have failed locating a theory of mind in chimpanzees arising from cooperation with researchers in several studies as we have encountered them in the previous sections, Tomasello and colleagues construct a chimpanzee theory of mind starting with species-normal and natural behavior, informed by *folk expertise* and *naturalistic observation*. If a nonhuman animal has a psychological property, we should expect to see evidence of it in its naturalistic environment in order to formally test for it.[140] In contrast, even-though the previous studies showed some cooperation with nonhuman animals, they have been non-naturalistic. It is one reason why for Tomasello and colleagues,

---

136. Andrews, "Beyond Anthropomorphism," 483–84; Reference made to Tomasello et al., "Do Chimpanzees *know* what Conspecifics *Know*?" 771–85.

137. Andrews, "Beyond Anthropomorphism," 484; Joseph Call and Tomasello, "Performance of Children and Great Apes," 381–95.

138. Chan and Harris, "Human Animals and Nonhuman Persons," 310–311; Refer also to Wittgenstein, *Philosophical Investigations*, 293.

139. "Folk expertise" is what one has when one knows one's subject well. Not all those who work with animals (ranchers, animal caretakers, trainers, farmers) are sensitive to their behavior. Being a folk expert requires having a certain quality of relationship that understands their personality, capability and intentions. Parents are folk expertise for their children. Career nannies have folk expertise about children. See more in Andrews, "Beyond Anthropomorphism," 478, 491, footnote 23.

140. Psychology as a product of evolution evolves coping with the natural social and physical environment of the species. Naturalistic observation and folk expertise go hand in hand. Andrews, "Beyond Anthropomorphism," 489–90.

perhaps the communicative situations of these latter (cooperative) studies may be unnatural for chimpanzees, who have not evolved for this kind of cooperative communication over monopolizable food resources and who do not normally experience in their individual ontogenies others helping them find food . . . . Chimpanzees' most sophisticated social-cognitive abilities may emerge only in the more natural situations of food competition with conspecifics.[141]

We can construe that nonhuman animals display mental states that suffice for the kind of reflective properties necessary for moral evaluations earning them an award of a pronounced moral standing or atleast to be decorated with moral status. Moreover, accommodating the folk expert understanding of nonhuman animals, in which we understand their thoughts about the thoughts of others, we need to be better informed by their normal and natural behavior revealed within their own environmental interactions along their own conspecifics or taxa. It is within their natural habitats that they will fully expose their true sophisticated social-cognitive abilities. Well knowing that mind-reading meta-representations have largely trusted the medium of language, we still lack a holistic picture of nonlinguistic mind-reading that is informed by folk expertise and naturalistic observation. So "we will not have a full understanding of the moral significance of nonhuman animals until we look at human mind-reading through the lens of nonlinguistic folk psychology."[142] And it is by understanding the nature of morality of nonhuman animals from their own perspective and on their own terms, what some refer to as the "speciocentric point of view," that we can go beyond a morality limited on anthropocentric presumptions. It is the *speciocentric* view that unlocks the moral condition of a nonhuman animal from its point of view, i.e., from a species–neutral point of view.[143] We would reliably interpret that nonhuman animals go through stress that is probably better understood by them from their own point of view than the point of view of their human care takers.

There are endless examples to show how nonhuman animals go through awful stress. For illustration, Singer and Mason note that humans eat 100 million tons of seafood, where one-third comes from fish farming. They argue that overcrowding of fish sometimes leads to stress, abnormal behavior, sea-lice infestations, abrasions, inadequate water circulation, painful suffocation, and high death rates. As if not bad enough, chicken is

141. Tomasello et al., "Do Chimpanzees *know* what Conspecifics *Know*?" 783.
142. Bermúdez, "Mindreading," 437.
143. Bradie, "The Moral Life of Animals," 564–65.

always maximumly raised in congested windowless sheds, littered with excrement and reek ammonia, which high ammonia levels give them chronic respiratory diseases, sores on their feet and hocks, chronic pain from bone disease and breast blisters. All these could make their eyes water, go blind, get broken hips and wings as well internal bleeding.[144] And it is from these poor methods of poultry and animal crowding in industrial farming that we trace the origin of both the bird flu (avian influenza A/H5N1) and the swine flu (influenza H1N1) epidemics.[145] It is from their own point of view that we can better get acquainted to what these nonhuman animals *want* as David DeGrazia argues[146] and *why* and *how* they want to move about their own lives. It is only when they can do what they want that they would typically experience pleasure or satisfaction as DeGrazia argues further; but when horses or primates, for instance, are continuously restricted in zoos/stalls/circuses/laboratories/farms/parks or confined in human homes as pets or deprived from doing what they want, they typically experience frustration, in which we seem not to promote their life holistically. Even if the current warden was to promote an animal's life by adjusting to its needs, a subsequent warden may not yield to its basic needs or wants, to an extent of frustrating it. Besides, think of different egg-laying poultry that only must lay eggs in cages throughout their lives in very tiny-crowded enclosures without being able to easily spread their wings or exercise but only to maximize profit in agribusiness for purely anthropocentric motives. To constraint cannibalism and aggressiveness on such farms, some chicken undergoes toe-clipping and debeaking but without anesthesia! Other nonhuman animals are painfully slaughtered or endure tail docking, castration, teeth clipping, ear notching and livestock dehorning and branding (with hot iron), all still unanesthetized or enforced against their fervent protests or wants! Also, as I grew up, we could wean and separate younger animals or poultry from their parents—since each child had some animals and poultry to make some money—whenever we wanted so that we could have new younger ones sooner and multiply our profits in school holidays, a practice that I find unethical recently, given that an unjustified triggering of harm is *pro-tanto wrong*, at least in anthropocentric views. Unfortunately, this seems to scarcely apply to nonhuman animals because their wants aren't respected. If but only if they would be respected and having voluntarily

---

144. See Singer and Mason, *The Ethics of What We eat*, 6, 24–28, 37, 122–33.

145. Deniss and Brown, "Pathogenic avian influenza," 19–38; WHO, "Pathogenic avian influenza."; Olsen, "Novel swine influenza viruses," 199–210; Wenjun, "Swine influenza virus."

146. DeGrazia, "Ethics of confining Animals," 738, 746; see also WHO, "H5N1 highly pathogenic avian influenza."

confined them in our compounds without their own will and sympathetic choice, we would morally endeavor to honor their rights entailed in fulfilling their wants without harming them if we were to appreciate a holistic approach to bioethics. We have to respect that every creature is entitled to a life of its own. We should not be indifferent to any entity's stress or pain. In conclusion, though nonhuman animals display mental states that to an extent satisfy some kind of reflective properties required for moral evaluations, such as fear, harm, stress, injuries, frustration, suffering, the question of whether they can self-reflect on their actions as human animals in relation to the normative structures remains pending.

Are Self-Reflections of Nonhuman Animals Guided by Norms?

The question is whether nonhuman animals as moral agents self-reflect and are guided by norms of approval and disapproval before executing their own motives. In retrospect, we not only saw Aristotle answering questions of normativity with the normative structure of virtues, that must be acquired and exercised in us by nature (habitually),[147] but also for Darwin, even-though morality can be found in nonhuman animals too, a true moral sense requires a capacity for self-reflection that can only be possessed by human animals.[148] Darwin's appeal to the superiority of the moral sense in human animals might still not succeed. In G. H. Lewes' critic at his contemporary Charles Darwin (inclusive of George Romanes), he wrote that "we are incessantly at fault in our tendency to anthropomorphize, a tendency which causes us to interpret the actions of animals according to the analogies of human nature."[149] We can say this humanistic mentality isn't a new discourse. While such weaknesses are revealed in different previous critics, the uniqueness of self-reflection in human animals is protected further. In defense of a reflective system of reasoning and decision making, Rowlands assigns the unique ability to reflect on or form judgements about what we ought to do to only a moral creature that is able to reflect on what it does, and ask itself whether this is, in the circumstances, a morally good thing to do or ask itself whether what it feels in these circumstances is the morally right thing to feel.[150] Such a normative self-control as the essence of morality

---

147. See *Nicomachean Ethics*, 1103a19–03b2, 1105a.

148. See Bradie, "The Moral Life of Animals," 549–51, 561; Darwin, *Descent of Man*, 36–48.

149. Lewes, *Seaside Studies at Ilfracombe*, 385. Quoted from Andrews, "Beyond Anthropomorphism," 471.

150. Rowlands, "Animals that Act for Moral Reasons," 523.

seems to be relatable to human animals. To put it differently in Korsgaard's tone, "the capacity for normative self-government and the deeper level of intentional control that goes with it is probably unique to human beings. And it is in the proper use of this capacity—the ability to form and act on judgements of what we ought to do—that the essence of morality lies, not in altruism or the pursuit of the greater good."[151] Just like Darwin, Rowlands, and Korsgaard, equally Aristotle neither counts nonhuman animals as reflective moral subjects nor as agents. Nonhuman animals are neither able to critically reflect on both their behavior and their motivation, nor to subject these to moral evaluations.[152] Even when we may claim that both are self-conscious, there is a unique difference between human animals and nonhuman animals in their exercise of self-conscious.

Though nonhuman animals are simply *conscious of their objects*, human animals are additionally *conscious that they fear the object*. We can explain this in Korsgaard's interpretation of Kant. For her "human beings have developed a specific form of self-consciousness, namely, the ability to perceive, and therefore to think about, the grounds of our beliefs and actions as grounds."[153] What Korsgaard means by being conscious of the ground as a ground is: "An animal who acts from instinct is conscious of the objects of its fear or desire, and conscious of it as fearful or desirable, and so as to-be-avoided or to-be-sought. That is the ground of its action. But a rational animal is, in addition, conscious that she fears or desires the object, and that she is inclined to act in a certain way as a result."[154] Nonhuman animals being *conscious of their objects* while human animals are furthermore *conscious that they fear or desire their objects* makes human animals quite distinct, which distinction is quite relatable to them being self-conscious about the normative principles of approval and disapproval of decisions. This perspective is no different from what psychologists understand with human reasoning and decision making. On the one hand, humans have a set of quick and intuitive systems that are largely shared with other animals, while on the other hand they have a more reflective system unique to them.[155] Nonetheless this position is challenged in other fields of morality. Some insist it is not only human animals capable of reflective

---

151. Korsgaard, "Fellow Creatures," 140.
152. See Rowlands, "Animals that Act for Moral Reasons," 527.
153. Korsgaard, "Fellow Creatures," 148–49.
154. Korsgaard, "Fellow Creatures," 148–50.
155. See Carruthers, "Animal Mentality," 382; Carruthers references to different studies including Evans and Frankish, *Two minds.*; Frankish, *Mind and Supermind*. See also Carruthers' other studies, "Dual Reasoning," 109–27; "Conscious Will," 197–213, and "Our Own Minds," 121–38.

moral endorsement—a kind of self-approval that involves approving one's own commitments having had beliefs about them—but also other animals possess metacognitive capacities as a precondition to being able to engage in reflective endorsement of one's moral sense. For example, nonhuman animals apparently have sympathy and the ability to think about their own mental states.[156] We need more evidence in their naturalistic environment, in addition to what we know that elephants or chimpanzees as moral agents discipline their younger ones or bury their dead relatives in grief and with dignity, evidence that can further approve or disapprove of the sympathy they feel and the mental-cognitive states surrounding their exercise of norms within their communities. In my understanding, this may be consistent with social norms that human animals may generally consciously apply in various particular instances, namely, social moral etiquette may require waiting politely in a line for one's turn at one moment, while in another moment, social etiquette may mean holding the door for the next person or allowing the elderly or pregnant person to use one's seat on public transport. Though nonhuman animals seem excluded from these conscious meta-cognitive states—such as when elephants bury their colleague, when chimpanzees beat up their young ones when they wrong or when they squeeze tree leaves to apply on their wounded bodies or when they sort wrangles between two youthful elephants—we may need to more precisely define what consciousness is. When we are conscious simpliciter of something as creatures, it is transitive consciousness (we are awake), as in, one is transitively conscious if she has thoughts about doing some gorilla trekking in Uganda. In contrast, states and other creatures may not be conscious of anything, i.e., intransitive consciousness. A creature may be intransitively conscious when it is asleep or otherwise unconscious. A state is intransitively conscious when we are consciously entertaining it—as when I think to myself that I can only do gorilla trekking in Uganda, Rwanda, and Congo.[157] Since we cannot deny states consciousness, similarly we are persuaded to confer onto nonhuman animals moral standing (as moral subjects). We have to be more sensitive of the fact that the notion of intrinsic value of nonhuman entities still suffers remarkable injuries in our whole discussion given anthropocentric and anthropomorphic oriented normative standards. If we further anthropomorphize normative systems in biomedical ethics, we would be imposing a human normative criterion while anthropocentrically rejecting the obvious conclusive evidence from evolutionary science, experiments by cognitive ethologists as well as results from neuroscience, that vehemently point to

---

156. See Driver, "Status and Character of Animals," 153, 158.
157. See Rowlands, "Animals that Act for Moral Reasons," 537–43.

shared capacities between human animals and other animals.[158] But if we are to pursue holistic bioethics, we ought to be extra sensitive to the fact that the minimum normative basics of our approaches to biomedical ethics are at the very least not distinctive to neither human animals nor nonhuman animals alone.

Moral Status and Moral Standing: From Nonhuman Animals to All Living Entities

We have encountered varied perplexities in our previous moral discourse as we advocated for an eventual awarding of moral status and moral standing to nonhuman entities. The discussed majority of principle-based frameworks interest themselves and largely presume than practically demonstrate how nonhuman entities lack some relevant forms of functional properties.[159] It is now clear to us that there seems to be largely no set of distinctive properties in these frameworks that convincingly confer moral standing and moral status to all entities. This basic confusion in biomedical ethics still somewhat remains. For instance, in relation to the theory of personhood, Childress and Beauchamp note this confusion:

> Person theory has not proven to be the key to a satisfactory model of moral status. Moral status does not require personhood, and personhood does not clearly entail moral status. In one theory, human embryos are declared persons and the great apes are not, whereas in another theory the great apes are persons and human embryos are not. Primates, for example, often

---

158. See Bradie, "The Moral Life of Animals," 558.

159. Summarily, a number of property formulations, some discussed while some not, that are necessary conditions for moral standing, moral status or both. They include: the capacity to experience pleasure and/or pain; the capacity for having desires; the capacity for remembering past events; the capacity for having expectations with respect to future events; an awareness of the passage of time, the property of being a continuing, conscious self, or subject of mental states, construed, in a minimal way, as nothing more than a construct out of appropriately related mental states; the property of being a continuing, conscious self, construed as a pure ego, that is, as an entity that is distinct for the experiences and other mental states that it has; the capacity for self-consciousness, that is, for awareness of the fact that one is a continuing, conscious subject of mental states; the property of having mental states that involve propositional attitudes, such as beliefs and desires; the capacity for having thought episodes, that is, states of consciousness involving intentionality; the capacity for reasoning; problem-solving ability; the property of being autonomous, that is, of having the capacity for making decisions based upon an evaluation of relevant considerations; the capacity for using language; the ability to interact socially with others. See Tooley, "Are Nonhuman Animals Persons," 548–49.

possess humanlike properties that some humans lack, such as a specific form of intellectual quickness, the capacity to feel pain, and the ability to enter into meaningful social relationships. Basing on human properties doesn't qualify as a comprehensive account of moral status, but the proposition that some set of distinctive human properties is a sufficient, but not necessary, condition of moral status.[160]

The same confusion still re-surfaces in other studies of Beauchamp: "It is fortunate for animals and humans who lack moral personhood that moral standing does not require personhood of any type. Some creatures have moral standing even though they do not possess even a single cognitive or moral capacity. The reason is that certain noncognitive and nonmoral properties are sufficient to confer a measure of moral standing."[161] An identical moral confusion, that there is basically any fixed framework of properties in bioethical principlism which credibly bestows moral standing and moral status to creatures, is not only explicit among the main protagonists of principlism but it appears often in other principle-based studies. In Frans de Waal's defense of the question whether animals have morality, "if we take the full-blown human phenomenon as a yardstick, they most definitely do not. On the other hand, if we break the relevant human abilities into their component parts, some are recognizable in other animals."[162] It is this breakdown in abilities that we have labored to do in the last couple of sections, and undeniably, nonhuman animals successfully qualified beyond this confusion as either moral patients or moral agents, befitting a moral status or standing, or even both.

If but only if we charitably interpret the discussed scientific evidence in and of itself, it would be an unfavorable argument to conclude that the search for a holistic approach isn't to an extent already implicitly presumed in some interventions of biomedical ethics. Even when nonhuman animals may not be credible candidates, human animals too fail to qualify since they lack one or more of the necessary prerequisites of moral standing or moral status.[163] Even when we have largely argued that nonhuman entities can be

---

160. Beauchamp and Childress, PBE, 70–71.
161. Beauchamp, "Failure of Theories of Personhood," 309–24.
162. De Waal, Good Natured, 6.
163. See Beauchamp, "Failure of Theories of Personhood," 309-24; Personhood of humans and nonhumans like apes, dolphins. DeGrazia, "Great Apes, Dolphins," 301–20; Relying on the thought of neoclassical theists like Alfred North Whitehead and Charles Hartshorne, nonhuman animals can be persons. Dombrowski, "Are Nonhuman Animals Persons? 135–43; Chan and Harris, "Human Animals and Nonhuman Persons," 320–21.

subjects of moral agency as moral or *proto* moral agents, the critic in Frans de Waal's terms, would be to inaccurately favor certain nonhuman animals (such as the great apes) as fulfilling some "component parts" of agency without these parts forming the *whole*.[164] Primarily, the pursuit of the "whole" could be atleast understood in a twofold perspective.

Firstly, I am of the view that if but only if nonhuman entities matter because of what they are, we should postulate a holistic fundamental standing toward them. We have a sincere moral obligation not only to treat them *decently*, but also not to cause them gratuitous pain. The obligation is only due to their nature themselves and to what would undermine their welfare, but not derived from our obligation to our own welfare.[165] In human terms, this is analogously captured in PBE, whereby it doesn't matter at all how much a parent loves her children's closest friends, the friends will neither eventually gain moral status by virtue of this close relationship nor will the lack of such a human relationship indicate any lack of moral status.[166] If we compare the same to our shared evolved neural architecture, we should evaluate the moral status of nonhuman animals in terms that are intrinsic to their own capacities, rather than in terms that satisfy our anthropocentric understanding of morality.[167] Part of the neurophysiological evidence we have to re-affirm, are the neurological structures in nonhuman animals that are homologous to the structures in the human brain responsible for affect, emotional responses, and reactions. Such evidence compels Tom Regan to undeniably portray nonhuman animals as *subjects-of-life*. They are subjects of life because they have beliefs and desires; perception, memory, and a sense of the future (including their own future); an emotional life (pleasure and pain); interests; the ability to initiate action; a psychological identity over time, and so on.[168] Altogether, the evidence in evolution, neuroscience, and cognitive ethology makes us prove that many nonhuman animals are indeed candidates for moral standing, or rather prove the existence of putative moral capacities. This evidence does not only partially support that they possess enough mindedness to count as moral agents and full members of a given moral community, it remains a harmless simplification backing-up my preferred holistic treatment of them, since this evidence supports

---

164. Frey, "Utilitarianism and Animals," 189–90; De Waal, *Good Natured*.

165. Copp, "Fundamental Moral Standing," 276; Copp references to Hooker, *Ideal Code, Real World*, 66–70.

166. See Beauchamp and Childress, PBE, 76.

167. See Bradie, "The Moral Life of Animals," 549.

168. See Bradie, "The Moral Life of Animals," 559; Regan, *Animal Rights*, 243–48, 285, 357.

nonhuman animals as moral patients or at least partial members of a moral community.

Evolutionary evidence supports the idea that there are no significant qualitative differences between humans and other animals. Neurophysiological evidence supports this conclusion insofar as homologous brain structures and systems implicated in the cognitive and affective capabilities of human beings are widespread in the animal kingdom. Finally, the evidence from cognitive ethology reinforces the view that a wide range of animals not only posses the relevant neural architecture necessary for sophisticated cognitive and affective behavior but that they manifest some degree of moral sensibility in their behavior.[169]

Secondly, I think that if but only if we are to fundamentally concern ourselves with the essence of morality towards human animals, morality must advance beyond the human welfare to include nonhuman life in equal measure. We should not stress a welfare that only caters for human animals living together successfully in their own human communities with little concern to the other nonhuman life, given that it is only by supporting other lives that we can ultimately support human survival or the holistic wellbeing of all. David Copp rightly supports this claim and believes that our duties regarding nonhuman animals are not derivative from duties we have to human animals, but our moral duties to nonhuman animals and to human animals alike have the same basis and are equally fundamental. In emphasis of this *thesis of the fundamental standing of nonhuman animals*, it is central to *common-sense morality* that the pain of nonhuman animals has moral weight. If we are to foster holistic welfare, not to torture a dog is not as important or weighty as not to torture a human infant.[170] Welfarism emphasizes that every creature's welfare counts fundamentally making human animals and nonhuman animals to have moral standing. So all "creatures are on a par except insofar as promoting the welfare of some creatures might be a more efficient way of promoting overall welfare than promoting the welfare of some creature."[171] In this regard, holistic welfare or well-being should be understood beyond satisfying human interests or preferences,[172] to include the whole chain of welfarism—not the maximum contentment but the overall welfare—that is, "the overall good matters morally; animal

---

169. Bradie, "The Moral Life of Animals," 567–69.

170. Copp, "Fundamental Moral Standing," 267–80. Copp references to Raz, *The Morality of Freedom*, 267.

171. Copp, "Fundamental Moral Standing," 283.

172. See Akhtar, "Animal Pain and Welfare," 499–500.

welfare is at least some part of the overall good."[173] Since every creature is morally significant in any holistic approach to bioethics we may envisage, critics of welfarism question whether if we take every creature as intrinsically valuable regardless of whether it is sentient or non-sentient, we should also include bacterias, germs, viruses and so on.[174] In defense Huebner is of the view that "viruses are nothing more than packets of RNA (or sometimes DNA) encased in protein . . . though mechanically complex . . . they are not the kind of entities that can want to threaten our wellbeing; they do not make plans or adopt deceptive strategies for navigating our immune systems; and they have not learned to outsmart our best antivirals."[175] Viruses are instrumentally useful in diagnosing infections and safeguarding our lives. Viruses can be harnessed in research and health care to handle illnesses, develop drugs and vaccines needed for our health and integral wellbeing. In our holistic search for functional bioethics, it all zeroes down to embracing the decent fair minimum in the overall welfare or well-being of all entities.

In arguing for a decent fair minimum appropriate to the holistic well-being of all entities, PBE is right that our global goal, for instance, should "be a decent minimum standard of health, not merely health care."[176] Construing the decent minimum, in Madison Powers and Faden Ruth's "Sufficiency of Well-Being Approach," we encounter a non-ideal theory that is concerned with the totality of social structure as having a profoundly integral effect on the essential dimensions of well-being, whereby, any inequality in the social determinants leads to some falling below a level of sufficiency. Even if we were to consider the permanent job of justice, our commitment to practical social justice requires us to embrace decent fair opportunities so that we neutralize limited resources, imagination, and sympathy by which some entities fall below a level of sufficiency.[177] Decent fair opportunities and minimums require an attitude of sympathy, not only to some but toward every creature

---

173. Hooker, *Ideal Code, Real World*, 68. See also more details in 33, 37–43.

174. See Copp, "Fundamental Moral Standing," 284.

175. Huebner, "Minimal Minds," 441.

176. Beauchamp and Childress, PBE, 298; A consensus that there is (at least) a right to a decent minimum of health care pervades recent policy debates. Buchanan, "Right to a Decent Minimum," 55–78.

177. See Powers and Faden, *Social Justice*, 57–79 (especially 57) and 78–79, 94–95; Rawls' guidance is helpful when he uses fair opportunity as a rule of redress, to overcome undeserved disadvantaging conditions, whether they derive from the natural lottery (distribution of advantageous and disadvantageous genetic properties) or the social lottery (distribution of assets or deficits through family property, school systems, tribal affiliation, government agencies), the rule of fair opportunity demands compensation for disadvantages. Beauchamp and Childress, PBE, 282–84.

in its own right as an equally valued social determinant without allocating varying degrees of moral status to a limited few. Whether I should forsake an ape in fire accident in preference to rescuing an old person takes great moral pains to decide since in favoring a decent fair minimum for all species we have denied a "theory of degrees of moral status that sorts creatures into higher and lower moral status."[178] The said sympathetic attitude extended appropriately—meaning it may be extended differently—towards all, should slash our speciesist tendencies that allocate higher or lower statuses to some creatures and not to the others. And this indeed is not tantamount to frustrating the Creator's original vision of each species.

What is unethical about speciesism in relation to the promotion of the wellbeing of all? In his discussion of hybridism, and response to creationists and naturalists, Darwin maintains "that species, when intercrossed, have been specially endowed with the quality of sterility, in order to prevent the confusion of all organic forms."[179] When apes mate, more apes are given life to. When chimpanzees mate, more chimpanzees. But when a chimpanzee and an ape interbreed, the resulting hypothetical hybrid is unimaginable (chim-pe)! It is why in Greene Mark's emphasis of this Darwinian creationist perspective, noting that the membership of a species consists of the original members plus those individuals that trace their ancestry, "God prevents 'the confusion of all organic forms' by enforcing reproductive isolation between species by making members of different species unable to interbreed and produce fertile young."[180] As Darwin has indicated above, we should firstly note that the creator's original vision of fertility within each species is intactly preserved without any interbreeding confusions from generation to generation.[181] Secondly, if speciesism entails "a) drawing a distinction be-

---

178. Frey, "Utilitarianism and Animals," 177–78.

179. Darwin, *On The Origin of Species*, 245.

180. Greene, "Origin of Species Notions," 581–87; see also De Queiroz, "Modern Concept of Species," 6600–07.

181. Although among the biologists and philosophers of science, there seems to be no single definition of what a species is, relying on the modern "biological species concept," a species is a group of interbreeding organisms with a reproductive isolation, see Mayr, *Origin of Species*.; in response to Mayr, some thinkers agree that "species are separately evolving *metapopulations*. That is, they are sets of spatially distinct subpopulations of sexually reproducing organisms that extend over time to form *lineages* (ancestor-descendant sequences of breeding populations) whose boundaries are determined in part by patterns of interbreeding," see Powell, "Nature of Species," 606; species and other taxa are more productively thought of as individual lineages, rather than immutable natural kinds. Powell, "Nature of Species," 606; about *individual lineages* in contrast to *immutable natural kinds/classes* in the context of biological *texa*, Powell references Ghiselin, "Solution to the Species Problem," 536–44, as the proponent and later endorsed by Hull, "A Matter of Individuality," 335–60. Species may be roughly

tween members of one's own species and others; and b) sometimes, in some ways, giving preference to the interests of members of one's own species,"[182] many times—even though we may not claim that every speciesism is wrong since there could be some ethical ways of restricting human concepts in their application towards nonhuman entities—we *unethically* (thinking of unethical application of anthropocentrism) restrict the application of these concepts to our fellow human animals or some living things, which literally means speciesism (akin to racism).[183] The challenge of this exclusive application can be traceable back to Aristotle's function argument, namely, "a living organism has the function of self-maintenance and reproduction, and things are good or bad for it insofar as they enable it to stay alive and healthy and reproduce."[184] Aristotle's moral account remains not only focused on living organisms just like his successors fall suit, but also includes and excludes some class of creatures.

To sort speciesist discrepancies in the contemporary era, species egalitarianism is suggested. "*Species egalitarianism* is the view that all living things have equal moral standing."[185] In different studies, like for Paul Tylor, it is biocentrism that grounds species egalitarianism. Taylor's biocentric view understands all living beings as having intrinsic worth and equally good *life of their own in their own way*. A plant like a nonhuman animal seeks a good of its own in its own way just like a human animal. All grow and reproduce, what can be understood as a trait of moral standing. They all have equal value since they are teleological centres of life as living things. In this sense, plants, nonhuman and human animals have not only equal value as far as being *teleological centres of life*,[186] but they are also *members of the earth's community of life* in the same sense and on the same terms, besides being *integral parts* of a system of interdependence.[187] This becomes obstructive or rather deadly to privilege or underprivilege one of the living

---

characterized as follows: independently evolving, spatiotemporally restricted metapopulation lineages that are poorly integrated, weakly cohesive, non-goal directed, non-developmental, and composed of largely non-differentiated, nonfunctional, and noncooperative parts. Powell, "Nature of Species," 609.

182. Hursthouse, "Treatment of Animals," 121–22.

183. See Hursthouse, "Treatment of Animals," 121.

184. Aristotle, *Metaphysics*, books 7–10; *On the Soul*, books 2–3; and *Nicomachean Ethics*, book 1, section 7. All in Barnes, *The Complete Works of Aristotle*. Cited from Korsgaard, "Interacting with Animals," 112, footnote 4.

185. Schmidtz, "Are All Species Equal," 628.

186. See Schmidtz, "Are All Species Equal," 632.

187. Taylor, *Respect for Nature*, 99, and also "Ethics of Respect for Nature," 217. Referenced from Schmidtz, "Are All Species Equal," 628–31.

entities as inherently *superior* or *inferior*[188] to others, or argue for degrees of equality within this interdependence. It is why Tylor morally embraces treating all living things with respect, a basic connection between self-respect and respectful care for the world as our only home in which we live. One reason to care about living things, for instance trees, is quite beyond their instrumental value as timber, aids in rain formation, medicine, fruit harvest, browse for wild animals and birds, shade and so on. It requires us not to satisfy trees that we are treating them appropriately, *but to satisfy ourselves*.[189] Lack of respect for woodlands or aesthetic beauties as part of a well-functioning system of a natural world may be an indication of lack of self-respect and satisfaction of ourselves. By all means each being remains uniquely incomparable and priceless in the network of interdependence. It ought to be common knowledge that with all entities, "we are not equal. We are not superior. We are not inferior. We are simply different."[190] And if human animals treat plants *no better than* they treat nonhuman animals, that is a failure of respect and self-satisfaction. "Failing to respect what makes living things different is not a way of respecting them. It is instead a way of being indiscriminate."[191] In the strive to improve ecology beyond any selective species preservation and respect, some radical biocentric environmentalists, such as deep ecologists and anthropocentric instrumentalists, reject any conservation triage—deserting some species to extinction—because it cannot be sustained along the notion that all species have equal intrinsic worth requiring equal treatment, i.e., "biocentric egalitarianism." Contrary to the triage approach, biocentric egalitarianism preserves all species regardless of their expected instrumental value.[192]

---

188. "Consider Mandeville's parable of the Roman merchant and the lion in his *Fable of the Bess*. The merchant, having washed up on a foreign shore, encounters a lion, who agrees that he will not eat the merchant if a good reason is given why he shouldn't. After the merchant argues that due to his greater reason and his immortal soul is superior, the lion responded: 'If the Gods have given you superiority over all Creatures, then why beg you an inferior?' The lion went on to skillfully dispose of all the merchant's arguments and concluded by underscoring his first criticism in the quote by eating the merchant." Bernard Mandeville's parable of the Roman merchant and the lion is accessible in Kaye, *Fable of the Bess*, 178–80. Retold by Garrett, "Animals and Ethics," 66.

189. See Taylor, *Respect for Nature*, 42–43. See an interpretation from Schmidtz, "Are All Species Equal," 634–35.

190. Schmidtz, "Are All Species Equal," 629.

191. Schmidtz, "Are All Species Equal," 630.

192. Powell, "Nature of Species," 617; more on *deep ecology* (inherent worth of living things) and the rejection of the triage approach, see Naess, "Long-Range Ecology," 95–100; more on moral philosophies rejecting *biocentric egalitarianism*, see Grey, "Anthropocentrism and Deep Ecology," 463–75; and more on the anthropocentric instrumentalists' rejection of the triage approach, see, for example, the two works, Takacs, *The*

In conclusion, moral standing and degrees in moral status have been consistently applied to each organism's capacity for sentience, social cognition, autonomous decision making, moral agency, metacognition, propositional attitude mind-reading, human language, self-consciousness, and to approve and disprove actions according to standard normative structures. Through an immense positive contribution of studies in this chapter, inclusive of different scientific approaches and principle-based theories, evidence has demonstrated a deeply shared heritage and affinity of nonhuman animals and nonhuman animals. Though beyond speciesism, welfarism, biocentrism, there is also species egalitarianism and biocentric egalitarianism. These moral accounts have aimed at respectfully harmonizing each life uniquely, but only life of the living organisms—if not mainly of human animals—while difficultly exclusively precluding the promotion of moral life of the nonliving things along the totality of life in the hierarchical order of forces. Our contemporary approaches to holistic biomedical ethics necessarily demand a revitalized reconceptualization of our approach to biomedical ethics, an approach that never precludes any creature or life force.

Having embraced rich evidence from different Western scientific approaches, it already strongly suggests a healthier complementary approach in our pursuit of holistic bioethics. Without forgetting the various shortcomings toward a possible holistic solution in bioethical interventions, I proceed with a complementary African approach to an understanding of moral status and moral standing appropriate for both moral patients and agents. For every created creature, both the living and nonliving—citing the African moral thought of *no creation is lifeless*—is embraced in the moral account of holistic bioethics. A holistic approach to bioethics is preferred since it embraces integrally the whole life without distinctions between higher and lower degrees of statuses, between living and nonliving things, between the visible and invisible realities.

Idea of Biodiversity.; and Norton, *The Preservation of Species.*

3

An African Approach to Holistic Bioethics

From a Black African context, the holistic approach supplies the missing gaps necessary to complement and integrally incorporate not only moral agents but also moral patients in a life of a triad-community—the three-dimensional community or tripartite community. If it is to qualify as a holistic approach to bioethics from African context, it has to consider all creation as having life (living and nonliving), deriving its normative content from an interactive solidary community of the living, the living dead (inclusive of the ancestors) and those to be born. To have a foretaste of the holistic sense, briefly think of "wolf-children"—children brought up in isolation from other human animals by nonhuman animals—to whom the social community is holistically exposed to morally provide the necessary social skills, moral support or linguistic ingredients that might enhance what lacks.[1] Likewise, a severely mentally dilapidated person in a permanently vegetative state (e.g., *anencephalic infants*[2]) should holistically enjoy both the moral status and the moral standing supplied by the sympathetic moral community since she remains a conscious responsible subject via the agency of other community members that make up the community moral agency. The question is whether the same moral community doesn't misuse its human moral patients who are already in pain, for instance, if it

---

1. See Chan and Harris, "Human Animals and Nonhuman Persons," 335.
2. "These are undoubtedly human beings. Yet they are born without a cortex, and although they sometimes possess a rudimentary brainstem, this lacks any covering of skull or skin. They are blind and response to touch and sound may occur. If not stillborn, most die within a few hours or days of birth. There is no cure or treatment." Information from the National Institutes for Health cited by Carruthers, "Animal Mentality," 390, 404.

harvests organs for donation. In the first instance, the holistic community sense shouldn't be erroneously misunderstood as being morally identical to a maximized utilitarian perspective of saving several community members by hastening a patient's death in order to gift her parts—heart, lungs, kidneys, liver, intestine, pancreas, ligaments, skin, parts of the eye, heart valves, heart tissues, bone, tendons—to the larger moral community. In the second instance, if we analogously translate the same human animal cases of pain to nonhuman entities, chicken may be stressed in cages or a primate could have a toothache, while wild nonhuman animals caged in zoos and parks—by contrast, black Africans are naturally used to free moving wildlife—for our enjoyment could have downheartedness or melancholy or depression comparable to the moral patient-hood depicted in the case of an anencephalic infant. Given this correlativity, we should morally recognize the moral standing of not only human animals but also equally nonhuman animals, not only living things but equally also nonliving things, so as to holistically protect every creature since every creature makes the future community survival possible.

FROM AN ANTHROPOCENTRIC TO A HOLISTIC VIEW

The Danger of a Strong Anthropocentric Point of View

The reader should recall that throughout our bioethical discourse, we have silently indicated that anthropomorphic[3] and anthropocentric perspectives have generally taken human moral systems as the only ones if not the cardinal and conceivably the exclusive guidelines against which to judge the moral systems of other creatures. The so called "anthropocentric point of view" is a perennial tradition which assesses the moral status of all animals in terms of how much they are like humans. Such an anthropocentric point of view takes "human morality as the standard for determining the moral standing of other animals. The more like us they are, the higher their moral status and the more their interests and well-being need to be taken into account."[4] Anthropocentrism gives "exclusive or primary consideration to human interests above the good of other species."[5] We can understand bioethical principlism as identifying itself with *strong anthropocentrism*, to a

---

3. In animal cognitive research, "anthropomorphism" is the attribution of uniquely human mental characteristics to nonhuman animals, raising questions of which properties are uniquely human. Andrews, "Beyond Anthropomorphism," 469.

4. Bradie, "The Moral Life of Animals," 564.

5. Schmidtz, "Are All Species Equal," 630.

larger extent, while to a smaller extent, it goes beyond humans and extends to animals but with limited or no ethical relationships with other systems of life such as the invisible communities (our ancestors and those not yet born) or other entities, like the environment, cosmos (ecology), inanimate entities, etc. Correspondingly, some moral thoughts can be cited as defending a *weaker anthropocentric sense* by claiming that creatures like animals have weaker duties to other entities to grant them atleast some partial moral status. Some argue for an *enlightened anthropocentrism*, for instance, strong indirect duties not only to protect the whole environment for humanity's generational survival but also to necessarily safeguard a functioning planet—climate, human and nonhuman animal life.[6] Among these three senses of anthropocentrism, we may primarily argue for a weaker sense of anthropocentrism in some interpretation, for instance, of the African account of moral personhood since it accords a partial or some moral status to nonhuman animals, rivers, lakes, mountains, forests and so on. The reason is some interpreters of the moral account of personhood do not accord an intrinsic value to some parts of the environment because these do not have the capacity for sympathy. This is because, these parts of the environment are neutral to the presence or absence of sympathy. For an entity to be receptive to sympathy, at the very least, it should be the subject or object of life. Since these parts of the environment do not count as either subjects or objects of sympathy,[7] it turns out ethically difficult to think of direct or indirect moral duties towards them or other nonhuman entities at large.

The African moral thought can also be cited as defending strong anthropocentric views. For instance, in Wiredu's African studies, he indicates two meta-ethical properties of the African moral thought: Secular (ethical naturalism) and religious (ethical supernaturalism). Ethical-naturalism accounts for moral properties in physical terms, where the source of ethics is "horizontal" (the natural or cultural world); whereas ethical supernaturalism invokes spiritual properties, considering the source of morality to be "vertical" (the spiritual realm). Wiredu settles for an ethical naturalism than a supernaturalistic view of the Akan people. In this light, his meta-ethics employs a naturalistic humanistic approach (human interests) to ethics, in which he is convinced of an axiological cultural thinking of his people. The approach is humanistic because they are the humans that are

---

6. See Molefe, *African Personhood*, 108; Literature on "enlightened anthropocentrism" include, Keurlatz, "Emergence of Enlightened Anthropocentrism," 48–71.

7. For an anthropocentric view, see Metz, "An African Theory of Moral Status," 399; Metz, "African Moral Theory," 81–99; Molefe, *African Personhood*, 81–82, 107–8; more on the anthropocentric view of African moral ideas, see Chemhuru, *African Ontology for Environmental Ethics.*; Behrens, *Environmental Ethics.*

the measure of all value and the summary of the entire project of morality, hence a strong sense of anthropocentrism.[8] Beyond scholarships defending a strong anthropocentric view of African ethics, numerous scholarships on African ethics describe it as having both a strong and a weaker anthropocentric sense. In reference to his book, *Animals and African Ethics* (2015), Horsthemke thinks that in African ethics, moral perceptions, attitudes and practices depict a strong anthropocentric sense on one side while on the other side, through values like *ubuntu* (humanness) and *ukama* (relationality), they strongly include nonhuman nature, which depicts a weaker anthropocentric sense.[9] However, confining the African moral account to an anthropocentric sense is to limit it as I will prove my position later on.

Generally, the natural world isn't any more intact, given the current over-reliance on disastrous anthropocentric principlism coupled with a ruinous anthropocentric arrogance that doesn't wish other creatures a respectful living of their own, more especially when these entities do not directly benefit humans. In wishing to rectify this and sustain a functioning planet suitable for the future generations—since the future generation (human beings) may not be intrinsically distinctive from our generation—need demands us transcending an enlightened sense of anthropocentrism by adopting a non or anti-anthropocentric view which aims at ameliorating the limited anthropocentric dimensions that only underline and respect the central importance of inter-human relationships in bioethics. "From the perspective of anti-anthropocentric environmental ethics, not only the other sentient animals, but also the members of the millions of species of non-sentient animals, and of plants, ecosystems, and the like, all matter morally as well. The feature conferring moral status that all these groups have in common has to be something extremely broad—being alive, having a good of its own, being an integral part of an ecosystem, or being part of nature."[10] The non-anthropocentric argument uniquely confers moral status to (even) non-sentient animals. It goes beyond the limited anthropocentric dimensions to include nonhuman living species as also mattering morally. Living entities matter morally in their own good and need demands us to

---

8. For Wiredu's rejection of ethical supernaturalism, see Wiredu, "Reply to English/Hamme," 234; Wiredu bases the articulation of his moral theory on the Akan assertion '*Onipa na ohia*', see Wiredu, "An African Culture," 194; For the Akan axiological thinking, see Wiredu, *Cultural Universals and Particulars*, 65; Wiredu, "African Philosophy in our Time," 1–27; Wiredu, "Social Philosophy in Postcolonial Africa," 332–39; Wiredu, "Oral Philosophy of Personhood," 8–18; Molefe, *African Personhood*, 79–80; Molefe, "A Rejection of Humanism," 59–77.

9. Horsthemke, "African Communalism," 64.

10. Hursthouse, "Treatment of Animals," 123.

be satisfied within our sublime rationality as humans that know and convincingly extend our respectful love towards them in the humblest means possible. This is in dialogue with what Rosalind Hursthouse notes:

> From the perspective of the major non-anthropocentric environmentalists, such as Aldo Leopold and Arne Naess, respectful love is something that should be extended well beyond the limits of our fellow autonomous agents and sentient others to *any living things*, because they have a good of their own . . . . We are not the beauty of the world nor paragon of animals. Our sublime rationality should enable us, especially now that we know as much as we do, to recognize that the living world contains myriad of wonders that should make us humble as well as be a source of delight. *This anti-anthropocentric, 'biocentric' claim, that any living thing is an appropriate object of respectful love, is more familiar in Eastern than Western* philosophy and one that we may find very hard to take on board. I do, but I can certainly find much that is true in it.[11]

The anti-anthropocentric, "biocentric" claim limits its horizon on living things as the appropriate objects of respectful love. Although some interpretations of the African account as mentioned above seem anthropocentric, the *life force* as understood in the relational community is deeply anti-anthropocentric and likewise extends respectful love not only to the living entities but also beyond them. This is because, confining anti-anthropocentric approaches to living species is to dichotomize what cannot be dichotomized, it is to limit what cannot be limited, given the African account whose moral-ethical solution towards the endangered integrity of the planet cannot be limited to animates alone. The life force must include the living and non-living communities, the visible and invisible forces.

Toward a Holistic view: Bioethics must be Local to be Global

To lower the widening degrees in moral status of organisms, the claim that human animals are the apex of biological existence has been dismissed as an arrogant speciesist claim—assumption of human superiority—from an African local context. Even when it is less disputable that human animals have putative moral responsibilities toward inanimate objects, plants, and nonhuman animals, nonhuman entities have largely been considered not to have any correlative moral obligations toward human animals.[12] We

---

11. Hursthouse, "Treatment of Animals," 132. *Emphasis is mine.*
12. See Tangwa, "Biomedical and Environmental Ethics," 388; Situating human

argue that the seeming lack of the reciprocal relational requirement of responsibility among nonhuman entities or, severely mentally dilapidated people in a permanently vegetative state (e.g., anencephalic infants) or wolf-children, is fully taken care of by the hierarchized life force of the African social community that competently takes full responsibility of every community member without any discrimination. But taken commonly, even when a nonhuman animal displays human-like capacities than a retarded child, speciesists would not treat it more considerably than the child, since nonhuman animals are not considered as responsible culpable moral agents, a trait reversed for human animals among all other earthly creatures. In interpreting the African moral thought however, we are of the view that the moral worth and value attributable to human animals that are not moral agents is symbolic and analogical and lies on the same continuum with the moral consideration given by human animals to nonhuman animals. To better appreciate this continuum of life, we emphasize promotion of life by every entity.

Every entity contributes to Bantu moral life and coexists with the whole and cannot be treated separately from the cosmic whole. Even if nonhuman animals displayed no similar human functional capacities, human moral sensibility and sensitivity would still treat nonhuman animals, other living creatures and inanimate entities with consideration and it cannot justifiably simply be linked by the idea of sharing similar capacities.[13] In the African world, it is through contextualizing other creatures that human animals better have self-knowledge—self-actualize themselves—as species that are plainly part of a one extended relational cosmic unity. Africanists like Tangwa note that human animals have indeed no special God-given privilege to subdue, dominate, and exploit the rest of creation as overlords of an impoverished once bio-diversified cosmos. It is one reason why the *Nso'* cultural attitude of *live* and *let live* toward nature and the rest of creation is that of a humble respectful coexistence with all, conciliation, and containment within the cosmic triad-community. Well knowing we find ourselves existing in the world at an unchosen *datum*—we may also find ourselves not existing, i.e., accepting life and death—about which it is too late to choose otherwise. This ought to give every human being a great sense of humility[14] before every earthly creature and life force. The African understanding of the earth harbors exceptionally the whole wide

---

beings at the apex of biological existence is a claim that is sometimes dismissed as too arrogant. Plants too have rights. Tangwa, *African bioethics in a Western frame*, 29.

13. See Tangwa, "Leaders in Ethics Education," 98–99.

14. See Tangwa, *African bioethics in a Western frame*, 71–72, 75.

range of cosmic forces. We note that "for the Nso', the earth *(nsaiy)* is a very potent force, to the extent that they do not cut the earth lightly (without ritual permission),"[15] otherwise they would disrupt cosmic co-existence since "the law of the earth *(nsër nsaiy)* is the strongest and brooks no breaking because the consequences of its violation are severe, metaphysical and unavoidable."[16] Moreover, Tangwa notes not only the fertility sacrifices (for plants, animals and humans), appropriate sacrifices and ritual cuttings of the earth *(gbar nsaiy)* with the sacred hoe of the Kingdom *(kisoo ke wong)*, but also incantations performed by the King *(Fon)*, the chief High Priest of the Kingdom, assisted by his three ritual helpers: *tawong* (father of the Kingdom), *yewong* (mother of the Kingdom) and *fai Ndzëndzëv* (chief great councillor of the Kingdom). Thusly, to safeguard this cosmic co-existence is visible in

> frequent offerings of sacrifices to God, to the divine spirits, both benevolent and malevolent, to the departed ancestors and to the sundry invisible and inscrutable forces of nature. The Nso' Year (Ya' Nso') always begins with fertility sacrifices. Through the course of the year, numerous other sacrifices are offered all over Nso' by the custodians of arable land *(ataangvën)*, lineage heads *(ataala')*, and *agaashiv* who normally combine the functions of medical doctor, priest, psychiatrist, counselor, and exorcist.[17]

Trying to see all as equal in biomedical approaches (bio-friendly) may not be the best way, but it is one way to a holistic approach to the solution. It is one reason we are compelled to believe in a non-speciesist continuum of life for the whole nature, even when every creature may pursue a different system of life goals or life force. However, our intervention in the life systems of human animals has to be holistically tilted towards maintaining a unified continuum of all. Towards all is to maintain this attitude of *live and let live*, which humbles humans more to be "cautious, more mistrustful and unsure of human knowledge and capabilities, more conciliatory and respectful of other people, plants, animals, inanimate things, as well as sundry invisible/ intangible forces, more timorous of wantonly tampering with nature."[18] Being *bio-friendly* with a respectful attitude of *live and let live* protects all the Other (inclusive of all entities and life forces), the moral agents as equally as

---

15. Tangwa, "Bioethics: an African perspective," 190; see Tangwa, *African bioethics in a Western frame*, 58.

16. Tangwa, "Bioethics: an African perspective," 190.

17. Tangwa, "Biomedical and Environmental Ethics," 389–90; see also Tangwa, *African bioethics in a Western frame*, 145, 158.

18. Tangwa, *African bioethics in a Western frame*, 41, also 157.

moral patients. It is the reason why to a black African, it is not only strictly a taboo to eat domestic animals meant for companionship such as dogs, cats, horses, donkeys, etc., but also "killing a pregnant animal is, however, strictly taboo and requires immediate ritual cleansing and purification, even if done accidentally."[19] Without distinguishing between moral patient-hood and moral agency, human beings and animals, human babies and animal babies, the African moral thought finds it simply "obvious that it is the unborn baby which makes the taboo necessary" while guarding "clearly against deliberate non-therapeutic abortion."[20] So it is unnecessary to strike a difference between which baby status it is. Paradoxically, while non-therapeutic abortion has been always held as wrong and sanctionable, infanticide was sometimes held as permissible amongst Nso'.[21] Considering infanticide (even without weeping) as permissible was believed by ancestors to promote life by avoiding an unacceptable consanguineal connection which may have polluted any collective communal interactive growth and conversion, for instance in cases of incest, since the moral cost of incest has not only been strictly held as a taboo till today, but it also necessarily requires moral purification and ritual cleansing. Collective growth critically necessitates appropriating ancestral wisdom to the current contexts.

The challenge faced in bioethical principlism, and scientific approaches discussed has been to apportion unique degrees of moral status as well as moral standing. Meaning, we could morally consider it as worse to exterminate a person than to exterminate a primate for research (the potentiality problem), implying that the human species have a special status and not the same status as other organisms.[22] But to focus on this distinction of moral status, say between the patient and the subject, living and nonliving, human species and primate, makes no moral sense in the African outlook since life remains a single unbroken unity without any privileged kinship to any, but for all to contribute toward its constant continuity. We encounter a parallel approach in Nussbaum's approach to an integral flourishing, atleast primarily towards nonhuman animals, where she stresses that "our ethically attuned awareness of the value of animal striving suggests that we ought to promote for all animals a life rich in opportunities for functioning and lacking many of the impediments that we humans typically put in the way

---

19. Tangwa, "Bioethics: an African perspective," 189.
20. Tangwa, "Bioethics: an African perspective," 197.
21. See Tangwa, "Bioethics: an African perspective," 197–98.
22. See Consequentialists argue that moral standing of pre-embryos, embryos, fetuses, and infants increases during gestation. Strong, "Status of preembryos," 457–78; Harman, "The Potentiality Problem," 173–98; Beauchamp and Childress, PBE, 82–83.

of animals' flourishing . . . animals matter because of what they are, not because of kinship to ourselves."[23]

And if nonhuman animals matter because of what they simply are—what is oftentimes unspoken but quite understood—but not because of their relationship to human animals labelled as a special status, the same understanding should clarify even the language of rights. Some argue that a nonhuman animal has a right only if a human animal has interest that merits its protection, not for the nonhuman animal's sake but rather for the human animal's own sake specifically. But if human animals and many nonhuman animals share numerous interests that merit protection by rights,[24] then the term "rights" is invariantly used in contexts across human animals and nonhuman animals,[25] which calls for our invariant understanding of the nature of biomedical ethics across them. Even if a human animal or a nonhuman animal is not aware of its right, it is no equitable basis for asserting that it does not have it and this doesn't change the fact that it still and will still possess it. The same thesis is in dialogue with the ethical approach of Black Africans. Their logic has already suggested that the relational community is the legal competent surrogate for an anencephalic infant or any community member who is in a permanently vegetative state, which is roughly close though limited to the principlistic thought, that a right can be exercised on one's behalf by an appropriate authorized representative such as a surrogate.[26] Even if some country laws—the would-be surrogates—do not (invariantly) acknowledge moral standing for nonhuman animals, and subsequently do not grant them legal rights, the befitting assumption would be, that just as human animals have rights against extermination or abuse in their flourishing, so do nonhuman animals correlatively. Here, correlativity firstly implies that whenever human animals have obligations to nonhuman animals, they too have correlative rights. Secondly, it implies not an obligation merely regarding nonhuman animals, but a direct rather than an indirect obligation to them.[27] Obligations to wildlife in Africa are getting threatened too.[28] But if the East African citizens get more aware—with

---

23. Nussbaum, "The Capabilities Approach," 240–41.

24. See Beauchamp, "Rights Theory and Animal Rights," 203–5.

25. Though humans may have many rights that animals do not hold, but eventually many rights are also shared. See more in Beauchamp, "Rights Theory and Animal Rights," 201, 204.

26. See Beauchamp and Childress, PBE, 403.

27. See Beauchamp, "Rights Theory and Animal Rights," 207.

28. Nussbaum gives an example of elephants that are highly endangered. Given that an adult elephant needs to eat about 200–250 pounds of vegetation per day to stay healthy, elephants must cover a lot of territory, and there can't be too many elephants

the help of principlism—of a direct obligation to conserve spacious natural woodlands for elephants, lions and chimpanzees so as to be their own-selves in their animal-hood, then these nonhuman animals will have a correlative right to natural habitats with a befitting roaming space without human encroachment.

Besides, if nonhuman animals matter because of what they simply are, it is an urgent sensitive concern not only to think of correlativity in relation to rights, but also in relation to justice. Justice is not only appropriate to human animals, but it should be understood to extend to all world citizens if we are to flourish and coexist together in our holistic approach. In Nussbaum's address to the "frontier of justice," she goes beyond ethics that only covers human capabilities responsible for the pain and suffering of nonhuman animals, to extend "justice to all world citizens."[29] In pursuit of an interdependent world in which all species cooperatively and mutually enjoy relationships of coexistence, for Nussbaum, we should enhance our perspectives to holistic ethics by treating each citizen justly. This is possible "if we adopt a type of paternalism that is highly sensitive to the different forms of flourishing that different species pursue."[30] Given that "human beings are entitled to 'being able to live with concern for and in relation to animals, plants, and the world of nature,' so, too, are other animals, in relation to species not their own, including the human species, and the rest of the natural world."[31] Living and flourishing decently in an interdependent social cooperation of many species with heterogeneous life forms is not contractarian or utilitarian in nature, instead, it should feature in principles that prevent the blighting of valuable natural powers.[32] To put it briefly, human cognitive capabilities and properties that could for example help to enter and maintain contractarian agreements, don't successfully count as standards for our direct obligations to nonhuman animals. What counts towards social flourishing is to justly treat nonhuman animals as both moral subjects as well as moral agents without any discrimination.

---

in one territory. South Asia and Africa, where most elephants live, have rapidly growing populations, and this growth has diminished the space where elephants can roam free. Humans won't like them near their habitation, since young males mix baldy with human villages. Moreover, hundreds of elephants are poached for the ivory market. In 1930, there were between five and ten million African elephants and somewhere around a million Asian elephants. Today, there are probably only about 35,000 to 40,000 Asian elephants left in the wild, and only about 600,000 African elephants. Nussbaum, "The Capabilities Approach," 245.

29. Nussbaum, "Frontiers of Justice," 2, 22.
30. Nussbaum, "Frontiers of Justice," 366–80, especially 375.
31. Nussbaum, "Frontiers of Justice," 392–401, especially 399–400.
32. See Nussbaum, "Frontiers of Justice," 346–52, especially 351–52.

A Holistic Approach to Life is a Homelike (Community) Dialectic Flourishing Relationship of the Local and Global approaches to Bioethics

It will be indeed an underestimation to approach bioethical concerns of our era less of a holistic approach. Indeed, to Africans, it "may be misleading to simply qualify their ethical concerns as being either eco-centred, bio-centred or anthropo-centred." [33] Their ethical concerns go beyond these limitations and so demands us to encompass a holistic horizon. The holistic approach to bioethics I am proffering is a way of minimum conditions and requirements that favor a flourishing union of relationships among creatures, in pursuit of their system of life goals appropriate both to the universalized bioethical life and the local native analysis of day-today life.

To favor a holistic flourishing, there must be a dialectic relationship between the universalized approach and the local approach to bioethics. The World Congress of Bioethics in Sydney, Australia (2004), without a concrete way forward emphasized "Deep Listening: bridging divides in local and global ethics."[34] The implicit global question ever since remained how can we bridge these divides? Borrowing the wording of Tangwa, in Henk ten Have's book *Global Bioethics: An Introduction* (Chapter 7), he tries to answer the question with two levels of global bioethics. One is a universal level of minimum principles and standards agreeable to all cultures and traditions expressible in an international language. Second is a multiplicity of different ethical approaches anchored in different contexts, cultural or religious settings. In between, local cultures and traditions are indispensable in the eventual interpretation and application of universalized standardized principles. And the life between suggests a dialectic relationship between the global and the local approaches to bioethics,[35] not forgetting that "the future of the human species can only be guaranteed if humanity itself is regarded as a collectivity or a 'global community.'"[36] We note a question of dialectic flourishing relationships both locally and globally. This dialectic relationship connotes what in modern times we understand as "solidarity." Hans-Georg Gadamer is of the view that solidarity teaches us that there is a tension between our would-be flourishing dialectic friendships. He thinks that "the Greek word that Socrates proposed and that one cannot accurately translate now, is *Oikeion*, the 'house-like/domestic,' the 'home-like/native.'"

---

33. Tangwa, "Bioethics: an African perspective," 188–89.
34. Tangwa, "Leaders in Ethics Education," 97.
35. See Tangwa, "An Introduction by Henk," 269.
36. Henk, "Global bioethics," 611.

"But that homeland and origin represent a connection, a kind of community, a kind of solidarity of a genuine kind ... home and house are the places of living together."[37] In explicating a homelike environment of living together, difficultly, Gadamer "opted for the Greek concept of *Philia*, as a translation of 'Solidarity,' .... Solidarity here means a promise of a payment of friendship, which is limited."[38] However a homelike community of living together shouldn't be confined to limitations, and to this difficulty, partly to which this thesis question has turned. Here solidarity as the dialectic relationship isn't limited though challenged. It can efficaciously make use of the normative structure of solidarity, atleast along the three abridged moral bonds of solidarity towards: The entire cosmos, interpersonal humanity, and universal institutions. So, this holistic dialectic relationship positively responds to the 1) Exploited cosmic-ecological relationships 2) Exploited interpersonal and humanistic collaborations and 3) Exploited structural-universal collaborations. In amending the globally exploited collaborations, as the holistic Other, the approach of holistic bioethics suggests conversion in the existing dialectic relationships by responding to them with respectful sympathy. It is bioethics of respect. Therefore, an African *sympathetic approach of solidarity* is the proffered engine of holistic bioethics, bioethics that necessarily *promotes life fully*. In promoting life fully, the African ethical system promotes an *integral community life, a homelike flourishing relationship,* by continuously promoting the norm of *solidarity, continued vitality,* the *hierarchical order of life* of *every entity within the corporate community*. So, promoting the life of solidarity in all relationships is the greatest pursuit of the African moral thought. It constitutes our humanness and suggests normatively that "an action is right just insofar as it is a way of living harmoniously or prizing communal relationships, ones in which people identify with each other and exhibit solidarity with one another; otherwise, an action is wrong"[39]if it doesn't sympathetically promote a flourishing solidarity or homelike life (community) in all relationships.

To promote solidarity within the African moral thought is to relationally promote healthy relationships by mending the exploited global collaborations. This is in dialogue with what the president of the International Association of Bioethics (IAB) Nikola Biller-Andorno recently underlined. She explored bioethics not on reasoning troubling autonomously rational individuals in their struggle to maintain abstract theoretical outlooks, but

---

37. Gadamer, "Friendship and Solidarity," 4–5. Earlier published as "Freundschaft und Solidarität," 56–68, and "Konstanten für Wirtschaft und Gesellschaft," 178–90.

38. Gadamer, "Friendship and Solidarity," 12.

39. Metz, "African and Western Moral Theories," 51.

rather "on the preconditions for flourishing human relationships as a way to address bioethical challenges in a globalized world."[40] But to maintain bioethics to flourishing human relationships alone is to limit it to "anthrospherical egalitarianism," namely, promoting only the intrinsic value of humans alone. It is why bioethics needs to go beyond its focus on human beings as autonomous individuals and emphasize the interconnectedness and the interrelations between human beings and the cosmic ecological environment. We go not only beyond "species egalitarianism" or anthrospherical egalitarianism, but also far than biocentrism, ecocentrism and holism to embrace an inclusive African "holistic moral egalitarianism," a suggested view that "all forces" and "all created things have life." Holistic egalitarianism grounds holistic bioethics. Even when we may agree that all created entities—not only living things—command respect, but it may also not be necessary to agree that every creature command equal respect.[41] But what remains as a minimum imperative within a Black African approach to bioethics, is that every creature has life and commands respect. And this attitude begins right from our local setting before getting global.

For a successful global approach to bioethics, the approach must be primarily successful locally. Global bioethics is only possible through local bioethics. It is only by not being blind to the undeniable different incarnations of regional moralities (local ethos) as raw materials on which we can ground a common morality. African studies note, for instance, that citizens should be able to claim their due rights not from international systems but rather from their immediate responsible states first. Given the unique yet dynamic African environment, need demands solutions from within Africa in the first place. Then after, it is the responsibility of Africa to adapt international norms to its specific situation and draft complementary regulations to supplement the internationalized guidelines. African may pick a vivid lesson from its own response to the Universal Declaration of Human Rights which created the African Charter on Human and Peoples Rights which came into effect in 1986. An analogous development in biomedical ethics drawing on the African outlook is inevitable and overduely right, so that Africa can aid the localization of the universalized perspective to bioethics.[42] Here, the operation of dialectics requires revitalizing bonds of solidarity toward interhuman relationships, structural and universal relationships and cosmic-ecological relationships, altogether encompassing a

---

40. Biller-Andorno, "Bioethics in a globalised world," 430–36.
41. See Henk, "Global bioethics," 608; Etieyibo, "African Philosophy and Nonhuman Nature," 164–65, 169–70.
42. See Tangwa, "Ethics in occupational health," 9.

holistic mission that builds bridges and promotes life not only locally but also globally. Building bridges implies developing a locally grounded bioethical approach that is shaped by a dynamic understanding of local cultures and informed by social-religious structural and institutional problems that impact the public's health as understood by the natives. It is from this local social approach to life that we can better understand and implement what is offered as universalized principlism and subsequently amend the exploited structural-universal collaborations that have even escalated organ transplant tourism recently from SSA.

THE AFRICAN RELATIONAL SOCIALITY OF THE VITAL FORCE AS THE MEDIA (VEHICLE) OF A HOLISTIC APPROACH TO BIOETHICS

In relation to some characteristics of the African moral thought, i.e., promotion of life, community harmony, continued vitality, solidarity and hierarchical order of forces, it is quite clear that African community ethics ultimately reveals itself at all costs in its holistic promotion, protection and revitalization of the *vital force* in all entities without discrimination. Studies like those of Tempels do not only understand the vital force as the central dimension in African thinking, but also as a consequence and goal of ethical conduct.[43] Tempels' pioneer approach to an African non-dichotomized moral thought rests on the ontological thesis that the world is an ordered, intimately interrelated multiplicity of forces: "Die Welt als eine geordnete, innig Zusammenhängende Mannigfaltigkeit von Kräften dar."[44] The interconnected multiplicity of forces as a non-dichotomized moral thinking is described by Placid Temples' relational ontological view of an African holistic life in contrast to Western principlism. Even *being is force* but force is not additional or accidental to being like it is claimed in Western thought:

> Für die Bantu ist das Sein etwas, das Kraft ist. Das sein ist Kraft, Kraft ist sein. Die europäische Formulierung "Kraft haben" verstehen wir Europäer ja unbewusst im Sinne unserer Philosophie. Wenn wir den Seinsbegriff der bantu als "etwas, das Kraft hat" formulieren, werden europäische Leser sofort den Schluß ziehen, daß auch für die Bantu "Kraft" nur etwas zum Sein Zusätzliches ist. Für die Bantu ist indes *Kraft keine Akzidenz*. Für sie liegt es in der Natur des Seins, Kraft zu haben, Kraft zu "sein." Kraftsein ist die Natur des Seins als solche. *Dem Bantu*

---

43. See Bujo, *An African Ethic*, 2–3.
44. Tempels, *Bantu-Philosophie. Ontologie und Ethik*, 74.

> ist die Lebenskraft das Sein selbst, so wie es ist, in seiner realen Totalität, die im Augenblick verwirklicht, und im Augenblick einer intensiveren Verwirklichung fähig ist. Um nun alle Verwirrung zu vermeiden, daß der europäische Leser den Terminus für etwas Akzidentelles ansieht, halte ich mich vorläufige an die Formel: Für die Bantu ist das Sein etwas, das Kraft ist.... Wo wir bestimmte konkrete Seinsweisen als Dinge betrachten, die existieren, sehen die Primitiven die konkreten Seinsweisen als Kräfte, die existieren. Wir sagen, dass die seinsweisen nach Art and Natur verschieden sind, die Bantu sehen Kraft, die sich nach ihrer Art und Natur unterscheiden, tierischen, pflanzlichen und rein stofflichen oder mineralischen Kräfte. *Da jedes Seine Kraft und nur insofern Sein ist, als es Kraft ist, kann der Begriff auf alles Existierende angewandt werden*: auf Gott, die Menschen, die verstorben und Lebenden, die Tiere, die Pflanzen und Mineralien. Alles individuelle Sein stellen sich die Bantu als Individuelle Kraft vor.[45]

Bantu understand the vital force as being itself in its entire totality. And since every being is force and can only be insofar as it is force, this substantive belief applies to everything that exists. Tempels struggles to explain the interrelation of these forces toward an unbroken constant that cuts across Bantu relational ontology of life without dichotomizing it, a vital force that cuts across rational living organism (e.g., animates) and irrational nonliving organisms (e.g., inanimates), visible and invisible worlds, communal systems of the past, present and future generations. In this perpetual interrelation, inanimates just like animates, both have *life*, and can revitalize or weaken the vital force:

> The Bantu say in respect of a number of strange practices in which we see neither rhyme nor reason, that their purpose is to acquire life, strength or vital force to live strongly, that they are to make life stronger, or to assure that force shall remain perpetually in one's posterity. Used negatively, the same idea is expressed when the Bantu say: we act thus to be protected from misfortune, or from a diminution of life or of being, or in order to protect ourselves from those influences which annihilate or diminish us.[46]

Tempels grounds the Bantu vital force as the vitology of *amaanyi, ntu, moyo*, which is newly understood as the universal vitality, to be the essence

---

45. Tempels, *Bantu-Philosophie. Ontologie und Ethik*, 27.

46. Tempels, *Bantu Philosophy*, 44–45; see also Bujo, *Ethical Dimension of Community*, 208–9.

of every entity—including God, spirits, human animals, nonhuman animals, plant, stone, time, beauty, wisdom, courage and so on. Sempebwa describes it as the *wesentliche Kraft*.[47] In understanding the *wesentliche Kraft* or vital force, for instance, the rendered close Luganda version is *amaanyi*, what Kasozi understands as "the all reality permeating dynamism." *Amaanyi*, so to speak, is a quality or expression of being. It is not an independent force existing free of the beings in the universe. *Amaanyi* designates a principle of activity in beings.[48] In African morality, the vital principle of activity can be manifested in varied modes across all entities, for instance as a magical force, without discrimination between both the living and the non-living organism.

Magical Force and Vital Force in African Moral life

There is a difference between vital and magical force. Whereas the magical force is ontologically an accident of being in the vital force, the vital force remains being itself. In essence, the magical force of the universe is neither evil or good in itself, it is a potential force at our disposal (everyone is potentially a witch, i.e., with latent or dormant power to some[49])—a "vorhandene Kraft" as Sempebwa refers to it.[50] The magical force is one of the vital force's (*amaanyi*) modes of manifestation that could be interpreted as neutral, if it is deemed to be indifferently—possess *amaanyi* in a neutral manner—disposed to human animals.[51] In principle, the neutral force or *vorhandene Kraft*, can be present in everything that exists in the African moral world. If one has only the necessary practical knowledge—requiring the media of another entity like human animals—one is usually able to dispense it. It does not matter which method is employed as Damman notes:

> Es handelt sich immer wieder um Erhaltung, Auffüllung und Ansetzen der magischen Kraft. Sie kann grundsätzlich in allem, was in der Welt besteht, vorhanden sein. Wenn man nur die nötigen technischen Kenntnisse besitzt, ist man in der Regel fähig, über sie zu verfügen. Dabei ist es nicht von Belag, welche Methode man anwendet. Allen ist gemeinsam, daß durch sie Vorstellungen, Gedanken und Wünsche realisiert werden

---

47. Sempebwa, *Reality of a Bantu*, 57–58; See Placid Tempels, *Bantu Philosophie*, 30–32.

48. Kasozi, *The Ntu'ology of the Baganda*, 54.

49. See Magesa, *African Religion*, 167.

50. Sempebwa, Reality of a Bantu, 63–64.

51. See Kasozi, *The Ntu'ology of the Baganda*, 55.

können. Für diese Denken ist die Welt der Vorstellung mit der Welt des Realen identisch.[52]

Another manifestation of the vital force is the *besondere Kraft*. This is a special force that is accessed by some spirits, tappable by a few human animals like medicine-persons, witches, priests, rainmakers, which tapping is for the good or ill of others within their communities, and this special force is referred to as the magical force. Besides, others have interpreted this force as a mystical force, which is believed to manifest itself in certain nonhuman animals, certain plants, certain objects, certain places and at certain times.[53] So on the one hand, the vital force is existent in human animals, while on the other hand, it is equally and abundantly alive in nonhuman entities.

Some human animals are believed to have a special magical force (*besondere Kraft*) since they have the knowledge or ability of how to tap or control this mode of vital force. Some human animals may possess it without knowing it since it may be found out through *muntu's word* or performance of *ritual rites*. This force can be released for particular use in the community to either do harm (in an antisocial or negative sense) or good (in a social or positive sense) to other human animals as well as to (their) nonhuman entities. Besides, it is not only released toward nonhuman entities, but these entities are also (in nature) credited with powers for good or for evil, which magic power influences the moral activities of human animals negatively or positively. Such nature with magical power includes rivers, trees, mountains, nonhuman animals, which may not be made use of without also seeking the intervention of the ancestral world of spirits. Such nature can be used in its entirety by human animals antisocially or socially. A specific example of the antisocial employment of the mystical power includes an instance of witchcraft or wizardry or sorcery, which is the malicious use of magical force.[54] This is believed to give birth to moral misfortunes, sickness or illness, accidents, tragedies, sorrowfulness, natural catastrophes, death, and various

---

52. Damman, *Die Religionen Afrikas*, 106.

53. Sempebwa, *Reality of a Bantu*, 57–58; See Tempels, *Bantu Philosophie*, 30; relatedness of entities to each other, see Lugira, *Ganda Art*, 5.

54. See Magesa, *African Religion*, 165–66; Mbiti, *African Religions and Philosophy*, 198–200; On the use of magic power, see Mbiti, *African Religion*, 165; On ability to tap magic power, see Sempebwa, *Reality of a Bantu*, 63; Roscoe states that Rivers in Buganda are "credited with powers for good or for evil." This magic power makes travelers, before crossing them, to throw coffee beans for safety. Large trees (*miti*) too are believed to have magical powers, making it difficult to simply cut them without seeking the intervention of the worshipped spirit (*Lubaale*). Failure to do this, it is believed to cause illness to the family. Roscoe, *The Baganda*, 288–89, 317–18.

unhappy mysteries that lead to unimaginable anti-social life. The malicious use of magical force disrupts community life and disharmoniously poisons interrelationships.

Nonetheless, the practice of medicine should not be confused with the magical force involved in witchcraft.[55] Here we note that the anti-sociality of sorcery is an antithesis of the mystical power used by medicine-persons positively. Since medicine persons have to appeal to the social totality of life to answer questions arising from Bantu moral life, to get rid of some suspicious ethical questions for instance regarding sorcery, we need to be acquainted with the totality of community life.[56] This means the practice of orthodox medicine cannot be arguably based on Aristotlean dualism which separates the spirit from the body but rather treat the human person at once as both spiritual and physical. It is for this reason, an African approach to the practice of medicine "generally aims not only at bodily health but also at psychical, mental and spiritual harmony and rhythm, not only for the individual but also for the community, including the living-dead ancestors and even the as yet unborn."[57] In engaging the totality of this triad-community

---

55. See Tangwa, "African Traditional Medicine," 42.

56. These suspicions and suppositions may not be based on the actual conduct of the alleged evildoer; they may have their origins long ago and may encompass the history of the entire family or clan fellowship. In other words, the tensions between two families or two clan fellowships can be handed on in such a way that they remain alive in the memory of succeeding generations. It is possible that someone may be suspected of being a sorcerer merely because he belongs to a clan fellowship that has been regarded historically as suspicious or evil. The very presence of such a person disrupts the community and poisons interrelationships. For instance, elderly persons whose existence may be felt as a burden; childless women who are suspected of harming children or even killing them. It is not possible to make ethical judgments about the idea and the practices of one is ignorant of their individual, familial, and social background. The basic concern everywhere is with preserving an order of things laid down in tradition, which is disturbed by wrong attitudes, tensions, unforeseen events, or external social changes. Questions of sorcery emphasize centrally the significance of the total life of the community, whose life is hampered by individual deviation that has its roots in jealousy, envy, rivalry and so on. Here, one must guard against the problem of retaliatory killings or actions. Bujo, *An African Ethic*, 134–36; Leading politicians, university students and graduates, medical doctors in hospitals, are known to consult or work side by side with medicine-persons. Mbiti understands African medicine-men as "specialists who have suffered most from European-American writers and speakers who so often and wrongly call them 'witch-doctors'—a term which should be buried and forgotten forever. Every village in Africa has a medicine-man within reach, and he is the friend of the community. He is accessible to everybody and at almost all times, and comes into the picture at many points in individual and community life." Mbiti, *African Religions and Philosophy*, 15, 167, 171.

57. Tangwa, "African Traditional Medicine," 43; Tangwa concludes at p. 44 in reference to his own village Catholic specialized hospital of Shisong: "African traditional

life, medicine persons socialize what is suspiciously anti-social. Baganda emphasize a difference in the goals pursued between unsociable (anti-social) use of magical force—like for sorcerers, witches, or wizards (*mulogo* or *musezi*)—and the sociable employment of magical force by a medicine-person (*muganga*). One uses the magical force negatively while the other uses it positively in the life of the other community members and their properties. One aims at disunity, harm, and the social evilness while the other aims at revitalizing the vital force by promoting unity, healing, eventually correctively counteracting the harm caused, and thereby guaranteeing the general social goodness of the entire community. In short, the medicine person aims at revitalizing the sociality of life that was anti-socialized by the sorcerer as Damman notes: "Der fundamentale Unterschied besteht lediglich in dem erstrebten Ziel. Der Zauberer handelt zum Schaden, der Medizinmann zum Nutzen oder zum Heel des anderen. Ein großer Teil seiner Tätigkeit besteht darin, den durch das Wirken der Zauberer verursachten Schaden durch Gegenmaßnahmen zu kompensieren."[58] Though this is not the only sense in which *amaanyi* can manifest in the relational community.

Moreover, the vital force or *amaanyi*'s mode of manifestation could be negatively or positively construed as specifically attractive. It can be positively attractive if it is beneficial to the human animals and their relationships, on the one side. For instance, the Baganda people without being coerced flock willingly the palace of their Kabaka (king), the king, till today. They testify how they feel attracted to his Highness' spiritual leadership, given their strong belief that it unites the relationship of the physical world of human animals with the spiritual world of the ancestral spirits. Kabaka is for this reason understood to be positively gifted with an attractive vital force. Yet again the vital force's nature of manifestation could be decoded as negatively horrid, if it is considered as frightful, hazardous, harmful, etc., to the human animals in their varied relationships with nonhuman entities like boulders, hills, thickets which have to be approached with carefulness.[59] Basically, the vital force manifests itself outstandingly and in a peculiar way not only through entities of hierarchically distinguished ranks like Kabaka

---

medicine is quite compatible with Western scientific medicine . . . . The communities that make use of the Shisong hospital know very well what particular ailments to take to the hospital and what to take to the traditional healers. Sometimes the doctors at the Shisong hospital will advise a patient to seek traditional healing, and quite often traditional healers refer patients with conditions they know they cannot handle to the hospital. At Shisong hospital, consultation and in-patient admissions have adapted to the African communal system."

58. Damman, *Die Religionen Afrikas*, 59.
59. See Kasozi, *The Ntu'ology of the Baganda*, 55.

and the elders who are held to be nearest to the eldest of the old, i.e., to *Katonda* (God); but also in spectacular natural objects, like boulders, hills, huge trees, principal rivers, etc.[60] We note two media of vital force: Human animals, and nonhuman entities.

Given this hierarchical order of forces that is characteristic of African morality, the higher one ranks hierarchically the more one is supposed to exercise the vitalistic force as an attractive media. The Kabaka's utmost hierarchical attractive authority since *time immemorial*[61] wins him a description as the *primus inter pares*.[62] To understand Kabaka as the first rank among all, a uniting attractive vital force, one needs to understand the notion of authority (*buyinza*), whose origin could be monarchial, an entitlement, or an acknowledgement that designates "power," "capacity" and "ability." *Ow'obuyinza* is the one with authority, ability and power; for instance, God almighty (*Katonda omuyinza wabyonna*), the monarchial Kabaka of *Buganda*, who is a legitimate source of authority with indisputable superiority and intelligence amongst all people (*Sabasajja*) in his *bwakabaka* (kingship).[63] Nevertheless, any Black African kingship cannot be successful without a well-functioning relationship with the people, take an example of the Bakuba in the Democratic Republic of Congo.[64] Such well-functioning relationships as intended by the ancestral wisdom and being supported continuously by the ancestral spiritual presence, analogously speak to current African leaderships. Africans cannot forever blame foreign powers for

60. Kasozi, *The Ntu'ology of the Baganda*, 54; Different accounts show the divinely derived power of the King (Kabaka) and how clans depend on his leadership, authority and influence. See Richards, *East African Chiefs*, 45–46; Fallers, *The King's Men*, 91; West, *The Mailo System in Buganda*, 1–2; Merkies, *Ganda Classification*, 98–99.

61. "From time immemorial the Baganda have known no other ruler above their Kabaka in their Kingdom and it is commonly accepted that they still do not recognize any other person whose authority does not derive from the Kabaka. The Baganda cannot exist as a people unless the Kabaka is the head of the political structure in his kingdom." Merkies, *Ganda Classification*, 98.

62. See Kabuga, "The Geneology of Kabaka," 205–16; Kaggwa, *Ekitabo kye Bika Buganda*.

63. More on Ganda concept of authority (authority), see Sempebwa, *Reality of a Bantu*, 176–89; *Buyinza* means authority or power, ability or capacity. *Ab'obuyinza* means, the authorities. Murphy, *Luganda-English Dictionary*, 54.

64. Within the Negro-African artistic objects, the Bakuba in the Democratic Republic of Congo have various genres of masks. One is the Broom, an imposing wooden mask. The fundamental idea behind this mask, without the people, the king deserves neither his name nor his kingdom. If the people are indispensable in this manner, then the king is obliged to rule in dialogue with it. Thus, the mask Broom intends to proclaim that the contribution or participation of the people is *necessary* for political and social equilibrium. This in turn means that a king or chief is legitimate only when he is fully acknowledged by the people. See Bujo, *An African Ethic*, 43.

the recent untold bioethical shortfalls when all the 54 African countries are atleast independent in some sense. Such blames weaken African potentials since they not only have a limited life span but also have outgrown their time. African countries need to work towards an ethical conversion and a sound bioethics that reconciles the recent reading of signs of the times with their rich ancestral history of harmony.

Several abuses of power—like self-enrichment, corruption, nepotism, conniving in exploitive organ transplant tourism—by many African heads of state and high ranked officials is anti-social to the admired relational harmony of vital force.[65] In contrast to ancestral hopes of continued moral vitality, contemporary high ranked government officials loot dreadfully their own people and enrich their own family fraternities at the expense of promoting a vital force befitting all country-people. They tarnish the credibility of their would-be standard media of vital force. Meaning, the current African dictatorships are incompatible with the African moral thought which obliges leaders to attractively revitalize the vital force for all within the three-community-dimensional fellowship. Here too, we need conversion beyond our own ethnicities.

Having understood the vital force as being itself, that *all reality permeating dynamism*, the *wesentliche Kraft* or *amaanyi* or *moyo* or *ntu*, in addition to human entities as media of vital force, even nonhuman entities like natural objects are existents or media of vitality. Natural objects of the earth and places of sacrifices aren't only seats of magical powers and powerful potencies of life but are also *abodes* of spiritual beings.[66] Nature's

---

65. See Bujo, *An African Ethic*, 151–153.

66. For the *Baganda*, natural objects and living things, e.g., hills, trees, snakes, forests, rocks and places of sacrifice are abodes of spiritual beings. a) The earth, the ground or soil is inhabited by the earth god called *Kitaka*. He is consulted by gardeners for the fertility of cultivated land and for good harvests. b) These hills located in *Bulemeezi* County in *Buganda*, Uganda, are abodes of the "lion spirits": *Bbowa, Nnambe, Lwanga* and *Kyangali* Hills. They are to be appeased with offerings. They are also a safety resort for people fleeing from all sorts of danger. c) The following rivers possess spirits which are credited with good or evil powers: Rivers *Mayanja, Ssezzibwa* and *Katonga*. An offering to these spirits in the form of coffee berries is hence mandatory before crossing the river. d) Many forests are inhabited by nature spirits called "*musambwa*" (singular), *misambwa* (plural)," e.g., the nature spirits *Nnabambe* and *Ntabambe*. "Misambwa" are consulted by hunters for protection against wild animals and for a successful hunting spree. e) Besides being abodes of spirits, certain trees are manifestations of those spirits. The nature spirit or "Musambwa Lubowa," for instance, is said to have been a tree at *Kalisizo, Buddu* County in Buganda. f) The python deity "Serwanga" was once a python that had its temple by the River *Mujuzi* in *Buddu* County on the shores of Lake *Nnalubaale* (Victoria). Sserwanga is believed to be a giver of fertility to young couples and is, too, an example of snakes that are manifestations of spirits. g) Certain spirits are custodians of places of sacrifices. Before the village *Namugongo* in *Kyanddondo* County

(stones, mountains, nonhuman animals, plants, trees) magical and mysterious power, think of water and its "cooling" ability, is noted by Damman among Bantu.[67]

The reality of the vital force to all media or abodes influences the essence of every existent. For the Baganda, "to be" for every existent is to be with vital force. The vital force unites thoroughly and works indistinguishably with each and every existent. Conceived from this point of view, all existents are in their innermost nature media of the vital force. And consequently, existence is the mutual or reciprocal influence prevailing between the various media of *amaanyi*.[68] To show how various media of vital force are relationally harmonized in unity, we cannot help exploring the inner life within the three-dimensional community, the three realms of the universe, the living, the living dead and those not yet born. To foster Bantu morality, *muntu*'s moral duty is to maintain this relational harmony by upholding the varied media of vital forces together, which is "morally good," while interfering with *this* harmony is "morally evil." It is why moral evil produces natural evil, since moral evil interferes with this ontological harmony of the three realms of the universe.[69] If we pick an example of adultery, being adulterous is morally threatened among Baganda to breed miscarriages, which disrupts the relational life of the three-dimensional community.

On top of this relational ontological harmony—various media of specific magical forces fusing into a unified vital force—is *Katonda*, who is the primogenitor of the spiritual beings, the creator, source and ultimate dispenser of the vital force to all media, both to the spiritual and physical beings (as abodes), for instance, nature spirits.[70] For Africans, God doesn't

---

in *Buganda* was taken over by the Christians, it was "guarded and controlled" by tutelary deities who could even determine when human sacrifices were to be offered there. Kasozi, *The Ntu'ology of the Baganda*, 48–49. Kasozi borrows some examples from the works of Roscoe, *The Baganda*, 313–20.

67. "Vor allem ist aber die organische Natur Sitz magischer Kraft. Besonders gilt dies für Pflanzen und Bäume, was sogar Seinen sprachlichen Niederschlag finden kann . . . in den Bantusprachen . . . . Wald und Feld, wo das Wachstum erfolgt, sind ebenfalls Sitz machtvoller Potenz. Dasselbe gilt von Wasser, dessen geheimnisvolle Kraft in seiner 'Kühlenden' Fähigkeit liegt. Ebenso werden gewisse Tiere als besondere Machtträger angesehen . . . . Ein besonders geformter Stein, ein bestimmter Berg oder irgendein Platz in der Landschaft sind zuweilen Träger besonderer Kraft." Damman, *Die Religionen Afrikas*, 7.

68. See Kasozi, *The Ntu'ology of the Baganda*, 55.

69. Kasozi, *The Ntu'ology of the Baganda*, 77–78, see also footnote 1; Roscoe, *The Baganda*, 350; Mbiti, *African Religions and Philosophy*, 245.

70. The ultimate source of *amaanyi* is "the one whom mount reveres and exalts as supremely good and powerful." *Katonda* is at once the name or attribute of a deity, and an expression of the highest rank or highest essential nature of a good. *Katonda* is

want or is not the cause of the arch-evil, death, but rather the hierarchically lower media or abodes of vital force like human animals or bad spirits.[71] On the one hand, the anti-sociality of human animals misleads them to manipulate directly or indirectly the power of the spiritual beings to cause good or skillfully inflict evil on other entities for their own benefit. On the other hand, Baganda believe that on top of *Katonda* being the ultimate dispenser of the vital force, *Katonda* actually guards against evil manipulations done through contingent human animals: "Katonda omukozi w'ebirungi y'anaddaabiriza balubaale bye bakoze," or to put it literally, "it is God, the benevolent one, who will fill up the gaps of evil caused by the evil spirits."[72] In filling up all in-balanced gaps in the natural world, God eventually dispenses the necessary vital force to all modes. In contrast to criticisms of varied manifestations of vital force, like attractive force, magic, wizardry, sorcery, along their negative or positive outward form of vitality in Black Africa, one has to appreciate a non-Western form of rationality, the conviction that is not only invisible powers are at work in the world and are beyond the explanation of human reason; but also the conviction that these

---

distinguished from the minor deities by the qualification "Katonda w'e Butonda" (the God of *Butonda* hill). The hill *Butonda* is his sanctuary and palace on earth. Though supremely good and powerful, *Katonda* is approachable, and may receive donations; though does not demand sacrifices. Hence, *Katonda* is propitiously transcendent and benignly immanent as different *muntu-deity* relationships reveal him as a "super-human person": God as *Kyetondeka* (one who fixed himself solidly), *Katonda* (creator), *Namugereka* (one who correctly determines, shapes or adjusts things), *Kawamigero* (one who ascertains "weights and measures"), *Bugingo* (one who creates with dexterity or skill), *Namugeta* (one who is skillful), God metaphorically titled *Ssemanda* (the master of charcoal), *Ssebintu* (one who possesses all things), *Liiso-ddene* (big eye), *Ssewannaku* (king of days), *Kagaba* or *Lugaba* (one who causes others to have or receive), *Ddunda* (shepherd or pastor), *Sseggulu* (master of heaven), *Nantalemwa* (omnipresent). Largely, Baganda names of God describe a conception of the qualities, attributes of God's nature. They also express *muntu*'s contingency, as well as his dependence on God. See Kasozi, *The Ntu'ology of the Baganda*, 54, 91, 93–96; Kyewalyanga, *Religion, Customs and Christianity in Uganda*, 99. In other sources, *Ssebintu* is referred to as "a very rich person," other attributes of God may include: *ssabazira* as "the bravest of the brave," "nnantawetwa, a resolved, determined person," "omubumbi, potter," "luwangula, the all-conquering one," "omusaasi, provisioner." Merkies, *Ganda Classification*, 84–85, 88–98; The word "semanda" is a compound containing the word "Amanda" i.e., charcoal. Hence the expression "Ssemanda agalimenya embazzi n'okuyunga": Charcoal both breaks and welds axes. It is powerful and hence used as a synonym for the Kabaka. Merkies, *Ganda Classification*, 104, footnote 11; See more on the *Ganda* concept of God as eternal, supreme, and benevolent, Sempebwa, *Reality of a Bantu*, 65–66.

71. Bujo, *Ethical Dimension of Community*, 17–18.

72. Kasozi, . . . *The Ntu'ology of the Baganda*, 97; see also footnote 10 and 12; Roscoe, *The Baganda*, 300, 460.

modes of vital force influence ethical behavior within African communities.[73] Thus all creatures have inbuilt manifestations of the vital force and eventually enhance or weaken life energy within Bantu morality.

Inanimate Entities and Ecological Systems have Life too, and are Permeated with Vital Force

Though we could quickly advocate for a global species-neutral thought, to which viewpoint numerous scholarships have contributed, some scholars like Gary Steiner have uniquely gone ahead to accord nonhuman animals *perpetual intelligence*—the ability to aptly react to their habitats so as to nurture their well-being, even when they may not fully exercise their capacity for concepts, intentions, and reflections. Even though Steiner's perspective remains restricted to living existents, he replaces social justice—that is not species-specific—with "cosmic justice," a wider universal conception that is part of "cosmic holism."[74] Cosmic holism is the view that "sentient beings, both human and nonhuman, have kinship relation to one another that binds them together in a moral community in which neither can properly be said to be superior or inferior to the other."[75] Even-though the cosmic holistic moral account can be plausibly defended as abandoning an anthropocentric moral stance that we have largely challenged; it is mostly apt for some living entities while difficultly doing so, it excludes not only *nonliving entities* but also *systems of forces* that embrace *every creation as lifeless*. In bioethical principlism, we have at different occasions noted how largely it is oriented to the cultural approaches of the industrial west, in which their emphasis of principle-based approaches nature is symbolically demonstrating against systems and extreme harmful climatic changes, and in which changes, natural resources are insatiably exploited and so demanding us to cultivate an attitude toward conservation or stewardship ethics. The African holistic therapy does not only demand revitalization of the vital force in animates, but also necessarily insists on reconciling biotechnological systems with the local African moral thought that grants life to inanimate objects, and thereby renews the entire ecological-cosmic life with the ancestral ideals. Bioethical technological principlism must not be uncritically imported at the expense of abandoning the local cultural African heritage that never dichotomizes systems, between living and nonliving entities. It

---

73. Bujo, *An African Ethic*, 128.

74. Steiner, *Animals and the Moral Community*, 61, 68, 104–5, 163. Referenced by Bradie, "The Moral Life of Animals," 566–67.

75. Steiner, *Animals and the Moral Community*, xiii.

AN AFRICAN APPROACH TO HOLISTIC BIOETHICS 87

is not profit or economic marketable principlism that ought to be made the norm—as the global North based biomedical interventions in Africa elicit manipulatively an exploitative mentality—but only holistic humanization should not be forgotten, inclusive of conserving the whole cosmos. A holistic humanization aims at constantly liberating life of all entities multidimensionally and hierarchically. Inanimate entities like minerals, stones, just like animate entities like plants, nonhuman animals, human animals are all built up with systems of forces made available by God.[76] God who is at the top of the ontological hierarchical harmony, remains the sole dispenser of the vital force which is employed by various creatures as lower forces. This is indistinguishable to Tempels' maiden interpretation of Bantu ontological worldview that "all beings in the universe possess vital force of their own: human, animal, vegetable, or inanimate. Each being has been endowed by God with a certain force, capable of strengthening the vital energy of the strongest being of all creation: man."[77] And if every entity hibernates a life force, then life of human animals solely depends on nature, implying that the cosmic elements enable a village community life to holistically function. Putting aside the lighted streets of Europe or the uncomplicated access to electricity, for Black Africans who don't access electricity all the time, the new moon, for example, is always a happy occasion for a village moral palaver meeting, which through dances, drinking and other activities consolidates community relationships. Besides, fire which is essential for cooking is shared with a neighbor whose fire has gone out or who lacks it.[78] This infers that when neighbors share fire, it is not only an opportunity to exchange current information regarding the village, for instance whose funeral rites are recently scheduled, whose traditional wedding is coming up next, but fire as a symbol of life also cements dialectic relational affinities. It is the reason the African moral thought transcends weak, strong and enlightened forms of anthropocentrism because we are not at liberty to ill-use any of the lesser forms of entities or forces; namely, the moon, fire, sun—I lack Vitamin D in winter and need a plane to catch the sun—even when they are below our hierarchical order as human animals. Destroying the lower forces

76. See Bujo, *Ethical Dimension of Community*, 218–19. "Because the culture of profit and money is made to have priority over humanization, the monster *Evu-Mana* of the African myth, which swallows up everything in its path, is accepted. The significance of the story may be clarified by the example of the radioactive waste which is offered to the Third World as an alternative for the reduction of debts. But is the danger of radioactive waste not more dramatic than excessive debts, especially if one realizes that this waste leads to the total destruction of that environment in which life emerges and develops?" See Bujo, *Ethical Dimension of Community*, 217–18.

77. Tempels, *Bantu Philosophy*, 46.

78. See Bujo, *Ethical Dimension of Community*, 220–21.

of inanimate life similarly destroys the higher forces of animate forces, since the vital force in the understanding of Black Africans is relationally hierarchical. Therefore, an African approach to bioethics can hardly succeed without indispensably reconciling the entire cosmos toward a holistic harmony.

To reconcile with the cosmos is to absolutely appreciate in bioethics not only animates but also those inanimate entities and the invisible systems, in which the inanimate physical *bintu* (things), too, are permeated with *amaanyi* necessary for a relational harmony. For Bantu, matter is therefore not inert but rather active, since it is permeated with vital energy, i.e., all existents are media of this all-reality-permeating-dynamism.[79] In the African sense, since we have asserted that all existents and invisible forces are media of vital force—which force can be positively or negatively used—these existents have value, at least derivatively or non-derivatively. This is in dialogue with Greene's conviction in his study "On the origin of Species Notions and Their Ethical Limitations," in which he presents four kinds of value: "Derivative Instrumental Value"—casual contribution to bringing about a valuable state of affairs, e.g., the instrumental value from mountains' causal contribution; "Derivative Projected Value"—to be valued by some suitable valuer, e.g., the rock owner projects value onto the rock; "Derivative Constitutive Value"—making a non-additive contribution to the value of a state of affairs by helping to constitute that state of affairs, e.g., in agricultural diversity; "Non-derivative Value"—to have it is to have value that does not derive from any other value or valuer, e.g., something is loved because it is good.[80] Briefly, the values that are derivative can be summarized as instrumental, projected and constitutive.

First, in explaining the derivative *instrumental* value, Greene employs Holmes Rolston III example of "life-support value." This is implicit in the provision of "environmental services"—such as the conversion of carbon dioxide to oxygen by photosynthesis or the breakdown and recycling of dead organic matter—or "ecosystem services"—an interactive community of biological life, in which there is provision of various resources such as food, medicine, fuel, energy, raw materials, and tourism—whereby, all entities involved contribute necessarily toward the continuation of life,[81] as well as to the general systems indispensable in achieving the integral common good. In relation to the common good, the economic value of functioning

---

79. Kasozi, *The Ntuology of the Baganda*, 54–55.

80. Greene, "Origin of Species Notions," 579.

81. Greene, "Origin of Species Notions," 580–2; More about "life support value," nature's recreational value as different from the economic value (as the instrumental value), Greene references to Rolston III, "Values in Nature," 115–21, 123–24; Rolston III, *Environmental Ethics*, 3–8, 17–18; Powell, "Nature of Species," 612–13.

healthy relationships of ecosystem services—which may include regulation and support services of atmospheric clean oxygen, carbon dioxide, air moisture levels, nutrient recycling, climate mitigation and disease control, natural pollination, seed dispersal, waste decomposition, productivity of food and provisioning of clean drinking water, decomposition of wastes, culturally spiritual and recreational welfare, and so forth—is estimated to *exceed the world's total gross domestic product*! Not only ecosystem services, but special diversity also provides "evosystem service," which includes the capacity for adaptive evolutionary and novel beneficial variations in the face of changing weather patterns. This points to the fact that evosystem services may grow increasingly beneficial in soothing the disharmony of our cosmos as climate or environment anthropogenic alterations impose higher levels of stress on ecosystems.[82] In unison, ecosystem and evosystem services forge an interrelatedness between ecological biodiversity and a holistic wellbeing of human animals. A holistic interrelatedness within the "life-support value" chain is foreseen, for instance, if culturally spiritual and recreational welfare or goods from hunting and fishing services have instrumental value, then, not only do the hunted or fished nonhuman animal species derive value from their contribution to recreation,[83] but also other entities that contribute to the health of the hunted, whether as prey for them or as contributors to a holistic ecological environment that sustains them. So the extinction of any entity's causal instrumental contribution—*inter alia*, extinction of ecosystem services or goods like soil formation, purification of air and water, detoxification, predation to regulate prey habitats, organic control of pests and diseases, flood protection, spices for food, wild and seafood, skins, fuelwood, fertilizers, biogenic minerals, medicinal resources, energy from hydropower, biomass fuels, ornamental services from furs, feathers, ivory, shells, spiritual and cultural therapeutic services, etc.—to the sustenance of the ecosystem means loss of "biomemetical value,"[84] i.e., the immediate utility of both the natural historical information and ecological/evolutionary utility.

Second, there is the aesthetic value of nature as the derivative *projected* value. The scope of nature's aesthetic value is not confined to what we find

---

82. Powell, "Nature of Species," 612–13. To show that species have instrumental value, e.g., providing resources like medicine, Powell references to Randall, "Preservation of Species."; and to show that species offer ecosystem services and their economic value, see IUCN, UNEP, and WWF, *World Conservation Strategy* (WCS); and to show that special diversity provides evosystem services, see Faith et al., "Evoystem Services," 66–74.

83. Greene, "Origin of Species Notions," 580–2.

84. See Powell, "Nature of Species," 624–25, note 44 and 51.

only as beautiful but goes further for the valuer to imagine the experience and natural beauty of seeing the interaction of Masaai or Karimojong people with their animals in their vegetational environment. So, nature acts as an object of "valuable intellectual stimulation." Third, a case can be made for the derivative *constitutive* value of an entity if it can be identified as a constituent of some valuable whole or state of affairs. Rolston and others presume that there is constitutive value in natural diversity, i.e., constitutive contribution of species to the ecosystems, wilderness and the biosphere.[85] Analogously, it is this *constitutive* value that Donald Regan claims in the triads consisting of (i) a natural object, (ii) a person's knowledge of that natural object, and (iii) that person's pleasure in her knowledge of that natural object.[86] My reader should recall that a Black African takes an inanimate natural object as constitutive of value basically in a Reganian perspective. Although value requires consciousness and natural objects may be said not to have value of their own, in dialogue with Regan, the same thesis remains at home with the ethics of Black Africans for whom there is value not only in the complex consisting of the natural objects, but also in *muntu*'s knowledge of them as well as her pleasure in her knowledge of these entities having vital force (life) and contributing to an integral common good. Regan's triad as well as the African outlook can be further conceptualized in dialogue with Frances M. Kamm's argument, in which entities count either in their own right (e.g., a work of art, a tree) or by acting for the sake of something (e.g., a bird, a person). In both cases, we have reasons to act in certain inclusive ways, for instance, not to destroy nonhuman entities:

> A work of art or a tree may count in its own right in the sense that it gives us reason to constrain our behavior toward it (for example, not destroy it) just because that would preserve the entity. That is, independently of valuing and seeking the pleasure or enlightenment it can cause in people, a thing of aesthetic value gives us (I think) reason not to destroy it. In that sense, it counts morally. But this is still to be distinguished from constraining ourselves for the sake of the work or art or the tree. I do not act for its sake when I save a work of art, because I do not think of its good and how continuing existence would be

---

85. Greene, "Origin of Species Notions," 580–1; More about nature's aesthetic value (as the projected value), natural diversity (as the constitutive value), Greene references to Rolston III, "Values in Nature," 115–21, 123–26; Rolston III, *Environmental Ethics*, 3–8, 17–19.

86. See For Donald H. Regan's triads in value and constitutive value to species, see "Duties of Preservation," 201–2, 208. Cited from Greene, "Origin of Species Notions," 581–82.

good for it when I save it. (Nor do I think of its exercising its capacities or performing its duties. Acting for the sake of these might also involve acting for an entity's sake, though it need not involve seeking what is good for it.) Rather, I think of the good of the work of art, its worth as an art object, when I save it for no other reason than that it will continue to exist. By contrast, when I save a bird, I can do it for its sake, because it will get something out of continuing to exist, and it could be a harm not to continue.[87]

That is, not to destroy or harm any entity is essentially to protect it and so we act for this entity's sake. So "an entity has moral status when, in its own right and for its own sake, it can give us reason to do things such as not to destroy it or help it."[88] Besides every entity counts in its own right and can give us this one reason to save it. However the moral challenge with principle based approaches is to insist that protections supplied by moral norms, including principles, rules, obligations, and rights, are provided only to entities that can be morally wronged by actions.[89] Pertinent to this are cases beyond this scope, where biomedical researchers in sub-Saharan Africa have intentionally infected human baby subjects with the HIV virus, subsequently injuring not only the parents but the baby itself as well as the *relational community* that originally gave and continues to give the baby life—since not only the baby counts in its own right but equally the extended relatedness the baby originally has to the triad-community remains indispensable. Conversely, one can indirectly wrong a neighbor by intentionally infecting her banana plantation with a mosaic virus but does not wrong the plantation directly, as principle-based approaches would put it, because a banana tree does not count in its own right. Contrarily, for an African, a banana tree counts in its own right and so it would be wronged given every entity's relational contribution to the integral life. Here the question is what entity—of which properties against moral principles—counts in its own right and what does not?[90] Kamm says if an entity gives us reason not to destroy it or help it, it counts morally. If we are to safeguard against any moral discrimination in the pursuit of a holistic bioethics, we ought to reevaluate our persistence in emphasizing how human animals count in a way that banana trees don't as well as the significance of the relational

---

87. Kamm, "Moral Status," 228–29.

88. Kamm, "Moral Status," 229. I take her understanding of moral status to mean *moral standing*.

89. See Beauchamp and Childress, PBE, 67.

90. See Morris, "Moral Standing," 257.

community, or rather, how inanimate objects are to be protected only insofar as they are valued by human animals or due to our specific relationships to other entities.

It is in the same dialogue that an African attaches a revered status to not only all entities, including banana trees, graves and tombs, land, national parks, environment, works of art, as counting in a way that benefits every entity, but also to all systems and forces holistically. All things in the cosmic systems are relationally interconnected since all natural forces hierarchically depend on each other, so that human beings can ecologically live in harmony only in and with the whole systems of nature.[91] This emphasis of interconnectedness by Africans south of Sahara, just like we highlighted, relies on their substantive ontological belief, that given the media of vital force, all existents remain ontologically related and holistically interact with each other with no isolated mode of being. To have vital force is "to be in relation to,"[92] not only to the *other* but to the holistic ecological *Other* (all life realities). Moreover, in grounding an ecological ethics that isolates none but includes all life realities, "it is decisive for the African worldview that one simultaneously be an animal, plant or mineral and that conservation of the universe needs no other argument than the unity of the whole. Consequently, it is no longer only sensitivity to pain or analogy of language which establishes an ethical obligation towards nature. The cosmic community with all beings, including those that are not animals, is an essential foundation on which African ecological ethics is based."[93]

This African approach to an ecological ethics is in dialogue with a derivative constitutive value of an entity as a constituent of some valuable whole. One of the adherents is Martin Gorke who argues for a *non-derivative value* of species so as to non-anthropocentrically assume a general duty of species preservation. Gorke's account endorses the context of "holistic ethics" as the possible way to defend and protect all species for their own sake. Consequently, in Gorke's holistic ethics, "not only all living things but also inanimate matter and entire systems have intrinsic (non-derivative) value."[94] However his account hardly considers the other communities of life that constitute the three-dimension community of Africans. Nonetheless, relying on the above accounts, like any species, the natural inanimate

---

91. See Bujo, *Ethical Dimension of Community*, 21–22.

92. Kasozi, *The Ntu'ology of the Baganda*, 56.

93. Bujo, *The Ethical Dimension of Community*, 225.

94. More on the switch from anthropocentric to non-anthropocentric ethics to justify holistic ethics, see Gorke, *Death of Our Planet's Species*, 129–33, 196, 203, claims that general duties of species preservation are rooted in moral intuitions (pp. 9 and 129). See, Greene, "Origin of Species Notions," 584.

object too has constitutive value as well as a non-derivative value for two reasons. It is constitutively and non-derivatively valuable as a means to promoting life. Besides, it is an essential constituent of a holistic complex whole of systems and forces, just like we could promote an integral ecological life. Given the two reasons, we therefore have a moral cause to imperatively promote every entity's relational existence so that we integrally identify fully with forces of all systems of the valuable one whole.

Holistic Bioethics as Sympathetic Impartiality toward the Other: An African approach to Solidarity

Principle-based approaches in bioethics note that obligations of beneficence accord special relationships of help or benefit in contrast to those with whom we have no such connections. Examples of care ethics reveal detachment of impartiality and embrace loyalty and attachment to relations we care about most and are closest to us: "With family, friends, and others of our choice, morality ordinarily allows us to practice beneficence with partiality."[95] This partiality is noticeable in Hume's sentimentalism as we discussed, where attachments of human animals are chiefly limited to friends, family and one's native country, notwithstanding the fact that sympathy with the sentiments gets weaker or fainter with distance.[96] This proportionate intercourse of sympathy reaches out most naturally but decreasingly from our intimate ties—frequent contacts and those whose lives we have heavily invested in or impacted—to wider acquaintances or those remote from us (strangers or persons in distant nations).[97] But to confine sympathy to human animals is to limit a holistic intervention of bioethics. Like we already put it, there are many striking cognitive capacities like sympathy among nonhuman entities. For instance, "apes seem to posses at least some of the ingredients of human moral psychology, such as sympathy for others and engagement in reciprocal social interactions."[98] But even if we were to specifically speak of human animals, given that this proportionate intercourse of sympathy reaches out naturally, it may be argued that our interactive attachments with the "Other"—holistically including all entities and relationships: Interhuman, ecological-cosmic and universal-structural systems—derive from

---

95. Beauchamp and Childress, PBE, 219. About care ethics see p. 36.
96. Hume, *Method of Reasoning*, 602–3, especially T.3.3.3.2.
97. Beauchamp and Childress, PBE, 91.
98. Carruthers, "Animal Mentality," 391. Carruthers references to De Waal, *Good Natured*.

the good or bad qualities evinced in our moral character.[99] This may then suggest that one's right dealings with or treatment of the Other evinces a likely indicator of one's moral character. The reader should recall that Bantu take personhood *qua* virtue, ethics, morality, character, or one's "healthy humanness"[100] (*obuntu-bulamu*) as close synonyms. One is cold-hearted or impartially sympathetic to the Other because her *obuntu-bulamu* likely manifests who she is in her dealings with the other human animals without anticipating a return favor. This Bantu outlook is in dialogue with our common-sense intuition as Carruthers argues,

> it is important to see that someone with the right sort of kindly character who acts to prevent suffering to an animal will do so for the sake of the animal. This is required for having the right sort of sympathetic attitude . . . . Certainly, someone acting to ease the suffering of an animal won't be doing it to try to make himself into a better person! Nevertheless, the reason why this attitude is a virtue at all will be because of the way in which the behavior is likely to manifest itself in the person's dealing with other human beings.[101]

Restricting sympathy and confining partiality to our own taxonomic characterizations and cultural zones is to be speciesist which still limits holistic bioethics. The Bantu outlook counteracts this limited partiality—both impartialism and a strong form of partialism as two extremes are forbidden in favor of moderate partialism—and sympathy with social "sympathetic impartiality." The golden rule of sympathetic impartiality firstly focuses on a milieu that works interdependently for the wellbeing of each and all, viz., the welfare of every human animal and every system of life, but not only some. Each *muntu* can only co-exist as a member of the whole human community if he belongs primarily to some particular cultural subgroup. This is the demand of morality that Menkiti describes in African ethics "as one of beingness-with-others."[102] And it is similar to Tangwa's moral assertion that "morality is not possible without altruism, empathy and sympathetic impartiality," which he considers to be "part and parcel of human nature."[103] It is equally the same moral mandate that Tangwa subscribes to: "Ethics is not about self-interest, not about bargaining, not about realism of the present moment but . . . about sympathizing and empathizing with fellow humans

---

99. See Carruthers, "Animal Mentality," 396–97.
100. Karlström, "Democratization in Buganda," 485–505.
101. Carruthers, "Animal Mentality," 399.
102. Menkiti, "Normative Conception of a Person," 324.
103. Tangwa, "Ethical principles," s3.

in need."[104] But this sympathy or empathy would be limited if it only incorporated the demands of the human community. Since *muntu*'s significant element of being, is "being in relation to," not only to the *other* but also to the *relational Other*, *muntu* and the Other beings in the cosmos are constantly in interaction with each other. *Muntu* can only be conceived as a being if interwoven in a holistic network of community relations with the Other beings and systems of life, which Otherness includes the supreme being (Katonda), the spiritual beings (*balubaale*, *mayembe*, *misambwa* and *mizimu*), the living species (Bantu, people, persons), the deceased clan members, *muntu*'s piece of land and domestic animals, properties, natural objects, etc. Missing out on being in a dynamic relationship with the Other *NTU* is the same as not-being. So it is not *muntu*'s atomic individualism, but her relational being-ness that can only succeed through the unity of functioning good relationships with the other *NTU* vital forces, which relational ontological harmony can give assurance of *muntu*'s healthy humanness.[105] This African reality ultimately re-affirms a non (anti)-anthropocentric stance since it grants life not only to inanimate entities but also captures relational systems that holistically enjoy respectful love along the communities of the living, the nonliving, those not born as well as the living-dead.[106] In the language of this study, it is this relationship I refer to as relational solidarity which goes beyond interpersonal relationships, cosmic-ecological relationships to include relational or structural systems as having a vital force evincing a necessary dynamic cooperation between *muntu* and Other community members. Hence for a black African, the invaluableness of life comprises

104. Tangwa, "HIV/AIDS pandemic," 229.

105. See Kasozi, *The Ntuʹology of the Baganda*, 82–84; Need to care for one's community member is shown in these Baganda proverbs: *Agali awamu gegaluma enyama* (Those i.e., teeth, which are together are the ones that bite, or united we succeed). Nason, "Proverbs of the Baganda," 249; *Endege ziba nnyingi neziyoogaana* (The bells are many (on the hunting Dogs) and they make a lot of noise. Or many bells on the legs make a loud sound. In unity there is strength). See Murphy, *Luganda-English Dictionary*, 408; *Tussa kimu, nga nkuyege* (People should unite like the worker termites, which react together when someone steps on them). Sekadde and Semugoma, *Ndimugezi*, 10; at this initial stage, the significance of the *Other* and sociability in the African moral thought, see Gyekye and Wiredu, *Person and Community*; Gyekye, *A Common Humanity*; Wiredu, "Oral Philosophy of Personhood," 8–18; Metz, "An African Moral Theory," 321–41; Metz, "An African Theory of Moral Status," 387–402; Ikuenobe, "Good and Beautiful," 124–63; Molefe, "African Philosophy Through Personhood."; Molefe,"Ubuntu and Development," 96–115; Just like Rickert, Black Africans at least understand culture as the *totality of all* (holistic sense): "Die *Gesamtheit* der Objekte, an denen allgemeinen Werte haften, und die Rücksict auf diese Werte gepflegt werden." See Rickert, *Kulturwissenschaft und Naturwissenschaft*, 27. *Emphasis is mine.*

106. See Bujo, *Ethical Dimension of Community*, 70.

both the biotic and abiotic environments, i.e., all the Other NTU. The question of the Other is in conversation with Miller and Spoolman's notion of ecology. In their chapter 3, "Ecosystems: What Are They and How Do They Work?," they understand ecology as the study of an ecosystem and "how its variety of organisms interact with their living (*biotic*) environment of other organisms and with their nonliving (*abiotic*) environment."[107] Analogously, their bio-protective ecology of the Other is inherently manifested within an African biotic-abiotic-approach to holistic bioethics.

To minimize what would make the Black Africans less human and less African, aiding every force to participate in the friendship of relational solidarity with the holistic Other, African scholarships interest their audience with the term "classless African solidarity."[108] This classless solidarity within an African thought is partly understood as the self-insufficiency of each nation, demanding all nations to be collectively available to each other, in order to reduce bioethical global inequalities as one unified whole. Classless solidarity points to an all-inclusive belonging, a solidary belonging based on reciprocity towards an interdependent life since we all share an equal vulnerability to bioethical challenges. In this regard, the African understanding of solidarity goes beyond repeatedly associating existence with health and only human vulnerabilities and benefits, which limits the broad theme of solidarity to a few species and systems that benefit humans as clarified in bioethical principlism, and UNESCO declarations (such as UDBHR). Solidarity goes beyond focus on human cognitive capacities to include the capacity to socially share with the holistic Other. It is the reason the African moral thought proposes solidarity not only as an additional approach to the traditional four principle-approach developed by Beauchamp and Childress,[109] but also as a penetrative harnessing instrument for the four principles. Biomedical interventions globally and locally in African settings will succeed better, if non-individualistic values like solidarity, are included. Moreover, global solidarity is possible if global symmetrical cooperations are not exploitive but rather inclusively classless and symmetrically reciprocal.[110] Therefore, although we are locally different, we stand in a need of a reciprocal collective commitment since we are similar within a global unity.

What we must guard against, is the quality of solidarity we offer mostly globally, which can jeopardize or safeguard collaborations, i.e., not only solidarity of exploitive collaborations that don't promote the universality

---

107. Miller and Spoolman, *Environmental Science*, 38. *Emphasis is mine.*
108. Bujo, *Ethical Dimension of Community*, 20.
109. See Tangwa et al., "Global health inequalities," 242–46.
110. See Tangwa et al., "Global health inequalities," 245, 49.

of life, but a lack of structural solidarity also has the same moral challenges. The underlying ethical conviction concerns the existential dynamism that holistically operates only in reciprocity, that is, through the genuine exchange of vital force across interpersonal and universal cooperations. The sociality of an African life upholds a qualitative continuous flow of life even across all structural systems of collaborations. The life, as vital force, which ensues from God is a task for all global partners to accomplish so that this life reaches full maturity, and this is only possible if all genuinely commit to act in solidarity.[111] To this end, the normative sense of solidarity is suggestive of two thoughts. One, actions are wrong insofar as they fail to respect genuine relationships of solidarity in which we share a quality of life with the relational Other. The quality of solidary commitment contributes either to the growth or reduction, promotes or impedes, increases or hinders the life of the entire system of collaboration. Such a holistic substantive belief guarantees the norm of relational solidarity that is necessarily appropriate for promoting not only an interpersonal solidarity, a cosmic-ecological solidarity in bioethics, but also a structural-universal solidarity. Two, the holistic existential sense gives prominence to an African account of community sympathy which extends love and respect to all entities, the *Other*, on the one hand, while extending the same to broader structural solidary collaborations on the other hand. If natural recourses are discounted in the developed world, while the miners in SSA endure inhumane anguish, any citizen of the developed world who secures such discounted resources participates fully in this cable of structural injustices. Here the chain of liability involves systems of structural collaborations, animate and inanimate objects, in which life may either be negatively or positively promoted.

But if to promote a cosmic life of integral solidarity would be fulfilled by promoting community sympathy, that is, *muntu* being morally sensitive and responsive to the painful suffering and plight of the "Other," it would be morally myopic to limit the scope of the Other to some entities or systems only, given that suffering or holistic moral life is not limited to *them* exclusively. The view that we need to extend the scope of our love and respectful sympathy to all entities and cooperative systems, for example, is suggested in the analogy of hearing, characteristic of the idea of sympathy in African languages. The human capacity to "here"—to be sympathetic—should be attuned to the voice of the Other. Analogously, it would then be a mischaracterization of the moral ear to be discriminatingly attuned to hearing the sound or voices of human beings, as the only Other. Human sympathy

---

111. See Bujo, *An African Ethic*, 87–88.

should be extended to include all the *other Other*.[112] And if we are to capture well the golden rule of sympathetic impartiality, our sympathy towards the Other ought not to discriminate since the idea of sympathetic impartially is, "a *human universal* transcending culture viewed as social forms and customary beliefs and practices. In being common to all human practice of morality; it is a universal of any non-brutish form of human life."[113] To that, respectful sympathy to all entities and systems which promote life merits an African approach to holistic bioethics with a non-anthropocentric trait, where it embraces the hierarchized Other with love as an object of sympathy in the moral community, which entity or system maybe different from us but ultimately makes our moral life possible if not contributing some part. Besides if our sympathy can harmonize more their life or means of function, while difficultly doing so, holding this sympathy back would disharmoniously desecrate them or injure their wellbeing, flourishing and operation, it compels us to morally appreciate all systems and entities as mattering, taking them as communal objects needing our respectful love and sympathy. Relying on compelling evidence established in this investigation as far as the moral standing and moral status for creatures is concerned, it is relatively uncontroversial to uncover that it would be both *pro-tanto* and *prima facie* wrong in every-way if any entity wouldn't receive our sympathetic respectful love. Otherwise, the moral costs involved should trigger our intellectual honest to realize a moral attitude towards holistic bioethics that contains all creatures. Difficultly, we cannot overcome the caveats and moral costs stated in bioethical principlism, or even achieve a complete moral life without simultaneously incorporating all creation and life systems interrelatedly, i.e., within the spirit of holistic solidarity.

AN AFRICAN HOLISTIC APPROACH TO THE PRACTICE OF MEDICINE, HEALING AND RECONCILIATION

One practical case, in which we can present a holistic approach to bioethics, in response to insufficiencies of principle-based approaches in bioethics, is the approach to the practice of medicine and healing. In contrast to principle-based bioethics, I argue that the practice of medicine and healing in the African outlook encompasses not only the ill body but the whole person. It is not the healing of this one person who is sick, but the relational healing of the community. And the whole process involves the whole creation and the three-dimensional community. The practice of medicine and healing is

---

112. See Molefe, *African Personhood*, 87–88.
113. Wiredu, *Cultural Universals and Particulars*, 31. *Emphasis is mine.*

not limited to the individual but incorporates an all-inclusive healing of the totality of the community.

The Practice of Medicine and Healing mean Sharing in the Totality of Cosmic Life

In the African mind, an animate patient (*muntu* force) takes an inanimate or an animate medicine (*kintu* force),[114] which force can positively or negatively influence *muntu*'s own ill life. The sociable positive application of magical force by a medicine-person (*muganga* or *musawo*) as we indicated for example amongst Baganda, paves way for both physical and psychological treatment (intended for an integral healing).[115] Gilges' experience of African medicine-persons makes him to qualify them as highly skilled, and with better effective therapies. He mentions an example in Zimbabwe: "How far he was herbalist and how far witchdoctor I could never fathom, but I regret that I shall never possess his knowledge of African psychology, and his art in the treatment of his fellow man . . . ."[116] The holistic palaver of healing (how far he was herbalist and how far witchdoctor) is obviously a narrative that applies the magical force to the integral life of the patient. The therapies given by the medicine person have to fundamentally heal *muntu* in her totality of life.

"African psychology" and their "art in the treatment" of their community members, in contrast to the ethics of principlism, appreciate a communicative ethics through a healing palaver in a unique way that allows the entire triad-community to participate in an unlimited narrative palaver, not only to discern ethical norms but also to determine healing of the entire community.[117] The precautionary necessity of the narrative dimension in the medicinal African palaver, is also embraced in principlism. Proverbial wisdom and maxims as used by medicine persons (since they are morally virtuous as approved by the community) in the medicinal palaver act as precautionary measures in similar ways as used in bioethical interventions—think of the "precautionary principle" or approach like better safe than sorry; look before you leap; an ounce of prevention is worth a pound of cure—as rough guides for decision making and remain unobjectionable.[118]

114. See Magesa, *African Religion*, 189.
115. See Sempebwa, *Reality of a Bantu*, 111–12.
116. Gilges, *African Poison Plants*, 20.
117. See Bujo, *An African Ethic*, 29.
118. In case of morally unacceptable harm that is scientifically plausible but uncertain, actions shall be taken to avoid or diminish that harm. World Commission on

In contrast to principlism however, the African narrative as a communicative ethical dialogue process considers *several narrative vehicles* that embrace the totality of life.[119] These vehicles as used by medicine persons continuously *appropriate* African indigenous moral wisdom to relevantly acquire its best contemporary form suitably medicinal to the patient. Though principlists consider principles at the heart of narrating their moral life, African narrativists see a communicative palaver at its core.[120] Like Bujo, Ikuenobe too insists that the role of virtue in an African social reality—for instance, that is necessary for understanding the informal methods (communal) of African moral education—cannot be understood outside the narrative dimension.[121] Listening to the medicinal palaver word as it is narrated by the medicine person to the patient is a competent way of learning something new and healing than simply being listened too. But still there is mutual communication because the patient narrates all her historical relationships inclusive of her life with the neighbors. It is within this line that we note that the African medicine narratives have been recently restructured and practiced as healing narrative competences—the recently novel *must-have* expertise through storytelling—in bioethics. They are presented as effective practices of medicine with an ability to acknowledge, absorb, interpret, and act on the stories and plights of others. Medicine practiced with narrative competence, called narrative medicine, has been proposed as a new skilled model for humane and effective medical practice. Narrative medicine examines and illuminates atleast 4 of medicine's central narrative situations: Physician and patient, physician and self, physician and colleagues, and physicians and community.[122] This is contributory to the holistic perspective dealt with here. So, with narrative competence, bioethical interventions can reach and join medicine persons and their patients. Moreover, other disease healing practices may not be known to Africans only. For instance, disease healing has been "universal. Although we do not like to admit it, it is widespread in the West under various disguises, from fortune-telling with

---

the Ethics of Scientific Knowledge and Technology (COMEST, under the auspices of UNESCO, *The Precautionary Principle*.; Cranor, "Aspects of the Precautionary Principle," 259–79; Beauchamp and Childress, PBE, 140, 249.

119. Examples of narrative vehicles include tales, legends, proverbs, maxims, fairy tales, symbols, parables, songs, music, dances, pantomimes, allegories, stories, events of the past, verbal spiritual invocations, riddles, myths, beliefs, customs, taboos, maxims or paradigms, sayings, anecdotes, fables, songs, idioms, rituals, statements, meaning of words, word groups, initiation rites and so on. See Bujo, *An African Ethic*, see the foreword. See Bidima, *La Palabre*.; Ndjimbi-Tshiende, *Systeme Palabrique Africain*.

120. McCarthy, "Principlism or narrative ethics," 65–71.

121. See Ikuenobe, *Communalism and Morality in African Traditions*, 162.

122. Charon, "The patient-physician relationship," 1897–902.

AN AFRICAN APPROACH TO HOLISTIC BIOETHICS

cards to the curing of disease by contact with relics."[123] So it is common in the Western approach to bioethics, that a non-African may fail to appreciate that the palaver of healing *uniquely* leads to regaining holistic health, not only to the patient but across the community members.[124] It is also common that some African medicinal practices may be disputed because their semantics at first glance aren't familiar to others—influencing some not to go beyond this shallow conceptualization. This doesn't mean that African medicine's rich scientific interpretations cannot be formally demonstrated.

Citing an example from Armel Ayimdji and colleagues, a prescription from African medicine person may run thusly: "This plant should be collected by a young man, early in the morning, before the daybreak. Once the plant is collected, the collector must run straightly at home without stopping on the way, and the plant must be used immediately."[125] To outclass any narrow conceptualization on the one hand, one must realize, as Armel Ayimdji and colleagues note, that such plants contain essential oils for which the concentration is very high in the early mornings and their volatility requires a very short delay between the collection and the usage. That is why some medicine doctors, without knowing this veiled scientific explanation which would be explained, let us say by pharmacologists or apothecaries, recommend that such plants be collected specifically by young men who can run fast. Briefly, the scientific specification of the collector is a young man—to minimize delay before usage—whose attitude is to run nonstop (given the volatility of an active inherent component), and the period of collection is early morning—since it is an essential oil that can liquify when it gets sunny. While on the other hand, scholarships have slowly realized that (also) bioethical principlism from a Western outlook tries through psychosomatic medicine, psychotherapy research and psychopharmacology—their trend of innovative thinking interfaces between medical and behavioral sciences—to reintegrate applicable African holistic practices of medicine that used to be heavily condemned.[126] So in restoring broken relationships, we shouldn't therefore condemn African realities, even of yesterday, say of disease and holistic healing, in which *muntu* influences "events that are beyond rational control"[127] in the sphere of bioethical principlism.

---

123. Maquet, *Africanity*, 65.
124. See Bujo, *An African Ethic*, 10–11.
125. Ayimdji et al., "Ontology for African Traditional Medicine," 247–50.
126. Cosci and Guidi, *Acta Psychotherapeutica, Psychosomatica et Orthopaedagogica* (*Psychotherapy and Psychosomatics*).
127. Maquet, *Africanity*, 65.

For a holistic human healing, need demands a holistic encounter with the entire cosmic life. For *Muntu* to be victorious, she needs to relax the tension between life and death by cultivating eco-friendships in the cosmos. First and foremost, in the physical treatment the medicine-person uses *inanimate* or *animate* forces such as plants, herbs powders, bones, seeds, wood, teeth and hair, roots, juices, leaves, liquids, minerals, charcoal and the like to revitalize or increase life forces in a patient or unhealthy *muntu*. In the second instance, the psychological treatment completes the holistic process, since the medicine-person does not merely treat a disease but treats the totality of the patient.[128] Treating the totality of *muntu* is achieving an integral health that Tangwa understands as the *value of all values* originating from the traditional Black Africa, where "health was seen as the value of all values—the value that made other values possible and achievable. As long as one was healthy little else mattered and all other achievements were with-in the bounds of the possible."[129] In upholding health as the value of all values, it always meant handling *muntu*'s totality of life that till today necessarily requires an integral approach to health. Achieving an integral health or practicing medicine holistically, differs from westernized biomedical principlism in a way that the African medicine-person can only wholly practice medicine if she doubles as a physician and as a psychiatrist, psychotherapist, psychologist, than treating solitarily *muntu*'s bodily disease or illness. Africanists like Tangwa speak similarly of the significance of the holistic cultural context in the practice of medicine: "Understanding of a disease, its perceived causes and possible remedies, are culture anchored. Within African culture it may not be enough to identify the physical cause of an ailment or illness, as there is a tendency to search for the cause of the cause in a regressive chain that can terminate only in God or else become interminable. The ontology of the African cultural universe recognizes non-material beings and presences, including dead-living ancestors, sundry spirits, divinities, gods, and God."[130]

This holistic sense presupposes handling the totality of the patient by the medicine-person, which means, the effectiveness of curing of maladies is not entirely dependent on the relevant medicine or mere physiological and individual symptoms like in principlism, but also on the totality of the relational cultural atmosphere surrounding the patient's contextual existence or sociality. We have already indicated that *muntu*'s social reality encompasses the actual psychological, moral and social relational realities

---

128. See Sempebwa, *Reality of a Bantu*, 111–112; Rwiza, *Environmental Ethics*, 65.
129. Tangwa, "African Perception of a Person," 43.
130. Tangwa, "African thought," 105.

of life across the visible and invisible communal realms. Meaning a disease may manifest that something in human relations is wrong. Thus, the diagnosis of the patient does not only embody the class of different diseases, but also, interpretation and re-interpretation of the external relational communal past and present conflicts.[131] This is one reason why in the African ethic prevails a palpable dissatisfaction regarding physical casualties as the sole sufficient explanation surrounding the realities influencing Bantu life. Falling sick may not necessarily mean being infected with a virus or a bacterium. One needs supplementary relational explanations, which may lie in the broader disruption of the relational media of vital force, for instance, in the spiritual world which is eventually accessible to only those human beings endowed with special powers, e.g., medicine-persons.[132] This outstanding uniqueness of the medicine-person in the African holistic approach to the practice of medicine is stated by Merkies in a similar fashion: "It is often reported by physicians working in the field of developing countries, that patients, after having consulted them, also seek the advice of their native doctors in whom they have no doubt a great confidence. This phenomenon may be explained that either the physician is believed to have no sufficient insight in the circumstances causing the disease or on account of the absence of well-established and trusted ritual in the procedure."[133] In patients seeking the advice of their native doctors, they are searching for a holistic healing beyond their physical diseases, a healing interconnected with their relational communal relationships that can never be diagnosed through the westernized principlistic approaches to medicine. Analogously, this holistic sense of practicing medicine explains why an African Christian goes to church in the morning and to the medicine person in the evening so as to search for practical answers regarding fear, suffering, illness, etc., within her social community, a perspective beyond the individual viral sickness.[134] This explains the significance of the medicine person, who holistically re-harmonizes the social totality of life by answering questions arising from *muntu*'s viral or bacterial or physiological sickness, but also moral fears arising from her externally lived relational community life, which questions couldn't be practically answered in the church service or reliance on a principle-based Western approach to bioethics. Just know that *muntu* wouldn't like to be studied or analyzed as a research subject in her illness but urgently

---

131. See Bujo, *Ethical Dimension of Community*, 182–85, 190.

132. See Kasozi, *The Ntu'ology of the Baganda*, 56–57, see also footnote 25; Lugira, *Ganda Art*, 116–18.

133. Merkies, *Ganda Classification*, 114–15.

134. Bujo, *Ethical Dimension of Community*, 17–18.

seeks effective solutions to ameliorate any ill-health and preserve functional relationships.

In promoting life holistically, the medicine-person treats *muntu* by participating in the life-giving dimension of a healing palaver that extends beyond the living visible community. In the African communal wisdom of a therapeutic healing palaver, *muntu*'s illness (misfortune) presupposes a necessity of a relational healing dialogue. In addition to several symbols, the dialogue employs the *word*—each hearer eats, drinks, chews, digests, and invests in it—since it possesses great medicinal power, it signifies life growth of *muntu* or death, medicine or poison, creates anew or destroys the community if badly chewed. But since the community is always both visible and invisible, the dialogue is not limited to the patient alone but includes the living community, the living-dead ancestors and the entire spiritual, supraspiritual or terrestrial world, namely, not only the spirits but also God himself.[135] The basis for dialogue is in the African logic of practicing medicine, where medicines (*kintu* forces) or poison remain ineffective without the influence of a *muntu* along an inclusive dialogue. Even when a medicine-person is sick, some other medicine-person must treat her, she cannot treat herself. The Baganda say: "Omuganga teyeganga" (A medicine-person does not treat oneself). She cannot increase her own life-force by herself, she cannot give herself life. She requires the influence of another *muntu* force to revitalize her own life. The ontological background is that sickness weakens *muntu*'s vital force.[136] So for a black African, it is only through *muntu*'s influence, such as a word, that an ineffective or innocuous poison becomes an effective or harmful poison. Analogously, the patient or weakened *muntu* force can only be holistically re-energized by a participatory dialogue of the Other cosmic vital forces, whether animate or inanimate.

The reader should recall that the goal of the entire holistic healing between *muntu* and the network of the cosmos, is to increase vitality, not only a biological force, but the entire vital force of the causal and ontological interdependence traceable back to the Creator of everything. No one is allowed to keep this vitality for oneself; everyone has to share it with the other members of the family and clan, so as to increase and promote life.[137] Not to share this vital force further is to keep it to oneself, insinuating that *muntu* has not only failed in increasing cosmic life as the goal of holistic healing but also desecrated the cosmos.

135. See Bujo, *An African Ethic*, 46; Bujo, *Ethical Dimension of Community*, 182–84.

136. Poison is not considered an effective substance in its own right. It is merely a force that remains innocuous until set to work by a *muntu*. Sempebwa, *Reality of a Bantu*, 111–12.

137. See Bujo, *Ethical Dimension of Community*, 16.

A failure in holistically sharing vitality leads to *ill-health*,[138] which means, human relations are in disorder with less respect for healthy humanness. Ill-health and its disorderliness go beyond *muntu*'s physiological helplessness (e.g., through malaria) to include her exercise of humanness in her external relational life. In the aftermath of the COVID-19 pandemic, some of the external relationships include lamenting parents from sub-Saharan African families. They are crying for their children exported as labor to other gulf countries but return without some of their organs, if not as corpses. There is concern about an increasing black market for human organs and organ trafficking, for instance, disguised atleast in the 98% of Ugandans seeking jobs in the Middle East, recruited as casual laborers, who sometimes die strangely or undergo through mysterious surgeries.[139] Several relatives grieve on receiving back their victimized community members or their dead bodies from the Gulf. In my view, such exploitation involving collaboration of the global networks with local systems lies outside genuine African morality. Besides, it is not within genuine morality of African natives to allow exploitive collaborations where dictators from Africa transport the wealth of their people to rich countries in the Global North or facilitate exploitative biomedical research, while difficultly doing so, the health services and moral systems in their own countries are collapsing.[140] A *muntu* as a patient can link her ill-health to such lamentations. But a holistic healing is only possible if we effectively reenergize the various life forces, viz., including illness of an individual *muntu* like malaria, fixing health systems, fixing exploitative dictatorial systems, overhauling the beggar status of foreign assistance, renewing life relationally among affected neighborhoods and so on, given that some of these toxic ethical concerns are largely homegrown.

Holistic Healing Entails Reconciliation with the Visible and Invisible Community, and the entire Cosmos

I treat reconciliation in relation to three areas: The visible community, the invisible community (most extensive) and the entire cosmos.

Firstly, *reconciliation entails the visible community* of Bantus. When *muntu* is sick, the community is also sick, suggesting that if *muntu* needs healing, the community too needs healing as well as reconciliation. Sickness

---

138. Okot p'Bitek uses the concept of "ill-health" to include African religion, witchcraft, vengeance ghost, curse, cult of ancestors, works of diviners. P'Bitek, *Africa's Cultural Revolution*, 88.

139. Ssejjoba, "Migrant worker loses kidney."; Draku, "Fly to death."

140. See Bujo, *Ethical Dimension of Community*, 193, 195.

or illness or suffering is experienced to the end in common as brothers and sisters (neighbors). Oftentimes since sickness concerns directly the living community members, the medicine-person, patient; they take part verbally in a healing palaver in order to achieve the physical and psychological healing through confessions of guilt. The shared, eaten, chewed, digested word and rites of reconciliation are the real therapy and medicine.[141] The aim is a new re-energized harmonious beginning, besides precautionary reconciliatory countermeasures that apply not only to the patient but also to the would-be ill-health of the living that may be linked to the community of the living dead.

Secondly, *reconciliation entails the invisible community*. It is a moral challenge to accord bioethical principlism, with its argumentative power of reason, a place for a productive reconciliation toward a holistic approach to bioethics. A fruitful reconciliation demands a holistic dialogue between the medicine-person with herself, with God, as well as with the social fellowship of Bantus. It is why the African dialogue-oriented palaver cannot reduce *muntu*'s healing and reconciliation to simply discursive rational bioethical principles.[142] In contrast, an African anticipates healing, not of her body only, but her entire totality.[143] Since African disease etiology is understood in its entire totality as a communal moral-spiritual issue—spiritual discordance or disharmony—[144] the holistic healing process must indispensably aim at a communal integrated wholeness that is unthinkable without a palaver (of rites) of reconciliation. This confirms why

> the "vital force" of which Africans speak is not only biological but fundamentally "spiritual" too, and this is why the healing process cannot treat the spiritual and psychological as "secondary" dimensions. The "physical" illness is usually the crystallization point of the invisible dimension in the community—many conflicts in the community, among the living and the dead, lead to a worsening of health, which finally finds "a biological" expression. For this reason, there is no genuine healing in traditional Africa without rites of reconciliation, which include both the invisible and visible community, including God.[145]

Reconciliation within a holistic approach to bioethics reestablishes the broken interpersonal relationships by demanding not only the dialogue

---

141. See Bujo, *An African Ethic*, 47.
142. See Bujo, *An African Ethic*, 48; Bujo, *Ethical Dimension of Community*, 38.
143. See Tangwa, *Contemporary Bioethics Problems*, 65.
144. Magesa, *What is not Sacred*, 93.
145. Bujo, *An African Ethic*, 97.

between the medicine-person and the patient alone, but also full participation of the entire community. In a healing dialogue, the patient supplies not only full information about her physiological illness but also the truest complete historical standing of her interrelationships. It could happen that one traces one's suffering back to one's own incorrect behavior in relation to the deceased family member, a scenario that may demand the patient to responsibly confess her quilt and be reconciled with the family for the healing process to be effectively completed.[146] This approach to a holistic reconciliation is well captured in Kivuto Ndeti's African medical anthropology. He asserts that "in African medicine, the concept of disease first takes into account the role of the spirits of dead ancestors. This concept is found in almost all African societies. Because of the organic and psychological relations that exist between the living and the dead, the spirits of the dead ancestors seem to take a keen interest in the affairs of the living. They regulate the general conduct of individuals in African societies in mysterious ways."[147] It is the reason, within a holistic reconciliation, the interrelationship between the living and the dead cannot be forgotten since *muntu*'s healing, before anything else, necessitates fixing her disrupted relationships with the past deceased. May be there is some past un-concluded indebtedness![148] For example, *muntu* must have paid all her debts to die peacefully and clear any future possibilities of ill-health that would demand rites of cleansing, communal confession, reconciliation, or delays to execute her will (*kiraamo*). And since the African thought is non-dualistic, sickness, health and reconciliation necessarily require a functioning unitary wholeness that cannot only be revitalized physiologically, but rather holistically. Ill-heath, sickness, healing, reconciliation concern and impact the whole clan and family community of the living and the living-dead, and subsequently demand their harmonious solidarity with the whole person of the patient without fail. We can concretely symbolize this invisible reality existent in the African palaver of a communicative community, in which nonverbal forms of dialogue are employed atleast in two ways. First, in *muntu*'s desire to achieve reconciliation with her departed ancestors, she asks for forgiveness at the grave of her deceased parent or ancestor. Here the grave symbolizes the presence of the deceased, allowing a nonverbal dialogue to take place, and an opportunity for the suffering patient to fully unload all the underlying loads of pain. The nonverbal unloading of a community member's suffering is therapeutically medicinal. Second, there is also a nonverbal dialogue of encounter with the

---

146. Bujo, *An African Ethic*, 46.
147. Ndeti, "African Traditional Medicine," 186.
148. See Bujo, *Ethical Dimension of Community*, 183–85.

natural environment, e.g., ancestral trees, rivers, rocks. Given the immanence of the vital force in all nature, it houses some of the frequented places for a communicative nonverbal dialogue between the visible and invisible community where a holistic approach to reconciliation takes place.

To accomplish an all-inclusive healing and reconciliation, the holistic approach to bioethics seriously incorporates the invisible world to wholly dialogue with all those who were victimized in the past and forgotten as well as those permanently incapacitated to participate physically or cognitively in the palaver. And since the ancestors exercise a genuine custodianship on the living community, "restoring the order of the relationship between the living and the dead is also restoring the natural order of things;" whereby, "belief in the ancestors as representatives of fatherhood plays a primordial role in African medicine"[149] and all symbolic techniques of healing within the entire social relationships.[150] One of the vastest moral challenge with the practice of medicine in bioethical principlism is to forget the victimized, the permanently damaged patients, those not present and their communicative bond with the past ancestral life and so doesn't blend with the anamnetic thinking entailed in the African anthropology. The reader shouldn't forget our emphasis that the African communal anamnetic palaver recognizes a "memoria-conscience" in which the participating creatures' interests are represented besides those not physically present and those who maybe cognitively or rationally incapacitated to take part in any contractarian settlements. Though principlism favors an advocatory ethics, whereby it overemphasizes individual autonomous rationality as central in intellectually formulating principles and agreements in the name of other creatures unable to express themselves logically—e.g., through surrogacy—an African approach goes further to represent interests of the illiterate, those with diminished autonomy and those permanently damaged, atleast at all levels (*micro*, *meso* and *macro*-ethical levels) as a holistic way of promoting a broader communal pursuit of humanness. It could be argued that the basic rules of the communal palaver are not systematically logical as the ethics of bioethical principlism, but they are practically lived out on a daily basis by a village Black African without forgetting the interests of both the individual and the community.[151] In brief, in contrast to bioethical principlism, an anamnetic-solidary-nature of the African discourse of palaver includes all those affected in the community without excluding anybody such as those

---

149. Éla, *My faith as an African*, 22.

150. Éla, *My faith as an African*, 51.

151. See Bujo, *An African Ethic*, 54–55; Bujo, *Ethical Dimension of Community*, 40–42.

incapable of physical presence or formulating intellectual logical inferences or the victimized of history. The absence of *muntu*'s physical presence doesn't mean an absence of a nonverbal communicative dialogue within an African moral thought. Such a nonverbal dialogue anamnetically includes not only those mentally dilapidated but also the invisible community of those not yet born, the community of the ancestors and most especially the victimized of the past. It is clearly evident how the victims of history are so central to an African anamnetic approach to bioethics.

In contrast to bioethical principlism, the African approach holistically reflects on the accumulated ancestral anamnetic wisdom that subsequently recreates anew today's communal life by promoting reconciliation which augments the solidarity of all forces. Then it is the anamnetic solidarity that deeply fosters reconciliation with the "community of victims"[152] or the "victimized of history," by recreating the memory of the great fore-parents to whom the victimized descendants owe their dignified social existence. The ancestors' "deeds encourage and stimulate their descendants, and thus establish a genuine solidarity in time among the generations."[153] To pass on identity as well as their collective lifetime experiences which are essential for a holistic approach to the bioethics of healing and reconciliation, the fore-parents, who worked tirelessly to preserve the first commandment as life for the later generations (their descendants) have to be integrated into the solidary wellbeing and reconciliation of community members. The commandment of life and its associated treasures of wisdom, both self-realization of the victimized *muntu* and the victimized group, all can only fully be achieved in anamnetic solidarity with the invisible community of fore-parents. Since the anamnetic solidarity is not limited to the victims of history, those to be born and the young generation are also included. For instance, as the young generation responsibly augments relations especially with the elderly, they also maintain their identity, which can only be properly understood in the light of their fore-bearers' history. That being so, remembrance of the ancestral forebears as benefactors towards a holistic reconciliation, basically belongs to ancestral veneration, which refers not only to the life still to be received, but also to the one already received.[154] Briefly, it stands clarified that the fore-parents cannot be disputed as architects of the current bonds of solidarity enjoyed by their descendants, and so remain communicatively alive among them. Moreover, when solidarity is tested with time given the ill-health or unhealed bonds arising from the

---

152. Bujo, *Ethical Dimension of Community*, 32.
153. Éla, *My faith as an African*, 15.
154. See Bujo, *Ethical Dimension of Community*, 30–31, 45, 202.

victimized of the past, it is reconciliation within an anamnetic dialogue that can revive an integral-inclusive life.

Concretely, the African mind of integration and inclusion exemplified in an anamnetic dialogue is put forward, not only negatively in victims of history, but also positively in care of the extended relational Other. In some positive injunctions among the Bantu, atleast three Ganda obligations focus on positively "taking care of one's kins" (*kufa ku b'oluganda*): "You ought to take good care of your children," "Children should take care of their parents," "You ought to take care of other members of your clan (*kika*) and help them whenever possible." At the chore of these injunctions, the significance of clan kinship or *muntu*'s relatives cuts across the community triad without forgetting one's fore bearers. It is why there is a prescription of conduct: "Be sure to know your relatives" (*Omanyanga ab'olulyolwo*).[155] These positive injunctions demonstrate how many Black Africans survive only thanks to their solidary environment, whereby each community incurs a debt—e.g., providing a conducive environment for personhood—by nurturing a community citizen, which debt is reciprocally paid back in later times. We note atleast financial, social, and moral injunctions. Concrete examples to illustrate these positive injunctions include *muntu*'s upbringing, medication, education, etc.;[156] whereby, it is not rare that family members closely cooperate to support financially, morally, or socially one of the village children with the hope that the child will be the future savior of the whole family and heir to the ancestral lineage. Besides the financial and moral injunctions, the anamnetic nature of social injunctions reveals that "instruction in general good manners is not left to the parents; on neutral ground, at least, any grown-up person present may take a hand."[157] This is because children do not belong to their biological parents alone, but the right and duty to reward or punish, or even pass on the accrued ancestral wisdom, goes beyond the nuclear family to relationally include the whole village as well as the clan lineage. In this regard, learning to be human is learned from childhood together with the community Other, meaning, the parents alone cannot offer their children the entire anamnetic wisdom of the ancestors and the elders.[158] To relationally embrace anamnetic wisdom within the African holistic sense, reciprocity of life remains central. However, the demand to interact reciprocally with the "living community," atleast cannot be restricted to an African thought. It partly transpires in principle-based approaches,

---

155. Sempebwa, Reality of a Bantu, 145–48.
156. See Bujo, *Ethical Dimension of Community*, 170.
157. Mair, *An African People*, 66.
158. See Bujo, *Ethical Dimension of Community*, 118, 150–51.

for example in Hume's reciprocity account: "A man who retires from life does no harm to society: He only ceases to do good; which, if it is an injury, is of the lowest kind. —All our obligations to do good to society seem to imply something reciprocal. I receive the benefits of society, and therefore ought to promote its interests ...."[159] Hume's thought incurs an obligation to benefit others while reciprocally receiving beneficial help from them, meaning we can neither claim any autonomous independence nor maintain that we can free ourselves from that indebtedness to our community (parents, public health, institutions, teachers). Analogously, principlism so emphasizes just like the Hippocratic oath, that the obligations of physicians to patients represent debts incurred in the course of becoming physicians to the larger society.[160] In this sense, a physician's beneficent care shouldn't be misconstrued as personal commitment, philanthropy or altruism, but rather as a solidary reciprocity akin to patient's donation of her organ after death.[161] And solidarity or reciprocity should be further understood as an alternative prosocial value-laden persuasive appeal, an act of "giving from the heart" that cannot be equaled to any commercial gain.[162] Though bioethical principlism appreciates reciprocity as one essential component of solidarity, the moral challenge remains that it scarcely incorporates the victimized of the past as well as their dynamic communicative action with the present generation, making it difficult to blend with the *anamnetic* thinking entailed in the genuine African holistic approach to bioethics. Nonetheless, this is not to claim that the *anamnetic* dimension has fully worked among black Africans.

As an illustration of failure of an *anamnetic* thinking in modern Africa, among some African countries is Rwanda, which was so Cristian to an extent that ninety per cent of the inhabitants identified themselves as part of the Catholic, Protestant, or Seventh-day Adventist Church in 1991.[163] With the onset of Christianity and colonialism in sub-Saharan Africa, the Rwandan genocide occurred in 1994. In 2017, Pope Francis officially

---

159. Hume, *Essays on Suicide*, 12.

160. Beauchamp and Childress, PBE, 229.

161. "Justice as reciprocity." Buchanan, "Justice as Reciprocity," 227–52; Chronic organ shortage can be ameliorated by coupling altruism with an emphasis on reciprocity and fairness. Siegal and Bonnie, "Closing the Organ Gap," 415–23; Should we suggest solidarity since the use of financial incentives to increase the supply of transplantable organs from deceased individuals should not be promoted. Childress and Liverman, *Organ Donation*, 258–59.

162. Guttman et al., "Altruism, Solidarity, or Reciprocity," 909–36.

163. See Longman, Genocide in Rwanda, 163–86; Longman, *Christianity and genocide in Rwanda*.

asked for forgiveness as a contribution to the "purification of memory" that would renew trust and assure us of the future of peace and solidary engagements.[164] On a positive note, for solidarity to reign again, the Pope's apology already indicated a purification of memory that can be analogously implied in the *memoria-conscience*, an anamnetic thinking or anamnetic solidarity traceable in a genuine African anthropology. On an undesirable note which depicts a non-genuine African anthropology, instead of resolving their differences through the known African palaver rites of reconciliation, where the silent goal of retribution is reconciliation that prevents further recurrence and rectifies the situation rather than punishment of one's neighbor,[165] as well as creating reconciliatory alliances with enemies, Rwandese resorted to weapons,[166] but which weapons did not promote life but instead destroyed it by annihilating each other's neighbor. However later on, after the genocide, studies prove how *gacaca* handled reconciliatory justice positively. *Gacaca* means "judgement on the grass," offered as a pragmatic and community-based conflict resolution procedure. *Gacaca* focuses on contextual local as well collective justice. *Gacaca* was lawfully established in 2001 with about 11,000 community courts that would try lower-level hierarchally organized networks of crime. It was estimated that Rwandan courts would take close to 150 years to try all the suspects accused of human rights crimes. It was accordingly clear that the International Criminal Tribunal of Rwanda (ICTR) set in Arusha was unlikely to try more than a hundred of the most prominent suspects, while over 100,000 suspects languished in Rwandan prisons. Positively, *Gacaca* rewarded over 60,238 prisoners who confessed their crimes and apologized, subsequently allowing promotion of reconciliation and reparations to victims.[167] It is in the same line of thought

---

164. At the Apostolic Palace, the Holy Father, Pope Francis, received in Audience His Excellency Mr. Paul Kagame, President of the Republic of Rwanda. The Pope conveyed his profound sadness, and that of the Holy See and of the Church, for the genocide against the Tutsi. He implored anew God's forgiveness for the sins and failings of the Church and its members, among whom priests, and religious men and women who succumbed to hatred and violence, betraying their own evangelical mission. In light of the Statement published by the Rwandan Bishops, the Pope also expressed the desire that this humble recognition of the failings of that period, which, unfortunately, disfigured the face of the Church, may contribute to a "purification of memory" and may promote, in hope and renewed trust, a future of peace, witnessing to the concrete possibility of living and working together, once the dignity of the human person and the common good are put at the centre. The Holy See, *Audience with the President of the Republic of Rwanda*.

165. See Metz, "An African Moral Theory," 321–41.

166. See Bujo, *An African Ethic*, 142–143.

167. Tiemessen, "Gacaca Justice in Post-Genocide Rwanda," 60; Graybill and Kimberly, "Truth, Justice, and Reconciliation in Africa," 8–9.

that the holistic approach to bioethics re-emphasizes the institutionalized ancestral tradition of rites of reconciliation which have been oftentimes criticized as primitive by colonialists and Christian missionaries.

A concrete instance of holistic healing inclusive of reconciling the community of victims with the victimizers (anamnetic solidarity) is in Archbishop Desmond Tutu's approach in The Truth and Reconciliation Commission he chaired after being named by President Nelson Mandela. Tutu sees "No Future Without Forgiveness" because true reconciliation cannot be achieved by denying the past.[168] This moral insight of reconciliation takes us back to the quality of social interrelationships we have labored to clarify till now. It is these qualitative or poor relationships that serve as crucial moral enablers or disablers of truth, forgiveness, and reconciliation in a holistic approach. The circumstance is no different to the apartheid, where the oppressor's humanity was (possibly) as dehumanized as the humanity of the oppressed.[169] The greatest good, according to Tutuism as a version of the African moral thought, is the good of the community that promotes a collective social harmony (friendship) instead of social disharmony. This is equivalent to asking whether harmony must be initially secured in order to perform what is eventually right? From an African prescription defended in this investigation, an action is right if it promotes life, meaning, *a shared relational social identity*[170] among community people. What is essential is for the act to identify itself with a functioning shared relational identity. This is no different to John Samuel Mbiti's view, that "it is not the act in itself which would be 'wrong' as such, *but the relationships* involved in the act: *if relationships are not hurt or damaged,* and if there is no discovery of the break of custom or regulation, then the act is not 'evil' or 'wicked' or 'bad.'"[171] Meaning an approach to holistic bioethics in an African sense is only possible if we familiarize ourselves with their understanding of a collective interactive relational identity, which if damaged or hurt, it gives off a sour or an unhealthy relationship. One may argue whether this can't justify a communal collective violence or any group actions of engaging in a war, such as what happened in the Apartheid of 1948 to 1994 in South Africa and Hutu/Tutsi 1994 genocide in Rwanda, as well as the Kenya post-election violence of 2007–2008, which violence left the mighty largely Bantu groups extremely divided? Suppose the apartheid oppressors expected their

168. Tutu, *No Future without Forgiveness*, jacket.

169. Tutu, *No Future without Forgiveness*, 35. Molefe, *African Personhood*, 28; Metz, "African Moral Theory," 84.

170. See Tutu, *South Africa's Truth and Reconciliation Commission*, 212–13; Metz, "African Moral Theory," 340.

171. Mbiti, *African Religions and Philosophy*, 208. *Empasis added.*

collective cruelty to promote an integral harmonious life, would they have acted rightly in the African sense even when their actions didn't eventually yield harmony (or promoted a harmonious living)? What if their oppressing acts were expected to yield disharmony, would they have acted wrongly even when their shared cruel actions never produced disharmony? The question we are supposed to answer is what relationships of shared identity precisely mean for Bantu.

Foremost, one barely notes any separation between the victims and the victimizers since they all collectively share an identity of one delicate existential community that needs cleansing at multiple levels, both local and global. Nonetheless, it is not until the oppressed as the community of victims and the oppressor as the community of victimizers are *relationally empowered* to be *human again*, that we can then ultimately and rightly speak of a holistic shared identity.[172] If but only if Tutuism is interpreted charitably, it means that the *shared identity* can rightly be spoken of if the normative outcomes positively promote a shared social solidarity as well as a holistic reformed healing inclusive of the victimized of past, as well as taking into account "the post-conflict reconciliation." In Tutu's interpretation of the African moral thought, post-conflict-reconciliation aims at reuniting both the victims and the victimizers. A shared identity implies a functioning relationship where the victims forgive the victimizers while the victimizers—who may have been in the past far more dehumanized—fully disclose facts which do not undermine a rich reconciliation and full account for the past evils committed in order to restore lively humanity.[173] If we recall what gave birth to the "National Unity and Reconciliation Act" of July 26, 1995, which established the "Truth and Reconciliation Commission" lead by Tutu, its mandate of reconciling the victims and the victimizers is firmly stated in chapter 2 of the Act—"Objectives of the Commission": "§3(1) the objectives of the Commission shall be to promote national unity and reconciliation in a spirit of understanding which transcends the conflicts and divisions of the past by . . . (c) establishing and making known the fate or whereabouts of victims and by restoring the human and civil dignity of such victims by granting them an opportunity to relate their own accounts of the violations of which they are the victims, and by recommending reparation measures in respect of them . . . ."[174] So in Tutu's approach, the mandate to be fulfilled was to attune South Africans to the realization that a genuine relational reconciliation is impossible without holistically incorporating the victimized with

---

172. See Molefe, *African Personhood*, 107.
173. Cordeiro-Rodrigues, "Towards a Tutuist Ethics," 426–27, 432–33.
174. Republic of South Africa, *Government Gazette*.

their victimizers, the past and the present into one shared identity. This is no different to the aftermaths of the humiliating colonial activities and slave trade, where the oppressed to date inclusively embrace the descendants of their past oppressors without discrimination. However, we cannot rule out the fact that oftentimes victims are also victimizers who are themselves likewise victims of some sort. We therefore find a chain of exploitive oppression broadening from one level to another, from racist dehumanization of the victim by the victimizer to probably commercial-economic manipulation, spiritual-religious as well as social-cultural colonization.

In contrast, Western principle-based approaches would probably question why such an African approach to the holistic bioethics of reconciliation would not compel white beneficiaries of the racist apartheid to fully account for their horrific victimizing injustices. Tutu himself, having held firm that our humanity will forever remain intertwined—the humanity of the victimizer in relation to the Kenya election/Rwanda genocide/South Africa apartheid's mayhems couldn't escape being interwoven in the sufferings of the victims whether one liked it or not—whereby in the process of dehumanizing another (exacting indescribable internal and external injuries) the victimizer is inescapably being dehumanized as well, dehumanized as much as, if not more than, the victimized. Unfortunately, as Tutu openly remarks, many in the white community assumed his slogan as provocative hate. They took Tutu as irresponsible and loved to hate him![175] What is forgotten here, is exactly what social relationships and their requirement of reconciliation mean for Bantu.

Tutu's cathartic holistic "atonement theory" states: "When you come forward to confess you are guilty, you will lighten the burden for us all."[176] The tutuistic holistic approach to reconciliation is conditioned on full disclosure by the victimizers and dialogue with the past victims to benefit the present as well as the future generation, an approach that neither ignores the victimized of the past nor relies on principle-based ethics of war—victor-loser tactic as the white community presumed—like what applied in the ethics after the World War II. What the ethics of principles must learn from the African thought, the *burden for us all* extends to include the social harmony with the dead given the hierarchical interconnectedness of life in the triad-community. Memory of the victimized of the past is part of it and valued since it causes relational peace to the hurt or damaged relationships of the past in order to heal the present and future relationships as Tutu recounts:

---

175. Desmond, *No Future without Forgiveness*, 35.
176. Cited from Battle, "Ubuntu Theology of Desmond Tutu," 177.

> There can be no peaceful presence as long as the spirits of the dead are not laid to rest. Therefore many relatives of murdered or disappeared persons ask the TRC to help them get back from the police the remains of their loved ones in order to bury them in a decent and dignified manner.... This is the way in which harmony between the generations is restored and maintained. The bringing home of the one who is lost, even the one who is guilty, *to the place of the ancestors is a vital aspect of the peace of the living.* [177]

Tutuism reminds us, that even if we were to talk of justice, it has to point to a *relational mutual harmony* as the *summum bonum*[178]—the greatest good—of Africans south of Sahara. Whereby anything that disrupts us from this collective good must be evaded like the plague. What dehumanizes me as a victim unescapably dehumanizes you as a victimizer. It is why Tutu argues that the principlistic "western-style justice does not fit with traditional African jurisprudence. It is too personal," given that the Black African moral thought purposes "the healing of breaches, the redressing of imbalances, the restoration of broken relationships. This kind of justice seeks to rehabilitate both the victim and the perpetrator, who should be given the opportunity to be reintegrated into the community he or she has injured by his or her offence."[179] Thusly, it should be vehemently re-echoed that wholeness of healing within the African moral outlook mutually accords respect to the tainted image of the victim—whereby even the supporters or implementers of an apartheid or a genocide or electoral malpractice are counted as victims—as well as the victimizer alike without forfeiting the truth but maintaining a concerted inclusive effort to the final goal of relationally re-integrating both the twin actors in sorting the mutual cost within the relational community, and mainly enable the victimized to see their victimizers as comrades before the ancestral guardianship.

The fact that the white community assumed Tutu's emphasis of a cathartic atonement way of life, inclusive of the victimizers and victims, as an irresponsible provocative hate cannot be taken lightly. One notices that it is indeed not less common for various exploitive studies not to account for the community of past victims. Several exploitive biomedical interventions between the Global North and South, include for example a candidate Ebola virus vaccine sponsored and funded from the Global North in 2015 with an intention of testing for safety and immunogenicity in a sub-Saharan

---

177. Battle, "Ubuntu Theology of Desmond Tutu," 180. *Emphasis is mine.*
178. See Tutu, *South Africa's Truth and Reconciliation Commission*, 29.
179. Tutu, *No Future without Forgiveness*, 51.

African country which had not registered any cases of the Ebola virus disease. Given that research ethics governance in biomedical ethics was generally a response to the misuse of human research participants in the Western world, with examples like the Tuskegee syphilis study and Nazi experiments that pushed for *Nuremberg trails*,[180] we can clearly refer to such African exploitative biomedical interventions as the Tuskegee studies of Africa, which interventions require admitting the earlier wrong done to the victims before any genuine present reconciliation can be fruitful.

More concretely, it should be recalled that the Tuskegee Syphilis Study was exposed in 1972, and in 1975. On record, the US government settled a lawsuit without clearly admitting wrongdoing. In 1997, President Bill Clinton welcomed five of the Study survivors to the White House and, officially apologized for an experiment he described as wrongful and racist. Despite that, numerous studies have described Clinton's apology as manipulative and unapologetic since he differentiated himself and his audience from the *past* generations and the whole system that were directly responsible for these ethical and scientific exploitations, what John Lynch referred to as "generational chronotope." For Lynch, in Clinton's powerful rhetorical strategy, he employed the generational chronotope which indeed reinforced whiteness, deflected attention from the endemic nature of racism in America and declared the *unethical past ethical*.[181] Clinton's generational chronotope—depicting an unethical past ethical—is indistinguishable to Western individualistic principlism, which is notable in arguments like that of Alasdair MacIntrye, in which the anamnetic life of solidarity lacks due to the dichotomization of *muntu*'s responsibility from that of her present and past community. He argues that choosing as an individual, "I may legally be a citizen of a certain country; but I cannot be held responsible for what my country does or has done unless I choose implicitly or explicitly to assume such responsibility. Such individualism is expressed by those modern Americans who deny any responsibility for the effects of slavery upon black

---

180. Nuremberg Code. *Trials of war Criminals before the Nuremberg Military, 1949-1953.*

181. See Lynch, "Generational chronotopes," 284–304; In 1932, the U.S. Public Health Service recruited 623 African American men from Macon County, Alabama, for a study of "the effects of untreated syphilis in the Negro male." For the next 40 years, even after the development of penicillin, the cure for syphilis of these men was denied. They were denied medical care for this potentially fatal disease. The attorney for the men, Fred D. Gray, unraveled the investigation and the lawsuit, till the events leading up to the Presidential apology, and further efforts to see that out of this painful and tragic episode of American history comes lasting good. Gray, *The Tuskegee syphilis study.*; When researchers take advantage of the social deprivation of their subjects, they become accomplices, not observers. Rothman, "Tuskegee," 5–7.

Americans, saying 'I never owned any slaves.'"[182] Even within a Western communitarian spirit as MacIntrye may argue, one basically sees the detachment of an individual from the relational community life, an attitude of no concern for injuries committed by one's ancestors in the past and how they affect a contemporary integral harmony if the two actors adamantly fail to reconcile or appreciate forgiveness with all its communitarian benefits.

Even if one were to emphasize Western communitarian ethics as non-individualistic, still African communitarianism remains unique in its anamnetic thinking that also encompasses a non-verbal palaver to include the injustices of the historical past and never deny responsibility of the unethical past. Different from principlistic communitarian ethics, Black Africa has the experience of transcendence through nonverbal communication making the communicative fellowship stronger. In African ethics, any genuine bioethical intervention must holistically include reconciliation and accepting ownership of all injustices. The anamnetic solidarity is concerned not only with infringements of rights in the present; it includes equally the injustices done to those who lived in the past—without excluding the guilt of the ancestors. *Muntu* is aware of the summons to accept responsibility for the inapt deeds of her ancestors, and the willingness to confess these injustices.[183] In the nonverbal anamnetic communicative fraternity, the three-dimensional fellowship is made anew in the holistic bioethics of reconciliation.

It is then notable that *reconciliation entails the invisible community*. On the one hand, the African thought of anamnetic solidarity as depicted in Truth and Reconciliation Commission inevitably brought together the victimized (patient) and victimizers to take cognizance of their past wrongdoing before reparation of the damage caused and embraced reconciliation without necessarily victimizing the said oppressor as a form of reparation. It is the holistic sense of reconciliation that prevents further recurrence of another segregative apartheid and rectifies the circumstances rather than punishing the victimizer. Besides Tutu, the medicine-person, doctor or healer's task of holistically reconciling the patient with the three-dimensional community is fulfilled. On the other hand, Clinton's generational chronotope strategy reinforced mightiness of the individualistic oppressor at the expense of the oppressed broader community. Failing to recognize the unethical past of Tuskegee Syphilis Study guarantees "No Future" since "Forgiveness" is impossible without a true integral reconciliation that entails accepting our past wrongs and re-emphasizing the glory of all peoples.

---

182. See MacIntrye, *After Virtue: A Study in Moral Theory*, 220–21.
183. Bujo, *An African Ethic*, 43–44.

Lastly, *reconciliation entails the entire cosmic totality of creation*. Amidst the tension between life and death, the therapeutic aspect lies not only in our qualitative relationship with visible and invisible world but also with the natural environment (the entire cosmos) which necessitates identifying plants, herbs, bones, animals, and minerals that possess that force—which can be positive or negative—which can liberate one from physical suffering and sickness. We have iterated enough that the African holistic approach to the practice of medicine goes beyond physical repair, like, "repairing" one's bodily organs since holistic health presupposes living in harmony with the cosmic creation. It is why a medicine-person does not only include the community of the living and the dead into the healing palaver, but also the natural environment; whereby, holistic healing is only possible where reconciliation with the entire cosmos has taken place.[184] So as healing goes beyond physical repair, likewise reconciliation entails holistic solidarity with the entire cosmos. Like Bujo puts it, destruction of the cosmos implies destruction of the network interrelationships unified by the vital force whose architect is God:

> The African person can only be understood as being characterized by interrelationships. The network of these relationships includes the entire cosmos and God himself. By seriously considering this sacred, cosmic and interhuman relationship, people should become aware of the fragile nature of their human existence. Human beings exist only in the state of becoming. Hence, human existence could break down if the cosmos is neglected . . . . Hence, it follows that insatiable greed for possessions and an uncontrollable wish to dominate creation can lead to a technology without culture.[185]

Even-though to a non-African, the communion or reconciliation of the living, the dead and the entire cosmos may seem incompressible in the practice of medicine or disease healing, it doesn't mean their cultural approach to a holistic moral life is to be meaninglessly discarded in any collective pursuit of a consensual universalized approach to bioethics. Each approach needs some space in the global discourse. It is thus clear as Richard N. Rwiza intones—reconciliation as "walking together" after violated community relationships, stemming from the Latin word *conciliare*, "come together," "to assemble" —that "we cannot achieve reconciliation in a cultural vacuum; we must read the signs of the times and be attentive to local

---

184. See Bujo, *The Ethical Dimension of Community*, 184–86, 190, 211–12.
185. Bujo, *Ethical Dimension of Community*, 212–213.

cultural and anthropological systems."[186] The practical examples picked from local African contexts in this investigation serve to prove numerous errors made by colonizers, explorers and missionaries when a Western standard of rationality was absolutized, as if it all alone encompassed every aspect of the truth in the pluralistic customary moralities that were evangelized, explored or colonized. Nonetheless, here reconciliation suggests *change* as far as *restoring the vital force of the community*, a deeper holistic *conversion* that restores relational life of both the colonized and the colonizer, an inculturated conversion that cannot take place within a cultural vacuum if it is to be transformative and remain locally relevant to the ideals of solidarity and communion.

RÉSUMÉ OF PART I: A HOLISTIC BIOETHICS INCLUSIVE OF, NOT ONLY HEROIC ANCESTORS, BUT ALSO THE VICTIMIZED OF THE PAST

The enquiry has been how best the local and global approaches to bioethics can be collectively shared in the world of bioethical challenges, since the approach to holistic bioethics can neither be Western or an African invention that people of other cultures could only either admire from a distance or be proselytized into it by Western or African bioethicists. Given the common affinities and heritage of creation that have been largely discussed herein, thanks to principle-based studies, each world can richly contribute its own treasured experiences towards a possible collective global solution appropriate to the current global challenges in bioethics.[187] I tried arguing for a holistic approach to bioethics that is not only cultural, but also transcultural and transglobal, viz., a bioethical journey toward a proportionate holistic horizon of life for all. I have endeavored not to take any, whether the African or the Western contribution as much more plausible than the other. My implicit general conviction has been not to tire of continuously making

---

186. Rwiza, "Opportunities for Reconciliation in Africa, 30–31. Rwiza dialogues with reconciliation rituals among the Acholi such as *mato oput* (literally "to eat together") that have promoted peaceful negotiations, rituals that shouldn't be discarded. The Ugandan government recognizes traditional mechanisms of justice like *mato oput* in the Uganda's Amnesty Act. *Mato oput* as a bitter drink of the Acholi people of Northern Uganda has symbolic ingredients for peace between the Uganda government and the Rebel Lord's Resistance Army (LRA), a rebel group since 1987. *Mato oput* is a traditional African forgiveness ritual that emphasizes deterrence, retribution, reparation and reform. To foster forgiveness and lasting community reconciliation, the criminal is deterred from repeating the offense and other community members too (pp. 33–35).

187. See Tangwa, "An Introduction by Henk," 268–70.

claims entirely with fear of making false claims or even fewer true claims, or those that would be challenged, but rather, I have tried at all times to strive to maximize the number of true claims, not necessarily intellectual syllogistic pursuits common in university academic halls, but rather in very simple experiences of an African world deep down in an African village and the nature world that surrounds *muntu*. This is no different to Kristin Andrews' conviction that "the best scientific methods are those that will maximize the number of true claims over the number of false ones, not the methods that will avoid false claims altogether."[188] In order to avoid this over-emphasized anthropocentric blind-spot or the worst methodological error of *anthropodenial*—what some refer to as false negative error or reverse anthropomorphism—[189] in biomedical interventions, we must be willing to make some claim that may turn out to be false, be open to being wrong, ask questions even when the answer turns out to be no, and challenge the proffered holistic approach in order to maximize its accuracy as Kristin Andrews relatedly puts it. For him, the willingness to be wrong is a risky willingness to reject the proffered holistic approach to bioethics when it is in fact true, while failing to reject the proffered holistic approach when it is in fact not true. We cannot therefore rule out that biomedical interventions or scientific progress does encompass errors and anyone who wants to avoid error at all costs ought not be a scientist, or rather a bioethicist.[190]

188. Andrews, "Beyond Anthropomorphism," 472–73.

189. The *false negative error* is synonymously referred to as *anthropodenial* by De Waal, Anthropomorphism Anthropodenial," 225–80; the same blind-spot is referred to as *reverse anthropomorphism* by Sheets-Johnstone, "Taking Evolution Seriously," 343–52; others say animals and human beings have shared inherited brain structures associated with emotional and mental capacities. De Waal labels this blind spot *Anthropodenial*, Bradie, "The Moral Life of Animals," 554, and 570–71.

190. See Andrews, "Beyond Anthropomorphism," 474; Sober, "Psychology Meets Evolutionary Biology," 85–99. According to Andrews, "in case of animal cognition, the null hypothesis is that animals lack the particular psychological property under investigation. For example, in what is known in psychology as the theory of mind research program, the null hypothesis is that animals do not have the ability to consider other's mental states or to attribute beliefs and desires to themselves or others . . . . So a type-1 error in this context can be seen as a false positive, whereas a type-2 error would be a false negative. If in fact chimpanzees do not have a theory of mind, then the researcher concludes that the chimpanzee does have a theory of mind, then the researcher is committing a type-1 error. Some critics of animal cognition studies take this methodological principle as reason not to accept animal psychological properties; because we fail to have the required evidence that, for instance, the chimpanzee has a theory of mind, we conclude instead that the chimpanzee does not have a theory of mind. They are several problems with this line of reasoning. First, the methodological principle does not permit the inferences to the nonexistence of chimpanzee theory of mind; rather, it requires that we remain agnostic about chimpanzee theory of mind.

Thusly, for all the scientific erring in my propositions, it is an opportunity for a deeper holistic dialogue across global partners, and more especially, between the African and Western scholarships—since both are perfectible. My only task was to claim that all created entities and cosmic systems primordially have life of their own and moral status deserving our protective respectful sympathy as the African moral thought has mandated us—no creation is lifeless. *Solidarity* is to relationally share a way of life with the *Other,* which goes beyond limitations of individualistic anthropocentrism and humanistic cooperations, to normatively include *all created entities* and *systems of life in the three-dimension community* as objects deserving our respectful sympathy. This reconstructs the limited principlism and it leads me to redefine bioethics *as respectful sympathy towards the relational Other.* Respectful sympathy goes beyond principlism because it incorporates a life outside medical bioethics and the living community of human animals to include inaminates, the community of the ancestors, so to speak, respectful sympathy embraces the African dimension of anamnetic solidarity. If we fulfil this, we would actually be on a path to doing holistic bioethics, a bioethics that can only be holistic if it is *interspecies,*[191] a bioethics that concerns itself with *interstates* to handle global biomedical exploitations. Holistic bioethics must be sensitive to local systems, global life and to all creation as having a moral status and a life of their own. Dealing with one species or *muntu* or state implies genuinely dealing with a wider corporate community of species, Bantus or states.

I have unraveled holistic bioethics as a hallmark of collective local and universalized efforts. It does not only include *integrating, contextualizing, inculturating* or *enculturating* bioethical principlism in local settings—going glocal—but also encompasses revising the universalized principlism to incorporate pluralistic customary moralities. Locally we can talk of adapting the universalized sense of bioethical principlism to an acculturated approach to bioethics, allowing blending with the host cultural realities, adjusting to a new cultural environment, incorporating, and balancing different cultural values against assimilation, imperialism and cultural superiority. For a successful *inculturation or enculturation of principlism*, we ought let go applying

---

From this it would follow that we don't know whether or not having a theory of mind is uniquely human, and hence, we don't know whether it is anthropomorphic to attribute a theory of mind to animals. Second, it has been argued that the methodological rule of thumb has resulted in a behavioristic bias for animal cognition research. One piece of evidence for the supposed behaviorist bias is that while false positives in animal cognition research have a widely recognized name ('anthropomorphism'), false negatives do not." Andrews, "Beyond Anthropomorphism," 473.

191. Matevia, "Biocommunitarian Theory of Interspecies Justice," 201.

to peoples of other cultures words like "primitive," "savage" or any "dreary vocabulary of inferiority," and take "acculturation in human intercultural interaction as an experience that always works both ways . . . the native and the foreign. . . . cultural differences ought no longer be permanent factors of tension between peoples; and that cultural similarities, just like cultural differences, should be constructively and effectively exploited, not denied."[192]

Local adaptations should be consistent with the unity of local socio-religious values. It is easy for natives to own values that are familiar to their *shared way of life* as derived from the cherished indigenous raw materials before welcoming those that are foreign or universalized. For instance, if it is African, solutions should be primarily home grown on African soils. So, a would-be functioning holistic bioethics on an African soil should be more consistent with the locally held value thought, viz., drinking directly from native wells, what the local populace easily accepts as its ancestral heritage—remember "the crocodile is only strong in the water" as the Angolans say—but not what contradicts or annihilates their valued shared way of life or ethical-moral constructs.

The African approach can also complement foreign principlistic approaches holistically. To put it in another way, the African approach speaks from within than from outside Africa, suggesting that African epistemic methods of medicine, healing and reconciliation uniquely complement the universalized method. The anamnetic solidarity suggests something new and penetrate bioethical principlism integrally. Challenges towards this holistic approach could partly spring from people who have been brought up in principlistic backgrounds that think in either/or formats. Insinuating that everything must be divided into two. If something is not physical, it must be spiritual, without finding out the homeomorphic equivalents—of what is spiritual or physical for Africans—of these categories of thought within other cultural milieus. The African holistic thought has repetitively indicated that if we belong together—as a cosmic unity—there is no need to dichotomize knowledge—that if something is not spiritual then it is physical—which is already whole and truth which is one. It is likewise meaningless to analytically divide between customary approaches and the universalized principles as the most credible ones. We need to think *transculturally* and *transglobally*, than only replicating the ancient primitive dualistic approaches to life, separating non-Greeks from Greeks, slaves from colonial masters, them from us, etc. The separation of *them* from *us* is holistically replaced by the relational Other, who cannot be understood

---

192. Onwubiko, "Re-encountering African culture," 92–93; Behrens, "Indigenous African bioethics," 6, 32–35; see also Tangwa, "Ethics in occupational health," 5, 9.

in a dualistic thinking, atleast in the African moral thought. Without these dualistic weights, we can embrace the contribution of a holistic thinking that grounds the normative approach of anamnetic solidarity, a holistic approach that incorporates not only our ancestors who lived a righteous life by forgiving their enemies in order to heal the relational community, but it also incorporates the *victimized of the past as well as their dynamic communicative action with the present and future generation.* We cannot live a holistic ethic *forwards* without understanding our heroic ancestors and victimized *backwards.* And this doesn't mean that we should "exceptionalize" an African thought or a westernized approach to bioethics, rather we must make each approach an integral part of the holistic bioethical worldview, appreciating our differences, while standing in a need of a collective commitment even when we are different, we are alike within a cosmic unity.

PART II

Holistic Solidarity, the Relational Other, and Eco-theological Bioethics

ABSTRACT OF PART II

The guiding question of *part II* is: How could the African understanding of solidarity contribute to the discourse in theological bioethics in dialogue with the Encyclical Letter *Fratelli Tutti* and Emmanuel Levinas' ethics of the other? I explore complementary reflections between the African worldview, Levinas and *Fratelli Tutti*'s accounts of the "other" in relation to solidarity. The example of Covid-19 pandemic as depicted in the encyclical letter has generally made *more visible* the failures of an economically globalized cooperation. With its insistence on a *monocultural model of life,* globalization has reluctantly welcomed the possible contributions of less industrialized cultures, more specifically, towards ideas of cooperative solidarity. *Fratelli Tutti* has proposed a significant general solution, as social friendship and fraternal love of the *other as my neighbor* or a *stranger*. Levinas has proposed an infinite responsibility to the *other as a stranger*, to which an African thought seeks to contribute a step further. So, what could an *African relational understanding of life* contribute to a sustainable dialogue in order to give new strength to universal cooperations and ecological life—creation as our home[1]—and more specifically contribute to the discourse of theo-

---

1. In reference to the thoughts of the German zoologist Ernst Haeckel, I use the term ecology/ökologie with the sense of the word οἶκος, oikos, meaning a house, home, a place to live in, with a broader implication of creation. Without forgetting the Greek sense of the word οἶκος, oikos as a house, a home, a place to live in—I similarly think of creation in its broader sense. Indeed, for Haeckel, the term *ökologie* explains more the "relation of the animal both to its organic as well as its inorganic environment." Thusly, ecology is defined broadly not only as "the study of the interrelationships of organisms with their environment and each other," but also as "the economy of nature," as well as

logical bioethics? In parallel reflections I draw between *Fratelli Tutti* and the African worldview, I add another aspect to *Fratelli Tutti*'s insistence on the general human fraternal social friendships and Levinas' ethics of the other. The complexity of the messy relational friendship as our earnest contemporary bioethical problem doesn't necessarily demand us a complex bioethical solution. For starters, we need a simple solution to melt this complex problematic. I propose that good bioethics demands a *relational friendship* visible in a *relational solidarity* inclusive of everything, everyone and every system (the "Other") as the relational social life of Africans suggests. I argue that holistic solidarity suggests respectful sympathy toward the Other which reminds us that genuine cooperation is the imperative of the presently required moral civilization. Secondly, in a simple lay person's language, I argue that there is no other fascinating and instructive language of our Creator than this language written in this created manuscript, the manuscript of our friendship of solidarity with the whole creation and systems of life (relational Other).

"the biology of ecosystems." See Pimm and Smith, "Ecology."

4

Towards Holistic Solidarity

FAILURE IN GLOBAL COOPERATIVE SOLIDARITY: COMPLEMENTARY SOLUTIONS BETWEEN THE AFRICAN THOUGHT, FRATELLI TUTTI'S APPROACH, AND EMMANUEL LEVINAS' ACCOUNT OF RESPONSIBILITY OF THE OTHER

To begin with, although to some extent the monocultural model of life—e.g., bioethical principlism, globalization—has registered some economic and bio-technological success globally, to another extent, global cooperations necessitate more of a collective engagement. We have already distanced our discussion from stressing a *monoculture* since our universal home is for every people and it cannot be identified with one specific culture, given that, it is impossible to cause the world to embrace a certain uniformity, but it is possible for one culture to enrich another or the collectivity of life. This is because the beauty of cultural differences could offer different practical solutions towards a common harmony without necessarily losing out on a people's solid identity. In interpreting the African thought, a monoculture seems indeed impossible given the unequal representation of different ideas in a world that is certainly globalized, agitating for a need to relationally incorporate every culture's view in redefining theological bioethics as well as drafting international regulatory declarations since we all share an equal vulnerability to relational global challenges. This holistic sense is by some means attempted in the encyclical Letter: *Fratelli Tutti*.

The Grand Imam Ahmad Al-Tayyeb and Pope Francis don't ignore the valued bio-technological advancements on the one hand. On the other hand, nonetheless, they note a failure in the *general global cooperation* that is visible in failed fraternities and social friendships[1] among brothers and sisters ("*fratelli e sorelle*").[2] Instead of leading to a more humane future,[3] rather this general cooperation is replaced with "globalized indifference" (FT 30),[4] a throwaway society (FT 18–20)[5] promoting individualism. All these are tearing humanity apart (FT 44, 166) and blocking humanity from an authentic cooperation (FT 49). "We say one thing with words, but our decisions and reality tell another story" (FT 23). For instance, we can choose the neighbor with whom we wish to share our world (FT 47),[6] making us to grow ever more distant from one another (FT 16, 21, 47). Precisely, the Covid-19 pandemic unexpectedly checked these cooperations, exposing our false securities and inabilities to work together, making us witness a fragmentation that made it more difficult to resolve global problems that affect us all (FT 7, 24, 280).[7] I can refer to two outstanding particular references of hoarding of COVID-19 vaccines, which vaccines are morally global public goods. First, according to the World Health Summit Meeting of 2021, disparities of vaccine injustices divided the world between those that have access to vaccines and those who do not. Disparities arose between the low- and high-income countries. Whereas the high-income countries only represented about 20 percent of the global adult population that was required to be vaccinated at that time, these countries held over half of the doses globally available—almost five billion—enough to vaccinate twice their populations.[8] Second, while as special guest during "The Dakar International Forum on Peace and Security," President Cyril Ramaphosa accused powerful nations of hoarding vaccines and imposing travel restrictions on Southern African nations in response to the Omicron variant, which South

---

1. With these words, "Saint Francis of Assisi addressed his brothers and sisters." Francis, "Encyclical Letter: *Fratelli Tutti*," 1. This greeting implies "fraternity" not forgetting that St. Francis of Assisi is a "saint of fraternal love. See Catholic News Agency (no specific author), "Fratelli tutti: Pope Francis calls for unity."

2. Fraternity extends "to all of humanity." According to the Vatican's editorial director, Andrea Tornielli, Francis is deeply concerned about "fraternity and social friendship . . . He therefore addresses all his sisters and brothers, all men and women who populate the earth: Everyone, inclusively, and in no way exclusively." See Winfield, "What's in a name?"

3. See also Francis, "Human Fraternity for World Peace," 6.

4. See also Francis, "World of Culture."

5. See also Francis, "Persons with Disabilities," 7.

6. See also Francis, "Popular Movements."; Catholic News Agency, "Fratelli tutti: Pope Francis calls for unity."

7. See also Pentin, "'Fratelli Tutti' Outlines Vision for a Better World."

8. To give a recent scenario, is the *World Health Summit Meeting* of 27th June 2021 in Uganda, Kampala.

African scientists had discovered and immediately took on the responsibility of informing the world about it, to which the payment in return was to impose a travel ban.[9] In analyzing both examples, I note that the crisis of vaccine injustices strongly remind us of the plea to promote the spirit of genuine solidary cooperations instead of practicing vaccine nationalistic insensitivities.

Besides, *Fratelli Tutti* expresses how the unregulated economic market interests have made us neighbors, but not sisters and brothers. These interests have led to an egotistic individualistic self-preservation that makes us think in terms of "them" and "those," but not "us," thereby founding a new culture of walls—walls in the heart, walls on the land—with a focus only on "my" world (FT 11–12, 27, 35–36, 166, 168).[10] The individualistic tensions in between constitute a real "third world war" fought piecemeal and the effects collectively harm the entire planet since the destinies of countries are so closely interconnected on the global scene (FT 15, 25, 57, 155, 259).[11] In these tensions, one notes not only a detachment from our human general roots since we remain deprived of a collective connection to our roots and ancestral wisdom (FT 19),[12] but it also confirms a growing loss of our sense of historical consciousness, making us fail in picking from our inherited past generations[13] and in building a functioning planet that we can pass on to the next generation. Putting the African thought together with *Fratelli Tutti*'s approach, there is a general need to reconstruct our unregulated economic interests and historical past into a functioning global cooperation. It is here we specifically require not only good bioethics but also functional relational friendships, where we are not only neighbors in commerce but also brothers and sisters. How can we achieve functional relational friendships?

Firstly, for a sustainable relational life, *Fratelli Tutti* and the African thought suggest we cherish again our historical ancestral roots—the containers of treasuries of knowledge—*appropriate* them, so that blending and dialogue-ing with other authentic cultural identities[14] may yield relational functional harmony between creatures and systems of cooperation. We have to learn from the great lessons or memory or witness of every nation's

---

9. Khoza, "Western nations' handling of Covid-19."
10. See also Benedict XVI, "*Caritas in Veritate*," 19.
11. Francis, "2016 World Day of Peace," 2.
12. Francis, "Diplomatic Corps accredited to the Holy See."
13. Francis, "*Christus vivit*," 181.
14. See also Francis, "Apostolic Exhortation *Querida Amazonia*," 37.

rich cultural *history*[15] as a great *teacher of life*[16] to profit our contemporary approach to life. Thus history—a coherent way of life, which also governs African day-to-day moral wisdom—makes us powerfully aware of the unity, integration and common destiny of the earlier nations.[17] To express this need for solidarity, similar to the African understanding of justice as *mutual aid* towards *muntu*'s neighbor, a concept that is historically powerful, *Fratelli Tutti* uses *a good Samaritan neighbor as its theological heart*. For a Samaritan to become a neighbor to the wounded Judean was a lesson that indeed crossed all cultural and historical barriers (FT 81). Traditionally, the imperative to love and care for others—love your neighbor as yourself (Lev 19:18)—appears to have been initially limited to relationships between members of the same nation. But the good Samaritan neighbor seems to *sympathetically* extend communion to the universal shared humanity without any discrimination. A Samaritan's *heart* welcomes every stranger as neighbor! (FT 57, 60, 84).[18]

Elsewhere, we cannot deny that some spirit of historical economic integrations have exemplified shared roots, a rich diversity and a capacity to work together (FT 10).[19] Some examples include: the dream of a united

---

15. For example, Israelite judges were instructed, if they couldn't find any grounds for a decision in the statute, case law or analogy to form their decision, they could legally refer to the light of the principles of freedom, justice, equity and peace of *Israel's historical heritage*. See Goodman, "Normative Traditions of Judaism," 15, 23, 26, 34, 46.

16. "Historia vero testis temporum, lux veritatis, *vita memoriae, magistra vitae*, nuntia vetustatis, qua voce alia nisi oratoris immortalitati commendatur?" Emphasis is mine to show how history is the witness of time. See Cicero (Karl Wilhelm Piderit), *De oratore*, 9. 36, 110. Wilhelm Piderit, a commentator in this book writes "*Vita memoriae* wird die Historie genannt, weil durch sie das Andenken an die vergangenen Zeiten lebendig erhalten wird . . . *vita mortuorum in memoria vivorum est posita*; die Vermittlerin der Vergangenheit für die Lebenden aber ist die Geschichte, ohne die es gar bald keine memoria mehr gäbe." Emphasis is mine to show how the past is taken as a life's teacher to negotiate today's challenges, i.e., the study of the historical past ought to be a great lesson or witness to the future.

17. Francis, "2014 World Day of Peace," 1.

18. In reference to their lived experiences as foreigners in Egypt, they are various biblical examples to prove historical jewish reasons why their *hearts* welcomed foreigners as neighbors in old Testament: *Stranger* as *alien*: "You shall not oppress or afflict a resident alien, for you were once aliens residing in the land of Egypt" (Ex 22:20–21); "You shall not oppress a resident alien; you well know how it feels to be an alien, since you were once aliens yourselves in the land of Egypt" (Ex 23:9). For the New Testament, the neighbor or brother is emphasized: "For the whole law is fulfilled in one statement, namely, 'You shall love your neighbor as yourself.'" (Gal 5:14); "If anyone says, 'I love God,' but hates his brother, he is a liar; for whoever does not love a brother whom he has seen cannot love God whom he has not seen" (1 Jn 4:20); "You have but one teacher, and you are all brothers." (Mt 23:8).

19. See also Francis, "European Parliament."

European union, Latin America, the United States of America, the African Union and so on. Contrarily however, the relational approach not only to non-exploitive global cooperations; but more specifically also, to an ecological life has been neglected. Today the humans and nature cry out in rebellion. The Roman poet Virgil (*Publius Vergilius Maro*, 70–19 B.C.) alerted us timely of the "tears of things" (FT 34) —*sunt lacrimae rerum*—to mean that the things or the universe feel(s) sorrow for the pains and sufferings of humanity. So, the creation's tears touch our mind, i.e., our heart.[20] But how? In deriving this claim, we can argue summarily, that there are tears of/for things and mortal things touch the mind. But since the Latin genitive *rerum* can either be "objective" or "subjective," the scholar David Wharton concludes that the semantic and referential indeterminacy is both intentional and poetically productive, suggesting an attractive implicational richness, which, if the genitive is translated subjectively, the phrase would mean that the things or the cosmic universe feel(s) sorrow for the pains and sufferings of humanity.[21] Moreover, in one of the finest works, Robert Fagles translates *sunt lacrimae rerum et mentem mortalia tangent* thus: "Even here, the world is a world of tears / and the burdens of mortality *touch the heart*."[22] In this context, I take the *mind* to connote *the heart*, hence formulating the compound word: *a thinking heart*. For instance, a Samaritan thinking heart welcomed every stranger, Greek or Jew. The thinking heart which relationally thinks without any discrimination can also be wounded by any injured creation. Pope Francis emphasizes relatively the same meaning in the Encyclical Letter *Laudato Si'* where he describes the unique relationship between the Creator, my neighbor, and the created earth itself. The creation as our

> sister now cries out to us because of the harm we have inflicted on her by our irresponsible use and abuse of the goods with which God has endowed her. We have come to see ourselves as her lords and masters, entitled to plunder her at will. The violence present in our hearts, wounded by sin, is also reflected in the symptoms of sickness evident in the soil, in the water, in the air and in all forms of life. This is why the earth herself,

---

20. "Sunt hic etiam sua praemia laudi; *sunt lacrimae rerum et mentem mortalia tangunt*. Solve metus; feret haec aliquam tibi fama salutem." In English: "Here also there be tears for what men bear, and mortal creatures feel each other's sorrow. Therefore, have no fear!" Maro, *Aeneid* (c. 29–19 B.C.), 462.

21. See Wharton, "*Sunt Lacrimae Rerum*," 259–79.

22. See Spiegelman, *Imaginative transcripts*, 11. *Italics added for emphasis.*

burdened and laid waste, is among the most abandoned and maltreated of our poor.... (LS 2)[23]

Unfortunately, our business as usual of hurting and injuring our only home goes on. Creation is consciously or unconsciously touched to realize its own limitations, and work out the meaning of its existential life, its extensive relationships, and its ecological harmonious network (FT 33). Given our human sensitivity, just like the Samaritan's *thinking heart* welcomed every stranger as a neighbor, it is the commitment of our thinking heart to embrace the tears of things into our relational harmony without appealing to any anthropocentric (LS 69, 116, 118–119, 122) or ethnocentric partisanships. Conversion calls us to be sensitive and cultivate a spirit of sacredness and kindred connectedness to all creation as our perpetual universal siblings.

Secondly, reconciliation is another step towards a relational friendship. *Fratelli tutti* talks of nourishing of goodness in our hearts—not with revenge—but with a collective shared hope of reconciliation and healing, truth and mercy, justice and renewed encounter, solidarity and peace (FT 225, 231, 242–243, 248, 251).[24] The collective remembrance of the victimized of the past (*memoria-conscience*) in the African view of reconciliation and healing is likewise emphasized by Pope Francis. For him, it is in reconciliation that humans "keep alive the flame of collective conscience, bearing witness to succeeding generations to the horror of what happened."[25] Moreover *Fratelli Tutti* understands social friendship as valuing forgiveness and reconciliation as means of resolving injustices (FT 241, 244, 246, 251). For Pope Francis, "justice is properly sought solely out of love of justice itself, out of respect for the victims, as a means of preventing new crimes and protecting the common good, not as an alleged outlet for personal anger" (FT 252).

In respecting victims in our pursuit of holistic reconciliation and justice, Agbonkhianmeghe Orobator is made to postulate how *Fratelli Tutti* by any other name would smell as sweet as *Ubuntu*, making Pope Francis to credit South African Anglican Bishop Desmond Tutu, among others, as an inspiration for his encyclical (FT 286). Tutuism is inspirational to Pope Francis' encyclical because it espouses—"no future without forgiveness"— above all, forgiveness and reconciliation with the victims as prerequisites for

---

23. Francis, "*Laudato Si'*."

24. See also Francis, "National Reconciliation."; Francis, "2020 World Day of Peace," 2; Francis, "Interreligious Meeting with Youth."

25. Francis, "2020 World Day of Peace," 2.

and the litmus test of preserving a shared relational social harmony.[26] Even though reconciliation appreciates dialogue,[27] *Fratelli Tutti* understands a constructive dialogue to be characterized by consensus but not relativism or individualism, inclusive of subsequent generations—without bracketing off victims—and all authentic cultural components (FT 50, 123, 198–199, 203, 206, 208–209, 211, 224, 271, 224),[28] which could foster an integral social covenant—a covenant that respects and coexists with other worldviews—since no one can possess the whole truth (FT 164–165, 180–182, 218, 221).[29] A cultivated social covenant can replace the false sense of security—individualistic interests in nuclear weapons—frenetic commerce with fraternal gratuitousness (FT 122, 138–140).[30]

However, promoting a globalized worldview does not *necessarily mean uniformity* based on interests of a particular cultural mode (FT 51–52, 100, 144, 257).[31] Given that history remains a good teacher—*die Vermittlerin der Vergangenheit für die Lebenden*—even when reality is one, humans have to historically appreciate the co-existential richness of each cultural contribution (polyhedron), an interdisciplinary dialogue while remaining solidly grounded in each one's original cultural *substratum* (FT 136–137, 145, 204, 215, 287).[32] To pick an example from *Fratelli tutti,* an interdisciplinary dialogue remained inescapable throughout the Coronavirus pandemic since it found the global community in the same boat, where one nation's problems applied to all, necessitating all to be saved jointly only as cooperating brothers and sisters with a common commitment to the common good (FT 5, 32,

---

26. See Orobator, "*Fratelli Tutti*' is Ubuntu."

27. See also Francis, "Ecumenical and Interreligious Meeting," 9; Francis, "*Evangelii Gaudium*," 228.

28. See Wenders (film director), "Pope Francis: A Man of His Word."; Francis, "Apostolic Exhortation *Querida Amazonia*," 108, 211; Francis, "Brazilian Political, Economic and Cultural Leaders."; "*Laudato Si*'," 123; John Paul II, "*Veritatis Splendor*," 96; "Aufeinander zugehen, sich äußern, einander zuhören, sich anschauen, sich kennenlernen, versuchen, einander zu verstehen, nach Berührungspunkten suchen—all dies wird in dem Wort Dialog zusammengefasst." (In my perspective, the German version brings out more clearly the conversational interaction (διά).

29. See also *Laudato Si'*, 231; *Caritas in Veritate*, 2; Pontifical Council for Justice and Peace, *Compendium of the Social Doctrine of the Church*, 207.

30. See also Francis, "Instrument to Prohibit Nuclear Weapons."; Benedict XVI, *Caritas in Veritate*, 67.

31. See also Francis, "Religious Liberty with the Hispanic Community."; Francis, "Address to Young People," 10.

32. See also Francis, "Human Fraternity for World Peace," 7; Francis, *Evangelii Gaudium*, 235.

54, 118, 121, 154)³³ This is no different to the unregulated economic interests visible in biomedical controversies which include numerous exploited cosmic-ecological relationships between the Global North and South, exploited interpersonal and humanistic collaborations as well as exploited structural-universal collaborations, lack of cooperative values and corruptive collaborations. To such unregulated economic interests arising from an individualistic monocultural mentality and the exploitive collaborations in biomedical interventions, the African moral thought and *Fratelli Tutti* redirect our moral pursuits back to our historical ancestral wisdom, which wisdom accords a Samaritan heart to each of us, a heart that welcomes and reconciles with every stranger as a neighbor within our social harmony, and constructively dialogues and reconciles with the other (FT 149).³⁴ The limitation for *Fratelli Tutti is to limit its* approach to human relationships with less emphasis on an extended relatedness.

The third way to revitalize a relational friendship in our home is to cultivate social harmony as the good for the other and "the good of all" (LS 95, 122). It is then that we can feel at home as we "live in harmony with all" (FT 4). Having stressed the significance of our historical roots as the *local* seeks to enrich the global (FT 42, LS 114),³⁵ *Fratelli Tutti* highlights that "no one people, culture or individual can achieve everything on its own: to attain fulfilment in life we need others" (FT 150). Relating to differences, makes us understand ourselves since other cultures remain differing reflections of the inexhaustible richness (FT 87, 147).³⁶ In dialogue with the idea of African personhood, we have at length presented black Africans as recognizing differences as self-insufficiencies—*muntu* can only be *muntu* through another *muntu*. To put it another way, the *other* is the mirror of my subjectivity); and therefore, an inevitable need for each other and contribution of pluralistic thoughts. Human worth lies not in each one's independence, but in the relational interdependence with the other, the readiness to relationally be part of the welfare or wellbeing of the other. The *other* in *Fratelli Tutti* is a good Samaritan, whose heart welcomes every stranger as her neighbor. This is the theological heart of *Fratelli Tutti*. On the other hand, the relational other is at the heart of the African moral thought, but with a profounder ethical implication as we shall explain later on.

---

33. See also Francis, "Human Fraternity for World Peace," 6; Francis, "Address to Civil Authorities."
34. See also Francis, "Civil Society and the Diplomatic Corps," 7.
35. See also Francis, *Evangelii Gaudium*, 234.
36. See also Second Vatican Ecumenical Council, *Gaudium et Spes*, 24.

The emphasis of the other in achieving social harmony can be recounted in the contribution of the renowned Jewish scholar Emmanuel Levinas' first philosophy as *ethics*—in contrast to the Heideggerian ontological problem of transcendence which invoked the Husserlian existential sense of *Dasein*, taking first philosophy as *ontology*. It is "the ethics of the other" that practically transcends ontology according to Levinas. The other as my neighbor is the "first one on the scene."[37] And the neighbor or the other's alterity as a stranger from me, is not relative to me but rather, generates the *ethical*: "The strangeness of the other, his irreducibility to the I, to my thoughts and my possessions, is precisely accomplished as a calling into question of my spontaneity, as ethics."[38] Moreover, it is within this ethical relationship that the strangeness of the other's face as a destitute dominantly demands *my response of care* and likewise transcends me as Levinas intones: "The being that presents himself in the face comes from a dimension of height, a dimension of transcendence whereby he can present himself as a stranger without opposing me as obstacle or enemy. More, for my position as *I consists in being able to respond to this essential destitution of the Other*, finding resources for myself. The Other who dominates me in his transcendence is thus the stranger, the window, and the orphan, to whom I am obligated."[39] The I, consisting in being able to *respond* with care to the Other's—though Levinas introduces the term the "Other," it isn't yet clear if it is restricted to the human stranger because he keeps on changing to/from the "other" without precisely explaining the difference—destitution points to another dimension of ethics. And since Levinas' ethics is the ethics of care of the other, some scholars have charitably referred to it as the *ethics of hospitality*.[40] There is an indivisible relationship between my infinite positive—Levinas barely thinks of a negative response—response and my being hospitable as far promoting life can be understood. "'Hospitality is yes to the other', but this yes is a second yes ('*oui, oui*'), coming as it does in response to the first yes, which is the Other him–or herself. The Other is not a no, not the one who I am not, but a yes, a 'positive' infinity constituting an infinite yes which elicits our affirmation and desire (yes). 'It is not I, it is the other that can say '*yes*.'"[41] To pronounce the second yes, *oui oui*, is the hospitality that encourages us to infinitely open with care our heated house in winter

---

37. Levinas, *Autrement qu'être ou au-delà de l'essence*, 109 and *Otherwise Than Being or Beyond Essence*, 87.

38. Levinas, *Totalité et Infini*, 13 and *Totality and Infinity*, 43.

39. Levinas, *Totality and Infinity*, 215. *Emphasis is mine.*

40. See Caputo, "Adieu-sans Die: Derrida and Levinas," 282.

41. Levinas, *Totalité et Infini*, 66 and *Totality and Infinity*, 93. Cited from Caputo, "Adieu-sans Die: Derrida and Levinas," 284.

without considering the strangeness of the other, with a risk of the other being a twosome or threesome. This means I cannot eventually just accept one and abandon the other two outside in a cold snowing winter, which gesture would indicate my in-hospitality. To overcome in-hospitality is to infinitely be responsible (infinite yes) to the stranger.

Levinas' sense of responsibility however seems paradoxical since it is a heteronomous "responsibility prior to freedom,"[42] a stance that challenges my freedom as an autonomous moral agent, if we were to appeal to principle-based accounts. In contrast, Levinas depicts an ethical responsibility in which I am not only to keep "standing in place of the other" but I am also "answerable for the other and his well-being," viz., I am committed to a "responsibility for the responsibility of the other."[43] The I's responsibility to the other is not an accident but a commitment of *an infinite actuality* as Levinas intones: "Responsibility for another is not an accident that happens to a subject, but precedes essence in it, has not awaited freedom, in which a commitment to another would be made.. . . . The word *I* means *here I am* (*me voici*), answering for everything and everyone. Responsibility for the others has not been a return to oneself . . . ."[44] Beyond my autonomy and the I as the source and measure of my responsibility or freedom as principlism would prescribe, and in order to promote my freedom or not limit it, I must ensure the other's freedom first. I must not only ensure her fulfilment of her responsibility, but also ensure her responsibility to others. This is the infinite responsibility for the responsibility of the other, which we can interpret as the transcendence that transcends transcendence transcendently. Furthermore, it means I am held responsible for her responsibility, *inclusive of her failures*, since she is infinitely the subject and object of my responsibility. Though I remain not the origin of her previous and current erroneous or irresponsible moral actions, I should never abandon her in her shortcomings because I remain in guilt with her even when I am personally guiltless.[45] In reference to the biblical story of Job in which our bearing of guilt of others who are overburdened with suffering is upheld,[46] Levinas postulates fur-

---

42. Levinas, *Autrement qu'être ou au-delà de l'essence*, 159 and *Otherwise Than Being or Beyond Essence*, 123.

43. Levinas, *Autrement qu'être ou au-delà de l'essence*, 150 and *Otherwise Than Being or Beyond Essence*, 117.

44. Levinas, *Autrement qu'être ou au-delà de l'essence*, 145–46 and *Otherwise Than Being or Beyond Essence*, 114.

45. See Levinas, *Autrement qu'être ou au-delà de l'essence*, 14, 148 and *Otherwise Than Being or Beyond Essence*, 11, 116; Levinas, *Totality and Infinity*, 197–200; Burggraeve, "Fraternity, Equality, Freedom," 18–21.

46. See Levinas, *Autrement qu'être ou au-delà de l'essence*, 156–57 and *Otherwise*

ther, how "each of us is guilty before everyone for everyone, and *I more than others*."⁴⁷ The Levinasian account helps us to deduce that there is no way the command of responsibility can be limited, be finite or be confined to our voluntarily chosen acts, because "responsibility as vortex—suffering of the other, my pity for his suffering, his pain over my pity, my pain over his pain, etc.—stops at me."⁴⁸ Accordingly, the infinity of responsibility is in charge of the totality of the other as Levinas accounts: "Not owing to such and such a guilt which is really mine, or to offences that I would have committed; but because I am responsible for a total responsibility, which answers for all the others and for all in the others, even for their responsibility. The I always has one responsibility *more* than all the others."⁴⁹ Though many have interpreted this Levinasian account of our infinite responsibility towards the other as paradoxical, we have to appreciate how he is trying to ground an ethics of intersubjective responsibility as the heart of his thinking which is clear in his account of face-to-face encounter with the other.

In interpreting the Levinasian account of alterity (the face-to-face encounter) —in repudiation of the phenomenology of the time—it reveals an ethical significance of the concrete other. In upholding the other, the account emphasizes the intersubjective relational interdependence of existential beings, the ethicization of existence, i.e., supplanting ontology with ethics, where the "I" encounters the other—trace of *illeity* in contrast to *ipseity*—not only at a precognitive level of an irrecusable ethical responsibility, but also at her embodied sensibility. For Levinas, discovering my responsibility and encountering the other's face seems to be the theological heart of ethics. This intersubjective responsibility allows us even to witness death only in the death of the other, since the infinity of responsibility lies in the face-to-face encounter of the other without waiting for any reciprocity. Thus for Levinas, what is ethical is the foundation of the other by me,⁵⁰ recognizing the ethical relation first "in the eyes of the other."⁵¹ But one of the challenges with this Levinasian account is, "the intersubjective relationship is a non-symmetrical relationship," in which "I am responsible for the

---

Than Being or Beyond Essence, 122.

47. Levinas, *Autrement qu'être ou au-delà de l'essence*, 186 and *Otherwise Than Being or Beyond Essence*, 146.

48. Levinas, *Autrement qu'être ou au-delà de l'essence*, 150 and *Otherwise Than Being or Beyond Essence*, 196 no. 21.

49. Levinas, *Ethics and Infinity*, 99.

50. See Bloechl, "Ethics as First Philosophy," 134–36. See more in Levinas, and *Ethics and Infinity*, and *Totality and Infinity*.

51. Levinas, *Totalité et Infini*, 188 and *Totality and Infinity*, 213.

other without waiting for reciprocity, were I to die for it."[52] If the I is the absolute starting point, the other is also absolute—or even more absolute—in the sense of transcending, exceeding, questioning, or overflowing this starting point of the absolute I. The other puts me (I) in question in such a way that I find myself infinitely responsible for the other, for whom I can never do enough or even ask for a mutual return. This is the asymmetrical character of the relation of alterity. I demand more of myself than I would ever have the right to demand of the other.[53] In other-words, Levinas' account of asymmetrical ethics—I-other or I-meets-other relationship—presents the other as almost a deity, let us say, as exceedingly transcending me without me transcending. Levinas excessively overemphasizes the ethics of asymmetrical alterity, hospitality, responsibility, which puts one under obligation to the stranger without the stranger reciprocating to the host's (my) total indebtedness, leaving the host in self-hostage—punishing oneself for someone else, or the subject herself being replaced for the other. The other has to be prioritized first and it is to her that I am first responsible or hospitable before minding my own self.[54] This can still mean, that for any arising intersubjective face-to-face moral conflicts between the I and the other, it may be correctly argued I have to show responsibility by surrendering my own way so that the other can have her way out. Moreover, if even I am responsible for my own hostage and her hostage, and for the errors that the other does to me and those she does to others, or may do, isn't this scandalous and destructive to morality itself? Although this thesis can be refuted since there is a concrete moral *response* of *yes yes* or *no no* to the face of the stranger, meaning the host is indeed fully active and participatory in the existential intersubjective ethics, but for the *I–other* relationship to be relationally symmetrical and more holistic, it needs to be grounded in an inclusive triad-community that fully embraces relationships beyond human communities. It would then be far-fetched to convince a Black African that we can talk of some genuine hospitality or responsibility or fraternity within a relationship of an unsymmetrical character!

Levinas scarcely preoccupies himself with an "ethical Other" outside an anthropocentric face-to-face encounter—I can face the "other" basically with mutual similarities like human speech. The account remains barely holistic, since it does not include nonhuman animals, the ecological system, so to speak, an all-inclusive life as presented in the African thought

---

52. Levinas, and *Ethics and Infinity*, 98.

53. See Levinas, *Totalité et Infini*, 24 and *Totality and Infinity*, 53. Referenced to by Bernasconi, "The Alterity of the Stranger," 62.

54. Levinas, *Ethics and Infinity*, 99. Subject as host, Levinas, *Totality and Infinity*, 299.

and other sciences. Even-though Levinas handles political obligations as responsibilities to the other, whereby the force of the face of nonhuman-others as ethical can be implied in different obligations inclusive of the environment, but in regard to "the force of things,"[55] the moral implications basically remain improbable. Applying analogies—an alterity politics which struggles to grant every face justice—and anthropocentric standards may be weak to encourage a holistic solidarity amongst creatures and universal systems of collaboration since the human face still remains highly prioritized throughout the Levinasian account of ethics. What we still need is a normative framework that is holistic. But the account remains restricted to the community of the living entities, challenging a possible Levinasian holistic normative account. Moreover, Levinas seems not to be interested in holistically constructing a normativity with norms as he notes: "My task does not consist in constructing an ethics; I only try to find its meaning."[56] And elsewhere, "responsibility is not comprehensible on the basis of ethics (i.e., moral rules or norms)."[57] But again, if ethics is for Levinas a *prima philosophia* (as foundational) it is difficult to understand—the same thesis is at home with the ethics of the Black African thought of relatedness—any ontological separation between *I* and the *other*, host and visiting stranger or neighbor, *ipseity* and *illeity*, between *forces of things*, as standing in the way of ethics.[58] But as a positive moral clue, although the Levinasian account of infinite responsibility— atleast not based on a cognitivist account given its emphasis on social affectivity—does not give us a set of rules but it reminds us to reorient our thinking to the ethical and *concretise ethics* relationally within our sociality as a *binding force* against any rational constructions and before any universal pursuits. Levinas stresses that "the force of the Other is already and henceforth moral,"[59] and "can be only as a moral summon."[60] The ontological translation of this *binding force* into a practical normative approach of solidarity is partly visible in Levinas' work, beginning with the account of hospitality. The question is how can we holistically practice an unconditional hospitality, not only to the stranger or neighbor but also across other cultural spheres which are subject to pluralistic contingent ethical conditions? To understand the Levinasian normative response

---

55. Levinas, *Otherwise Than Being or Beyond Essence*, 158.
56. Levinas, *Ethics and Infinity*, 90.
57. Levinas, *Otherwise Than Being or Beyond Essence*, 120.
58. See Bernet, "The Encounter with the Stranger," 59.
59. Levinas, *Totality and Infinity*, 225.
60. Levinas, *Totality and Infinity*, 196.

of solidarity, we need to combine Levinas' concept of hospitality with his understanding of responsibility.

Critics highlight that Levinas stresses responsibility as an infinite command, but he does not practically show how it produces moral fruits. But if we embrace the humanitarian emphasis of Levinasian account, it is in my "hands-on hospitality" (my infinite yes) from which "visible responsibility" and "practical solidarity" ensue, meaning "The more I answer, the more I am responsible,"[61] re-emphasizing the ethical dimension that, "the epiphany of the face is ethical."[62] It becomes clear that Levinas' account of ethical responsibility to the face of the other is contrary to principle-based accounts that rely on the moral subject's autonomy. For Levinas, responsibility is a matter of response, it is my infinite obedience to a command, not from any universal principles or common morality, but from the unique "other," "the epiphany of the face." So all ethics is necessarily rooted in the face-to-face relation that I have with the singular other. Therefore, my responsibility for the other permits no delegation and no justification in terms of any universal principles.[63] This makes responsibility to find its source only in the epiphany of the face of the stranger, not to kill her—clashing her life—but rather to acknowledge her as she is and wholeheartedly promote her relational well-being.[64] It is this *prioritized* practical relation, first, with my neighbor which secondarily "gives meaning to my relations with all the others."[65] And since the antithesis of the stranger is the I, the I remains "the non-interchangeable par excellence, the I, the unique one," who "substitutes itself for others."[66] When I meet the face of my neighbor, it is my subjectivity that turns into responsibility: "*Moi, c'eat-à-dire me voici pour les autres*"—"*me, that is, here I am for the others*,"[67] which points to "fraternity of proximity."[68] It is the reason why for Levinas fraternity is the result of my response to the face of the other: "It is my responsibility before a face looking at me

---

61. Levinas, *Autrement qu'être ou au-delà de l'essence,* 119 and *Otherwise Than Being or Beyond Essence,* 93.

62. Levinas, *Totality and Infinity,* 79, 199.

63. See Bernet, "The Encounter with the Stranger," 53–54.

64. Burggraeve, "'Fraternity, Equality, Freedom,'" 2.

65. Levinas, *Autrement qu'être ou au-delà de l'essence,* 202 and *Otherwise Than Being or Beyond Essence,* 159.

66. Levinas, *Autrement qu'être ou au-delà de l'essence,* 149 and *Otherwise Than Being or Beyond Essence,* 17.

67. Levinas, *Autrement qu'être ou au-delà de l'essence,* 233 and *Otherwise Than Being or Beyond Essence,* 185.

68. Levinas, *Autrement qu'être ou au-delà de l'essence,* 104 and *Otherwise Than Being or Beyond Essence,* 82.

as absolutely foreign that constitutes the original fact of fraternity."[69] Here fraternity unambiguously signifies "an ethical solidarity" between me and the other,[70] which is not my own choice as a creature, or even before I am responsible toward the other, but I am made as a creature to be in *solidarity primordially*.[71] Against my individual existence or autonomous I as principlism would claim, I am pre-originally bonded—"pre-original condition" indicating an "alliance" or a "covenant"—in a fraternal solidarity without my preceding choice or even before any commitment or contract undertaken or ethical relationships.[72] Akin to the African concept of relatedness that doesn't stop at blood fellowships but includes non-blood relationships to the other, in the Levinasian account too, it is a relationship primordially "without alienation."[73] So for Levinas, the primordial covenant of ethical solidarity proceeds any shared commitment or responsibility as well as our created-ness or being-ness. Against all logic, it is "a relationship of kinship outside all biology."[74] So it is my view as well—that fraternal ethical solidarity is not to be naturally reduced to simple biological fraternity (blood-bonds), even when belongingness has given birth to some virtues, because reducing solidarity to tribalism, ethnocentrism, claiming African-ness or European-ness, posing as the majority group or industrialized nation and so on, does not make us inadvertently linked with each other. Moreover, being the biological siblings or world citizens is something we do not choose. We have to outdo this natural fraternal solidarity (one's own other) and aim at a universal ethical solidarity (the "different other," the "foreign other") which concretely expresses the normative idea of solidarity with all communities of people and their systems of collaboration, naturally extending responsibility towards the "different external other," i.e., "bond of blood and soil."[75] Here, the unlimited ethical human fraternal solidarity as the foundation or pre-condition of social moral order with the different external other doesn't

---

69. Levinas, *Totalité et Infini*, 189 and *Totality and Infinity*, 215.

70. See Levinas, Quatre Lectures talmudiques, 182, and "Four Talmudic Readings," 185.

71. See Levinas, *Autrement qu'être ou au-delà de l'essence*, 117, 140 and *Otherwise Than Being or Beyond Essence*, 110, 192, 195 no. 5.

72. See Levinas, *Autrement qu'être ou au-delà de l'essence*, 12, 104, 109, 212 and *Otherwise Than Being or Beyond Essence*, 10, 82–83, 87, 166.

73. Levinas, *Autrement qu'être ou au-delà de l'essence*, 143 and *Otherwise Than Being or Beyond Essence*, 146.

74. Levinas, *Autrement qu'être ou au-delà de l'essence*, 109 and *Otherwise Than Being or Beyond Essence*, 87 ; Bloechl, "Ethics as First Philosophy and Religion," 131.

75. See Burggraeve, "'Fraternity, Equality, Freedom," 10–13; See also Levinas, *Totalité et Infini*, 256–57 and *Totality and Infinity*, 279.

rest on mutual similarities like anthropocentrism would emphasize cognitive properties, it rests rather on the radical irreducibility of everyone for everyone else, the community ethical "we" or the community proximity that ensues from the responsibility of everyone for the other. It doubly comprises individuals who in their alterity are unique, as well as summons all others in their irreducible unique alterity, emphasizing not only equality for all,[76] but relationally also "responsibility for oneself and the other."[77] In summary, even-though "the whole humanity, in the eyes looks at me," it is because of the irreducible other, "the infinity of the other,"[78] that responsibility becomes an inescapable fraternal solidarity between "brothers among brothers,"[79] sisters among sisters, world siblings among siblings.

In the section entitled "The Nations and the Messianic Time," in Levinas' *In the Time of the Nations,* as a recognition of the Torah before Sinai, Levinas asks, can't the "participation in the history of Israel . . . be assessed by the degree to which their *national solidarity is open to the other, the stranger?*"[80] In relation to this study, needless to say, different scholarships later show how we should understand that Levinas is faced up with the test of the messianic order as defined by hospitality but seeks to go beyond all revelation or any election confined to a certain people, in search of a universal fraternal solidarity—since the Torah opens up to universal humanity—suitable to universal siblings who must be welcomed independently of their qualities. The other doesn't have to qualify, merit, or earn the welcome of solidarity because we are just giving her *her* due as a created entity. It is God commanding this hospitality and He is translatable to this fraternal solidarity. So, the notion of God orders—kind of *ordo ordinans*—me to the neighbor. It is only by *welcoming the stranger whom God loves that God can be God.* This means that God is God only if I am speaking to the stranger, the neighbor, the stranger, the universal sibling.[81] The universal fraternal solidarity as a kind of *ordo ordinans* doesn't discriminate between the Jewish and the non-Jewish as well as between an African and a European neighbor. John Caputo captures this point in his interpretation of the Levinasian account of hospitality: "Hospitality is Jewish, the essence of the Torah, but it

---

76. See Burggraeve, "'Fraternity, Equality, Freedom,'" 14–15; Levinas, *Totalité et Infini,* 257 and *Totality and Infinity,* 279–80.

77. Levinas, *Totalité et Infini,* 190 and *Totality and Infinity,* 214.

78. Levinas, *Totalité et Infini,* 188 and *Totality and Infinity,* 213.

79. Levinas, *Totalité et Infini,* 256 and *Totality and Infinity,* 279.

80. Levinas, *Beyond the verse,* 97, Cited from Caputo, "Adieu-sans Die: Derrida and Levinas," 288. *Emphasis is mine.*

81. See Caputo, "Adieu-sans Die: Derrida and Levinas," 289–90, 298–99, 302–3, 307–9.

is also universally human; hospitality is humanitarianism itself, but it is not merely human, for it is also divine.... The Jewish and the non-Jewish, the divine and the human, reach across and touch each other."[82]

Although here Levinas seems to focus on the other in whom we see God—as the theological heart, on the other hand, he indeed reminds us of the Good Samaritan neighbor as the theological heart of *Fratelli Tutti*. The Good Samaritan "thinking heart" extends friendship not only to the stranger but also to the universal shared humanity surpassing the narrow-mindedness of not only of that time, but also of our time. The ongoing scandals of exploitative global collaborations, depicting evils of irresponsibility and injustices, which are labelled as globalization or "polished civility," so thinks Levinas, can be undone by revitalizing our primordial responsibility of our fraternal ethical solidarity "prior to all civilization"[83] In our pursuit of holistic bioethics, literally we cannot dichotomize sciences, say theological bioethics from religion or from our way of life, like global collaborations. "Everything that cannot be reduced to an inter-human relation represents not the superior form but the forever primitive form of religion."[84] It is why the responsible "justice rendered to the Other, my neighbor, gives me an unsurpassed proximity to God."[85] So Levinas categorically notes that "the ethical order does not prepare us for Divinity; it is the very accession to the Divinity."[86] Though many times unspoken, it remains quite understood how we are reminded of the hierarchical order of forces among Africans, to which God remains at the Apex and the ultimate Giver of the vital force that makes life holistically and morally possible, not only for "inter-human" relations as Levinas thinks, but for all Other forces in the life principle.

Precisely, the African logic of relational solidarity as well as Levinas' account of the ethics of the other are similarly upheld by *Fratelli Tutti* (FT 83, 90, 94, 98),[87] as a creative openness of heart—a movement outwards towards others—a fraternal social friendship that seeks freely (*gratis*) the best for others. Elsewhere, the encyclical describes this creative openness of heart as an innate supreme sense of fraternity that excludes no one and acknowledges each person as unrepeatable (FT 1, 3, 8, 26, 41, 77–78,

---

82. Caputo, "Adieu-sans Die: Derrida and Levinas," 290.

83. Levinas, *Autrement qu'être ou au-delà de l'essence*, 182 and *Otherwise Than Being or Beyond Essence*, 198 no. 6; Burggraeve, "'Fraternity, Equality, Freedom," 22, footnote 17.

84. Levinas, *Totalité et Infini*, 52 and *Totality and Infinity*, 79, no. 5.

85. Levinas, *Difficult Freedom*, 18.

86. Levinas, *Difficile liberté*, 137 and *Difficult Freedom*, 102, no. 3.

87. See *Summa Theologiae* II–II, q. 27, a. 2 resp; see also *Summa Theologiae* I–II, q. 26, a. 3, resp; q. 110, a. 1, resp.

88, 95, 97, 99). To note however, in *Frattelli Tutti*'s emphasis of *the other* as a humanistic fraternal friendship,[88] or even Levinas' account of our infinite face-to-face encounter of *the other*, these twin friendships to *the other* are quite anthropocentrically limited. Though it has been many times unspoken in this study, but it is quite understood that *the relational Other* would not be limited to relationships between human beings or simply be built along linguistic human standards but rather it does not only transcend but it interconnects with and to all creation in the three-dimension community. It is by achieving the relational Other, understood as *holistic solidarity*, that we can close, for instance, gaps in genuine collaborations, limited friendships, the current ecological debt etc. But we need primarily to broaden the meaning of our "neighbor" by expanding the meaning of the relational "Other" beyond "the limited other." It is the broad definition of the Other that makes us more aware of what holistic solidarity entails.

THE THEOLOGICAL HEART OF A HOLISTIC SOLIDARITY IS THE RELATIONAL "OTHER"

Once the question of the *Other* is answered, the course to holistic theological bioethics becomes clearer. We have already rejected defining the other in anthropocentric terms, but rather preferred a *relationship in terms of the Other*. In understanding this relationship, scholars like Augustine Shuttle, have labored to understand the same as *African humanism*.[89] Shutte describes a conflict in a convent between some German and African nuns in South Africa. When an investigator studied their conflict, she came to understand how the Germans took good nuns to spend adequate time in chapel as well as use spare time industriously in knitting and sewing; whereas the African nuns understood a good nun to spend spare time in conversing with each *other* and sympathizing over problems the *other* experienced. One group valued the vital law of industriousness while the other sympathetic

---

88. This humanistic perspective seems apparent with *Fratelli Tutti*'s reference to Aquinas—out of ourselves towards others, John Paul II—a "law of *ekstasis*" operating as the lover goes outside the self to find a fuller existence in another, and Karl Rahner—man moves beyond himself. *Fratelli Tutti* references to Wojtyła, *Love and Responsibility*, 126; Rahner, *Kleines Kirchenjahr*, 30; Aquinas: *Scriptum super Sententiis*, lib. 3, dist. 27, q. 1, a. 1, ad 4: "*Dicitur amor extasim facere et fervere, quia quod fervet extra se bullit et exhalat*"; see also Francis, *2020 World Day of Peace*, 8.

89. "In all free time they would settle down comfortably to converse, their hands empty, but their hearts and minds full. They saw the German sisters as barbarians, caring only about practical matters and wasting their energies on trivial pursuits." Shutte, *Ubuntu*, 27–28.

communalism. Put differently, one group employed a relational approach while the other a rational approach. Here my interest is not which group of nuns had the best value system. Not at all. Like Shutte discerns, I too think we inevitably need each other in constructing an adequate infrastructure befitting us all, yes of course. Indeed, we necessarily don't need one approach, but rather, we must stand, not in neglect but, open to the enrichment of both value systems of industriousness (rational ontology) and sympathetic communalism (relational ontology), without emphasizing any as overriding the other. But unfortunately, this kind of limited humanism, is the *other*—but not the *Other* I am interested in.

The Other has been largely also understood as an ecological issue. Retrospectively, before Holmes Rostoln III published "Is There an Ecological Ethic?" in 1975 highlighting an anti-anthropocentric ecological ethics,[90] some principle-based scholarships had dealt with ecological issues in different journals on environmental ethics. One is Lynn White's publication "The Historical Roots of our Ecologic Crisis," she examined *the relationship between religion, particularly Christianity, and attitudes toward nature*, arguing that the problems of bioethical interventions arose from *anthropocentrically centered Christian cultural heritage*.[91] In fighting for nature intrinsic values, in yet another study of Christopher D. Stone, a legal theorist had published some study in 1972 "Should Trees Have Standing? Toward Legal rights for Natural Objects."[92] Another publication from 1974 by John Passmore, "Man's Responsibility for Nature: Ecological Problems and Western Traditions" stressed enlightened anthropocentrism in response to Lynn White's publication of 1967. In reference to ecological problems, Passmore notes that "we are rapidly causing to degenerate our sole habitation, that narrow strip of soil, air and water—the biosphere—in which we live and move and have our being."[93] Even-though he further concedes that "the West needs more fully to realize that it 'depends on things' and so far to . . . 'glorify' nature,"[94] he insists on maintaining rationalism and individualism of Western thought.[95] In our continued search of what the Other really entails amidst human individualism, one notes one major forgotten thesis in White's study of the relationship between nature and religion, i.e., religion remains and will forever remain a significant, if not the only component in

---

90. See Rostoln III, "Is There an Ecological Ethic?" 93–109.
91. See White Jr., "Ecologic Crisis," 1203–7.
92. See Stone, "Should Trees Have Standing?" 450–2.
93. Passmore, *Man's Responsibility for Nature*, 3.
94. Passmore, *Man's Responsibility for Nature*, 194.
95. See Passmore, *Man's Responsibility for Nature*, 99.

which human beings holistically interact with nature as life-centered. Our conversion needs to transcend the standard anthropocentric language of awarding moral standing only to conscious entities and attributing instrumental value only to unconscious entities of our ecosystems. Otherwise, the question of the Other will forever remain a discourse within a discourse. To this thesis, we shall return later, for now, the question *what the Other is* should be fully answered.

In trying to find the meaning of "the Other" our "neighbor," the church in dialogue with the ethics of the Black Africans, wonder how better we can care for the world and its systems—our dwelling historical common home, our planet—in which we live as we care for ourselves and prepare for our future generation.[96] The church too—just like the Black African thought already iterated in the triad-community—believes that the solutions benefit not only the living but also those who will come after us, since this earth—passed on to us by our ancestors only to use but not to possess it, for sustenance without excluding or favoring anyone, is only loaned to us as God's gift by the future offsprings—"is lent to each generation, to be handed on to the generation that follows."[97] The relational sense is broadened in the sense that "I cannot know myself apart from a broader network of relationships, including those that have preceded me and shaped my entire life" (FT 89). Similarly, the African understanding cannot sustain contextual theological bioethics without realizing the primacy of this relationship of interconnectedness, a relational friendship that penetrates ecological violence to embrace *with respectful sympathy* all forces of life, spheres of the living and non-living creatures excluding none, a genuine relationship that should defend any would-be nature's disastrous reaction to its misuse. This should be what the holistic sense of our neighbor (the Other) ought to entail.

This explains why the African thought has moved from simply approaching bioethics as a multidisciplinary mode of inquiry limited to human boundaries, to viewing it as an omnipotent energy (vital force) cutting across all our ecological, biological, and cultural systems of life. Many times, unspoken in this investigation but quite understood, bioethics nurtures an interdependent peaceful coexistence without taking any creation and system of collaboration as lifeless. In the life principle as discussed among *Ba-ntu* people, we indicated that *ntu* (the omnipotent vitality) flows in the wholeness of cosmic life—in the sense affirming Lynn White's thesis above of the religiously life-centered interactive bond. This interrelatedness,

---

96. See Francis, *Political, Economic and Civic Leaders*; *Fratelli Tutti*, 17.

97. Portuguese Bishops' Conference, *Responsabilidade Solidária pelo Bem Comum*, 20; See *Laudato Si'*, 178, 159; John Paul II, "*Centesimus Annus*," 31; *Fratelli Tutti*, 17, 102, 117, 120, 178.

interdependence, and interconnectedness of all beings, makes the Black African holistic wisdom not to exclude anything as lifeless. Put differently, everything sacramentally has potency, including inanimate and inorganic objects. Metaphysically, every creation or reality ("Other") as a sacrament points to an external actual interpretation of the vital force that makes us experience God's omnipresence. In my opinion, this is the prior and primary practical principle that describes the recognition or sense of life on which sustainable eco-theological bioethics ought to be hinged. This is in dialogue with what *Fratelli tutti* points at as the "first principle of the whole ethical and social order."[98] It is natural and inherent, a renewed hope deeply rooted in every human heart and takes priority over others (FT 55,120.)[99] For its excellence, although *Fratelli Tutti* limits this application of this first principle to nations, their territories and their resources, it still emphasizes that this principle necessarily precedes any societal institutional mightiness; given that, it flows inalienably from the dignity granted to each *muntu* as created by God (FT 124).[100] Moreover, to foster the virtues of social solidarity, social peace, social harmony and intercultural dialogue, *Fratelli Tutti* suggests we strive towards the best of others and the future generations (*agathosyne*), as well as edification for an integral excellence in a community of belonging (*benevolentia*) (FT 11, 36,112–116, 146, 169).[101] However still the emphasis of the Other, my neighbor, remains largely along inter-human relationships.

So, to broaden the sphere, atleast, of an eco-theology, *Fratelli Tutti* proposes further, that to penetrate the current ecological deafness of the world, we need to "hear every voice including the voice of nature, where one feels "himself a brother to the sun, the sea and the wind" (FT 48). This is the same positive understanding of pope Francis in *Laudato Si'*: "When we speak of the 'environment', what we really mean is a relationship existing between nature and the society which lives in it. Nature cannot be regarded as something separate from ourselves or as a mere setting in which we live. We are part of nature, included in it and thus in constant interaction with it" (LS 139).

Emphasizing the theological heart of bioethics as the Other is partly to highlight an integral interaction with nature as similarly recapitulated

---

98. John Paul II, "*Laborem Exercens*," 19.

99. See also Pontifical Council for Justice and Peace, *Compendium of the Social Doctrine of the Church*, 172; Paul VI, "*Populorum Progressio*," 268.

100. See United States Conference of Catholic Bishops, "Pastoral Letter Against Racism."

101. See also Francis, *"Civil Society and the Diplomatic Corps."*; John Paul II, "Representatives of Argentinian Culture," 7; Francis, "2016 World Day of Peace"; Francis, "Popular Movements."

by 2004 Kenyan Nobel Peace Prize winner and founder of the Green Belt Movement Wangarĩ Muta Maathai. The first woman ever in Africa to be internationally crowned as a Nobel Peace Prize laureate in recognition of her efforts as a Kenyan peace activist and environmental conservationist, cites our bond to natural ecosystem.[102] For her, "nature is not something set apart, with or against which we react. It is not a place to fear as something within which we might lose our humanity . . . it is instead something within which human beings are unfolded."[103] It an integral pursuit of life in which both humans and nature are twin actors. Given that we are "unique yet integral to creation" within this complex crisis involving the two twins, "the circle of life" that is practically described as the "dance of life," from an African relational thinking, the Tanzanian moral theologian Rwiza Richard suggests one possible ethical movement within this dance, either a movement that enhances or a movement that destructs the unity of life in *our only home*. So *muntu*'s choice is very clear, either ethical or unethical, *muntu* is positively attentive to the "integrity of creation" or affects "the universe negatively by destroying the balance inbuilt in it," and so *muntu* less partakes "in sympathetic communion" with other creatures.[104] Rwiza extends an affirmative invitation in regard to how we care for our common home:

> There is a need to reconsider the way we take care of the environment. The integrity of creation is the appreciation that everything is interrelated and also interconnected. The fundamental ecological insights implied is that all things exist in interrelated networks. Nothing exists in isolation. This is a basic insight into the cycle of life that points to the integrity of creation. It invites us to experience the divine in and through environment. It is the issue of rediscovering our roots: our link with the cosmos. This can energize our faith and lead to ecological spirituality.[105]

In a different voice, in rediscovering the African spirituality (religiosity) of experiencing the divine in and through the created objects and systems of forces, *muntu* either promotes or demotes a holistic life, enhances or weakens solidarity, along the circle of life or continuum of life. So, when we hear nature's voice positively, we increase the vital force—emphasizing how the *vitalogical* African outlook calms harmful attitudes towards nature—while not heeding to its voice, we lessen the integral life force of nature. In this sense, Rwiza would say, we "sin against the integrity of the

---

102. Wangari, *Unbowed*.
103. Wangari, *Replenishing the Earth*, 93.
104. Rwiza, *Environmental Ethics*, 10–13.
105. Rwiza, *Environmental Ethics*, 34.

environment," indicating not only "a deficit of integral ecological ethics,"[106] but also "integrity calls for solidarity in facing ecological problems."[107] In the same dialogue, just like Black Africans have consistently stressed, the perspective of the Other or my neighbor broadens beyond inter-human friendships to cultivate a holistic ecological friendship respecting laws of eco-solidarity that have been violently disrespected.

In any African setting, in relation to their understanding of the Other, we cannot avoid the spiritual interactive bond between the three-communities. Given the spiritual beliefs attached to all creation, clan totems and taboos, natural resources too are preserved not only in reverence and fear of ancestral punishments but also fear of destroying the dwelling places of the deities and ancestors that can roughly react to descendants. But if missionaries had successfully convinced the local people that God didn't reside in their huge forests, lakes, rivers or mountains like Mt. Kilimanjaro, but in heaven, then these natural resources would have lost their spiritual significance or sacredness (inviolability) and would already have been insensitively exploited. And the source of our misery is in most times the aftermath of our exploitative attitudes of such natural resources, such as deforestation, unlawful mining, illegal fishing etc. But as far as stewardship of God's creation and the pursuance of ecological reconciliation, without being speciestic, it is the reason "Africans have always revered natural resources, believing that some of these are home to the deities and that destroying them can be catastrophic."[108] This means that Black Africans will embrace a holistic approach with an attitude of respectful sympathy which extends to the Other in form of the revered natural resources and the invisible community of the living dead.

Some other simple examples of the Other are self-revealing in concrete circumstances before any *muntu* down in some village. As Africans commonly say, "the danger that threatens the hunting dog also threatens the hunter," so "from an African religio-cultural perspective, the moral imperative to protect human life necessarily warrants the protection of sacred forests, trees, rivers, mountains, streams, and animals."[109] Primarily, beyond being ancestral dwelling places that must be approached with fear and trembling, "in African spirituality, there has been a spirit of conserving African forests. They are taken to link the present to the past generations

106. Rwiza, *Environmental Ethics*, 10.
107. Rwiza, *Environmental Ethics*, 35.
108. Centre for Social Justice and Ethics (CSJE) and Alliance of Religious and Conversation (ARC), *Stewardship of God's Creation*, 81. Cited from Rwiza, *Environmental Ethics*, 41.
109. Orobator, "Ethics of HIV/AIDS Prevention," 149.

and preserved for coming generations. Forests are symbols of harmonious co-existence of the earth, plants, animals and humans."[110] Rightly and so ethical if we respect the integrity of the Other and so the Other is indeed my protective skin, the maker of the salutary air I need, without which I will never survive with my family the next few hours. And so "when there is something wrong in the forest, there is something wrong in the community" as many African sages would popularly say and—as the wisdom of the Guinean proverb asserts similarly: "The forest is our skin and if one removes the skin of the human being, the end result is death."[111] It is common knowledge to a Black African that the community of those not yet born borrowed us this forest skin, this environment as intact as it was, only to be used well and briefly, improved, and let life continue because it doesn't belong to us but to the survival of the rest of the community and the sustainability of the future generation.

This is in dialogue with heathy-humanness among Baganda in which *omuntu-mulamu* (person) is a pro–active leader (*omukulembeze*), by emulating the ancestors who planted trees and forests that they knew very well they would not make use of in their lifetime, but for the generations after them.[112] It is extending respectful sympathy to the Other as the future community of those not yet born. This is the attitude of *live and let live* as the maxim of the Kom people envisages it: *Wà kæ àjvà wa fayti tinteŋ*, literally meaning, "when you harvest garden eggs, fix its branches."[113] Not fixing the branches or taking care of the forest skin is to undermine harmony of the fellowship since one member would be acting immorally by not increasing life for the next harvesting member. "In African societies, immorality is the word or deed which undermines fellowship."[114] "Any action which increases life or vital force is right, and whatever decreases it is wrong."[115] In this instance, increasing life and fully participating in a harmonious fellowship necessarily implies increasing life for the triad community without eliminating any. In conversation with the ethic of *Ukama* held by the Shona people of Zimbabwe, "one should always live and behave in a way that maximizes harmonious existence at present as well as in the future."[116]

110. Rwiza, *Environmental Ethics*, 35.
111. Bujo, *The Ethical Dimension of Community*, 217.
112. See Nnabagereka and Ssentongo, OBUNTUBULAMU, 7–62.
113. Mbih, "Foundation of kom proverbs," 14.
114. Kasenene, *Religious Ethics in Africa*, 21.
115. Kasenene, *Religious Ethics in Africa*, 140.
116. The ethic of *Ukama* implies an ethical concern for the well-being of future generations because of the primacy it gives to kinship/relatedness and the immortality of values. So genuine existence is one that is based on solidarity with others in human

Muntu's primodial committment to Other-creation-types is associated with an unbroken shared rythm of the vital force, which guarantees *muntu*'s future survival only in her respectful sympathy to every creation-type in the present. This relational coexistence, i.e., relational solidarity, between the present visible community, the past invisible community and the future community among black Africans is further evidence of the necessity to broaden the understanding of the Other as Mbeki similarly challenges us.

In Thabo Mbeki's speech at the adoption of The Republic of South Africa Constitution Bill, the deputy President of South Africa by then analogously noted: "I am an African . . . . I owe my being to the hills and the valleys, the mountains and the glades, the rivers, the deserts, the trees, the flowers, the seas and the ever-changing seasons that define the face of our native land."[117] The whole created world is not only included in the African thought of the Other but subsequently awarded equal citizenship to human animals as Mbeki poetically continues: "The dramatic shapes of the Drakensberg, the soil-colored waters of the Lekoa, iGqili noThukela, and the sands of the Kgalagadi, have all been panels of the set on the natural stage.. . . I should concede equal citizenship of our country to the leopard and the lion, the elephant and the springbok, the hyena, the black mamba and the pestilential mosquito."[118] The Other does not only include the beauty of nature, but coexistence of life further holistically extends to the community of the living dead, the victimized of the past in Mbeki's speech: "I owe my being to the Khoi and the San whose desolate souls haunt the great expanses of the beautiful Cape—they who fell victim to the most merciless genocide our native land has ever seen, they who were the first to lose their lives in the struggle to defend our freedom and dependence and they who, as a people, perished in the result." Furthermore, while focusing on a reconciled peaceful relational coexistence with the Other, Mbeki doesn't separate *remembering* the victimized ancestors of the past on the one hand, and putting the present victims on the other: "Today, as a country, we keep an audible silence about these ancestors of the generations that live, fearful to admit the horror of a former deed, seeking to obliterate from our memories a cruel occurrence which, in its remembering, should teach us not and never to be inhuman again." Moreover, in favoring a holistic solidarity with the Other, while expressing the union between the victimized of the past with their victimizers, Mbeki adds: "I am formed of the migrants who left

---

society at present, the past and the future. Murove, "The Shona Ethic of Ukama," 179–89, 181.

117. Mbeki, *I am an African*.
118. Mbeki, *I am an African*.

Europe to find a new home on our native land. *Whatever their own actions, they remain still, part of me.*" And I claim I am an African because "I come of those who were transported from India and China, whose being resided in the fact, solely, that they were able to provide physical labor, who taught me that *we could both be at home and be foreign . . .* " since "South Africa belongs to all who live in it, black and white,"[119] and no room should be accorded race and color to ascertain who is human and who is sub-human, and so be enriched or impoverished, forgotten or remembered. The attitude towards the Other should be embracing the invisible interconnectedness of life but not at the expense of dichotomizing between victimizers as humans and victims of the past as sub-humans, human and nonhuman animals and so on.

In the same vein, if we are to think about the Rwanda genocide, Véronique Tadjo shows how the genocide did not only locally occur within Rwanda and to Rwandans alone, but also sought reconciliation along the interconnected tripartite community life as well as affected the global community: "Yes, I went to Rwanda but Rwanda is also here in my country. The refugees are scattered all over the world, carrying within themselves the blood and fury of the abandoned dead."[120] And if we are to holistically cultivate an attitude towards the Other of moral solidarity, it should be also clear to me that "Rwanda is inside me, in you, in all of us. Rwanda is under our skin, in our blood, in our guts. In the very depths of our slumber, in our waking hearts."[121] In arguing for an interconnectedness to the Other which guarantees life between the living (visible community) and the nonliving (invisible community), Tadjo warns us of "The Wrath of the Dead."[122] In underscoring recent scholarships, she "found it impossible to talk about post-genocide Rwanda without invoking the presence of the dead and their continuous impact on the memory of the living."[123] The open question is how impactful are the dead as the other Other? Tadjo is convinced that they remain in every neighborhood haunting the living, angry at being killed or having been unpeacefully buried, and fearful of being forgotten by those whose memory is "starting to fade." Their rage keeps piercing the *eardrums of the surviving victims* which makes the days and nights quite unbearable. For them, as for the living, their desire is to be heard by the community, without which they can no longer exist, and it is to this community they

---

119. Mbeki, *I am an African*. Emphasis is mine.
120. Tadjo, *The Shadow of Imana*, 37.
121. Tadjo, *The Shadow of Imana*, 37.
122. Tadjo, *The Shadow of Imana*, 39.
123. Tadjo, "Lifting the Cloak of (In)visibility," 3.

would like to reveal the secrets of life.[124] In Tadjo's other narrative, "lifting the cloak of (in)visibility,"[125] though the inhuman genocide may be interpreted as "another form of invisibility" where victims were invisibly "anonymous,"[126] Tadjo takes it to be "the belief that there is no separation between the spiritual and material worlds."[127] In closing the gap between the dichotomies of victims and victimizers, dead and living, invisible and visible communities, leading to self-dehumanization and depersonalization, a holistic approach inclines towards immortality. Personal immortality in form of the "hidden world"[128] as we discussed it in the Africa thought resurfaces again in the post genocide narrative that "the dead will be reborn in every fragment of life, however small, in every word, every action, however simple it may be. They will be reborn in the dust, in the dancing water, in the children who laugh and play as they clap their hands, in every seed hidden beneath the black earth."[129] The Other, as the victim and the victimizer, all embrace the same humanity. Though both get dehumanized, the victimizer self-dehumanizes herself. This self-dehumanization and the fact that we have the hidden power to overcome it is well captured in Steve Biko's famous powerful words in 1971—in *I Write What I Like*—against the inferiority complex as he was brutally humiliated by the Apartheid state police. He states that the "most potent weapon in the hand of the oppressor is the mind of the oppressed." This self-dehumanization must be counteracted by holistically rescuing and recovering the subserviated humanity back to its status of Otherness, of both the victimizer and victim alike in relation to the three-dimensional hierarchical community.

To conclude in very simple terms, we shouldn't forget, it is before *sunset* that some African *village meeting, dance* or *ancestral rite* would take place, may be under a tree (be nice or kind to trees, "Seid nett zu Bäumen,"[130] as some Austrian organization has it for a motto), meaning, *muntu* can't live a happy moral life without living in full social communion with her happy neighbor or the Other (sun, tree) or members of the three-dimension community! Though *muntu* seems like a host of other creatures at this earthly house, her hospitality doesn't make her a master of this hierarchical house given that although she is a host, she likewise remains a guest

---

124. See Tadjo, *The Shadow of Imana*, 41–42, 45.
125. Tadjo, "Lifting the Cloak of (In)visibility, 1.
126. Tadjo, "Lifting the Cloak of (In)visibility, 4.
127. Tadjo, "Lifting the Cloak of (In)visibility, 1–2.
128. Tadjo, "Lifting the Cloak of (In)visibility, 3.
129. Tadjo, *The Shadow of Imana*, 46.
130. Ginkgo Gardens.

at this house as she journeys towards the invisible community. Therefore, in good bioethics, a successful holistic solidarity entails us being more, at least eco-responsible in our increasing numbers worldwide and activities that have incurred, not only an ecological violence but also an ecological debt, demanding us to cultivate more an attitude of nature-relatedness (ethnoecology) and never denying our contingency as fixed in sympathetically respecting relational creatural networks. This presupposes eco-theological bioethics along human eco-responsibility. Thusly, for the survival of each creature, we not only need each creature whether animate or inanimate, each life force and system, but also need each creature for the survival of the integral fabric of earthly life! To incorporate every entity in the integral community life to which we are also necessarily part of the survival, we have to communion with every entity with total respectful sympathy. We should never underestimate as critics sometimes aver, that already the rest of the creatures, though quite oftentimes unspoken but quite understood, simply through their orderly being, are far better morally faithful to the life vital laws and are already cooperating with the ecological broad systems than the economically exploitive increasing numbers of human beings. We cannot repudiate observable evidence that nature indeed listens to our heartaches, proves to us that we are never lonely and accepts us as we are, by never limiting the brightness of the sun and stars—dankness gives us meaning to appreciate their sunniness or starkness—the smooth hugs of the wind or the beautiful melodies of the singing birds of the air not only to one homestead or one entity. The question is whether we should continue choosing—in our anthropocentric linguistics—to act blind to these simple obvious facts!

As a promising unifying signpost, indeed *Fratelli tutti* and the "Document on Human Fraternity" by Pope Francis and the grand Imam of Al Azhar, recently led the United Nations to declare 4 February each year as the International Day of Human Fraternity, beginning in 2021. It is indeed a huge step towards cooperation of religions as well as a global promotion of peace, solidarity, harmony and intercultural dialogue.[131] Our efforts now, in a simple layperson's language, are to broaden this practical fraternal solidarity—translating from an intercultural social epistemology—in the holistic sense possible. To establish the heart of bioethics, along human eco-responsibility, is to be in solidarity with *the Other* ("with all") as the new culture and lifestyle of *our home*, a non-negotiable practical sustainable way of life that fosters a relational friendship, for example, without exploitation, self-victimization, dichotomization of life, racism, and excluding the

---

131. Vatican News staff writer, "'International Day of Human Fraternity'"; United Nations, "International Day of Human Fraternity."

victimized ancestors. We can refer to functional solidarity with the Other as the heart of bioethics. It is here that respectful sympathy must not only penetrate relationships between individual entities within their populations and between individual entities of distinctive populations, but also all systems that interconnect the above. It is again from here that we can holistically nurture a "social global covenant" between ourselves, as well as between us, the creation and the cooperative systems that bring us together. It is yet from here that we must resolutely revere the Other as mother earth, if it is to continue healthily contributing to the integral continuum of life favoring the flourishing of all. We have to continue overturning the current sub-moral human-oriented harmful risks—such as poaching, illegal ivory, encroachment of human beings on animal habitats and natural vegetation through deforestation—notable to various African traditional and World Heritage Sites such as Serengeti National Park and Kilimanjaro National Park both in Tanzania, the East African Great Rift Valley, the Lacustrine zone of eastern Africa, Victoria Falls on the Zambezi River in the southern part of Africa, endangered snow on Africa's highest mountain Mt. Kilimanjaro, and so many.

CONTRIBUTIONS OF AN AFRICAN HOLISTIC APPROACH TO THE THEOLOGICAL BIOETHICS OF THE OTHER

In addition to our discussion, some other authorships have assessed *Fratelli Tutti* and the African thought as generally complementing each other on themes like humanistic cosmological friendship, solidarity and interdependence[132] without identifying what the African worldview can uniquely offer to the broader discourse in theological bioethics. To be more precise with good bioethics, holistic bioethics has to transcend every kind of social charity, social love, social solidarity, social dialogue, social covenant, constraints of social systems, etc., to embrace the Other as my holistic neighbor. It is why the theological heart of an inclusive theological bioethics has to be in solidarity with and holistically embrace the tears of every creation and vital force in every local context together with every global system of cooperation, into one unity of an interconnected social reality. But some reality reveals that some local contexts have historically stood alone with almost no friendships!

132. Opongo, "'Fratelli Tutti' and 'Ubuntu.'"

Systemic Biases and Contradiction of African Native Methodologies

In 1659, the congregation of *Propaganda Fide* warned missionaries sent to China and Korea not only against compelling the faithful to disown their own traditions except if they obviously contradicted religion and morality; but also, not to transport France, Spain, Italy or some other European country to China. The mandate was to introduce faith but not any European country among the faithful.[133] The understanding of the congregation has always been that the "Catholic Church is neither Belgian, nor French, nor English, nor Italian nor American; it is catholic. This is why it is Belgian in Belgium, French in France, English in England, etc. In Congo, it must be Congolese."[134] Some of these contradictions have origins, we should not forget, from historical biases that the black color was cursed as clearly documented in 1873. The Catholic church, under the Congregation of Indulgences published a special prayer for the conversion of Ham's cursed black offsprings due to the sin of their father Ham (cursed by Noah): "Let us pray for the most miserable Ethiopian peoples in Central Africa, who form a tenth of humanity, so that God Almighty may take away from their hearts the curse of Ham and give them the blessings of Jesus Christ, our God and Lord."[135]

And a little later, when Europe undertook continental expeditions in Africa, the missionaries came with soldiers, explorers and merchants, who belonged to their colonizing nations, with their own view of life. Already this left a suspicion—"dubious intentions"—in Christianity's descent on the African Black soil given the subsequent dehumanizing and inhuman

---

133. "Nullum studium ponite, nullaque ratione suadete illis populis ut ritus suos, consuetudines et mores mutent, modo non sint apertissime Religioni et bonis moribus contraria. Quid enim absurdius quam Galliam, Hispaniam, aut Italiam, aut aliam Europae partem in Sinas invehere? Non haec, sed fidem importate, quae nullius gentis ritus et consuetudines, modo prava non sint, aut re spuit aut laedit, imo vero sarta tecta esse vult." Collectanea Sacrae Congregationis de propaganda Fide, *Decreta Instructiones Rescripta Pro Apostolicis Missionibus*, no. 135.

134. Congregatio de Propaganda Fide, Sylloge praecipuorum documentorum recentium summorum pontificum et sacrae congregationis de propaganda fide, *necnon aliarum SS. Congregationum Romanorum: ad usum missionariorum*, no. 206. Cited from Bujo, *An African Ethic*, xiii.

135. "Oremus pro miserrimis Africae Centralis populis Aethiopum qui decimam partem universi generis humani constituunt, ut Deus omnipotens tandem aliquando auferat maledictionem Chami a cordibus eorum detque illis benedictionem unice in Jesu Christo Deo et Domino nostro consequendam." Ex Sancta Congregatione Indulgentiarum, "Oratio pro Conversione Chamitarum Africae Centralis ad Ecclesiam Catholicam," 678.

injustices. The pertinent moral question is whether the contemporary application of theological ethics is only "amnestic," whereby an injustice happened and the Global North cultures were defeated, they lost and their case closed and forgotten, or "anamnetic," whereby we ought to remember the community victims of the dehumanizing historical colonization, slave trade, genocide, numerous biomedical exploitative collaborations, where natives were robbed of their cultural heritage, and their wealthy expropriated—e.g., African mummies in English museums.[136] The moral burden of our intellectually oriented theological ethics is to convince an African down in some village of a just and truly loving God amid all these inhuman injustices. Not forgetting that the God that an African believes in *up to the present time* is holistically alive in her daily totality of life, in the present, past and future community. A God who is greater than every reality, *semper major*, is unfortunately contrarily visualized as *semper minor*.

To partly contribute to the modern discourse of moral theology, methodologies used should succeed in meeting sub-Saharan Africans at their deep roots. It is no progress generally debating universally oriented academic moral theology with little accessibility outside the world beyond the Global North. Some recent church documents, which were supposed to heal such historic wounds in African communities and make the fruits of the Second Vatican Council accessible to even non-European churches, remained inaccessible. Studies show that although the encyclical *Rerum Novarum* (1891) courageously confronted contemporary challenges and led to a new era of Catholic moral thought; nevertheless, it must be admitted that the doctrine initiated by Leo XIII remained Eurocentric and outside the reach of sub-Saharan Africans. When the Pope published this encyclical, only six years had passed since the partition of Africa among Western powers at the Berlin Conference in 1885. The injustice which this partition along colonialism had done to the African psyche, and its consequent historical chronical conditioning of the African continent and Africans themselves, was not mentioned in the papal encyclical, nor the cruel slave trade of that time, even when the encyclicals, *In Plurimis* (1888) and *Catholicae Ecclesiae* (1890) took it up. In contrast, within the different European-American theological ethics "schools," since the methodologies

136. Differently, questions in research arise: What would the museums in Paris, London or Berlin be without artefacts from the Third World, which was so much victimized and exploited? How unscrupulously were the countries of the Third World economically exploited for the creation of a Western paradise to which the people of these countries have no rights, since now they are called "indebted" by their very exploiters? Bujo, *The Ethical Dimension of Community*, 32, 133–35, 162, 140–41; See also The Roxie Walker Galleries (about 2686 B.C.–A.D. 395). "Egyptian death and afterlife: mummies."

employed and the problems addressed concern a Western cultural principlistic context as proven by the choice of essay contributors, such moral encyclicals like *Veritatis splendor* (1993), *Humanae vitae* (1968) are widely received. This inconsistence suggests how these church teachings scarcely pay sufficient heed to today's multicultural world, and one gets a feeling that neither the critics nor the defenders of such encyclicals are particularly interested in how their message is fully received in non-western cultures.[137] We shouldn't forget that the intended propagated Catholic message is universal in nature (καθολικός, *katholikos*) and the regional churches shouldn't receive an altered impression.

A similar impression is consistent with most recent encyclical such as Benedict XVI's *Caritas in veritate* to which Agbonkhianmeghe Orobator in relation to Africa's burden of underdevelopment laments thus: "Reading Pope Benedict XVI's encyclical *Caritas in veritate* (2009) on integral human development elicits wonder about whether the pope had anything in mind other than European Catholicism."[138] It is not the goal of this investigation to dwell on encyclicals but if we get more specific to bioethics and pick out Paul VI's moral encyclical *Humanae vitae*, it is with this document that bioethical principlism and its natural law oriented obligatory norms of ethical conduct, i.e., autonomy-individual debates, were clearly generated in Catholic theological ethics.[139] Three years later, the worldwide debate of autonomy-individual thoughts in Catholic moral theology is well represented in Alfons Auer's book *Autonome Moral und christlicher Glaube* (1971), to which the corrective response of the moral encyclical *Veritas Splendor* never escaped Auer's influence as moral theologians corroborate. The old-yet-new question remained whether there is a revealed true moral theology to the church alone and who can confirm and declare the universal moral principles. The other question was whether all ethical wisdom proceeded from principlistic, and anthropocentric standards exclusively inherited by humans in the Catholic church. Basically, Auer, just like philosophers and theologians before him (like Aristotle, Thomas Aquinas) argued within the framework of natural law, where reason is decisive in interpreting social

---

137. Scholarships show more documents whose moral lessons remained not fully successful in the Global North include Catechism of the Catholic Church (1993), the new Code of Canon Law (1983). Bujo, *An African Ethic*, 73–74, 148–50; See a deeper analysis in Bujo, *Ethical Dimension of Community*, 165.

138. Orobator, "*Caritas in veritate* and Africa's Burden," 320.

139. Paul VI, "*Humanae vitae*," 11, 14. "For its natural adaptation . . . God has wisely ordered laws of nature . . . . The Church, nevertheless, in urging men to the observance of the precepts of the natural law" (HV 11) and, ". . . its very nature contradicts the moral order . . . (HV 14)

reality and positing ethical norms. Thomas' tractate on the law indeed grants humans the prerogative of reason and autonomy earned at creation,[140] a position that takes us back to emphasizing strong anthropocentrism. Besides the earlier on mentioned injustices and unhealed historic wounds (Africans as victims) all don't fit in an African milieu of theological ethics that champions a holistic anamnetic thinking.

If we are to embrace a holistic approach to theological bioethics, it requires localization of theological ethics, which shouldn't occur outside the riches of one's own tradition, culture or "father/mother's home," and if such an approach disrespects people's context, it must be turned down. This does not only show "us how necessary an inculturated moral theology is, if the Gospel is to be proclaimed in Africa in a way that does justice to human persons,"[141] but also "re-encountering culture becomes indispensable for living Christianity in my father's home."[142] Put differently, it would be fallacious to presuppose that what is good for the Global North must equally be good in every home and for all cultures everywhere in the Global South. Indeed "if the good news of Jesus is to make its home among every people, it cannot identify itself with one specific culture, not even a global or monoculture."[143] In the same vein, John Paul II makes a similar clarion call in 1995 during his visit to Malawi by encouraging local churches not to accept any way of life that diverts people from their own rich traditions:

> I put before you today a challenge—a challenge to reject a way of living which does not correspond to the best of your traditions, and your Christian faith. Many people in Africa look beyond Africa for the so-called "freedom of the modern way of life." Today I urge you to look inside yourselves. Look to the riches of your own traditions, look to the faith which we are celebrating in this assembly. Here you will find genuine freedom—here you will find Christ who will lead you to the truth.[144]

---

140. In STh I–II Prol. " . . . man is said to be made in God's image, in so far as the image implies *an intelligent being endowed with free-will and self-movement* . . . it remains for us to treat of His image, i.e. man, inasmuch as he too is the principle of his actions, as having free-will and control of his actions."(. . . homo factus ad imaginem Dei dicitur, secundum quod per imaginem significatur *intellectuale et arbitrio liberum et per se potestativum*; . . . restat ut consideremus de eius imagine, idest de homine, secundum quod et ipse est suorum operum principium, quasi liberum arbitrium habens et suorum operum potestatem); see also Bujo, *An African Ethic*, 76–80;

141. Bujo, *An African Ethic*, 74.

142. Onwubiko, "Re-encountering African culture," 107.

143. Bujo, *An African Ethic*, xii.

144. John Paul II, "Ecclesia in Africa," 48.

Unfortunately, the riches inherent in each individual tradition have suffered the greatest on the African continent. Yet in the holistic pursuit of a theological bioethics—in testimony of an African communitarianism that respects "EACH" one's identity as an individual without relegating the community of "WE"—the encyclical *Veritas Splendor*, just like John Paul II's message to the *Ecclesia in Africa* above, emphasizes the uniqueness of our own homes, the individualities of our traditions and the soundness of our local ways of life as inhabiting riches that should guide but never be underestimated in journeying toward the "WE" community. Although humans are endowed by God to set "down laws by virtue of a primordial and total mandate" (VS 36), "*this universality does not ignore the individuality of human beings*, nor is it opposed to the absolute uniqueness of each person" (VS 51).[145] It is our true individuality that leads us to an authentic universality. It is the reason why we can't draw the same rightful conclusions in all contexts, except in majority of cases (*ut in pluribus*) in regard to the natural law (*lex naturae*) and general principles (*prima principia communia*); and even if we did draw conclusions they can't be entirely the same, given that each draws particular just or unjust conclusions not from common morality or general universalized principles but rather from cultural-specific and contextual customary moralities.[146] Accordingly, it would be misleading for theological ethicists to assert an absolute validity of their moral thoughts without being keenly attentive to the louder voices of the cultures in context. It must be said that appreciating a locally inculturated functioning framework of theological ethics should interest each moral theologian.

In order to overcome such systemic biases and ameliorate numerous contradictions unfavorable to local moralities, in the recent modern Africa, although the Roman Catholic church started incorporating local traditions—like in the spheres of music, dance, initiation rites, funerary rites—the incorporations came along with great controversial changes, destructions, partial or total loss[147] of what Africans would genuinely preserve as positive

---

145. John Paul II, "*Veritas Splendor*"; see also Aquinas, *Summa Theologiae*, I-II, q. 94, a.2.

146. STh I-II q. 94, a.4c: "Consequently we must say that the natural law, as to general principles, is the same for all, both as to rectitude and as to knowledge. But as to certain matters of detail, which are conclusions, as it were, of those general principles, it is the same for all in the majority of cases, both as to rectitude and as to knowledge; and yet in some few cases it may fail . . . " (Sic igitur dicendum est quod lex naturae, quantum ad prima principia communia, est eadem apud omnes et secundum rectitudinem, et secundum notitiam. Sed quantum ad quaedam propria, quae sunt quasi conclusiones principiorum communium, est eadem apud omnes ut in pluribus et secundum rectitudinem et secundum notitiam, sed ut in paucioribus potest deficere . . .).

147. See Van Binsbergen, "The hermeneutics of race," 4–5.

values befitting a future African context-oriented approach to theological bioethics. Oftentimes, Christian instructions have equaled to destruction of a people's precious cultural values and religious heritage (the Other) without any tolerance.[148] Among the destroyed positive communal values within African tradition after the arrival of a Western-oriented Christianity, regard marriage life. If for example, a spouse psychosomatically threatened the marriage institution—other marital problems include cases of cruelty— it is the entire family or community palaver that diagnosed the historical root of the problem, helped the partner go through psychiatric exercises, before ultimately reconciling and reintegrating the holistically healed moral patient into the marital community. On the whole, these practices were condemned by Christian missionaries and dismissed as superstition without offering an alternative practical solution. The so called "universal Christian culture" carried with it a strong sense of absolutism and an individualistic attitude, making marital problems pertaining to the community families a private discussion with the priest,[149] other than the variedly experienced religious community palaver (council of elders). This leads to some African theologians to suppose that we can scarcely refer to African religion as more individualistic and superstitious "than certain devotional and sacramental practices of Christianity, which can be superstitious and idolatrous."[150] From varied North-South exploitative consequentialistic collaborations to the Tuskegee Syphilis Study, the candidate Ebola virus vaccine trials in Africa, genocides and apartheid, the three hegemonic Eurocentric forms of colonialism, partition of Africa, civilization and Christianity, rejection of African traditions, all largely manifest lack of a holistic approach to the ethics of the Other given the unethical inequalities and un-relatedness amongst God's beautiful creation.

African Religiosity offers a Rich Context to the Other

Worthy to note, the majority of African ethnic groups have never conducted a religious war in the name of their religious convictions. It is striking how most of the ethnic convictions in Black Africa have been historically receptive to other new religions such as Christianity and Islam without any notable persecutions toward their missionaries. That is why, it is an ordinary life to encounter siblings or clan relatives in today's Africa who belong

---

148. See Bujo, *The Ethical Dimension of Community*, 137.
149. See Bujo, *The Ethical Dimension of Community*, 106–7, 129–30.
150. Orobator, *Religion and Faith in Africa*, xx.

to different denominations, confessions, religions, or sects.[151] For a Black African, what counts most is not only how the new religion humanizes the world but also how it holistically contributes to an integral hospitable life. Unfortunately, this virtue of hospitality has routinely been misinterpreted as an African weakness since natives hardly make any resistance to foreigners, the Other, who in return lightly take African culture as simply inferior. Even-though the significance of African hospitality may not make sense to some foreign outlooks, to Black Africans, hospitality is not a weakness but whoever never shares withholds the life force from the Other, and inevitably poisons the relational vital force.[152]

In retrospect, the hospitable sharing of life richly indicates how the black continent has always immanently had a rich religious culture from the beginning, and so it was not Christianity or even Islam alone (the foreign Other) which could have civilized Africans. In fact, it was in the name of their religious culture and their God that the Africans offered Christianity the possibility of spreading (fertile soil) at the expense of their culture. It is moreover worth noting that there is no worse degree of total alienation that affects a Black person more than the loss of her cultural identity.[153] Loosing cultural identity is tantamount to losing one part of the Other, i.e., one's property since one's culture is identified as one's property in the African sense. The rich culture as a *fertile soil* is an appropriate context we endorsed already. The cultural-specific context is upheld by Paulinus Ikechukwu Odozor in his Morality *Truly Christian, Truly African*,[154] where he charges moral theologians with circumstances where everything in theological ethics cannot be negotiable or be open to bargaining.[155] Notions of negotiating and bargaining are relatable to inculturation in cultural contexts in which we should be open to Christianizing the African categories of thought as well as Africanizing Christianity in equal measure, i.e., a genuinely holistic approach to bioethics should be originally sympathetic to context.

This is in dialogue with Paul VI's clarion call when he was in Uganda in 1969: "You may, and you must, have an African Christianity."[156] To contextualize his message, he was endorsing an enculturated African approach to theological bioethics. The imperative for inculturation arises from the

---

151. See Bujo, *An African Ethic*, 162–63.
152. See Bujo, *The Ethical Dimension of Community*, 162.
153. See Bujo, *Ethical Dimension of Community*, 137, 139; Bujo, *African Theology*, 11–21.
154. See Odozor, *Morality Truly Christian, Truly African*.
155. See Odozor, *Morality Truly Christian, Truly African*, 162.
156. Paul VI, "The Bishops of Africa."

fact that principlistic Western culture has neither the last nor necessarily the best word on what it means to be human nor does the expression of Christianity with which it is identified constitute the only or best expression of the Christian faith.[157] We can scarcely converse univocally while seeking solutions to multicomplex realities, among which are African contextual challenges in relation to the new religious beliefs (the Other). It is here that a dialogic palaver would work. But with the awareness that not everything in theological ethics can be negotiable or be auctioned for bargaining, as well as the fact that we are not culturally neutral, even when we learn from other cultures within a genuine dialogic palaver between Christianity and the native African religions, it doesn't mean at all deserting native values. Though I have neither argued that it necessitates Africans advancing their own new distinctive brand of theological bioethics but their intervention in bioethics should materialize from a conversational palaver ethic between the universalized global discourse and the contextualized accumulated local wisdom—think of Bantu philosophical theology—whose richness cannot simply be underrated.

Argued differently, as far as Africans' rich spiritual-religious reality, we agree with Emmanuel Orobator Agbonkhianmeghe, a Jesuit theologian and a true son of the African soil, that "Africa is a deeply religious continent," explaining the "exponential growth of Christianity and Islam," just because "the African is a believer" and so "African's experience of faith did not begin with the advent of missionaries—Christian or Muslim."[158] Indeed comparing Western Christianity with African Traditional Religion—labelled as Paganism or Heathenism by some—Tangwa likewise sees "nothing wrong" in *his* (this) "dual-membership."[159] He is proud of this dual-membership, i.e., being an *African Christian* or an *African Muslim*. In similar terms, an *African Christian* is the term Orobator Agbonkhianmeghe employs in his *Theology brewed in an African Pot*. Why is he an African Christian? "Until my baptism as a Catholic, I lived the early part of my life with the milieu of African religion, being familiar with the gods, goddesses, divinities, deities, and ancestors of my people. I participated in many worship rituals in my

---

157. See Odozor, "An African Moral Theology," 594–98.

158. Orobator, *Religion and Faith in Africa*, 19. He argues that exponential growth of Christianity and Islam "is predicated on their essential relationship with African Religion. The latter is the ground in which they are planted. Without this vital relationship neither Christianity nor Islam would be recognizable as *African* religions" (p. 154, *Italics in original*). Orobator upholds "an existential symbiosis" as prevalent "between Christianity and African Religion, and between African Religion and Islam" (p. 171). So, it is the African religion as "the *ground* or *bedrock* on which the other two stake their claims to the African soul . . ." (p. 73), emphasis original.

159. Tangwa, *African bioethics in a Western frame*, 96–98.

family and developed a strong awareness of the communion between the human and the divine in daily life. As an African, prayer, praise, worship, and celebration were part of my upbringing."[160] Without being torn apart, he finds a satisfying and enriching unison between his African religious heritage and Christian faith contrary to what many writers believe about African Christians or Muslims. But if the Christian or Muslim faith remains culturally impervious in Africa, then one has no choice other than to refer to them as foreign religions. However, such a claim would raise more unnecessary questions. This explains why great contemporary African theological scholarships are against such perspectives. Indeed, Orobator Agbonkhianmeghe recently presented further his firsthand experience in *Religion and Faith in Africa* as a Catholic who also remains part of his native Igbo religion. I am no different either since being Catholic doesn't disconnect me from staying true to my Afrocentric Christianity which necessarily bares an imprint of the core values of my ancestral spirituality (Baganda). I remain true to Rome while remaining true to Africa. Theology empowers me to trust my faith as I trust my culture. In my opinion, this is not animistic or a syncretistic unhealthy spirituality, but a view to sit well in an African setting. It means my faith has to be incarnated in the soil's Africanity on the one hand, while on the other hand, I ought to approvingly appreciate that contemporary religious coexistence is my daily ecumenical tolerance, at least in theological bioethics.

Our discussions have shown how destruction of cultural contexts has been readily visible in biomedical interventions in sub-Saharan Africa, where the African art of holistic healing, reconciliation, and practice of medicine have not been adequately promoted but rather repressed in favor of Western principlistic methods of medicine. Promoting westernized principlism shouldn't mean erasure of Africanness. Some major contributors to this destruction, are the hospitably received foreign religions, to which Christianity belongs. And since Christian moral theology confronted the African religious approach to morality with its claim of absoluteness mixed with elements of Western culture, it is more than clear that the African moral thought hardly got a chance to contribute anything positive to a universalized approach to theological ethics.[161] For theological African scholarships, "no single culture has a monopoly on the gospel. No single culture can exhaust the mystery of salvation. No religion has a monopoly on the

---

160. Orobator, *Theology Brewed in an African Pot*, 10.
161. See Bujo, *Ethical Dimension of Community*, 24, 29.

truth."[162] Indeed absolute monocultural thoughts have no place in today's contemporary bioethics discourses.

It is one reason Agbonkhianmeghe rejoices "in the fall of the old demons of cultural imperialism that were content to foist foreign pantomimes disguised as Christian truths on places and peoples with rich cultural capacities for receiving, translating, and incarnating the Good news of the risen Christ according to their own genius and in their mother tongue."[163] Notwithstanding the fact that the same Christianity can gradually contribute to recent re-reinvigorations of the once true but condemned values in Africa, we need to ground a theological bioethics relevantly acceptable to an African soil with a distinctive African stamp since we neither holistically embrace Christ's message from barely a cultural vacuum nor do we need to abandon decisive contextual treasures of our culture so as to be children of a loving God. My claim here is in dialogue with the strong conviction of the African Catholic bishops: "Africa is not helpless. Our destiny is still in our hands. All she is asking for is the space to breathe and thrive. Africa is already moving; and the Church is moving with her, offering her the light of the Gospel."[164] It is the richness of the context, which when appreciated, then can we embrace a holistic approach.

Put differently, since Africans have no other alternative, they will remain forever Africans as their context dictates, no matter what may arise, meaning, whenever they are challenged with competitive principlistic theological bioethical interventions, they will resolutely return to their African religiosity (their Africanity) without disassociating themselves from the substantive beliefs of their ancestral fore-parents. So, for any religiosity that disregards this medicinal aspect of African spirituality should be ridiculed as misguided as well as misguiding a continent in which the future of Christianity seems the clearest. And of course, we can quickly observe how unimaginable it would be to talk of African theological bioethics without an African religion! Therefore, we cannot succeed in grounding a moral theology, appropriate for an African setting, without appreciating the holistic sense of the relational Other, which cannot be understood outside their own understanding of life as religiously immanent in every entity within the three-dimensional community.

---

162. Orobator, *Religion and Faith in Africa*, 172.
163. Orobator, *Religion and Faith in Africa*, 172–73.
164. Catholic Bishops for Africa, "Special Assembly for Africa," 42.

An African Life is not Secular but Holistically Religious

"Wherever the African is, there is his religion,"[165] so intones Mbiti. In a different voice, an African cannot separate God's immanence in her entire community life, every creation has spiritual life, given it derives from, proceeds, and returns to God, just as some traditional church theologians like Aquinas believe. In answering whether we can treat separately the science of the creator and creatures, angels, corporeal creatures, and human morality in sacred doctrine, without grouping them together under one class of subjects, Aquinas' answer is negative. He is convinced of one formality, a "one science" (*una scientia*) which "yet extends to everything" (*quae est una et simplex omnium*).[166] In relationship to *una scientia*, Aquinas further confirms an inherent spiritual life in each creature. For him, "even irrational animals partake in their own way of the Eternal Reason, just as the rational creature does."[167] Moreover, since every creature has a vital force, it can even vitally deliver beyond its nature as already stressed in Bantu moral life where an inanimate object (dry leaves) increases the life force of an animate sick *muntu*. Ofcourse this substantive belief cannot be disputed in the area of pharmacognosy and other modern scientific practices of medicine. Potentially, nature can provide varied remedies for some ailments. This conviction is no different to Bujo's reading of Aquinas' works. "The *potentia Dei absoluta*, which leads to the *potentia oboedientialis*, means that God awakens an utterly unsuspected potentiality in a creature, allowing it to attain a goal undreamed-of in its own nature, as, for example, would be the case if God were to raise a stone, a plant, or an animal to eternal vision in bliss."[168]

Procedurally, I am considering an integral holistic mission of theological ethics without dichotomizing the whole moral thought, separating human beings as super beings from the communal unity of God's entire natural creation. It has become clear that an African ethic safeguards this non-dichotomized holistic mission by operating in a "community," which is life-giving in both its visible and invisible dimensions, thus appreciating the totality of life as a single unity.[169] To an African, the whole totality of life is religiously or spiritually rich, given that a Black African's *Weltanschauung* is permeated by a universal dynamic vital force. This vital force

---

165. Mbiti, *African Religions and Philosophy*, 1–2.

166. STh I q. 1, a. 3.

167. "quod etiam animalia irrationalia participant rationem aeternam suo modo, sicut et rationalis creatura." STh I–II q. 91, a.2 ad 3.

168. Bujo, *An African Ethic*, 98.

169. See Bujo, *An African Ethic*, 99–101.

is synonymously understood by others as characteristically "religio-spiritistic."[170] So Africans are not only deeply religious but live in a world social reality they regard as spiritistic religious.[171] It is for this reason Kasozi concurs with John Samuel Mbiti, E.A. Ruch and K. C. Anyanwu that for Africans, "their world view is imbued with such a religious disposition that a spiritual condition or state or mode of being is regarded as either forming or influencing the inmost being of nearly every natural object or phenomenon. In other words, almost every natural object or phenomenon is ingrained with a spiritual condition or state or mode of being."[172] Such a spiritual disposition does not mean that Africans are animistic, superstitious or polytheistic like I have denied above, but rather, that *muntu's* monotheistic religious aspiration permeates her entire life as a unity. This is emphasized in the theology of Mulago: "La vie religieuse des Bantu semble pouvoir se résumer dans le culte rendu à leurs ancêtres et leur monothéisme. Mais ces actes de religion s'accompagnent presque toujours de croyances et pratiques parareligieuses. Et comme la religion imprègne toute la vie du Muntu, comme celle de l'homme africain en général, on comprend aisément qu'elle soit l'élément central de la culture bantu et al clef de la compréhension de la vision du monde négro-africain."[173] Moreover, the spiritual condition envisaged in every entity as the vital force shouldn't be literally emphasized as an African religious affiliation, prompting one to question who founded this religion, whether there is some sacred scripture to prove it, or whether it is some centralized institution with a leader, but rather to unfold the social reality of an African moral account that is simply one single indivisible unity:

> Der Begriff afrikanische Religion meint hier das traditional religiöse System der afrikanischen Völker, das sich ohne Religionsstifter, ohne aufgezeichnete heilige Schriften und ohne zentralisierte und institutionalisierte Organisation entwickelt hat. Zu ihren verschiedenen sowie die Realität der körperlichen (sichtbaren) und geistigem (unsichtbaren) Welten, die jedoch ineinandergreifen, so dass es keine scharfe Trennung zwischen dem, 'religiösen' und dem 'weltlichen' Leben gibt.[174]

---

170. Kasozi, *The Ntu'ology of the Baganda*, 53.

171. See Roscoe, *The Baganda*, 271; Ssemwogerere, *Katekismu ya Mapeera*, 257.

172. Kasozi, *The Ntu'ology of the Baganda*, 47; Kasozi partially picks the examples from Roscoe, *The Baganda*, 313–20; Ruch and Anyanwu, *Philosophical Trends in Contemporary Africa*, 122. Nature like hills, trees, snakes, forests, rocks, rivers, are the places of sacrifice and abodes of spiritual beings.

173. Mulago, *La religion traditionnelle des Bantu*, 9.

174. Mbiti, "Der Tod in der afrikanischen Religion," 201 ; In different scholarships, a couple of questions are shot at the African religion : Who was its founder? What

Owing to the single indissoluble unity of an African social reality of life, what suggests no sharp division between the "religious" and the "secular" life, it is yet another reason why it is difficult in practice for an African thinking to be dichotomous. To put it in another way, the human being acts in a secular manner with an intimate relationship to the religious dimension. This intrinsic connection makes it impossible for Black Africans to speak of some autonomous creation or any entity that must be distinguished from the religious dimension. Given that we have iterated the Black African world as only one, there is no practical possibility to think of this world as first profane and then religious, but both in one unity, which when disharmoniously tampered with, sanctions or taboos—which are inexistent in bioethical principlism—ensue in.[175] This indissoluble-unity-oriented approach to life strikes no "distinction between plants, animals and inanimate things, between the sacred and profane, matter and spirit, the communal and the individual."[176] Approaching life realities non-dichotomously is one reason why "African people are characterized by a holistic type of thinking and feeling. For them, there is no dichotomy between the sacred and the secular, and they regard themselves as being in *close relationship with the entire cosmos*. Total realization of the self is impossible as long as one does not peacefully co-exist with minerals, plants and animals."[177] Moreover, for coexistence to succeed, religiosity is holistically inscribed in all created life—not forgetting that inanimate things have life too—akin to how the well celebrated Mbiti puts it:

> Die Religion ist ins Leben des Volkes 'eingeschrieben', und man unterscheidet nicht zwischen Säkularen und Sakralen. In dieser Tradition versteht sich der Mensch als religiöses Wesen. Die Menschen leben ihre Religion, wann immer sie als Menschen handeln: auf Reisen, beim Bebauen ihrer Felder, beim Jagen oder Fischen, bei der Partnersuche oder bei medizinischer Behandlung. Auch dient die Religion zur Erklärung der Geheimnisse der Natur.[178]

---

is its Holy Book or sacred script? Who is the head of the faith and who are its most authoritative theologians? What is the approximate membership of the faithful? Others describe African religions as somewhat vague, non-doctrinaire, non-proselytizing, unsystematized and unorganized. Tangwa, *African bioethics in a Western frame*, 10, 197.

175. See Tangwa, *African bioethics in a Western frame*, 75–76; Bujo, *An African Ethic*, 96.

176. Tangwa, *African bioethics in a Western frame*, 41.

177. Bujo, *The Ethical Dimension of Community*, 208. *Emphasis is mine.*

178. Mbiti, "Die Vielfalt der Religionen," 49–50.

This indicates how the religious nature, for example, of *muntu* comprises both somatic and spiritual dimensions, suggesting an ultimate *intergralistic* conception of *muntu*[179] within her environment in which she cultivates her daily food, grazes animals, gets water from rain, and recreates. It would be an empty life to develop a lasting practical approach to the science of theological bioethics without considering the spiritual union with the integral nature, the visible community and the ancestral invisible community. Some scholars recently conceptualized this relational ontology as "harmonious monism"[180] while others had already hypothesized it as *bondedness*. The well-known Malawian theologian Harvey Sindima noted that any "alliance of progress, science and technology" shouldn't lead "to social and spiritual bankruptcy" that separates "nature and people" from "God."[181] For him, all creation is revered and shares in an intimate life of bondedness with the divine. For him, we can hardly talk of an African idea of community without its synonymousness with bondedness and oneness of life with each other and in communion with nature.[182] So "unless people cultivate a sense of bondedness to nature they cannot care about nature" and it is why "any model of transformation that does not take into account the value of nature does not stand a chance."[183] Otherwise attempts to achieve high productivity at the expense of appreciating the holistic approach to nature have been extensively counter-productive.

To demonstrate this counter-productivity, with the widely encouraged use of fertilizers on the African soil without testing their salt compatibility to African soils, African soils have consequently gotten burnt.[184] High productivity on land is also visibly abused along livestock farming. One of the most authoritative reports to date, the United Nations Food and Agriculture Organization (FAO) confirms that the livestock sector is not only "responsible for a significant share of environmental damage,"[185] it "is a major stressor on many ecosystems and on the planet as whole. Globally it is one of the largest sources of greenhouse gases and one of the leading causal factors in the loss of biodiversity, while in developed and emerging countries it is perhaps the

179. Kasozi uses the term *intergralistic* which to me seems to refer to *muntu* as a unity composed of and interacting with several integral parts. Kasozi, *The Ntu'ology of the Baganda*, 66.

180. Ijiomah, "Logic in African Worldview," 29–35, see also his *Harmonious Monism*.

181. Sindima, "Community of Life," 542.

182. See Sindima, "Ecological theology in African perspective," 137–47.

183. Sindima, "Community of Life," 549.

184. See Sindima, "Community of Life," 550; Rwiza, *Environmental Ethics*, 68.

185. FAO, "Livestock's Long Shadow," 284.

leading source of water pollution."[186] This authoritative FAO report does not only indicate that "by 2025, 64 percent of the world's population will live in water-stressed basins,"[187] it further informs how ecosystems offer us varied environmental services and goods, that are valued globally at US$33 trillion of which US$14.9 trillion are offered by wetlands. Unfortunately, an estimated 50 percent of world wetlands have vanished over the last century. By all means, need demands us to instantly appreciate a holistic approach in the science of theological bioethics so as to mitigate ecological violence of the relational Other, the threatened flood controls, groundwater replenishment, shoreline stabilization and storm protection, sediment and nutrient regulation, climate change, water purification, biodiversity conservation, recreation, and cultural tourism. It is due to the ecosystems' suffering from over-extraction, desertification, deforestation, over-fertilization, chemical runoff from farms, air and water pollution and poor livestock farming methods.[188] This makes Aaron J. Cohen and other scholars to thusly conclude that "ambient air pollution contributes substantially to the global burden of disease, which has increased over the past 25 years, as a result of both demographic and epidemiological trends and increasing levels of air pollution . . . estimated that air pollution levels in 2030 in China would need to decline by 29%, and those in India by 20%, to maintain per-person mortality at 2010 levels . . . ."[189] Precisely we notice that the extended relational Other is under extreme attack!

We recognize how the religiosity or spirituality envisaged in the Other—every creation and every system or force as having life—has lost its relational impact as understood by Bantu. It is a clarion call that we see life in the Other again as indispensable to us in living out a holistic solidarity. Then we have a sound reason to nurture respectful sympathy towards our climate, for instance. This is in dialogue with *Laudato Si'*. It notes, "the climate is a common good, belonging to all and meant for all" (LS 23). One notices a general problem cutting across a would-be-functional local-global solidarity, a problem that needs closing a dichotomized thinking with a holistic approach to save our mother earth, i.e., combining local autonomy with universal autonomy, local thinking with the universalized thinking, religious with secular, sacred with profane and so on. Ethical controversies from the bad scientist who fails to ascertain which appropriate livestock

186. FAO, "Livestock's Long Shadow," 267.

187. FAO, "Livestock's Long Shadow," 127.

188. FAO, "Livestock's Long Shadow," 51, 69, 79–123, 90–93, 112–16, 127–28, 188–200.

189. Cohen et al., "The global burden of disease," 1916–17.

methods and fertilizer compositions are suitable to a particular locality than another, to poor or corruptive policy makers who fail doing pilot studies before permitting certain livestock farming methods or fertilizers to be widely used on the life of innocent mother nature. Such are examples of chemically toxic Persistent Organic Pollutants (POPs) which are injurious not only to human life and livestock, but also generally hazardous to mother earth's *water, soil,* and *air,* since they are their commonest means of transportation. Indeed, if the quality of those three deteriorate, our life span, life for livestock, food production, environment, and the air we breathe, all get highly endangered, i.e., the Other, who equally has divine life.

We should note that the incomprehensibility (by some) of the African holistic religious thinking, the unity of secular and religious, doesn't necessarily entail meaninglessness or irrationality or exclusion in the discourse of bioethics, given our current pluralistic thinking. Indeed, getting convinced of the inherent truth in some categories of thought may delay, but at some time, it will come to pass. Of-course another may rightly commit an ethnocentric fallacy by imposing her own interpretation of this relational holistic thinking as irrelevant to her own cultural values or to the universalized principlism, without grasping the fact that Africans conceive of this theonomous force not simply as a myth but as a substantive religious belief, just like we Catholics believe in the sacrament of penance without mythologizing it. For Black Africans, it is the holistic relational life to which every force of ethics (Other) participates within a friendship of solidarity on which a black African accordingly grounds holistic theological bioethics but not simply basing it on rational ontology.

No Creation is Lifeless: From Eco-bioethics to a Mutual Cosmic Friendship with the Other

In modern interventions of bioethics, to eliminate the tension between life and death, it has invented complex life-threatening principles that have instead disharmoniously set asunder cosmic vital forces. Already earlier scholarships, like those of Andrea Vicini, indicate the necessity of cultivating an integrative holistic approach of theological bioethics encompassing all sciences and relationships by citing the African moral thought.[190] Moreso, the African moral thought is already agitating for not only humanization and dialogue with non-Western cultures, but also relearning the symbol of nature.[191] Relearning the symbol of nature is "to emphasize that human be-

---

190. See Vicini, "Bioethics," 169–87, especially 181–86.
191. See Bujo, *The Ethical Dimension of Community,* 216–18.

ings are part of nature."[192] It doesn't grant humans the status of superiority and domination[193] over other creation types, but in an African sense, it demands *muntu* to exercise a unique responsibility by genuinely according respectful sympathy to all creation. We have indeed already examined how this holistic view signals solidarity that includes all forces and components of the earth community. To some Black Africans, human beings being part of nature (*bintu*) grants them only a centre place in-contrast to being masters, for example, among Baganda. *Muntu* sees the universe in terms of oneself, "and endeavors to live in harmony with it. Even where there is no biological life in an object, African people attribute life to it, in order to establish a more direct relationship with the world around them. In this way the visible and invisible parts of the universe are at man's disposal . . . man is not the master in the universe; he is only the centre."[194] This means, humans aren't to masterfully exploit the *bintu* because they all have life, but in "recognition of man's ontological unity with all natural forces . . . man is the friend and beneficiary of nature,"[195] namely, the ontological friendship of man and nature is worth tenaciously nurturing for any flourishing of a holistic approach to theological bioethics, at least with some explanations.

In the first instance, the different conceptions which Africans "use to define their ethical norms or to generate their creatively constructed moral values arise from and are essentially connected with the way in which they conceptualize man and nature. This is in essence an ontological basis, since it is mainly concerned with *man's being in relation with other beings*."[196] Secondly, though there is the ontological hierarchical reality of *muntu* in her relationship with other beings, still the "the human task is not the enslaving domination of nature since *the human being is not above the cosmos but part of it* and can come to full self-realization only in union with other

---

192. Henk, "Global bioethics," 603–4.

193. See Rwiza, *Environmental Ethics*, 106–7.

194. Mbiti, *African Religion*, 39.

195. Sempebwa, *Reality of a Bantu*, 72–73. Ganda take Dogs for hurting because they remember certain smells, certain voices and certain words. Dogs can also remember the animal which was hunted, all done under the command of *muntu* (here p. 73). However, moral law is based on their conception or view of human nature as a whole (here p. 14 and p. 16); "In the African conception, there is no separation between "being" and "doing"; consequently, one may say that the human person is what he does. If action defines the being of the human person, it is also true that the human person's action is defined on the basis of his being." Bujo, *An African Ethic*, 124; "Being" and "doing" are fulfilled with interaction. In the mind of the Baganda "people, the universe is not barely a stage of natural things and events, but more so a cultural world, a world of interaction." Kasozi, *The Ntu'ology of the Baganda*, 46.

196. Sempebwa, *Reality of a Bantu*, 19. Italics mine.

cosmic beings, which ultimately have their *consistence in God as the inexhaustible source of life.*"[197] And since *muntu* remains only part of the cosmos, the ontological friendship presupposes she enjoys life, just like any other entity, from the same ultimate dispenser and source of the vital force (God). Even-though for Nso', this ontological friendship (interrelationship) may seem "humanly centred," it is not in the sense that moral consideration and concern are limited to human beings.[198] If we were to award moral status by hierarchically positioning humans at the summit of biological life, we would be morally speciesist. And this would be less of the relational life existent between the three-dimensional community as an unabridged continuum of all life forces, which Africanists like Tangwa grasp as eco-bio-communitarianism. Precisely eco-bioethics implies

> . . . interdependence among human beings, superhuman spirits, nonhuman animals, plants, and inanimate objects and forces . . . . In effect, the line separating human beings from the other ontological entities that populate the world, in the African world view, is neither hard and fast nor straight and clear. Since a human being can conceivably transform or be transformed (with or without knowledge or consent) into any of the other ontological entities, in this life or in the life after death, no human being can confidently claim to know that he or she is not the "brother/sister" of any other thing in existence.[199]

We are charged with a novel task to ground a holistic approach to theological bioethics that is both particular to the substantive ontological moral beliefs as well as to the universalized bioethical principlism, that is, a holistic approach that is particularly relevant and universally attractive and could be widely shared. Our earlier emphasis is that we can derive a moral approach from cultural realities—a way of life of a group of people—before we expand it universally.[200] Tangwa's *eco-bio-centric* attitude in bioethics is basically a view of *live* and *let live*.[201] I take Tangwa's interpretation of the African moral thought to be shaped by its ecological, biological and cultural diversity; whereby, the distinction amongst all "nature" diversities forms one single uninterrupted continuum (vital force) as God's creation. Therefore, it is not only humanistic but rather interdependent of all created entities and forces. This is the attitude of *live* and *let live*—which encompasses

---

197. Bujo, *The Ethical Dimension of Community*, 218. *Italics mine.*
198. See Tangwa, "African Perception of a Person," 39.
199. Tangwa, "African Perception of a Person," 42.
200. Tangwa, *Contemporary Bioethics Problems*, 45, 60.
201. Tangwa, "Biomedical and Environmental Ethics," 394.

eco-ethics, environmental ethics, developmental ethics, medical ethics, bioethics[202]—understood as a cosmic unity.[203] Though the life of *muntu*'s interrelatedness with the victimized in the ancestral community and how every force and created object dynamically participates in this cosmic unity isn't yet clear with Tangwa. But at least we can note that it is this cosmic unity that can guarantee a relational justice in Afrocentrism.

As understood by the Congolese and Kenyan thinkers, Afrocentrism is "cosmology," a kind of archaeology of African *gnosis*—a system of knowledge, whereby even in death, one's existence becomes part of the cosmos.[204] In this Afrocentrism, there is certainly "the recognition and acceptance of interdependence and peaceful coexistence between earths, plants, animals and humans."[205] Meaning we must quickly think anew ecologically. We can no longer distinctively separate death from life, creation from its Creator, but rather non-dichotomously recognize His presence within creatures as well as the creatures' presence in Him. This spiritual interdependent experience sacralizes cosmology—to yield into sacred cosmology.[206] I still claim that this is not an animistic or superstitious theological bioethics when I refuse undressing nature of its divinity, given that animism in the African sense, at least according to Orobator Agbonkhianmeghe's recent studies, "affirms the basic belief that all of reality is enfolded in a divine caress and animated by the life-giving breath of the Spirit. Trees, animals, and water are sacred elements, and human beings have the duty to care for and protect them. To destroy or pollute them incurs the wrath of the gods and goddesses with which they are associated and also the sanctions of the community."[207] Even when we succeed fooling ourselves or even misinforming fellow humans, we cannot successfully do this to the invisible community, comprising of our ancestors, spirits and God. Anyone violating the laws of the eco-systems

---

202. Tangwa, "Biomedical and Environmental Ethics," 388. African healers and medicine practitioners closely guard and pass on holistic codes of ethics, that are homeomorphic equivalents in other traditions or specifically, to bioethical principlism. Here homeomorphic equivalents have an implication of similar forms as Raimon Panikkar in different scholarships notes—he advocates for literal translations for words or activities without taking any univocal word-to-word translation. Panikkar, "Homeomorphic equivalents," 21–47.

203. Tangwa, *Contemporary Bioethics Problems*, 12–14, 25–26, 36, 45–46, 60.

204. African gnosis is the way Africans conceptualize the world inclusive of their rich historical past. See details in Mudimbe, *The invention of Africa*.; Creatures may sometimes openly and directly manifest a dead person on earth as her personification. See Magesa, *What is not Sacred*, 89.

205. Tangwa, *African bioethics in a Western frame*, 41, 57.

206. See Rwiza, *Environmental Ethics*, 108–9.

207. Orobator, *Religion and Faith in Africa*, 104–5.

awakens the wrath of the ancestors, which wrath will only be mutually soothed not only by her own efforts, but also by the community of her clan family as well as the community of the un-born. It becomes clear that the greatest enemy to the cosmic environment is us. So communal sanctions restrict *muntu* from threatening, hurting and mistreating mother earth.

Contrastingly, in the same dialogue with the ethics of Black Africans, we cannot claim an ethic, "just as an eco-bio-communal one may not necessarily forestall all dangers to the environment."[208] But to fix this danger, we must reiterate how the African community life is not restricted to humans or simply to living beings alone. Just like Setiloane states, "the term community is inclusive of all life (*bios*): animals, the habitat (the land), flora, and even the elements," and so "the success of life is found in the ability to maintain a healthy relationship with *all*."[209] Yes, healthy relationships with all since no creation is lifeless. Here, the quality of a healthy relational life can be fully reinforced or weakened. In the wording of Magesa, just like I have intoned in the previous sections, Black Africans perceive everything with reference to promoting or reducing life. "It is no wonder, then, that Africans quickly draw ethical conclusions about words and actions of human beings, or even of "natural" cosmological events, by asking questions such as: Does the particular happening promote life? If so, is it good, just, ethical, desirable, divine. Or does it diminish life in any way? Then it is wrong, bad, unethical, unjust, detestable."[210] In any case, we cannot talk about promoting healthy relationships in the physical world of the living community alone.

The entire three-dimensional community has life. Beyond anthropocentrism and biological propagation, even in Orobator Agbonkhianmeghe's interpretation of the African moral thought, "life represents an expansive reality and a continuum. Life is not construed only as a reality constituted by the living; it also includes the ancestors and the yet-unborn—in other words, all the constituents of nature."[211] This perspective encourages us to cultivate a commitment with all members of the three-dimensional community. It is the reason the "African Religion emphasizes the mutuality and interdependence that underline the communion and solidarity of human beings and the rest of creation."[212] And in addition to our earlier emphasis, that there is immanence of spiritual life in every creation, Magesa too emphasizes that "*all space is sacred* because its physical material appearance

---

208. Tangwa, "Biomedical and Environmental Ethics," 392–93.
209. Setiloane, "A biocentric theology and ethic," 79.
210. Magesa, *The Moral Traditions*, 77.
211. Orobator, *Religion and Faith in Africa*, 111.
212. Orobator, *Religion and Faith in Africa*, 109.

contains the invisible powers that make life possible: the world of the spirits is integrated into that of space. In space as well as time, sacrifices and offerings are made to *strengthen the community's soul.*"[213] We must listen to and feel the sacredness of the earth, the cosmos or nature, if we are to embrace the holistic rhythm of life. Current examples include international ecumenical eco-congregations that vitally promote a network of communal environment action and partnership, well knowing that the ecosystem existed before us, was loaned to us, and its integrity demands our present responsible protection. Think of the Southern African Faith Communities' Environment Institute (SAFCEI), which fosters commitment to live in sustainable harmony with the earth as custodians and co-partners of all God's gifts of creation—implying some sort of ecological spirituality with the community. Such communal spirituality with all, according to Bujo means "the whole cosmos is implicated in this communal vision. Being as relation does not only return to the three dimensions of the African notion of community, but also to being in and with the world."[214] As I identify with my deceased relative so must I identify with deforested trees.

Such an interpretation of the relationality of the communal African thought is not only restricted to the living entities that have a *telos*, but also to the *ecocentric* attitude of *live* and *let live*, i.e., even the non-living entities have a *telos* worthy of consideration, they too have a good of their own. In favoring green technology as a response to global warming—increase in the temperature of greenhouse gas levels of the Earth's atmosphere through human activities such as fossil fuel burning—the African metaphysics doesn't dichotomize between entities but remains sustainably *ecocentric*. It appreciates, like I argued already ethnoecology, an ethics of "nature-relatedness"[215] as Segun Ogungbem calls it, where Africans balance the resources of the ecosystem by appreciating the sacredness in every created object as one way of upholding the moral code of carefully using what one only needs from nature. Otherwise, since every object has moral significance, there would be need for ecological/cosmic salvation whenever a single object is tempered with, whenever a certain rhythm of life force is upset. It is only then that we shall realize the usefulness of the trees' interplay in safeguarding us and our environment from heavy winds, floods and arresting global warming—which is currently modernly pursued at some cost through removal of

---

213. Magesa, *What is not Sacred*, 58. *Emphasis is mine.*

214. Bujo, "African Thought," 117.

215. Ogungbemi, "Environmental Crisis," 330–37; Ogungbemi understands this "ethics of nature-relatedness" as a moral code to "keep a reasonable balance among the various resources constituting the ecosystem." See also the same article edited by Pojman and Pojman.

carbon dioxide from the environment. Here some countries are already expensively employing modern technology to reduce environmental carbon dioxide and hazardous anthropogenetic interferences through certificates of "carbon credits." However, in simpler ways of our semi-illiterate communities, it is only by healing mother earth through the experiences of our responsible community relationships that we can better heal the relational Other. Being eco-responsible and all the boldness it involves, demands our dependable commitment in response to the ecological violence melted on our one and only common home. We can boldly offer respectful sympathy to the Other, for instance, to nature by planting a tree for each event in one's life and promote environmental education rites among initiates. It is only when we offer respectful sympathy to the Other as a friendly attitude towards the environment, that it will continue to sustain the ecosystem with limited complaints.

It is the same expected friendly attitude of *live* and *let live* toward nature that other scientists, moral theologians, bioethicists, biomedical researchers for example, have to bear witness to. This earnest attitude of *live* and *let live* is well put in the *Kisumu declaration of moral intergrity*: "We solemnly pledge that, in carrying out this research, we will maintain the utmost respect for all participants and experimental subjects and objects, including any plants and animals."[216] The same friendly attitude of *live* and *let live* can be analogously likened to the moral friendship of solidarity espoused in the African moral thought of *muntu*'s character (personhood) as easily translatable to her external exercise of morality. It can also be associated with Aristotlean virtue ethics which is still very relevant in today's biomedical interventions. Even-though for Aristotle, *arete* (ἀρετή) reveals the sense of "moral excellence" or "goodness of character," in some commentaries on Nicomachean ethics, it is probable that ἔθος, "habit" and ἦθος, "character" (ethical, moral) are kindred words. A moral or an ethical virtue is the product of habit (ethos). In the sense, what one's habit oftentimes does, is a command of one's character. Moreover, it could be one reason why for Aristotle, intimate relationships involving daily "dealings with one another as good and trustworthy" hold persons together more than "bonds of justice" do, i.e., that moral friendships are nobler than friendships of utility.[217] And since we can virtuously actualize our external performance with

---

216. Tangwa, "Vulnerable human beings," S19; Tangwa, "Ethics Committees," 162.

217. "Civic friendship, then, looks at the agreement and to the thing, but moral friendship at the intention; hence the latter is more just—it is friendly justice. The cause of conflict is that moral friendship is nobler but friendship of utility more necessary; and men begin as being moral friends and friends on grounds of goodness, but when some private interest comes into collision it becomes clear that really they were

a well-disposed internal state, it is these moral friendships we need most (than ever before) to broaden out respectful sympathetic attitude of *live* and *let live,* not only towards human animals but broadly towards all cosmic objects, an attitude that must replace exploitative elements of *taking more than we give.* In Mahatma Gandhi's efforts to convert human hearts towards a sympathetic attitude of *live* and *let live*—being compassionate toward our fellow creatures—are still famously eulogized to date by millions of people after 75 years of his demise. To Gandhi's mind he said: "I hold that the more helpless a creature, the more entitled it is to protection by man from the cruelty of man." Gandhi was powerfully committed to nonviolent means towards creatures, emphasizing that, "the greatness of a nation and its moral progress can be judged by the way its animals are treated." In short, for a holistic approach to theological bioethics to be both particular and universally effective, it must be attractive and widely shared as a sympathetic moral life of friendship—but not of utility—toward all cosmic entities. This is the normative concept of solidarity translating from a lived social epistemology of a Black African life. It is a holistic solidarity of a respectful sympathetic communion with all creation that is not only beyond being scientific, but also neither exclusively Catholic nor African per se.

A Holistic Theological Bioethics demands Participatory Solidarity in the Principle of Life

To ground an African approach to the moral theology of holistic solidarity, I partly take up Mulago's guiding participatory principle as the normative order of "vital participation." For theological bioethics to be ecclesiologically suitable to the African church—the community as the church vehicle—beyond being simply an intellectual concept, the question of vital participation as known by Bantu Africans demands to be implicated in a true relational palaver, i.e., "dialogue and communal participation" as Mulago notes:

> Für uns ist es keine Frage, dass die lebensnotwendige Teilhabe, wie die Bantu kennen, als Grundlage einer spezifischen afrikanischen Theologie dienen kann. Um eine solche Theologie

---

different. For most men pursue what is fine only when they have a good margin in hand, and so with the finer sort of friendship too." (ἡ μὲν οὖν πολιτικὴ βλέπει εἰς τὴν ὁμολογίαν καὶ εἰς τὸ πρᾶγμα, ἡ δ' ἠθικὴ εἰς τὴν προαίρεσιν. ὥστε καὶ δίκαιον τοῦτο μᾶλλον ἐστί, καὶ δικαιοσύνη φιλική. αἴτιον δὲ τοῦ μάχεσθαι, διότι καλλίων μὲν ἡ ἠθικὴ φιλία, ἀναγκαιοτέρα δὲ ἡ χρησίμη. οἳ δ' ἄρχονται μὲν ὡς οἱ ἠθικοὶ φίλοι καὶ δι' ἀρετὴν ὄντες· ὅταν δ' ἄντικρυς ᾖ τι τῶν ἰδίων, δῆλοι γίνονται ὅτι ἕτεροι ἦσαν. ἐκ περιουσίας γὰρ διώκουσιν οἱ πολλοὶ τὰ καλόν· διὸ καὶ τὴν καλλίω φιλίαν). Aristotle, *Eudemian Ethics,* 7.1243a30–37.

zu erarbeiten, bedarf es der Geduld, des guten Willens und der Klugheit, aber auch des Mutes. Der Mittelpunkt einer solchen ekklesiologisch orientierten Theologie, davon sind wir überzeugt, wird die Erfahrung der "gemeinschaftlichen Teilhabe" sein. Dazu gehört der Symbolismus, durch den sie erfahren wird, und ihr Kulminationspunkt, der Sakramentalismus, der die heilige Menschlichkeit des Wortes weiterträgt Mittel der Verwirklichung und Manifestation.[218]

This participatory principle reinforces communion through exchange of life, firstly, between the visible and the invisible community, i.e., all created elements in these worlds, animate or inanimate, are penetrated and moved by an efficient life force—*Tous les éléments, animés et inanimés, sont pénétrés et mus par une force indifférenciée, sorte de vertu efficiente.*[219] This African anthropology—"*union vitale*"—correlates to the normative structural principle of the life force—"*Force vitale*"—a mutual harmonious interdependence of all beings with the whole, where everything in the triad-community participates in solidarity with the life force, as Ndombe portrays Mulango's theology:

> Mulago greift hierzu den Begriff der "vitalen Partizipation," der Teilhabe auf . . . Dieses partizipatorische Prinzip gilt nicht nur als Leitbild der normativen Ordnung (Solidarität im Handeln), sondern verstärkt die Gliedschaft durch die der Gemeinschaft zugrunde liegenden Erfahrung des Austausches von Leben und Lebensernegien. Darunter ist zu verstehen, dass die sichtbare Welt der Lebenden mit der unsichtbaren Welt (Gott, Ahnen, Verstobene) in Wort und Ritus symbolisch kommuniziert. Da Bleibenden und das Verbindende im Leben der Gemeinschaft artikulieren sich in der Einheit als communio. Es ist festzuhalten, dass mit dem Gendanken der "union vitale" die Besonderheit der afrikanischen Anthropologie zutage tritt . . . . Mulago erblickt im Structurprinzip der Lebenskraft (Force vitale) eine gegenseitige Interdependenz allen Seins, eine Interkommunikation alles Seienden. Weiterhim muss festgelegt werden, dass jede Handlung im Interesse der Gemeinschaft geschieht. Alle Riten sind von Hause aus Gemeinschaftshandlungen. Sie dienen

---

218. Mulago, "Bantu Strukturprinzipien der Gemeinschaft," 72.

219. Originally envisions Mulango the life force so : "Cette force vitale . . . est l'agent caché qui fait agir, qui procure la puissance et l'efficacité." Mulango, "Symbolisme dans les religions traditionnelles et Sacramentelisme," 471.

dem Zweck, das Leben jedes Einzelnen in Harmonie mit dem Ganzen zu bringen.[220]

Secondly, the participatory character of the normative structure of solidarity within the Bantu moral thought upholds that every entity (e.g., *muntu*), is not only a link in a chain of vital forces, a living link that is simultaneously affected as it also influences Others, but also a link that establishes bonds of life with the preceding generations, as Temples states: "Die Bantu können sich ja den Menschen nicht als ein unabhängiges, für sich selbst bestehendes Wesen vorstellen. Jeder Mensch, jedes Individuum ist gleichsam Glied einer Kette von Lebenskräften, und zwar ein lebendiges, beeinflussendes und beeinflusstes Glied, das die Verbindung mit den vorhergehenden Geschlechtern und den unter ihm stehenden Kräften herstellt. Das Individuum ist notwendig ein dem Clan verhaftetes Individuum."[221] Every link between members of the community as the dynamic participatory character intimates the unity of life. Here, life means "living with," "sharing," "giving" and "participating" in a strong sense of belonging thereby generating a solidary vitality of relationships. Contrary to the limited universalized principlistic ethics, the African community (triad) sense does not only include the living and the dead—the preceding generation—as we have already stated, but also the unborn, whereby the family extends to include grandparents, blood relatives, relatives by marriage, the ancestors and those to be born.[222] Moreover, when the African conception of life emphasizes communality of participation and mutual interdependence, it indistinguishably draws attention to a collective sharing of the cosmic world inclusive of the ecological natural environment, a solidarity that must not be manipulatively exploited.

220. Ndombe, *Verständnis der negro-afrikanischen (Bantu-) Weltanschauung*, 209.

221. Tempels, *Bantu-Philosophie. Ontologie und Ethik*, 67.

222. "Die partizipatorische Grundstimmung der afrikanischen Gesellschaft stellt ihren Grundcharakter dar: die Einheit des Lebens. Hierin gründet der Gemeinschaftssinn, der denn Einzelnen dazu führt, nicht sein eigenes Leben zu Leben, wohl aber das Gemeinschaftliche in inniger Verbindung mit anderen Angehörigen der Sippengemeinschaft zu fordern. Der Lebensbegriff wird freilich in einer dynamischen Dimension verstanden. Das Leben in der Gemeinschaft schließt somit die Verpflichtung ein, es durch sein Verhalten und Handeln zu bewahren und weiterzugeben. Auf diese Wiese partizipiert das einzelne Mitglied geradezu an der Fortbewegung einer inneren Erfahrung der Begegnung und Kommunikation. Leben heißt in diesem Sinne 'mitleben', 'teilhaben', 'teilgeben' und 'teilnehmen'. Da entsteht ein Wachstum an Gefühlen, das in ein starkes Zusammengehörigkeitsgefühl mündet. Dies erzeugt wiederum eine Vitalität von Beziehungen innerhalb der Familie. Letztere beschränkt sich entgegen der westlichen Auffassung nicht auf kleinen Kreis, sondern sie umfasst die Lebenden, die Toten und die noch Ungeborenen. Die Familie wird as Großfamilie begriffen. Sie schließt die Großeltern, Blutsverwandte und angeheiratete Verwandte ein." Ndombe, *Verständnis der negro-afrikanischen (Bantu-) Weltanschauung*, 155–57.

"Die Afrikanische Lebensvorstellung schließt die Kommunalität, die Partizipation und Interdependenz, d.h. gegenseitig Abhängigkeit, ein ... Der Begriff "Partizipation" deutet auf die kollektive Teilgabe und Teilhabe an der Welt und Umwelt hin, auf das Verhältnis zur Umwelt, die nicht manipuliert und ausgebeutet werden darf."[223]

Thirdly, our participation in this solidarity can increase or decrease the life force. Given human sensitivity and sensibility within this participatory solidarity, our positive contribution toward the cosmic-ecological flourishing increases integral life, while our manipulative activities toward nature crash the general flourishing of life, hence not promoting a holistic life. Life remains the most precious and sacred moral thing that is perpetually threatened by death across all cosmic nature, the Other. Like *muntu* continuously tries to identify all the enemies of life in order to defeat death, so should *muntu* likewise identify herself as the greatest enemy to the sacredness of cosmic-ecological life's flourishing. Since there is immanence of God (religious) in the innermost depth of every created Other and given that theology is our reflection on the cosmic existence in reference to our creator, the moral struggle for life and against death as mandated by the African moral thought cannot be a privilege of *muntu* only but practically cuts across the entire cosmos permeated with the creator's immanence. Such an uninterrupted interaction of life between creation makes *muntu* and the cosmos to inescapably complement each other to such an extent that no creatural force can exist without interdependence.[224] Every creation is the delicate cosmic Other, the stranger, the neighbor. So, the Other as a visiting stranger should be accorded hospitality by being welcomed without reservation as a blessing. It is only then that she participates as it were primordially in the life of solidarity. This is simply respecting the trans-ethnic vital laws of friendly relationships, even from the extended Other. The spiritual vital force in the Other can offer medicinal knowledge or beneficial skills which increase life or harmfully contaminate the community. Whenever *muntu* reinforces life for the whole group, she guards against evil. It is not only *muntu*, but also the family group has to extend relationships to other groups in order to strengthen its own group, for instance through intermarriages or pacts.[225]

---

223. Bujo, "Verantwortung und Solidarität," 795–804. Cited from Ndombe, *Verständnis der negro-afrikanischen (Bantu-) Weltanschauung*, 154–55.

224. See Bujo, *Ethical Dimension of Community*, 209.

225. See Magesa, *What is not Sacred*, 96; Kagabo, "Alexis Kagame," 238; In black African thinking, "hospitality, daily friendship, and dialogue with the members of other ethnic groups are vital laws admitting of no exception. One who is not a member of my own group is ultimately also the 'property' of the other just as I myself am, and this means that I owe him respect and esteem. Thus one is ultimately related to all human

And given that *muntu* can only guard against her own death as longer as she guards against the death of the community, the Other, an interdependence of life in which all life forces mutually interact in participatory solidarity, confirms Mbiti's African cobweb theory that "the world of forces is like a spider web, of which one single thread cannot be caused to vibrate without shaking the whole netweb."[226] In scrutinizing Mbiti's spiderweb approach in relation to both principlism as well as the African anthropology of the Other, on the one side, one can't fail to reiterate *muntu*'s inextricable needed holistic friendship with the cosmos, reminding *muntu* of assuming her participatory protective stewardship of the environment if he is to promote a life of genuine solidarity. *Muntu*'s stewardship entails a unique religious friendship visible in the holistic understanding of participatory solidarity within a pursuit of grounding a holistic approach to theological bioethics. It is in this holistic approach, as the reimagined place of relational communion, that we disconnect lived practice from abstract theological rhetoric. On the other side, theological ethics' approach is largely limited to a methodology of discursive rationality (*ratiocinatio*) without encompassing the holistic spheres of the living, living dead and those not yet born. Despite this fact, the immanence of God throughout a Bantu participatory community palaver along the world of the ancestors aids Bantu to transcendentally construct their own meaning of life inclusive of the entire cosmos, i.e., harmony is reinvigorated with all the vital forces of nature—"vital force" as "interpenetrating and permeating."[227] This is what we have described as participatory solidarity—vital participation by Mulango—which is not only relatable to the interaction between the cosmos as described in Placide Tempels' world of forces among the Bantu but also akin to the spider's web theory of Mbiti: If one touches a single strand, the entire web shivers in respectful sympathy. And this is one reason why for the medicinal palaver intended to heal *muntu*, cosmic elements like plants, minerals, wood, bones, animals are employed in the praxis to increase *muntu*'s life force.[228] This is to suggest that a sustainable harmonious interdependence is only achievable if *muntu* constantly realizes that she belongs together with the Other as part of nature and with the whole cosmos. In a nutshell, various scholarships of Tangwa, Tempels, Kagame, Bujo, Mulango, Aquinas as examined above conceive one science (*una scientia*), viz., *une science, une connaissance, une vérité autres*, that which is out there, preceding all historical new bioethical

---

beings." Bujo, *An African Ethic*, 5–6.

226. Tempels, *Bantu Philosophy*, 60.
227. See Setiloane, "A biocentric theology and ethic," 80.
228. See Bujo, *An African Ethic*,19, 55–56.

questions.[229] It is this one science as the code of life forces, though interactively net-webbed with varied forces that are hierarchically ranked back to the Creator, it guarantees holistic solidarity at the heart of theological bioethics. My argument is that every force participates in this *one friendship of solidarity* as dispensed by the Creator, with room to increase or decrease life for all—at least warranting an *ecological conversion*—with a capacious future that even when perfected holistic bioethics is being yearned for, we remain assured of the *continuous necessity for conversion*.

A HOLISTIC APPROACH TO THEOLOGICAL BIOETHICS OF ANAMNETIC SOLIDARITY WITH THE RELATIONAL OTHER

Every Creation and System immanently Speaks a Godly Language as a Sacrament

I argue that all created entities, given their inherent divinity, are understood as sacraments of the vital force that can promote or weaken moral life in an African sense. My focus is not to discuss sacramentalogy such as what we find in Karl Rahner, where the church is the "basic (or fundamental) sacrament of the salvation of humankind,"[230] while Jesus Christ is the beginning, the chief agent and the fullest manifestation of all the Sacraments, in fact he is the "primordial sacrament of salvation."[231] But when I attach divinity to all created entities, one can approximate this in some African theological scholarships.

Some African theological scholarships such as of Rwiza have emphasized an integral approach to theological bioethics but limited it, as several scholarships have done in our previous discussions, to an interrelated system where nonhuman beings are upheld as having intrinsic value.[232] But even when Rwiza is charitably interpreted, in his further emphasis that we not only "need to discover God in all the beings he has created and to find his life-giving spirit in the community of creation that they share,"[233] but also appreciate the intrinsic values in all created entities since by "caring

---

229. See Mudimbe, "An African practice of philosophy," 32.

230. Rahner, *The Church and the Sacraments*, 18.

231. Rahner, *Meditations on the Sacraments*, xv. See also Rahner, *The Church and the Sacraments*, 18.

232. See Rwiza, *Environmental Ethics*, 56.

233. Rwiza, *Environmental Ethics*, 99.

for creation implies promoting the value of creation."²³⁴ But still he remains speciesistic given that he remains inexhaustive to the fact that the aforementioned ecological wisdom in *Laudato Si'* of God, the neighbor and the earth being in a practical relationship, necessarily includes non-living objects and other cosmic collaborative systems that shouldn't be bracketed off from the communion of life since they can speak a godly language to us. In my approach, the African holistic thinking of caring for our one and only common home is non-speciesistic, given that the vital force (*amaanyi*) cuts across the tripartite-community-worlds. There is immanence of spiritual life in every material reality of the physical world that is accessible to human beings, i.e., even when spiritual beings are ontologically transcendent, they find their operative function in the symbols of material beings in the physical world of *muntu* as Kasozi has argued. On account of this inherent religiosity existent in every material reality inclusive of natural phenomena, Africans substantively believe in normatively conferring sacredness to every entity of the created universe within the hierarchical order of life. The universe is sacred since God and spiritual beings manifest their being and presence in it through various media of vital force, which ultimately confers inextricable solidarity of life to the components in the three-dimensional community or worlds or realms of the cosmic universe.²³⁵ African theological scholarships emphasize this African cosmic-ecological inextricable unity—as a sacrament—of life upon which, as a natural source, life realities are drawn from but also linked to the Creator. "This understanding of ecology, both human and environmental, resonates with a uniquely African spirituality and approach to creation in which creation acquires a sacramental dimension as a text inscribed all over with the action of God who triumphs over death to save both humanity and the cosmos."²³⁶ Meaning, all created entities morally carry along the inherent divinity as sacraments.

One illustration of this holistic nature of life can be observed in African rituals or rites. Akin to Christian religious sacraments that impart divine grace, initial rites in Black Africa, make the invisible visible to humans thereby firmly harmonizing the life of the living community in solidarity with that of all invisible life forces: "Riten machen das Unsichtbare sichtbar und stärken den Menschen, der darauf angewiesen ist, im Hier und jetzt in Harmonie mit allen Kräften und Wesen zu leben."²³⁷ Just like fairy tales,

---

234. Rwiza, *Environmental Ethics*, 171.

235. See Kasozi, *The Ntuology of the Baganda*, 56–57, see also footnote 25; Lugira, Ganda Art, 116.

236. Orobator, *Religion and Faith in Africa*, 119.

237. Sundermeier, *Das Menschenbild Schwarz-Afrikanischer Religionen*, 69–70.

proverbs, riddles, initiation rites have a holistic sapiential character and augment solidarity of life across generations and communities with God. In initiation rites, when a child is born, she is ritually accepted into her family community. She is brought into harmony with the whole of the cosmic order where each member is responsible for her upbringing[238] inclusive of those community members in the invisible realms. As a result, initiation rites symbolically aid *muntu* to make the invisible life visible in the initiate's solidary contact to social networks. In making the invisible visible, socio-religious initiation rites show intensively the solidary interrelationship of life and death between human beings, God, and the world, and how life ultimately triumps.[239] For Tossou, amid the interplay between life and death, the solidarity of life for an African as sacramentally symbolized in initiation rites triumphs. No different from Mveng, who likewise takes African rigorous initiation rites as symbolic sacramental celebrations of the great drama of life and death, where death is necessary in order to find true life: "Le rite d'initiation, dans toute l'Afrique, apparaît, comme une célébration symbolique et en quelque sorte sacramentelle du grand drame de la vie et de la mort. L'homme y apprend à mourir pour retrouver la vraie vie."[240] Initiation rites sacramentally symbolize what is invisible as a visible life reality in the three-dimensional realms of the community. Here the community is the sacrament too.

Some media reveal the invisible realities of the visible life in every *muntu*'s upbringing. Some are the therapeutic initiation rites that involve the tripartite form of the community. An example is the "Initiations spirito-somato-thérapeutiques" according to Jean de Dieu Mubaki Mvuanda. Since we already know that an illness can destroy the socio-religious harmony by distracting a holistic interaction of the spiritual, metaphysical and the physical realms, this initiation finds a medium that unifies them through the means of the healing art of the Black Africans via the physical realm to attain a mystical alliance.[241] Where moral theology has over stretched to

238. See Ndombe, *Verständnis der negro-afrikanischen (Bantu-) Weltanschauung*, 177; Mvuanda, *Initiations traditionnelles africaines*, 274–77; Bujo, *An African Ethic*, 24–27.

239. "Die Stammesinitiation als eine der wichtigsten sozio-religiösen Institutionen bei vielen Völker Afrikas, wo die Beziehung des Menschen zu Gott, von Mensch zu Mensch UND VON Mensch und Welt am intensivsten veranschaulicht wird, gehört zu den privilegierten Bereichen, wo das Symbol beheimatet ist. Sie Symbole betreffen hier vor allem das Zusammenspiel von Leben und Tod und den Triumph des Lebens über den Tod durch Neugeburt." Tossou, "Afrikanische Symbolwelt und Theologie," 47.

240. Mveng, "Structurés fondamentales de la prière négro-african." Cited from Ndombe, *Verständnis der negro-afrikanischen (Bantu-) Weltanschauung*, 180.

241. Four types of initiations according to Mvuanda: 1) "Initiations occultes ou

limits, the African theological scholarships supply a theological bioethics that holistically integrates the spiritual, metaphysical and the physical life, not only of *muntu*, but also the totality of cosmic networks of life. Given that the Creator of everything and every force is in every creature and unity of life force, without necessarily inferring that every creature is a god, "every reality contains the face of God and thus calls for respect."[242] This is the sacramental unity described by Mvuanda as a mystical alliance, an alliance where a sick *muntu*'s life is holistically re-energized not only bodily, but physically as well as spiritually in solidarity with other cosmic forces. The liturgy of rites indisputably reveals the highest form of God's immanence endorsing a cosmic sacramental solidarity that includes every creation (nature) in the three worlds:

> *One can only save oneself by saving the cosmos as well.* It is therefore, not surprising that in many African rites participation of the entire nature in liturgical action can be observed. All beings, organic and inorganic, living and inanimate, personal and impersonal, visible and invisible, act together to manifest the universal solidarity of creation. This is most important for African spirituality, because *the cosmos in its variety of forms, speaks a language which reveals the highest form of life*, namely, God, who triumphs over death. With this view, the *cosmos has a sacramental dimension* for the African person.[243]

Another distinguishing illustration is the ancestral community's role in linking the living community with the Creator. In the holistic sense, the entire cosmos as a sacrament of life, the visible community and invisible world

---

ésotériques" (secrètes): Mvunda understands the initiation rite as the entry into a secret covenant concluded between the elders, the ancestors and the initiate through the ritual action of the camp leader or a priest. 2) "Initiations spirito-somato-thérapeutiques": For the African anthropological understanding, man forms a unity. It also requires the initiation of the future priest-healer (*prêtre-guérisseur*), who sees himself as a representative or incarnated power of the invisible world (*Initiations traditionnelles africaines*, 262). This initiation guarantees entry into the status of a medicine man. The tension between modern medicine, which starts from a purely scientifically based experience, and African therapeutics, which closely follows traditional knowledge, is thus this. 3) "Initiations d'intégration sociale de la jeunesse": This form gives young person maturity and a new status of existence in a ceremonial process. It prepares them for the development of the person, including the newborn. 4) "Initiations socio-politiques et initiations professionnelles" : Socio-political and professional initiations. Mvuanda, *Initiations traditionnelles africaines*, 260–273 ; see also Ndombe gives an interpretation of Mvuanda's four rites of initiation in German, Ndombe, *Verständnis der negro-afrikanischen (Bantu-) Weltanschauung*, 174–75, footnote 545.

242. Rwiza, *Environmental Ethics*, 12.
243. Bujo, *The Ethical Dimension of Community*, 210. Italics mine.

of the ancestors imply each other in an uninterrupted interconnectedness; whereby, the ancestors link those alive to God as the original source of life. To borrow the language of Christology from an African theological scholarship, according to Nyamiti, before any encounter with Christ as our "divine Brother-Ancestor," we firstly meet our "own traditional ancestors."[244] *Ancestors as our true siblings in Christ* ("sister/brother-ancestorship")[245] remain indispensable in our efforts to establish an African approach to theological bioethics. It is within this context (from below) that Bujo likewise establishes his "proto-ancestor Christology."[246] For him, if to be truly Christian is not to be opposed to being truly African, "Jesus Christ is the Proto-Ancestor, the Proto-Life-Force, bearer in a transcendent form of the primitive 'vital union' and 'vital force.'"[247] In this sense, ancestors vitally "play a sacramental role for their surviving defendants. They are God's sacrament, for through them we are so strongly directed to the proper Giver of life, that they become for us the locus of God's revelation. *The cosmos becomes a sacrament, which brings us to notice that life comes from God. All creation speaks a godly language, assumes sacred importance*, which calls for reverence."[248] We cannot establish an eco-theological bioethics befitting an African theological scholarship outside African contextual categories, namely, cosmos viewed as a sacrament, all creation speaking a godly language, and seeing Christ as a Proto-Ancestor—the Greatest of the great ancestors.[249] To establish a bioethics not only befitting the living, but rather a proto-ancestral bioethics, Bujo rightly intones that "a truly dynamic Christianity will only be possible in Africa when the foundation of the African's whole life is built on Jesus Christ, conceived in specifically African categories."[250] Conceiving Jesus Christ in local categories is similarly put by the Ugandan theologian Emmanuel Katongole by inspiringly clarifying the holy marriage between what is counted as universal (Christianity) with what sacraments are in specific

---

244. Nyamiti, *Christ as our Ancestor*, 144.

245. Nyamiti, *Christ as our Ancestor*, 117–18; Nyamiti believes, even amidst diversities, there are enough common African ancestral beliefs in most communities, proving an ancestral-brother relationship that is hierarchically and eternally linking to God, "Christ as our Ancestor-Part I," 8–29; Nyamiti argues that there are enough similarities between Christ's brother-relationship to men and that of the African brother-ancestor to show us that the two types of relationships have the same fundamental structure, see in "Christ as our Ancestor-Part II," 1–20; "African brother-ancestorship and Christ's relationship to men," 16–19.

246. Bujo, *African Theology*, 81. See also Bujo, *Afrikanische Theologie*, 79–98.

247. Bujo, *Afrikanische Theologie*, 81, see also 83–84.

248. Bujo, *The Ethical Dimension of Community*, 19. Italics mine.

249. See Bujo, *Afrikanische Theologie*, 87–91.

250. Bujo, *African Theology*, 91.

contexts. He analogously likens it to "the politics of the incarnation, the story of God who 'dwells among us' and who invests local existence with an eternal significance."[251] Both the global and local approach necessitate a responsive local fertile soil. And it is from this local African context that God's immanence in every creation and force is understood as key.

The African understands God as immanently present in all creatures, and who sacramentally dispenses the vital force to every entity. This solidarity of the entire cosmic life is emphasized by the Baluba of Kasai in Congo Kinshasa, when they refer to each *muntu* as *Muntu-wa-Bende-wa-Mulopo*. *Bende* is the first human being and *Mulopo* is God. Each human being comes from *Bende*, as the origin of everything, while *Bende* comes from *Mulopo*. Each one of us reflects God and each should promote and discover this reflection of God in the Other. This presupposes not a community of "we" based on trust, but one based on a continued solidarity of life originating from God.[252] The solidarity of community life with God remains the antecedent to the primacy of trust. This sacramentality or African spiritual tradition cuts across all cosmic creation and it originates from God, which is analogously synonymous to God's creative breath traditionally referred to as the "breath of life" —Gen 1:2: Hebrew *ruaḥ*, Greek. πνεῦμα, Latin. *Spiritus*—the mysterious, unseen, and irresistible presence and operation of the Divine Being in all creation as the principle of life to inert matter.[253] In addition to this traditional thought of God's creative breath, the African thought of transcendence and immanence of God in the innermost depth of every creation is depicted by Kessler, a systematic theologian, who refers to this God's creative immanent breath as Creator Spiritus. "God penetrates all his creatures with his presence. Therefore, we must not treat any of his creatures (any element, plant or animal) recklessly but deal with them in a sensitive manner, with empathy and reverence. Whoever commits a fault against a creature, commits a fault against God, the Creator himself."[254] Kes-

---

251. Katongole, *The Sacrifice of Africa*, 144.

252. See Bujo, *An African Ethic*, 59–62.

253. Genesis 1:2: "And the earth was without form, and void; and darkness was upon the face of the deep. And the Spirit of God moved upon the face of the waters." The significant word is spirit, *rûaḥ*, רוּחַ. Commentaries on *the spirit of God*, show how the Hebrew Narrative of the Creation expresses the mysterious, unseen, and irresistible presence and operation of the Divine Being. It is the "breath" of God which alone imparts light to darkness and the principle of life to inert matter. The word for "wind," Heb. *ruaḥ*, Gr. πνεῦμα, Lat. *spiritus*, has been accepted as the most suitable term (literally or metaphorically) to express the invisible agency of God—the symbol of the invisible operation and influence of the Almighty. See The Cambridge Bible for Schools and Colleges Commentary.

254. Kessler, *Schöpfungsspiritualität und Schöpfungsethik*, 71. Translation from Bujo,

sler's call for an empathetic reverence towards every entity is to seek for a solution towards ecological crisis as the pressing issue of the 21st-century.

Talking of reverence towards nature is comparable to Emmanuel Asante's concept of *pan-vitalism*. Pan-vitalism commends a bio-centric theology that celebrates *reality (be-ing) as inseparable*, approving the kinship of all creatures. And because "reality is inseparable. The African is kin to all creatures—gods, spirits and nature."[255] And it is why "the whole of nature must be understood as sacred because it derives its being from the Supreme Being who is the Creator-Animator of the Universe."[256] In dialogue, other scholars interpret the bio-centric theology of pan-vitalism as eco-pneumatheology. Our century can borrow a bioethical contribution from the African approach to eco-pneumatheology—think of dogmatic bioethics or Christian ecological bioethics as Kuzipa Nalwamba and Johan Buitendag argue. They maintain that African vitalogy as a potent animating cosmic-spirit that interpenetrates all that is, without being identical to it, articulates ecological pneumatology in reference to nature and spirit underlying the interrelatedness and interconnectedness of the divine and creation, and of creation within itself. For them, vital force in every object as representative of African relational ontology and cosmology is construed as *presence* within which divine action takes place, appropriates the Spirit's active work in non-interventionist terms, in terms of contributory efficacy and interrelationship within that *presence*.[257] This Creator-cosmic Spirit firmly reiterates our emphasis at the beginning, not only of how the Bantu wisdom teaches an inherent gradual growth of being, which is in a precise dialogue with what the Catholic doctrine of Grace teaches, but also teaches how the Divine-creative-redemptive-presence throughout creation—no creation is lifeless—attunes us to a holistic unreserved renewal of our relationship with every created object. This view is analogous to the popular theological notion of *Creatio continua* in which, not only the creation's continuous existence, but also the conservation (*conservatio*) of all creatures and systems of life, is contingent on the active godly presence, and in which continuous relationship of conservation, we are part and unceasingly invited by God in this relational progressive work as co-creators. Stressing binaries between creation and the Creator, humans and nonhumans are beyond an operative intimate relationship of bondedness between God and nature in the African worldview. We cannot therefore help but rather reawaken our holistic

---

The Ethical Dimension of Community, 215.

255. Asante, "Pan-Vitalism in Africa," 290.

256. Asante, "Pan-Vitalism in Africa," 292.

257. Nalwamba and Buitendag, "Vital force."; Sakupapa, "Spirit and ecology," 422–30; Tempels, *Bantu-Philosophie. Ontologie und Ethik*, 27–30.

sensibilities and embrace an integral attitude of sympathetic respectful love towards every created object and all systems in all our pursuits of bioethics.

To realize holistic solidarity, each created creature is contingent on the Other, while disharmony is implied in injuring of one's relationship with the Other. This gives an impression, that in grounding an African approach to eco-theological bioethics, the sacramentality of the cosmos presupposes that for holistic solidarity to be achieved, human beings must bear in mind that they are automatically infringed with a theological commitment towards creation, while concomitantly entitling creation an ethical religious right to be respected with sympathy. Given that Bantu do not think in "either/or"—ancestors or descendants—but rather in "both/and"—holistic and non-dualistic—constructs, their holistic religious thinking finds a dialogue in the thinking of *Laudato Si'*, which suggests an integrative approach, for instance in ecological ethics, since "we are faced not with two separate crises, one environmental and the other social, but rather with one complex crisis which is both social and environmental" (LS 139). This analogously suggests that a genuine holistic thought wouldn't dichotomize between a universalized ethos and customary ethos, environmental and social, anthropocentric and cosmic bioethics, secular and religious, the living and living dead, given that it is basically one religious unity and therefore no need for highlighting bioethical concerns of the descendants without handling concerns of the ancestors.

At the apex of our search for an approach to theological bioethics is God from whom all other entities and forces derive their sacramentality. Since an African holistic thinking is religious, therefore an African approach to theological bioethics cannot be without God as the dispenser of the vital force to all other entities in the hierarchical order of life. It is one reason "the Supreme Being (*Katonda*), God, is believed to be 'the ultimate explanation of the genesis and substance of man and all things'. The religious relationship between the magical force, God, and Spirits is hence described as: *Verhältnis zu Einer Überlegenheit.*"[258] Though we should note, that in this spiritual or religious interrelationship,[259] humans are incapacitated to approach the

---

258. Sempebwa, *Reality of a Bantu*, 57–58; see details in Tempels, *Bantu Philosophie*, 30; for a deeper and specific explanation of categories by different studies and their relationship to each other, see Lugira, *Ganda Art*, 5; Mbiti, *African Religions and Philosophy*, 16; Roscoe, *The Baganda*, 271–73; Kagame, *La Philosophie bântu-rwandaise de l'Être*, 107–8.

259. "Es ist einerseits eine Macht vorhanden, die dem Menschen überlegen, der gegenüber er Objekt ist. Andererseits existiert diese Macht nicht für sich beziehungslos. Sondern der Mensch steht in irgendeinem Verhältnis, sei es positiver, sei es negativer Art, zu ihr. In diese Definition sind auch die Momente des Aktiven und des Passiven, die in allen religiösen Vorstellungen miteinander verbunden sind, eingeschlossen. Das

absolute Being alone. Firstly, when an African speaks more often about her fellow *muntu* rather than about God; it is believed, as *muntu* pays heed to the moral wellbeing of a fellow *muntu* to whom she closely interacts with, she subsequently pleases God and so "life is promoted"; and likewise, a *muntu* who disrupts another's wellbeing precisely offends God and thereby damages the entire community since "life is not promoted." Secondly, when Africans invoke spirits or pray more often to ancestors/fore-parents than to God, it is the role attached to the mediator that must be significantly remembered.[260] The holistic life between the visible and invisible moral communities references significantly to the architect of vital force, who is God. This operative immanence of God in everything convinces Black Africans to even attach religiosity to their daily moral life, like their farming welfare as proving not only the prime awareness of God's providence but also their main motive for petitioning God.

It is also why verbal spiritual invocations, on the one hand as positive outward forms of the vital force, are oriented toward good wealth and health of the people, increase in good garden harvests like crops and animal numbers, fertility of fields and more children, while on the other hand as guarding against negative outward forms of the vital force, protect *muntu* from enemies and danger, war and unhappiness, etc. So, for *muntu*, God's protection and guardianship of morality is not only evident in prayers expressed in Bantu names, but it is holistically evident also in bidding farewell, greetings, salutations, blessings, proverbs, verbal spiritual invocations, etc. Concrete examples among Ganda include: i) The personal name Kyalimpa, which means, "whatever He (God) will offer me"; ii) The proverb *Kyaterekera omulamu, tekivunda*, literally means, "what God destines for the living cannot rot a way"; iii) The farewell verse *Katonda akuume*, implies the wish: "let God guard you."[261] Even in Rwanda one bids farewell to somebody by the words *Imana ikulinde*, i.e., "May God protect you!" The immanence of the spiritual in the material and all systems of life already gives us reason why a number of African ethnic communities believe that numerous moral norms come directly from God and He is the topmost guardian of the moral law and of morality in general.[262] Commonly in Rwanda and Burundi, the

---

Passive ist das Erfahren der Überlegenheit, das Aktive das Verhalten des Menschen." Damman, *Die Religionen Afrikas*, 3–4, see more on pp. 7 and 106.

260. See Bujo, *The Ethical Dimension of Community*, 17–18; Bujo, *An African Ethic*, 1–2.

261. Kasozi, *The Ntuʹology of the Baganda*, 95–96, see also footnotes 8 and 9; see also Tokumboh, *Salvation in African Tradition*, 23 and Byabazaire and Waliggo, "Incarnating Christianity in Uganda," 113.

262. The theonomous view is outstanding amongst the Maasai of east Africa, Gikuyu

noun *Imana* refers to the creator deity, giving rise to numerous theophorous names like "Ndikumana," I'm with God; "Nzeyimana," only god is my hope; "Habyarimana," God alone gives birth or begets (not humans), "Hakizimana," God heals. Congolese and Ugandans name "Byaruhanga," meaning "God's property."

In numerous contexts, *muntu*'s daily moral life questions, without imposing any coherences, are not only practically religiously contextual—not oriented toward abstract principles—but also equally anthropocentric, cosmic, and theocentric. Agbonkhianmeghe Orobator testifies from his own experience that "knowing or encountering God is not a monopoly of religious and theological experts. As Africans, we know God from birth; we grow up in an environment filled with many experiences of God, and we live in communion with many spiritual beings and entities. We are never isolated from faith; we share a common space with God, the supreme Being."[263] So from childhood, *muntu* practices theological bioethics in daily palavers, which can either be symmetrical or asymmetrical. These palavers necessarily entail a life of an anamnetic solidarity since it is not possible to overlook the collective experiences of ancestors, the victimized of history and the "remembering" dimension of the word.[264] The anamnetic dimension already suggests God as the architect of vital force which permeates all life realities, embracing a *theonomous* view of an African approach to theological bioethics.

The theonomous view of an African approach to theological bioethics can also be understood with a modern practical illustration. In retrospect, if only the reader would recall the disuniting consequences from the partition of Africa at the Berlin Conference of 1885 and slave trade, numerous African clan-family communities were scattered without their own free will. The deformed boarders separated clan-family members hence one reason why Africans hardly spoke of nations in the Western sense, but of the artificially created states by their colonizers. As the rightful belonging of families was disrupted—and still being disrupted today due to contemporary continental immigrations—so was the disruption of the rightful graves of *muntu*'s ancestors. For *muntu* to stick to her historical natal moral wisdom in our current boundary situations, in which everything has spiritual life, in case of death and burial outside one's native place—*muntu* is buried to her

---

of Kenya, Akamba of Kenya, African Pygmies, Banyarwanda of Rwanda, Barundi of Burundi, Baganda of Uganda, Akan of Ghana and Ivory Coast, Bassa of Cameroon, Bahema and Bashi and Banande and Bakonzo of Democratic Republic of Congo, just to mention a few. See Bujo, *The Ethical Dimension of Community*, 17–18, 25.

263. Orobator, *Theology Brewed in an African Pot*, 140.

264. See Bujo, *An African Ethic*, 2,161–62.

ancestral land— somebody-parts are transported to the native birthplace for burial. Others remove some soil from the grave and bring it to the family or lineage of the deceased, which family "buries" it on the ancestral native soil of the deceased. This bit of the taken-earth bonds the deceased person to the natal home and keeps the clan-family-community bonding alive proving a dynamic anamnetic spiritual solidarity.[265] It is very clear how an African is attached to her natal treasuries of wisdom which cannot lose the theonomous character that is further associated with the palaver.

This suggests how impactful theological bioethics in the African World can only result from a theological ethical palaver that appreciates every component and force of life of African realities as having divine life. Indeed we need a dialogic palaver (LS 199) with modern sciences and local religious realities—from church leaderships to the lowest local citizen—precluding any monopolies or absolutized thoughts. If we could for example make use of the palaver language that guides African ecclesiology, viz., that is the word, the globalized bioethical principlism should see the word as too comprehensive to be dictated by one single cultural thought. Moreover, if and only if the universalized theological ethics was to impose its own interpretation exclusively without the relevant localized theological ethical palaver, this would fail to do justice to the localized meaning of the word, which is comprehensively greater for Africans in contextual efficacy than the universalized perspective.[266]

Among the recent expressions of the palaver in pursuance of the *synodal spirit* was the recent international theological congress in Nairobi, Kenya, which took place July 18-23, 2022. According to the Vatican correspondent, Christopher White, the Pan-African Catholic Congress on Theology, Society and Pastoral Life, made explicit the African proverb that "until the lions have their own historians, the history of the hunt will always glorify the hunter." The lions (Africans) are not only writing their own history today in their pursuit of a synodal spirit (walking together), but they are shaping their own future as well as that of the global Catholic Church, given that, although in 1900, an estimated 2 million Catholics lived on the African continent, today, the number stands approximately at 236 million, necessitating a broader palaver. In this congress, the lions viewed an inclusive *palaver as synodality in action*. In the spirit of synodality, all of us are called from our different walks of life to get seated at the same palaver table since no one can be saved alone in the African sense—the congress frequented the ancestral palaver of wisdom that "if you want to walk fast,

---

265. See Bujo, *The Ethical Dimension of Community*, 154-55.
266. See Bujo, *An African Ethic*, 156-59.

walk alone. But if you want to walk far, walk together."[267] The broad and large universal ears of the approach to bioethics ought to create an appropriate mutual theological discerning palaver suitable for a pluralistic cultural environment, otherwise the universalized theological bioethics will forever remain missionary bioethics since it continues to assume that whichever moral concerns worrying the principlistic West ought to equally worry the African world! I will try to illustrate with further practical examples, though not exclusively, a holistic approach to theological bioethics founded on an anamnetic solidarity perceptible in Bantu political life, dances, attachment to land, marriage and sexual life as well as their practice of medicine and reconciliation.

A Theological Bioethics Relevant to Muntu's "own" Religious Rhythm

To reiterate in a lay person's language what an anamnetic holistic thinking entails for a Black African, I will demonstrate further with three simple examples: Political leadership, African dances and land ownership. Our discussed perspective of a holistic unity clearly confirms that it is impossible to define *muntu* in purely secular or purely religious terms, since she is both at once. Where one of these two dimensions is lacking, one can no longer speak of *muntu qua* human person; and likewise, one cannot separate "autonomy" from "theonomy" in an African genuine reality as it is in principlism. *Muntu*'s dynamic social realities necessarily unify the visible and the invisible life, i.e., they invoke the presence of the ancestors as true living and physically present participants through various community palavers that accompany each practice. *First*, in the political sphere, if Kabaka or chief ceases to holistically communicate the vital force as a political spiritual mediator between the visible living community of his people and invisible community of the living dead as we hinted on it already, he despises the ancestors since he fails to do justice to the concerns of the living dead, and thus damages the entire community in its triple dimension of the living, the dead, and those not yet born.[268] To the contrary, in recent instances where neo-colonizers are inattentive or in cases where the colonizers abstracted this

267. Addressing the congress via video, Cardinal Mario Grech, secretary general of the synod, told participants in Nairobi, "The religious, cultural, philosophical traditions of Africa have such rich resources, examples and values and practices that really can correlate with the concept of synodality." "The synodal spirit is alive in Africa," he said, "rooted in the diverse and inculturated ways of being the church in local contexts." White, "Synodal spirit is alive in Africa."

268. See Bujo, *An African Ethic*, 95–96.

religious dimension, making it difficult for Chiefs or Kings to intermediate the concerns of the ancestors and their living descendants, chaos arose. This can partly explain the onset of the post-colonial genocides—episodes of tragic mass violence—and conflicts in many African states like Rwanda, Burundi, Democratic Republic of Congo, Nigeria, Namibia and Sudan. In the recent 6 chaptered book, *A History of Genocide in Africa* authored by an expert in African history Timothy J. Stapleton, he clarifies how in numerous African regions where genocides have happened, there seems to have been an identical historical imposition of a colonial outlook which was quite inapt for the local religious settings.[269] Such genocides would never have happened in a purely genuine religious Black African context, besides these states being highly Christianized or Islamized like we mentioned of the Rwanda genocide. *Second*, any true African dance and music, even liturgical dances as part of religious liturgies for example during offertory among African Catholics, reveal the interconnectedness of life, which to an African makes solidarity manifest itself anamnetically:

> Within the framework of the idea of *memoria*, dance is no mere choreography in which human beings reveal their ability and talent. Rather, it is a language that intends to communicate the deeper dimension of the *total reality of life*. To see a kind of folkloristic beauty in African dance is to fail to grasp the depth of the transcendental experience which is expressed by the person dancing. An African dances his own life in every existential events: births, marriage, and death, the new moon, political events, and so on. A dance can tell about pain and suffering, about joy and sadness, about love and thankfulness. It is always a *cantatory narrative poiēsis*, in solidarity with the entire fellowship.[270]

An African dance is a holistic narrative that recreates the present life anew in solidarity with the historical collective experiences ("memoria"), consequently bringing to life transcendental experiences that are in totality with the entire reality of *muntu*'s life. The *third* straightforward example is land which is not only the root of *muntu*'s existence, but it binds *muntu* with her departed clan relatives, that is, it joins the visible living with the invisible realms anamnetically as we have just indicated in the preceding section. The modern era (*mulembe*) unites Bantu, the spirits and God plus their cosmic-ecological environment of *bintu*—inanimate and animate entities.

---

269 Stapleton, *Genocide in Africa*, in the 6 chapters about six African states (11–156), more specially 1–10 and 157–76.

270. Bujo, *An African Ethic*, 40. Italics mine.

The distant past—*emirembe n'emirembe*—supplies securely the foundational moral codes to the modern era binding together all Bantus and all *bintus* i.e., all *muntu* forces and all *kintu* forces, so that all these forces are continuously revitalized anew within *muntu*'s actual time force. And since time defines experience and space for Bantu, they are very much inseparably tied to their land. The land provides them with the roots of existence as well as binds them to their departed, who are buried in their land and ultimately earning them an ineradicable burial right to their historical ancestral land. Thus land (place) anamnetically signifies Bantu expected future, their modern dynamic present as well as their experienced past, a holistic ontological rhythm unifying their daily life.

To create some burial space on land, in the first instance, it is the reason parts of the "clan land" is not used for subsistence, but as a common burying ground—taken up by graves. Mair is right to observe how the Ganda *butaka,*—part of land to which all clan members have rights—especially any member of the clan may claim the right of burial.[271] The *butaka* rights are not individual rights but rather common rights, absolute and so collectively held by the members of the clan (*bataka*). Even the Kabaka—*Sabataka*, the senior landowner who is the king—cannot contravene these rights otherwise the King would be disrupting the anamnetic holistic rhythm of spiritual guardianship of the clan ancestors, so to speak the lineage continuity and solidarity.[272] In other instances, graves of the departed relatives are also on people's own private land. Here graves justify not only as evidence for "long undisturbed occupation," but also this land acquires the same form of status and rights as the *butaka*.[273] As no one can contravene burial rights on one's ancestral ground in order not to disrupt one's anamnetic spiritual solidarity with the ancestral world, likewise no one can contravene the extension of human rights to encompass the dead in the African world. In both local practical examples mentioned briefly, African dances and attachment to land, one cannot separate *muntu*'s entire life from her religious/spiritual attachment if one is to discern her holistic approach to theological bioethics. Thusly, we have to ground a holistic approach to theological bioethics relevantly fitting *muntu* in her own simple interpretation of her own relational rhythm of life that extends beyond the clan family, tribal nation and death, i.e., holistic solidarity. What is religiously and relationally good is what is ethically worth to pursue, and what is ethical is what promotes solidarity.

---

271. See Mair, "Baganda Land Tenure," 187–89.

272. See Mair, *An African People*, 156–57, 162–64; Roscoe, *The Baganda*, 134; Sempebwa, *Reality of a Bantu*, 195–98.

273. Mair, *An African People*, 164; Sempebwa, *Reality of a Bantu*, 199.

Holistic Theological Bioethics Founded on Anamnetic Solidarity: Example of Sexuality

The Indissolubility and Immortality of African Marriage: Eschatological Character

Oluganda nkovu terugwa kumubiri: Solidarity is an indelible scar; it can never be permanently lost.

BAGANDA PROVERB

Referencing a holistic anamnestic solidarity of the African thought, I defend an eschatological moral character of an African marriage as indissoluble and immortal in contrast to principlistic Western marriages. An African marriage is covenantal given that it embraces holistically the triad-life of the community. However, theological bioethics that simply emphasizes principlism becomes irrelevant since it fails to take cognizant of an anamnetic character of an African ethics.[274] Such an anamnetic thinking has already stressed a holistic unity of "profane" (as secular) and "sacred" —as religious or spiritual—also explainable in the morality of an African marriage. In the African sense, for the consummation of marriage life shared between husband and wife, God and the ancestors must be religiously (spiritually) and hierarchically included. For an African marriage to be religiously and hierarchically inclusive—with view of attaining full humanity—it cannot simply be a "contract" but a "covenant" that binds the husband and the wife into the solidarity of the tripartite community, with an obligatory covenantal vital force which transcends the living to incorporate the coming generation. It is one reason Black Africans presently pay more attention to covenantal weddings as constituting a marriage force *than* contractual civil or ecclesiastical weddings.[275] Analogously, even if we have a universal moral imperative as human beings, that of sympathetic impartiality, we cannot rule out its diverse applications in different cultural contingencies. This is no different to the fact that just as all humans have a language capacity as one of their biological constitutions universally, different cultural contingencies remain with particular language derivations of their own. Even when we could undoubtly cite marriage as a *cultural universal*, its contextual form in various particularistic arrangements remains culturally colored. This distinctive understanding is comparable to Tangwa's assertion, whereby "in Western

---

274. See Bujo, *An African Ethic*, 39.
275. See Bujo, *An African Ethic*, 96.

cultures, marriage is generally understood as a union between two individuals ("a man and a woman?") to the *total exclusion of all others*, till death do them part, while in African cultures it is understood not in terms of *exclusion* but rather *inclusion* of many others."[276] Here a covenantal marriage is identified with inclusion of the extended lineage while a contractual marriage is identified with exclusion. More concretely, the differences can be illustrated as follows.

In contrast to fixed contractual arrangements, a traditional African wedding is a dynamic covenant that lasts a *whole lifetime*, a commitment that goes beyond the decisions of the visible two partners to include the decisions and program of life of the entire living clan fellowship and invisible community.[277] This means, principle based Western marriages are instituted contractually between two autonomous individuals,[278] with their autonomous programs, while African marriages are covenantally (alliance) sealed between two generational communal families, two broader clan lineages, without excluding the worldly and otherworldly communities holistically in the moral accountability of the "marital discourse" or "the intended marriage to be consummated." Since it is a holistic alliance, homage must be paid to everyone including the ancestors who founded communal norms so that the intended union can be blessed. In several circumstances in east Africa, civil law demands consent of the extended family community before recognizing a marriage as legally binding. To protect tenaciously the community common responsibility, an African attitude of holistic anamnetic solidarity guarantees an enduring moral support towards the spouses in ups and downs, better or worse, rises and falls, come rain or come shine. Besides we note uniquely that African marriages are in community stages (processes) while principle based church and civil marriages take place at one point in a time. Although principle-based marriages can cease to exist at one point in time just as they began at one point in time through a contract; a holistic African thinking understands a generational guaranteed marriage union as indissoluble.[279] Regrettably, several Christian and civil marriages contracted in disregard of the holistic anamnetic solidarity of the African

---

276. Tangwa, *African bioethics in a Western frame*, 148.

277. See Bujo, *Ethical Dimension of Community*, 33.

278. Here marriage is depicted as an individualistic contractual agreement of two partners by their own selves alone. We can base this claim on western principlism, depicted in paragraph 2 of Article 16 of the Universal Declaration of Human rights, "marriage shall be entered into only with the free and full consent of the intending spouses." *Universal Declaration of Human Rights* at 70: 30–Article 16.

279. See Bujo, *An African Ethic*, 18–19; Bujo, *Ethical Dimension of Community*, 94, 152–53.

understanding of marriage end up prematurely. Studies of Kisembo, Magesa and Shorter prove that marriages were more stable in Black Africa, like Uganda of 1950s, than it is turning out recently. The modern concubinage (trial marriage) was also unknown but became something normal recently in competition to monogamous Christian marriages.[280] We can thus qualify the African understanding of marriage in an approach to ethics as embracing a holistic anamnetic solidarity of life, a covenant between the tripartite community that indissolubly lasts a whole lifetime.

An integral stage of marriage, that holistically proves the norm of an anamnetic solidarity in the African ethics, is the payment of dowry (*le vesement de la dot*), whereby it does not only seal the physical and spiritual bonds between the two-family lineages, but also socially guarantees a stabilized life of the consummated marriage: "... ainsi le gage est un être d'union. *Il signifie la solidarité de deux familles,* puis il scelle les liens physiques et spirituels enter elles. Socialement, le vesement de la dot es une garantie de la stabilité du mariage."[281] Since *muntu* desires a stabilized life, he endeavors shielding against tension between life and death by pursuing an anamnetic solidarity that is realizable in a marriage bond. The theological scholarship of Bujo reveals that the communicative-fellowship-character of the act of dowry is one of the clearest examples of the meeting point of anamnetic solidarity—it is the locus not only where the departed, the living and those yet to be born hierarchically meet, but also all forces of the relational ontological rhythm of life are repeated, renewed and revitalized (like time, the whole drama of history, and so on), as in, every force actively participates as an actress and not just as a mere spectator.[282] A full participation of the three-dimensional community promotes solidarity not dramaturgically but holistically while difficultly abandoning one's active role which conflicts with the intended norm of a lasting solidarity as coded by the ancestors. A lasting solidarity suggests an indissolubility of the marriage covenant which lies in the symbolic character of *le Gage de l'alliance ou la dot* (the pledge of the alliance or dowry) as laid down in Ndombe's interpretation of Mulago. Marriage is indissoluble because the sacred character of *le Gage de l'alliance ou la dot* signifies a unified communion of the two families: "Darüber hinaus wird die Ehe als ein unauflöslicher Bund betrachtet. Diese Überzeugung gründet darin, dass die so auf die Gemeinschaft angelegte Ehe die Einheit der Familien herbeiführt." Ihren symbolischen Charakter, bemerkt Mulago, erlangt

---

280. See Kisembo and Magesa and Shorter, *African Christian Marriage*, 71–72.

281. Mulago, *L'union vitale bantu*, 54–55. Italics mine.

282. See Mbiti, *African Religions and Philosophy*, 133; Bujo, *An African Ethic*, 34–36; Bujo, *Ethical Dimension of Community*, 103.

die Ehe im afrikanischen Kontext durch die Mitgift ("le Gage de l'alliance ou la dot") die als Symbol erhält einen sakralen Charakter in diesem Bund. Es wird zum Bindeglied."[283] However the symbolic character of marriage isn't fulfilled through money. We need to distinguish between bride price as money and the intended significance of bride wealth or dowry. The symbol of the *Mitgift* (*le Gage de l'alliance ou la dot*) is a dowry gift or bride-wealth but not money as bride price. Bride price as money isn't accepted because it doesn't express the sacramental dimension as the normal custom of offering cows and goats. Money as dowry would turn a person into a mere thing. The cow (dowry) symbolizes the life force as a real sacrament.[284] The symbol of life as dowry (*Mitgift*) does not only solemnize marriage but also appreciates and pledges commitment that one—Bantu groupings are patrilineal while others are matrilineal—will be treated well or compensating for her loss in her family:

> The custom of presenting a gift to the bride's people . . . is an important institution of African societies. It is a token of gratitude on the part the bridegroom's people to those of the bride, for their care over her and for allowing her to become his wife. At her home the gift "replaces" her, reminding the family that she will leave or has left, and yet she is not dead. She is a valuable person not only to her family but to her husband's people. At marriage she is not stolen but is given away under mutual agreement between the two families. The gift elevates the value attached to her both as a person and as a wife.[285]

The symbol of the dowry pledges an African marriage a sacred character of a continued *lasting survival* of the family community life. The lasting character (indissolubility) of the marriage sacrament serves to extend a unifying link to the living and ancestral relatives; whereby unless one has close relatives to remember her after death, like a flame she would simply vanish out of human existence.[286] Procreation and offsprings are central and every adult's desire, man or woman. African scholarships insist on the great value attached to procreation, explaining why, just like fatherhood is believed to be the plenitude of manhood, similarly,

> . . . for African women in particular, motherhood is considered the plenitude of womanhood and, in spite of increasing Western

283. Ndombe, *Verständnis der negro-afrikanischen (Bantu-) Weltanschauung*, 235, footnote 782.
284. See Bujo, *Ethical Dimension of Community*, 98.
285. Mbiti, *African Religions and Philosophy*, 140.
286. See Mbiti, *African Religions and Philosophy*, 26.

influences, very few African women indeed would willingly and voluntarily accept to remain childless under any putative set of circumstances.

In Africa the idea of a childless marriage or of marriage for mere companionship and sexual gratification, accepted without question in other places and cultures, is one that, if not totally absent, is considered to be a veritable oddity. In Africa, infertility and childlessness are the main causes of breakup of marriages as well as the justification for the widespread practice of polygamy and sundry other forms of marriage.[287]

One cannot talk of an eschatological solidarity in the African sense of a holistic anamnetic solidarity without leaving behind offsprings. Marriage plays a decisive role in African moral eschatology as Bujo summarizes: "This idea is based on the eschatological concept that the individual and the entire community in their double dimension of the visible and the invisible world can only survive in the offspring. Whoever dies childless is forgotten and endangers the clan community whether he wills it or not."[288] As a prophylactic medicine against eschatological moral setbacks, it is why Black Africans argue against lifelong spouseless-ness and celibacy because one withdraws from the community anamnetic solidarity with the Other hence offending against the law of promoting life abundantly which is visible in the celibate's unwillingness to share in the growth of life biologically.[289] Failure to get married means, one has rejected the corporate community; and in return, the corporate community has rejected her as cursed.[290] One is not willing to grow in healthy humaneness (personhood) since she is not willing to positively contribute to the community growth and its social capital. However, if *muntu* is to pursue the immortality of personhood without losing focus on the future eschatological solidarity with the other living-dead of the family, it must be everyone's earnest responsibility to get married so as to promote, not simply life, but promote it *abundantly* by having children—progeny as future health insurance among Kom people—who would survive her in personal immortality.[291] The underscored eschatological

---

287. Tangwa, "Assisted conception: an African perspective," 300.
288. Bujo, *Ethical Dimension of Community*, 33.
289. Bujo, *An African Ethic*, 7.
290. Mbiti, *African Religions and Philosophy*, 133.
291. Tangwa claims that "having children is still the main reason for marriage and a good reason for polygamy." Tangwa, "Cameroon," 946; Mbiti, *African Religions and Philosophy*, 26; Procreation is viewed as security, health insurance, and source of financial help among old age in Kom proverbs: The first states: *Wayn nin ghi inkà mi id- viyn*, which means, "a child is one's firewood or pension at old age." The second states: *nji*

hope crowns *muntu* as immortal insofar as she survives in her living descendants. It is in accent to this that Alexis Kagame originally developed his idea that, even though *muntu*'s body dies, in reality it survives, because it is transmitted to the descendants through procreation.[292] The bioethics of immortality—eschatological character—of *muntu* cannot be fathomed without a chain of living progenies. It is by fulfilling the obligation of procreation that *muntu* will be, not only sure of a future health insurance through caring descendants who survive her, but also prepare for her personal immortality. The eschatological character pertinent to the indissolubility of the marriage bond and *muntu*'s immortality as far as she is survived by descendants, distinguishes the African moral thought from the principlistic Western conception of marriage. Since Africans take marriage to promote life and last for eternity, even marriages to in-laws after a spouse's death aren't against this moral idea of indissoluble solidarity, since one remains faithful by maintaining fidelity to one's family community as a living social sacrament.[293] Moreover, since the marriage union is sealed through the gift of dowry—whose absence is a sign of prostitution and whose presence is a symbolic sign of constitution of persons with the cosmic reality—in case of death, the dowry is not necessarily returned as if it were a bride-price, because the existing alliance eschatologically continues.[294] Besides, a total separation, which is an equivalent of proper divorce is rare in any genuine African setting (as we shall substantiate more later). The Bashi, for example, categorically stress to their offsprings desiring any marriage blessing that "marriage is a life-long affair. There is only one son-in-law and one wife. A son who respects his parents marries only once and never twice. He is son-in-law of exactly one person."[295] An African marriage is understood to be indissoluble and eschatologically immortal, constituting a holistic anamnetic solidarity with the Other.

Contrarily, trial, civil as well as Christian marriages are short of the indelible eschatological moral character present in African marriages since they don't anamnetically incorporate the two extended lineages of both couples into an indissoluble solidarity with the invisible community. In any

dvinà yi nyong wayn, which means, "when a sheep grows old, it sucks the breast fed by its offspring." What these proverbs mean is that one must take good care of his/her progeny because they are one's source of security (insurance), health and financial sustenance at old age. Mbih, "Foundation of kom proverbs," 15.

292. See Kagabo, "Alexis Kagame," 235–36; Kagame, "Le Fondement ultime de la morale bantu," 233.

293. See Bujo, *An African Ethic*, 16.

294. See Bujo, *The Ethical Dimension of Community*, 97.

295. Bujo, *The Ethical Dimension of Community*, 96.

case, the indelibility is guarded in the sense that even *death does not dissolve the lifelong covenantal force of marriage* established between these two lineages as represented by the covenantal union of the two members. Since death cannot dissolve the dynamism of the vital force of marriage, it cannot likewise disunite the profane from the sacred, as well the visible and the invisible community, a stance that still confers the said indelible moral character even beyond death in the African holistic anamnetic thinking. Indeed, different studies support this indissoluble solidarity to last. For example, the linguistic relationship between the Luganda word *kufa* (to die) and the verb *fuula* (transform or change). On death, *omuntu afuula bufuuzi mbeera gyabaddemu, naye taggweerawo ddala*, meaning that *muntu* simply transforms or changes her state but does not perish, viz., one remains a *muntu* but in another form. When Baganda say *gundi afudde* (someone has died), they are indicating *gundi afudde embeeraye* (someone has changed her state). In attestation, some proverbs prove how we are just reserved on burials after death: *Kitaka talya atereka buteresi* (the earth does not eat but stores or puts in reserve or keeps). And so, after burial, one would say: *Munaffe tumuterese bulungi*, meaning, we have "stored," "reserved" our friend well.[296] Death cannot therefore dichotomize *muntu*'s life, the profane from what is sacred, the secular from what is religious. Both are in a solidarity. So, marriage and death indelibly incorporate an anamnetic holistic moral character suggesting no life dichotomies like in principle based Western perspectives. The Baganda wisdom counsels us that *oluganda nkovu terugwa kumubiri*; meaning, solidarity is an indelible scar, which can never be permanently lost. In that, the eschatological character pertinent to the indissolubility and immortality of the marriage bond, suggests an anamnetic solidarity even after death in the African approach to theological bioethics, distinguishing the African moral thought from the principlistic Western conception of marriage.

Polygamous Marriages Promote Holistic Solidarity than other aspects of Sexuality

Authorized polygamous marriages in Africa have always been confronted with monogamous settings as the only reasonable forms of marriage. The official teaching of the Catholic church, as assertively implemented by missionaries, has always preconditioned polygamists to dismiss all their spouses except *retain one of them after the others* before receiving the sacrament of baptism. By forcing a spouse to dismiss the first or second official partner in

---

296. Nsimbi, *Olulimi Oluganda*, 11; Sempebwa, *Reality of a Bantu*, 67.

favor of one of them,[297] the Church precisely encourages divorce contrary to African morality that cannot abandon the sanctity of any legitimate and authorized marriage either socially or religiously[298] since marriage guarantees an anamnestic solidarity. The African moral thought looks at dismissing a legitimately married spouse as precisely suppressing *muntu*'s dignity besides clearly looking at Western principlistic thoughts as plainly imposed on other cultural settings as pure Christianity without caring if they stifle the local forms of thought.[299] Given that adultery is always and everywhere morally condemned, which basically suggests a minimum moral code, in African contexts where every marriage is sealed through the gift of dowry, polygamy is as legitimate with the same intensity as it is in monogamous Christian settings, and adultery is as equally condemned in Africa as it is in other settings. But when the other wives who were in the polygamous marriage are sent away without hearing them out, in order to baptize the once polygamous husband, the church's response towards polygamy seems as if only restricted to the reception of sacraments in relation to what canon law stipulates without being cautious of their extended relational pastoral consequences, especially to the vulnerability of the dismissed wives in the community.

If we refer back to African Anthropology that is not limited to monogamous marriages, the justification remains that the second or third legitimately married wife remain legitimate spouses, and the husband their legitimate husband, and it follows that the husband's infidelity to his second and third wife—likewise their infidelity to him—is just as much adultery as is his infidelity to his first wife. What counts as intrinsically evil (*intrinsece malum*) would logically apply to a polygamous marriage[300] in the same weight it applies to any monogamous marriage. And so African polygamous marriages can never be understood as institutionalized prostitution because it is the same quality of respect demanded from spouses in polygamy as in monogamy. The substantive belief remains as always, for instance, that a *muntu*'s standard of dignity could be maintained only by means of the *desired marital bond* that is either legitimately monogamous or legitimately

---

297. John Paul II, "*Sacrae Disciplinae Leges*," 1148 §1. "When he receives baptism in the Catholic Church, a non-baptized man who has several non-baptized wives at the same time can retain one of them after the others have been dismissed, if it is hard for him to remain with the first one. The same is valid for a non-baptized woman who has several non-baptized husbands at the same time"; see more elaborations in Bujo, *The Ethical Dimension of Community*, 114–15.

298. Bujo, *The Ethical Dimension of Community*, 117.

299. See Bujo, *The Ethical Dimension of Community*, 35.

300. Bujo, *An African Ethic*, 21.

polygamous, suggesting atleast, that the heart of an African polygamous setting is not immoral, moreover it socially excludes divorce cases and adultery, or it makes them atleast rare,[301] because almost every *muntu* gets a spouse to actively contribute to the promotion of life holistically. Given that the desired marital bond by every *muntu* creates voluminous chances through polygamy for each *muntu* to be lawfully married, it shields not only every individual but the whole community against prostitution. In contrast, monogamy has consequently made it not anymore practically attainable for every *muntu* to marry, implicitly compelling some to indulge in prostitution in order to survive socially and economically.[302] But the consequence of polygamists being forced to dismiss all their spouses except *retain one of them after the others* before receiving the sacrament of baptism is challengeable in an African social reality, where Africans protect any legitimate marriage thereby considering it immoral to dismiss any spouse from the community. In comparison to the death of one's partner, which would otherwise expose one to adultery or prostitution, a scenario that doesn't promote life. So, to defend the spouse's communal protection that goes beyond the principle-based approaches to economic autonomy, the *marital alliance as an indissoluble covenant* includes the entire clan communities of the two once marrieds, which ultimately favors the social-economic welfare of the remaining spouse and the children. Since the covenantal marital alliance is not interrupted by the spouse's death, the remaining spouse and the children are forever protected by the clan community which includes the surviving dependants, who all-together live in a kind of mystical community with the deceased, who remains a living person in the *memoria-conscience* of the descendants.[303] The covenantal marital alliance survives in a mystical alliance where the descendants, surviving children and spouse, the clan community, the deceased spouse and ancestors remain in an eternally indissoluble holistic solidarity through rites, supplications, prayer invocations, sacrifices and offerings.

The inevitability of promoting a continued sense of solidarity and vitality of the vital force in an indissoluble mystical alliance explains why, if

---

301. Even when a marriage does not result in procreation, which may sufficiently suggest a cardinal reason for divorce, further platforms are in place to correct this attitude beyond Mbih's study, "Foundation of kom proverbs," 15; Bujo, *An African Ethic*, 10; Bujo, *The Ethical Dimension of Community*, 112; For the Baganda, adultery (*bwenzi*) is a man sleeping with a married woman, which is forbidden. It is, however, not wrong for a married man to sleep with an unmarried woman because polygamy is permissible, and the married man could and is expected to marry this unmarried woman. Sempebwa, *Reality of a Bantu*, 159.

302. See Bujo, *Ethical Dimension of Community*, 109–110.

303. See Bujo, *Ethical Dimension of Community*, 110–12; Bujo, *An African Ethic*, 38.

muntu is not yet married, *muntu* never feels fulfilled. So, a married *muntu*, with offsprings, is "more respected as a person" than the contrary. Eventhough sterility and barrenness can lead to psychological trauma, this is catered for in a polygamous marriage. For instance, a wife might not necessarily feel miserable since she identifies herself with the other children as her own—analogous to adopting them socially or emotionally. In case of barrenness or sterility, for the Gikuyu (Kikuyu) of Kenya, the first wife as the mother of all further wives and children, and who consents to the subsequent wives, looks for the second wife, confirming polygamy as an alternative way to get the desired offsprings, offsprings that are important for inheritance (heirs)[304] as a prerequisite for a flourishing mystical alliance that reflects an earthly solidary sociality. Here polygamy does not only exhibit the African sense of solidarity and the strong sense of family spirit, but the sense of solidarity also created by polygamous marriages extends to other clan families and lineages, since each marriage introduces more new members from other clan lineages, creating numerous new alliances and social relationships.[305]

While polygamy promotes life in an African moral sense solidarily, similarly the church's tradition perceives, citing Aquinas' commentary on the sentences, mainly on "various laws about marriage," that polygamy does not contradict atleast the main purpose of marriage, i.e., the function of the male sperm in propagation of the species within a wholly communitarian setting, even when it contradicts secondary purposes, it can be permissible atleast under certain conditions[306] when the vital force for all is holistically reinforced. Serving as an example of permitted scenarios of polygamy in the church tradition, Martin Luther (1483-1546) allowed his protector Duke Philip of Hesse (1504-1567) to live in polygamy. Luther in 1520 wrote, "I so much detest divorce, that I prefer bigamy to divorce" (*Ego quidem ita detestor divortium, ut bigamiam malim quam divortium*).[307] Moreover, Luther's younger disciple, Philip Melanchthon (1497-1560) just like the German Protestant reformer in Strasbourg, Martin Bucer (1491-1551), supported polygamy by advising Henry VIII of England—atleast best known for his six wives—in 1531 to marry a second wife (Anne Boleyn) so as to solve his marital problems of fathering a male heir since Catherine of Aragon (first wife) had not succeeded: "Although I do not want to concede polygamy,

304. See Bujo, *Ethical Dimension of Community*, 111–14.

305. See Bujo, *Ethical Dimension of Community*, 113–14.

306. On various laws about marriage, Thomas Aquinas, 4 Sent. d. 33 q. 1 a. 2c, q. 2a 2 sol 2, on polyandry, q. 1 a. 1 ad 8.

307. Luther, *De captivitate Babylonica ecclesiae*, 559. Quoted from Bujo, *The Ethical Dimension of Community*, 105, 116.

generally . . . nevertheless in this case, for the sake of the utility of the Kingdom and perhaps also for the sake of the king's conscience, I declare that it will be most secure for the king to take a second wife, the first not being rejected, because it is certain that polygamy is not prohibited by divine law."[308] In the inevitability of promoting anamnetic solidarity and continued vitality, polygamy's vital force remains permissible atleast in some circumstances within the church tradition as well as in the African moral outlook. The aspect of promoting an anamnetic solidarity needs to be complemented with respectful sympathy towards the Other, since an anamnetic solidarity may be argued to lack within other sexuality aspects, like homosexuality, sex in menopause, in vitro fertilization (IVF), embryo transfer (ET), embryo donation, insemination, anal sex etc. This is because, even though some characteristics of the African moral thought, namely, continued vitality, solidarity, hierarchical order, community life and healthy humanness, may not be promoted, the African moral thought still respectfully extends sympathy to every the Other, given that every the Other has a life force that may simply be different from us.

Even-though theological ethics has variedly argued against some sexuality aspects basically basing on the mightiness of human reason and Aquinas' emphasis of natural law, a moral justification that for instance anal intercourse and homosexual unions contradict what is given by nature seem to be lacking.[309] The question is whether theological bioethics won't take cognizance of cultural-specific and contextual customary versions of ethics, like in Africa, as well as contemporary scientific evidence from evolutionary science, cognitive ethology and results from neuroscience, for instance, that some entities have homosexual orientations. These renewed sexual questions are appropriate to contemporary moral theologians since the church is one of most relevant communities and the biggest nongovernmental owner of healthcare systems in Black Africa—whereby, in short of the Catholic church's contextual role in Africa where all kinds of new bioethical interventions are infiltrating the continent unceasingly, we can hardly achieve lasting holistic theological bioethics.

Contra principlism, given that African marriages go beyond natural law debates to promote immortal solidarity and continued vitality of life,

---

308. "Etsi enim non velim concedere polygamiam vulgo . . . tamen in hoc casu propter magnam utilitatem regni, fortassis etiam propter conscientiam regis, ita pronuntio: tutissimum esse regi, si ducat secundam uxorem, priore non objecta, quia certum est, polygamiam non esse prohibitam jure divino." Melanchthon, "De Divortio Henrici VIII," 526. Quoted from Bujo, *Ethical Dimension of Community*, 105.

309. Homosexuality is "contrary to the natural law." *Catechism of the Catholic Church*, no. 2357–59; ST I–II q. 94 a. 3 ad 2.

the vital force of sexuality in an African approach to theological bioethics can only be understood within a covenant constituted between two human genders, reestablishing not an individualistic autonomous good but rather a three-dimensional communitarian-anamnetic framework of solidarity. In this regard, African marriages, as we illustrated in the symbol of dowry, are understood in the communal dimension of sexuality, where all community members supportively ally behind the individual. So, the rightful desire to marry must be understood in its community-life-promoting dimension.[310] It is from this basis that some aspects of sexuality, for instance homosexuality, don't sit well in an African milieu which understands *muntu* only in the duality of man and woman, a fundamental African anthropology recognizing both a *bipolar* and a *tripolar* family life. It is the bipolarity that generates the triad man-woman-child as an active community. Even where there is no progeny—descendants as offsprings—the existing childless bipolarity can generate a triad, for instance, through polygamy.[311] So the extended clan fellowship is only guaranteed through the duality or bipolarity of a man and woman giving off life. This conviction makes it difficult for Baganda to morally appreciate any sexuality aspects of anal intercourse or sodomy (*lusiyaga*). Just like any sexuality outside the duality of a man and woman, *lusiyaga* is considered too an abomination (*kivve*), since sexual relations are based on promoting life values of marriage and lineage solidarity.[312] Since sexuality is not a private or an autonomously individualistic-personalistic matter focused on procreation only—as bioethical principlism would claim—it is a holistic enrichment of life within a community (social parenthood) context that legitimates sexuality. Sexuality enriches life by keeping together the community entrusted to us by our ancestors but loaned to us by our descendants, but which community has a commitment to continuously renew this life fully.[313]

If an African approach to theological bioethics is grounded on the substantive belief of promoting life which warrants a continued friendship of solidarity to every creation including God, there are a couple of religious rites in sexuality that cannot be counted any more as promoting life and so would hinder solidary friendships. Unlike the ancestral wisdom which killed twins in some groups or introduced female circumcision as a means of preparing girls—*rite of passage* within practicing cultures—for a future

310. Bujo, *An African Ethic*, 18, 36, 38; Bujo, *Ethical Dimension of Community*, 103.

311. Bujo, *An African Ethic*, 6–7.

312. Sempebwa, *Reality of a Bantu*, 160–61; Haydon, *Law and Justice in Buganda*, 278–79.

313. See Bujo, *An African Ethic*, 37–38.

courageous life in the clan fellowship, which contributions were believed to have increased and protected the community vital force (life) in their time—today's holistic biomedical scientific findings veto against all these forms, for instance of Female Genital Mutilation—clitoridectomy, excision, infibulation and all other harmful procedures—as unjust brutality.[314] Studies show 91.5 million women and girls who undergo through "female genital cutting" or "female circumcision" in Africa by 2008,[315] while the official UNICEF figures (2020) show atleast 200 million women and girls in 31 surveyed countries worldwide.[316] Moreover, one hears of other groups like the Gikuyu who forbid men from marrying uncircumcised females. Not only the Gikuyu, but also among the Nso', it is a purely secular and profane ritual of initiation[317] into adulthood. Whether arguing for the necessity of male or female circumcision rites in nurturing the young into adulthood, fully socializing boys to be holistic males and equally holistic girls to be females, there is "no strictly moral argument against female circumcision that would not equally apply to male circumcision."[318] First, since both male and female sexes are prone to body integrity, and if that is the argument advanced against female circumcision, it would turn out unethical treating equal sexes (female and male) unequally. Second, we now know of lifelong sufferings of circumcised women, not like it was unbeknownst to us in former times, with urgent questions that urgently seek corrective criticism of an African attitude from the universalized bioethical perspective. A holistic approach requires an urgent enrichment of the African cultural palaver with positive elements of the universalized approach to bioethics.

More to sexuality, although African polygamy has always been recognized as having the covenant character like any valid form of marriage, respected and promoted a woman's dignity since the husband has always sought the permission or voluntary pleading of the first wife, promoted women economic independence, protected them from prostitution and allowed greater stability in marriage life; nevertheless, today's modern

---

314. Female circumcision includes—Clitoridectomy: partial or total removal of the clitoris; Excision: partial or total removal of the clitoris and the labia minora; Infibulation: narrowing of the vaginal opening through the creation of a covering seal; Or other harmful procedures to the female genitalia for non-medical purposes, see Garcia-Moreno, Guedes and Knerr, "Female genital mutilation."; Bujo, *An African Ethic*, 132–33, 138, 140–41.

315. Yoder and Khan, "Women circumcised in Africa," 1–19.

316. End FGM European Network and U.S. End FGM/C Network and Equality Now, "Female genital mutilation/cutting."

317. See Tangwa, *African bioethics in a Western frame*, 109.

318. Tangwa, *African bioethics in a Western frame*, 113, see 133.

polygamy fulfils less the ancestral ideal of promoting a holistic life. For illustration, even-though it has always been normal, perhaps even contextually necessary to have a large number of children through polygamy—even to a childless *muntu*—in order to compensate for wide infant mortality rates, provide a source of social capital and health security in old age, create more possibilities for the clan community to enjoy immortality of life through many descendants after death, replace childlessness with social parenthood, it is less feasible having many children in this economically challenged modern generation. Besides the education of children has been the task of the extended family or clan fellowship, which is less appreciated in the modern individualistic living conditions of families. Turning against these modern lifestyles mean being morally against promoting the community vital force as currently fostered by elders. Be that as it may, modern polygamy additionally ignores the first wife and still forgets the covenant life character of any marriage. Moreover, to promote life is to act against any wars of sexual violence waged against the bodies of women south of the Sahara, an instance that centrally disrupts women doing theological bioethics in sub-Sahara. Besides sexual violence resulting from patriarchal attitudes, some polygamous marriages do not promote the unity of the extended clan community and so differ from the original holistic ideal as it was institutionalized by our ancestors in the name of life, whereby the modern first wives neither consent nor know about the existence of the second wives (or third) wives. Moreover, some windows' economic independence is abused, and their property robbed. And moreover, numerous questions arise regarding the physical and psychological sufferings of the co-wives, other women, their sisters as well as other relatives.[319]

As if not enough, in other instances of sexuality, the community sometimes breaks the rules of the community palaver and imposes its own will on the candidate for marriage. While in some instances, infertility is being overemphasized as an undesirable condition, in others, childless couples can be exposed to community contempt or social scourge and trauma to an extent of breaking down the existing marriage. Today, taking the dignity and emancipation of women seriously, we see that the holistic life—at which the ancestors originally aimed—can hardly be attained by means of polygamy.[320] In these modern perspectives of sexuality, life is not promoted as it would originally be recommended by the ancestors themselves

---

319. See Phiri, "Why does God allow our husbands to hurt us?" 10–30; Kiruki, "Polygamy," 119–47; Baloyi, "Polygamy in the African Christian context," 164–81; Bujo, *An African Ethic*, 133–34, 138–40; Bujo, *Ethical Dimension of Community*, 118, 131.

320. See Tangwa, "Assisted conception: an African perspective," 301–2; Bujo, *An African Ethic*, 136–38.

if they lived today. This necessitates appropriating theological bioethics of sexuality befitting a modern holistic approach to life. This justifies why the extended community fellowship is always interested in an individual sexual life as we have presented in the case of marriage. The relational community can never abandon *muntu* alone given that her well placed sexual life in the triad-community revitalizes holistic anamnetic solidarity of the Other, while her misplaced sexuality doesn't promote life and so poisons the entire community atmosphere of the Other. Whatever lacks in one's sexuality is taken care of through the community's mandate to extend respectful sympathy to every the Other.

RÉSUMÉ OF PART II: HOLISTIC ANAMNETIC SOLIDARITY AS THE THEOLOGICAL BIOETHICS OF THE OTHER

We have tried to answer the question: How could the African understanding of solidarity contribute to the discourse in the holistic approach to theological bioethics in dialogue with the Encyclical Letter *Fratelli Tutti* and Emmanuel Levinas' ethics of the other? I have argued for a holistic anamnetic solidarity across every entity and system of creation within the three-dimensional-community which can be appreciated in theological bioethics and whose theological heart is the relational Other.

There is failure in friendships, cooperations, reconciliation, and numerous failed concerns as exploitation between the Global North and South is rampant in African contexts. We incorporated *Fratelli Tutti*'s meaning of *other* as my neighbor and the tears of every creation; with Levinas' meaning of the *other* as the stranger; and with the Black African meaning of the *Other* as everything created and all forces and all bioethical concerns existing in the community of the living, the community of the ancestors and the community of those to be born. It is the Other that is bioethically wounded and cries before our sympathetic hearts to be listened to and included in the circles of our solidarity. It wouldn't be a holistic solidarity if not integrating all networks of the triad-community, that is, the living community, the living dead inclusive of our ancestors and those to be born in a relationship that is inclusive of God at the apex of the hierarchical forces. Life as religiously immanent in every entity and every force participates in this *holistic solidarity*, with room to increase or decrease life for the wounded or rejoicing Other.

But even if the truth of theological bioethics was to be understood as revealed to us or not, we can scarcely reflectively access it using singularly principlistic coded categories of thought or even aptly act upon this truth without its appropriate incarnation in the familiar sensibilities of our cultural social realities. It is the reason such a holistic anthropological stance of SSA finds it rather unbecoming to separate the religious from the secular, body from the soul, and more so emphasizing only *muntu*'s body healing without healing the totality of her life holistically.

Holistic theological bioethics primordially demands us a collaborative commitment to fulfill God's will as handed down to us by our ancestors, a will to promote life cosmically in the dialectic three-dimensional community—the anthropological foundation of an African approach to bioethics contextualized within an enterprise of a relational social premium. The relational community can never abandon *muntu* alone given that her well placed sexuality, for instance, in the triad-community revitalizes holistic anamnetic solidarity of the Other, while her misplaced sexuality disrupts life and so poisons the entire community atmosphere of the *relational Other*. Also, marriage and death indelibly incorporate an anamnetic holistic moral character suggesting no life dichotomies like in principle based Western perspectives. The eschatological character pertinent to the indissolubility and immortality of the marriage bond, suggests an anamnetic solidarity even after death in the African approach to theological bioethics, distinguishing the African moral thought from the principlistic Western conception of marriage. Holistic solidarity additionally means extending respectful sympathy to the *relational Other* in her/its/his unique creatureliness.

5

Conclusion

In the two PARTS, the work advocated for a holistic approach to bioethics in which I advanced ways in which we could amalgamate the African approaches to bioethics and the universally oriented principle-based approaches. The work dealt not only with some tension between African and Western approaches to biomedical ethics, but it also brought together both the African and the Western approaches to bioethics in dialogue with the *ethics of the Other* (inclusive of nonhuman animals) in Emmanuel Levinas and the encyclical *Fratelli Tutti*. Here we grounded the theological heart of theological bioethics as the holistic *Other*.

Largely, contemporary bioethical interventions have remained Western-principle-based—built on Western socio-cultural-moral theories—while demands of bioethics in an increasingly pluralized diversified world are not only contextual but also global in nature. The lodged caveat cuts across biomedical exploitations as general weaknesses and inadequacies of an entire system. To efficaciously respond to such weaknesses, Western principle-based approaches cannot be incarnated successfully in African contexts if they are not complemented by a contextualized normative understanding of solidarity. On the other hand, the local contexts need equally to simultaneously contribute to the universalized principles so as to inclusively handle biomedical challenges that are global in nature and not restricted to one cultural perspective, hence demanding agreeable intercultural solutions.

In trying to provide some solution, I faithfully engaged rather in an ethic rooted in the relational interconnectedness of life as substantively believed by Black Africans, translating into not only the normative ethics of a holistic anamnetic solidarity but also defined the theological heart of theological bioethics as the relational Other. This is what I have basically termed "holistic bioethics," in which I tried systematically to embrace and bring together both bioethical principlism and the African moral thought.

In confirming the holistic sense, the African ethical system promotes an *integral holistic community life* by continuously promoting the norm of *solidarity, continued vitality*, the *hierarchization of life* of every entity across the corporate community, i.e., the living, the living dead, those not yet born and all living and non-living entities.

The study confirms rich contributions on the ethics of nonhuman animals from principle-based studies. Along their strong emphasis on anthropocentrism, with scientific evidence from philosophical ethics, evolutionary science, experiments by cognitive ethologists, results from neuroscience, it has become clear that even though empirical science can operate without necessarily proclaiming moral values, bioethics cannot without practical life values and indeed we shouldn't have biomedical interventions without morals. Having appreciated that there is no creation or system of forces that is lifeless, we saw it as a primordial imperative to awakening our collective commitment to revitalize our respectful sympathy towards every creature and system of cooperation. So, *bioethics is respectful sympathy towards the relational Other*, because every entity has at least some moral status, and we need to stand in solidarity with all against any exploitations.

While upholding the moral status of every Other, which is synonymous to the African understanding of God's immanence in every created object, I built eco-theological bioethics whose theological heart is the relational Other—my neighbor, the ecosystem, the stranger, my government, my compound, an animal, an ancestor, exploited and failed relationships such as interpersonal, universal and cosmic—as the ethical object of holistic solidarity. For a holistic solidarity, there is no division of life or cosmic realities or problems into pairs, either/or formats. It has become very clear to me that the general weakness that gives birth to all these shortcomings in bioethics is the fact that we have removed the Other from her rightful primordial place. It is onto the Other that we can locate all the discussed bioethical controversies. And likewise, the solution lies onto reordering the Other.

To achieve a holistic approach to theological bioethics, we rely on the primordial command to offer respectful sympathy towards every created entity or life force (Other). When we offer respectful sympathy towards the Other (past, present and future realities), we revitalize holistic anamnetic solidarity of the Other, while if we refrain from extending sympathy to the Other, we poison the anamnetic solidarity. Increasing a holistic life with the Other guarantees one's entrance in ancestor-hood, whereby the living enjoys an anamnetic solidarity with the ancestors. This suggests augmenting a moral bond of an eschatological character to an extent that Africans speak not only of an immortality of personhood or the living community remaining in an eternal symbiosis with the community of the dead and the community of the expected descendants, but also those who excel in the earthly community by respecting the Other, e.g., their marriage bond, even after death of their spouses, they still fully enjoy this bondedness and immortality.

Our creator is a God of life. The true God-given life extends not only to humans but to every creature and vital force, and it is indeed richer than any principle or approach. Cultivating the theological heart of theological bioethics as the Other serves as the best convincing witness and alternative to any possible holistic solidarity, an approach that at least respects a decent minimum of every creature and global system, which Other should become a global priority. It is through the otherness of the Other who is different from me yet unique and similar to me that we can holistically survive as human beings in the future. Our security is contingent only on the security of the relational Other. These relationships with the Other form us without us necessarily forming them or them having reciprocal responsibilities to us. My grandmother (100 years) always tells me that I will be no more at that point when I will stop being sympathetic to the relational Other.

I have unraveled an African understanding of solidarity as a version of holistic bioethics and as a hallmark of collective local and universalized efforts. A two-way dialogic palaver: It does not only include a holistic endless dialogue of localizing principlism, *integrating, contextualizing, inculturating, indigenizing* bioethical principlism in local settings (going glocal), but also encompasses revising the universalized principlism to incorporate pluralistic customary moralities. Locally we can talk of adapting the universalized sense of bioethical principlism to an indigenized approach to bioethics, allowing blending with the host cultural realities, adjusting to a new cultural environment, incorporating, and balancing different cultural values against assimilation, imperialism and cultural superiority.

The reader ought to take to heart the fact that this project of holistic bioethics doesn't offer the last word on nonhuman animal ethics, holistic anamnetic solidarity, the relational Other and intercultural eco-theological bioethics. And in this bioethical discourse, I tried to avoid any moral myopia and parochialism by cautiously presenting, not just reasons for their own sake—since not all reasons are in actual fact fine reasons, and not all fine reasons may well be relevantly sufficient to drive the point home—but sufficient reasons that this study deemed best as relevantly adequate in interpreting the ordinary *shared way of life* as lived by Black Africans themselves, what supported the study's ultimate conclusions without being morally myopic. To be relevant, the biomedical ethical investigations drew from and relied on simple ordinary moral experiences practically visible in the social reality surrounding Black Africans south of Sahara. Nevertheless, the investigation has not avowed any exceptional status of being exempt from corrective revision. One aspect stands tall, the conclusions motivate further in eco-theological bioethics, and so the various arguments sketched throughout this investigation do not infer any absolute permissibility.

Bibliography

Ainslie, George. "Impulse Control in Pigeons." *Journal of the Experimental Analysis of Behavior* 21 (1974) 485–89.
Akhtar, Sahar. "Animal Pain and Welfare: Can Pain Sometimes Be Worse for Them than Us." In *The Oxford Handbook of Animal Ethics*, edited by Tom L. Beauchamp and R. G. Frey, 495–518. Oxford Handbooks. New York: Oxford University Press, 2011.
Alexander, Deniss J., and I. H. Brown. "History of Highly Pathogenic Avian Influenza." *Revue Scientifique et Technique* 28 (2009) 19–38.
Andrews, Kristin. "Beyond Anthropomorphism: Attributing Psychological Properties to Animals." In *The Oxford Handbook of Animal Ethics*, edited by Tom L. Beauchamp and R. G. Frey, 469–94. Oxford Handbooks. New York: Oxford University Press, 2011.
Aquinas, Thomas. *Providence, Part II*. Edited and translated by Vernon J. Bourke. Vol. 3 of *Summa contra Gentiles*. Notre Dame, IN: University of Notre Dame Press, 1975.
———. *Summa Theologiae: Prima Pars*. Edited by John Mortensen and Enrique Alarcón. Translated by Laurence Shapcote. Latin/English Edition of the Works of St. Thomas Aquinas 14. Lander, WY: Aquinas Institute for the Study of Sacred Doctrine, 2012.
———. *Summa Theologiae: Prima Secundae*. Edited by John Mortensen and Enrique Alarcón. Translated by Laurence Shapcote. Latin/English Edition of the Works of St. Thomas Aquinas 15. Lander, WY: Aquinas Institute for the Study of Sacred Doctrine, 2012.
Aristotle. *The Complete Works of Aristotle*. Edited by Jonathan Barnes. 2 vols. Bollingen Series. Princeton, NJ: Princeton University Press, 1984.
———. *Ethica Nicomachea*. Edited by J. Bywater. Oxford: Clarendon, 1894.
———. *Eudemian Ethics*. Edited by F. Susemihl. Leipzig: Teubner, 1884.
———. *Eudemian Ethics*. In *Athenian Constitution. Eudemian Ethics. Virtue and Vice*, translated by H. Rackham, 190–483. LCL. Cambridge, MA: Harvard University Press, 1981.
———. *Nicomachean Ethics*. Translated by H. Rackham. LCL. Cambridge, MA: Harvard University Press, 1934.
Asante, Emmanuel. "Ecology: Untapped Resource of Pan-Vitalism in Africa." *African Ecclesial Review* 27 (1985) 289–93.
Auer, Alfons. *Autonome Moral und christlicher Glaube*. Düsseldorf: Patmos, 1971.
Ayimdji, Armel, et al. "Towards a 'Deep' Ontology for African Traditional Medicine." *Intelligent Information Management* 3 (2011) 244–51.

Baloyi, M. Elijah. "Critical Reflections on Polygamy in the African Christian Context." *Missionalia* 41 (2013) 164–81.

Bateson, Melissa, and Alex Kacelnik. "Rate Currencies and the Foraging Starling: The Fallacy of the Average Revisited." *Behavioural Ecology* 7 (1996) 341–52.

Battle, Michael. "A Theology of Community: The Ubuntu Theology of Desmond Tutu." *Int* 54 (2000) 173–82.

Beauchamp, Tom L. "The Failure of Theories of Personhood." *Kennedy Institute of Ethics Journal* 9 (1999) 309–24.

———. "Rights Theory and Animal Rights with Animals." In *The Oxford Handbook of Animal Ethics*, edited by Tom L. Beauchamp and R. G. Frey, 198–227. Oxford Handbooks. New York: Oxford University Press, 2011.

Beauchamp, Tom L., and James F. Childress. *Principles of Biomedical Ethics*. 8th ed. New York: Oxford University Press, 2019.

Beauchamp, Tom L., and David B. Morton. "The Upper Limits of Pain and Suffering in Animal Research." *Cambridge Quarterly of Healthcare Ethics* 24 (2015) 431–47.

Beauchamp, Tom L., and Victoria Wobber. "Autonomy in Chimpanzees." *Theoretical Medicine and Bioethics* 35 (2014) 117–32.

Beekman, Madeleine, et al. "How Does an Informed Minority of Scouts Guide a Honeybee Swarm as It Flies to Its New Home?" *Animal Behavior* 71 (2006) 161–71.

Behrens, G. Kevin. "African Philosophy, Thought and Practice and Their Contribution to Environmental Ethics." PhD. diss., University of Johannesburg, 2011.

———. "Towards an Indigenous African Bioethics." *South African Journal of Bioethics and Law* 6 (2013) 32–35.

Bekoff, Marc, and Dale Jamieson. "Cognitive Ethology and Applied Philosophy: The Significance of an Evolutionary Biology of Mind." *Trends in Ecology and Evolution* 5 (1990) 156–59.

Bekoff, Marc, and Jessica Pierce. *Wild Justice: The Moral Lives of Animals*. Chicago: University of Chicago Press, 2009.

Benedict XVI, Pope. "*Caritas in Veritate*: In Charity and Truth." Vatican, June 29, 2009. https://www.vatican.va/content/benedict-xvi/en/encyclicals/documents/hf_ben-xvi_enc_20090629_caritas-in-veritate.html.

Bentham, Jeremy. *An Introduction to the Principles of Morals and Legislation*. Edited by J. H. Burns and H. L. A. Hart. The Collected Works of Jeremy Bentham. Oxford: Clarendon, 1996.

———. "Of the Limits of the Penal Branch of Jurisprudence." In *An Introduction to the Principles of Morals and Legislation*, 307–35. London: Payne and Sons, 1780.

Bermúdez, José Luis. "Mindreading and Moral Significance in Nonhuman Animals." In *The Oxford Handbook of Animal Ethics*, edited by Tom L. Beauchamp and R. G. Frey, 407–40. Oxford Handbooks. New York: Oxford University Press, 2011.

———. *Thinking without Words*. New York: Oxford University Press, 2003.

Bernasconi, Robert. "The Alterity of the Stranger and the Experience of the Alien." In *The Face of the Other and Trace of God: Essays on the Philosophy of Emmanuel Levinas*, edited by Jeffrey Bloechl, 62–89. Perspectives in Continental Philosophy. New York: Fordham University Press, 2000.

Bernet, Rudolf. "The Encounter with the Stranger: Two Interpretations of the Vulnerability of the Skin." In *The Face of the Other and Trace of God: Essays on the*

Philosophy of Emmanuel Levinas, edited by Jeffrey Bloechl, 43–61. Perspectives in Continental Philosophy. New York: Fordham University Press, 2000.
Bible Hub. "Genesis 1:2." Bible Hub, n.d. Commentary. https://biblehub.com/commentaries/genesis/1-2.htm.
Bidima, Jean-Godefroy. *La palabre: Une juridiction de la parole*. Paris: Michalon, 1997.
Biko, Steve. "Black Consciousness and the Quest for a True Humanity." In *I Write What I Like: Selected Speeches*, edited by Stubbs Aelred, 87–98. Chicago: University of Chicago Press, 1978.
Biller-Andorno, Nikola. "IAB Presidential Address: Bioethics in a Globalized World—Creating Space for Flourishing Human Relationships." *Bioethics* 25 (2011) 430–36.
Bloechl, Jeffrey. "Ethics as First Philosophy and Religion." In *The Face of the Other and Trace of God: Essays on the Philosophy of Emmanuel Levinas*, edited by Jeffrey Bloechl, 130–51. Perspectives in Continental Philosophy. New York: Fordham University Press, 2000.
Braddon-Mitchell, David, and Frank Jackson. *Philosophy of Mind and Cognition*. Oxford: Blackwell, 1996.
Bradie, Michael. "The Moral Life of Animals." In *The Oxford Handbook of Animal Ethics*, edited by Tom L. Beauchamp and R. G. Frey, 547–73. Oxford Handbooks. New York: Oxford University Press, 2011.
British Museum. "Egyptian Death and Afterlife: Mummies." British Museum, n.d. https://www.britishmuseum.org/collection/galleries/egyptian-death-and-afterlife-mummies.
Brooks, Rodney A. "Intelligence without Representation." *Artificial Intelligence* 47 (1991) 139–59.
Buchanan, Allen. "Justice as Reciprocity versus Subject-Centered Justice." *Philosophy and Public Affairs* 19 (1990) 227–52.
———. "The Right to a Decent Minimum of Health Care." *Philosophy and Public Affairs* 13 (1984) 55–78.
Bueno-Gómez, Noelia. "Conceptualizing Suffering and Pain." *Philosophy, Ethics, and Humanities in Medicine* 12 (2017). https://doi.org/10.1186/s13010-017-0049-5.
Bujo, Bénézet. *African Theology in Its Social Context*. Translated by John O'Donohue. Maryknoll, NY: Orbis, 1992.
———. *Afrikanische Theologie in ihrem Geselleschaftlichen Kontext*. Düsseldorf: Patmos, 1980.
———. "The Awakening of a Systematic and Authentically African Thought." In *African Theology in the 21st Century: The Contribution of the Pioneers*, edited by Bénézet Bujo and Juvénal Ilunga Muya, 107–49. Nairobi: Paulines Africa, 2003.
———. "Differentiations in African Ethics." In *The Blackwell Companion to Religious Ethics*, edited by William Schweiker, 423–37. Wiley Blackwell Companions to Religion. Oxford: Blackwell, 2005.
———. *The Ethical Dimension of Community: The African Model and the Dialogue between North and South*. Translated by Cecilia Namulondo. Nairobi: Paulines Africa, 1998.
———. *Foundations of an African Ethic: Beyond the Universal Claims of Western Morality*. Translated by Brian McNeil. New York: Crossroad, 2001.
———. "Verantwortung und Solidarität: Christliche Ethik in Afrika." *Stimmen der Zeit* 202 (1984) 795–804.

Burggraeve, Robert. "'Fraternity, Equality, Freedom': On the Soul and the Extent of our Responsibility." In *Responsibility, God, and Society: Theological Ethics in Dialogue*, edited by Roger Burggraeve et al., 1–22. Leuven: Peeters, 2008.

Buyondo, Jude Thaddaeus. *The Critique of Bioethical Principlism in Contrast to an African Approach to Bioethics*. Eugene, OR: Wipf and Stock, 2024.

Byabazaire, M. Deogratias, and John Mary Waliggo. *Incarnating Christianity in Uganda: Proceeding of the Second National Theological Week*. Masaka, Ug.: Katigondo National Seminary Press, 1983.

Cain, Joanna M. "Is Deception for Reimbursement in Obstetrics and Gynecology Justified?" *Obstetrics and Gynecology* 82 (1993) 475–78.

Call, Josep, and Michael Tomasello. "Does the Chimpanzee Have a Theory of Mind? 30 Years Later." *Trends in Cognitive Science* 12 (2008) 187–92.

———. "A Nonverbal False Belief Task: The Performance of Children and Great Apes." *Child Development* 70 (1999) 381–95.

Callahan, Daniel. "Principlism and Communitarianism." *Journal of Medical Ethics* 29 (2003) 287–91.

———. "Universalism and Particularism: Fighting to a Draw." *Hastings Center Report* 30 (2000) 37–44.

Camp, Elisabeth. "Thinking with Maps." *Philosophical Perspectives* 21 (2007) 145–82.

Caputo, John D. "Adieu—sans Dieu: Derrida and Levinas." In *The Face of the Other and Trace of God: Essays on the Philosophy of Emmanuel Levinas*, edited by Jeffrey Bloechl, 276–311. Perspectives in Continental Philosophy. New York: Fordham University Press, 2000.

Carruthers, Peter. "Animal Mentality: Its Character, Extent, and Moral Significance." *Oxford Handbook of Animal Ethics*, edited by Tom L. Beauchamp and R. G. Frey, 373–406. Oxford Handbooks. New York: Oxford University Press, 2011.

———. "An Architecture for Dual Reasoning." In *Two Minds: Dual Systems and Beyond*, edited by Jonathan St. B. T. Evans and Keith Frankish, 109–27. Oxford: Oxford University Press, 2009.

———. *The Architecture of the Mind*. Oxford: Clarendon, 2006.

———. "How We Know Our Own Minds: The Relationships between Mindreading and Metacognition." *Behavioral and Brain Science* 32 (2009) 121–38.

———. "The Illusion of Conscious Will." *Synthese* 159 (2007) 197–213.

Catholic News Agency. "*Fratelli Tutti*: Pope Francis Calls for Unity in New Encyclical." Catholic News Agency, Oct. 4, 2020. https://www.catholicnewsagency.com/news/46083/fratelli-tutti-pope-francis-calls-for-unity-in-new-encyclical.

Chan, Sarah, and John Harris. "Human Animals and Nonhuman Persons." In *The Oxford Handbook of Animal Ethics*, edited by Tom L. Beauchamp and R. G. Frey, 304–31. Oxford Handbooks. New York: Oxford University Press, 2011.

Chappell, Jackie. "Avian Cognition: Understanding Tool Use." *Current Biology* 16 (2006) R244–45.

Chappell, Jackie, and Alex Kacelnik. "Tool Selectivity in a Non-Primate, the New Caledonian Crow (*Corvus moneduloides*)." *Animal Cognition* 5 (2002) 71–78.

Charon, Rita. "The Patient-Physician Relationship: Narrative Medicine; A Model for Empathy, Reflection, Profession, and Trust." *Journal of the American Medical Association* 286 (2001) 1897–902.

Chemhuru, Munamato. "The Import of African Ontology for Environmental Ethics." PhD diss., University of Johannesburg, 2016.

Childress, James F., and Catharyn T. Liverman. *Organ Donation: Opportunities for Action*. Washington, DC: National Academies Press, 2006.

Cicero, Marcus Tullius. *De oratore*. Leipzig: Teubner, 1862.

Clark, Andy, and Josefa Toribio. "Doing without Representing." *Synthese* 101 (1994) 401–31.

Clark, Stephen R. L. "Animals in Classical and Late Antique Philosophy." In *The Oxford Handbook of Animal Ethics*, edited by Tom L. Beauchamp and R. G. Frey, 35–60. Oxford Handbooks. New York: Oxford University Press, 2011.

Clouser, K. Danner, and Bernard Gert. "A Critique of Principlism." *Journal of Medicine and Philosophy* 15 (1990) 219–36.

Cohen, Aaron J., et al. "Estimates and 25-Year Trends of the Global Burden of Disease Attributable to Ambient Air Pollution: An Analysis of Data from the Global Burden of Diseases Study 2015." *Lancet* 389 (2017) 1907–18.

Collectanea Sacrae Congregationis de Propaganda Fide. *Decreta Instructiones Rescripta pro Apostolicis Missionibus*. Rome: Polyglotta, 1907.

Collett, Thomas S., and Matthew Collett. "Memory Use in Insect Visual Navigation." *Nature Reviews: Neuroscience* 3 (2002) 542–52.

Collin, Allen. "Assessing Animal Cognition: Ethological and Philosophical Perspectives." *Journal of Animal Science* 76 (1998) 42–47.

Congregatio de Propaganda Fide. *Sylloge Praecipuorum Documentorum Recentium Summorum Pontificum et Sacrae Congregationis de Propaganda Fide, necnon Aliarum SS. Congregationum Romanorum: Ad Usum Missionariorum*. Rome: Polyglotta, 1939.

Copp, David. "Animals, Fundamental Moral Standing, and Speciesism." In *The Oxford Handbook of Animal Ethics*, edited by Tom L. Beauchamp and R. G. Frey, 276–303. Oxford Handbooks. New York: Oxford University Press, 2011.

Cordeiro-Rodrigues, Luis. "Towards a Tutuist Ethics of War: Ubuntu, Forgiveness and Reconciliation." *Politikon* 45 (2018) 426–35.

Cranor, Carl F. "Toward Understanding Aspects of the Precautionary Principle." *Journal of Medicine and Philosophy* 29 (2004) 259–79.

CSJE [Centre for Social Justice and Ethics] and ARC [Alliance of Religious and Conservation]. *Stewardship of God's Creation: A Catholic Environmental Toolkit for Catechists and Seminarians*. Nairobi: Catholic University of Eastern Africa Press, 2014.

Cudney, Paul. "What Really Separates Casuistry from Principlism in Biomedical Ethics." *Theoretical Medicine and Bioethics* 35 (2014) 205–29.

Damman, Ernest. *Die Religionen Afrikas*. Stuttgart: Kohlhammer, 1963.

Daniels, Norman. "Wide Reflective Equilibrium in Practice." In *Philosophical Perspectives on Bioethics*, edited by L. W. Sumner and Joseph Boyle, 96–114. 2nd ed. Toronto Studies in Philosophy. Toronto: University of Toronto Press, 1996.

Darwin, Charles. *On the Origin of Species: A Facsimile of the First Edition*. Edited by Ernst Mayr. Cambridge, MA: Harvard University Press, 2000.

———. *The Descent of Man and Selection in Relation to Sex*. Princeton, NJ: Princeton University Press, 1981.

———. *The Expression of the Emotions in Man and Animals*. 3rd ed. Oxford: Oxford University Press, 1998.

———. *The Formation of Vegetable Mould through the Actions of Worms with Observations on Their Habits*. Chicago: University of Chicago Press, 1985.

DeGrazia, David. "The Ethics of Confining Animals." In *The Oxford Handbook of Animal Ethics*, edited by Tom L. Beauchamp and R. G. Frey, 738–68. Oxford Handbooks. New York: Oxford University Press, 2011.

———. "Great Apes, Dolphins, and the Concept of Personhood." *Southern Journal of Philosophy* 35 (1997) 301–20.

———. *Taking Animals Seriously: Mental Life and Moral Status*. New York: Cambridge University Press, 1996.

Dennett, Daniel C. *Brainchildren: Essays on Designing Minds*. Representation and Mind. Cambridge, MA: MIT Press, 1998.

———. *Kinds of Minds: Towards an Understanding of Consciousness*. New York: Basic Books, 1997.

De Queiroz, K. "Ernst Mayr and the Modern Concept of Species." *Proceedings of the National Academy of Sciences USA* 102 (2005) 6600–607.

Descartes, René. "Animals Are Machines." In *Animal Rights and Human Obligations*, edited by Tom Regan and Peter Singer, 60–66. Englewood Cliffs, NJ: Prentice-Hall, 1976.

De Waal, Frans B. M. *The Age of Empathy: Nature's Lessons for a Kinder Society*. Toronto: McClelland and Stewart, 2009.

———. "Anthropomorphism Anthropodenial: Consistency in Our Thinking about Humans and Other Animals." *Philosophical Topics* 27 (1999) 225–80.

———. *Good Natured: The Origins of Right and Wrong in Humans and Other Animals*. Cambridge, MA: Harvard University Press, 1996.

———. *Primates and Philosophers: How Morality Evolved*. Edited by Stephen Macedo and Josiah Ober. University Center for Human Values Series. Princeton, NJ: Princeton University Press, 2006.

De Waal, Frans B. M., and Lesleigh M. Luttrell. "Mechanisms of Social Reciprocity in Three Primate Species: Symmetrical Relationship Characteristics or Cognition?" *Ethology and Sociobiology* 9 (1988) 101–18.

Dombrowski, Daniel A. "Are Nonhuman Animals Persons? A Process Theistic Response." *Journal of Animal Ethics* 5 (2015) 135–43.

Draku, Franklin. "Ugandans Fly to Death in Hunt for Jobs Abroad." *Monitor*, June 16, 2022. https://www.monitor.co.ug/uganda/news/national/ugandans-fly-to-death-in-hunt-for-jobs-abroad-3850172#.

Driver, Julia. "A Humean Account of the Status and Character of Animals." In *The Oxford Handbook of Animal Ethics*, edited by Tom L. Beauchamp and R. G. Frey, 144–71. Oxford Handbooks. New York: Oxford University Press, 2011.

Dyer, Fred, and Thomas Seeley. "Distance Dialects and Foraging Range in Three Asian Honeybee Species." *Behavioral Ecology and Sociobiology* 28 (1991) 227–34.

Éla, Jean-Marc. *My Faith as an African*. Translated from the French by John Pairman Brown and Susan Perry. Nairobi: Action, 2001.

Emery, Nathan J., and Nicola S. Clayton. "The Mentality of Crows: Convergent Evolution of Intelligence in Corvids and Apes." *Science* 306 (2004) 1903–7.

End FGM, et al. *Female Genital Mutilation/Cutting: A Call for a Global Response*. End FGM, Mar. 2020. https://www.endfgm.eu/editor/files/2020/03/FGM_Global_-_ONLINE_PDF_VERSION_-_06_2.pdf.

Etieyibo, Edwin E. "African Philosophy and Nonhuman Nature." In *Debating African Philosophy: Perspectives on Identity, Decolonial Ethics and Comparative Philosophy*, edited by George Hull, 164–81. London: Routledge, 2019.

European Union. "Directive 2010/63/EU of the European Parliament and of the Council of 22 September 2010 on the Protection of Animals Used for Scientific Purposes (Text with EEA Relevance)." Official Journal of the European Union L 276 (2010) 33–52. https://eur-lex.europa.eu/LexUriServ/LexUriServ.do?uri=OJ:L:2010:276:0033:0079:EN:PDF.

Evans, Gareth. *Varieties of Reference*. Edited by John McDowell. Oxford: Clarendon, 1982.

Evans, Jonathan St. B. T., and Keith Frankish, eds. *Two Minds: Dual Systems and Beyond*. Oxford: Oxford University Press, 2009.

Faith, Daniel P., et al. "Evoystem Services: An Evolutionary Perspective on the Links Between Biodiversity and Human Well-Being." *Current Opinion in Environmental Sustainability* 2 (2010) 66–74.

Fallers, A. L. *The King's Men*. London: Oxford University Press for the International African Institute, 1964.

FAO. *Livestock's Long Shadow: Environmental Issues and Options*. FAO, 2006. https://www.fao.org/3/a0701e/a0701e.pdf.

Francis, Pope. "Address at the Ecumenical and Interreligious Meeting with Young People." *Osservatore Romano*, May 9, 2019.

———. "Address to Authorities, Civil Society and the Diplomatic Corps." *Osservatore Romano*, Sept. 27, 2018.

———. "Address to Young People." *Osservatore Romano*, Nov. 25–26, 2019.

———. "*Christus Vivit*." Vatican, Mar. 25, 2019. https://www.vatican.va/content/francesco/en/apost_exhortations/documents/papa-francesco_esortazione-ap_20190325_christus-vivit.html.

———. "Document on Human Fraternity for World Peace and Living Together." *Osservatore Romano*, Feb. 4–5, 2019.

———. "*Evangelii Gaudium*: On the Proclamation of the Gospel in Today's World." Vatican, Nov. 24, 2013. https://www.vatican.va/content/francesco/en/apost_exhortations/documents/papa-francesco_esortazione-ap_20131124_evangelii-gaudium.html.

———. "Ecumenical and Interreligious Meeting with Young People." Vatican, Sept. 5, 2019. https://www.vatican.va/content/francesco/en/speeches/2019/may/documents/papa-francesco_20190507_macedoniadelnord-giovani.html.

———. "For the Celebration of the 53rd World Day of Peace: Peace as a Journey of Hope; Dialogue, Reconciliation and Ecological Conversion." Vatican, Jan. 1, 2020. https://www.vatican.va/content/francesco/en/messages/peace/documents/papa-francesco_20191208_messaggio-53giornatamondiale-pace2020.html.

———. "For the Celebration of the World Day of Peace: Fraternity, the Foundation and Pathway to Peace." Vatican, Jan. 1, 2014. https://www.vatican.va/content/francesco/en/messages/peace/documents/papa-francesco_20131208_messaggio-xlvii-giornata-mondiale-pace-2014.html.

———. "For the Celebration of the XLIX World Day of Peace: Overcome Indifference and Win Peace." Vatican, Jan. 1, 2016. https://www.vatican.va/content/francesco/en/messages/peace/documents/papa-francesco_20151208_messaggio-xlix-giornata-mondiale-pace-2016.html.

———. "Meeting for Religious Liberty with the Hispanic Community and Immigrant Groups." Vatican, Sept. 26, 2015. https://www.vatican.va/content/francesco/en/

———. speeches/2015/september/documents/papa-francesco_20150926_usa-liberta-religiosa.html.

———. "Meeting with Authorities and the Diplomatic Corp." Vatican, June 6, 2015. https://www.vatican.va/content/francesco/en/speeches/2015/june/documents/papa-francesco_20150606_sarajevo-autorita.html.

———. "Meeting with Authorities, the Civil Society and the Diplomatic Corps." Vatican, Jan. 18, 2018. https://www.vatican.va/content/francesco/en/speeches/2018/january/documents/papa-francesco_20180119_peru-lima-autorita.html.

———. "Meeting with Political, Economic and Civic Leaders." Vatican, July 7, 2015. https://www.vatican.va/content/francesco/en/speeches/2015/july/documents/papa-francesco_20150707_ecuador-societa-civile.html.

———. "Meeting with the Academic and Cultural World." Vatican, Sept. 22, 2013. https://www.vatican.va/content/francesco/en/speeches/2013/september/documents/papa-francesco_20130922_cultura-cagliari.html.

———. "Meeting with the Brazil's Leaders of Society." Vatican, July 27, 2013. https://www.vatican.va/content/francesco/en/speeches/2013/july/documents/papa-francesco_20130727_gmg-classe-dirigente-rio.html.

———. "Message for the World Day of Persons with Disabilities." *Osservatore Romano*, Dec. 4. 2019.

———. "On the Occasion of the World Meetings of Popular Movements." Vatican, Feb. 10, 2017. https://www.vatican.va/content/francesco/en/messages/pont-messages/2017/documents/papa-francesco_20170210_movimenti-popolari-modesto.html.

———. "*Querida Amazonia.*" Vatican, Feb. 2, 2020. https://www.vatican.va/content/francesco/en/apost_exhortations/documents/papa-francesco_esortazione-ap_20200202_querida-amazonia.html.

———. "Reconciliation Liturgy." Vatican, Sept. 8, 2017. https://www.vatican.va/content/francesco/en/speeches/2017/september/documents/papa-francesco_20170908_viaggioapostolico-colombia-incontrodipreghiera.html.

———. "To the European Parliament." Vatican, Nov. 25, 2014. https://www.vatican.va/content/francesco/en/speeches/2014/november/documents/papa-francesco_20141125_strasburgo-parlamento-europeo.html.

———. "To the Members of the Diplomatic Corps Accredited to the Holy See." Vatican, Jan. 13, 2014. https://www.vatican.va/content/francesco/en/speeches/2014/january/documents/papa-francesco_20140113_corpo-diplomatico.html.

———. "To the Participants in the World Meeting of Popular Movements." Vatican, Oct. 28, 2014. https://www.vatican.va/content/francesco/en/speeches/2014/october/documents/papa-francesco_20141028_incontro-mondiale-movimenti-popolari.html.

———. "To the United Nations Conference to Negotiate a Legally Binding Instrument to Prohibit Nuclear Weapons, Leading towards Their Total Elimination." Vatican, Mar. 23, 2017. https://www.vatican.va/content/francesco/en/messages/pont-messages/2017/documents/papa-francesco_20170323_messaggio-onu.html.

Francis, Pope, and Ahmad Al-Tayyeb. "A Document on Human Fraternity: For World Peace and Living Together." Vatican, Feb. 4, 2019. https://www.vatican.va/content/francesco/en/travels/2019/outside/documents/papa-francesco_20190204_documento-fratellanza-umana.html.

Frankish, Keith. *Mind and Supermind*. Cambridge Studies in Philosophy. Cambridge: Cambridge University Press, 2004.

Frey, R. C. "Moral Standing, the Value of Lives, and Speciesism." In *Ethics in Practice: An Anthology*, edited by Hugh LaFollette, 192–204. 3rd ed. Blackwell Philosophy Anthologies. Oxford: Blackwell, 2007.

———. "Utilitarianism and Animals." In *The Oxford Handbook of Animal Ethics*, edited by Tom L. Beauchamp and R. G. Frey, 172–97. Oxford Handbooks. New York: Oxford University Press, 2011.

Frisch, Karl von. *The Dance Language and Orientation of Bees*. Cambridge: MA: Belknap, 1967.

Gadamer, Hans-Georg. "Friendship and Solidarity." Translated by David Vessey. *Research in Phenomenology* 39 (2009) 3–12.

Gallagher, Colleen M. "A Christian Consideration of Human Vulnerability in Healthcare and Research." In *Religious Perspectives on Human Vulnerability in Bioethics*, edited by Joseph Tham et al., 135–41. Advancing Global Bioethics 2. Dordrecht: Springer, 2014.

Gallistel, Charles R. *The Organization of Learning*. Learning, Development and Conceptual Change Series. Cambridge, MA: MIT Press, 1990.

Gallup, G. Gordon. "Chimpanzees: Self-Recognition." *Science* 167 (1970) 86–87.

Garcia-Moreno, Claudia, et al. *Understanding and Addressing Violence against Women: Female Genital Mutilation*. World Health Organization, 2012. https://iris.who.int/bitstream/handle/10665/77428/WHO_RHR_12.41_eng.pdf?sequence=1.

Gardner, Allen Robert, et al. "Categorical Replies to Categorical Questions by Cross-Fostered Chimpanzees." *American Journal of Psychology* 105 (1992) 27–57.

———, eds. *Teaching Sign Language to Chimpanzees*. Albany: State University of New York Press, 1989.

Garrett, Aaron. "Animals and Ethics in the History of Modern Philosophy." *The Oxford Handbook of Animal Ethics*, edited by Tom L. Beauchamp and R. G. Frey, 61–87. Oxford Handbooks. New York: Oxford University Press, 2011.

Gert, Bernard, et al. "Common Morality versus Specified Principlism: Reply to Richardson." *Journal of Medicine and Philosophy* 25 (2000) 308–22.

———. *Bioethics: A Return to Fundamentals*. New York: Oxford University Press, 1997.

Ghiselin, M. "A Radical Solution to the Species Problem." *Systematic Zoology* 23 (1974) 536–44.

Gil, Mariana, et al. "Learning Reward Expectations in Honeybees." *Learning and Memory* 14 (2007) 491–96.

Gilges, W. "Some African Poison Plants and Medicines of Northern Rhodesia." Occasional Papers of the Rhodes-Livingstone Museum 11. Rhodes-Livingstone Museum, Livingstone, Rhodesia, 1955.

Giurfa, Martin, et al. "The Concepts of 'Sameness' and 'Difference' in an Insect." *Nature* 410 (2001) 930–33.

Goodman, Lenn E. "The Individual and Community in the Normative Traditions of Judaism." In *Religious Diversity and Human Rights*, edited by Irene Bloom et al., 15–53. New York: Columbia University Press, 1996.

Gorke, Martin. *The Death of Our Planet's Species*. Translated by Patricia Nevers. Washington, DC: Island, 2003.

Gosling, Samuel, and Oliver P. John. "Personality Dimensions in Nonhuman Animals: A Cross-Species Review." *Current Directions in Psychological Science* 8 (1999) 69–75.

Gould, James L. "The Locale Map of Honeybees." *Science* 232 (1986) 861–63.

Gould, James L., and Carol Grant Gould. *The Honey Bee*. Scientific American Library. New York: Freeman, 1998.

Gray, Fred D. *The Tuskegee Syphilis Study: The Real Story and Beyond*. Montgomery: New South, 2013.

Graybill, Lyn, and Kimberly Lanegran. "Truth, Justice, and Reconciliation in Africa: Issues and Cases." *African Studies Quarterly* 8 (2004) 1–18.

Greene, Mark. "On the Origin of Species Notions and Their Ethical Limitations." In *The Oxford Handbook of Animal Ethics*, edited by Tom L. Beauchamp and R. G. Frey, 577–602. Oxford Handbooks. New York: Oxford University Press, 2011.

Grey, William. "Anthropocentrism and Deep Ecology." *Australian Journal of Philosophy* 71 (1993) 463–75.

Guttman, Nurit, et al. "Should Altruism, Solidarity, or Reciprocity Be Used as Prosocial Appeals? Contrasting Conceptions of Members of the General Public and Medical Professionals Regarding Promoting Organ Donation." *Journal of Communication* 66 (2016) 909–36.

Gyekye, Kwame. *Beyond Cultures: Perceiving a Common Humanity*. Ghanaian Philosophical Studies. Accra: Ghana Academy of Arts and Sciences Press, 2004.

Gyekye, Kwame, and Kwasi Wiredu, eds. *Person and Community: Ghanaian Philosophical Studies*. Washington, DC: Council for Research in Values and Philosophy, 1992.

Hare, Brian, et al. "Chimpanzees Know What Conspecifics Do and Do Not See." *Animal Behavior* 59 (2000) 771–85.

———. "Do Chimpanzees Know What Conspecifics Know?" *Animal Behavior* 61 (2001) 139–51. https://doi.org/10.1006/anbe.2000.1518.

Harman, Elizabeth. "The Potentiality Problem." *Philosophical Studies* 114 (2003) 173–98.

Holy See Press Office. "Audience with the President of the Republic of Rwanda." Vatican, Mar. 20, 2017. https://press.vatican.va/content/salastampa/en/bollettino/pubblico/2017/03/20/170320c.html.

Haydon, Edwin Scott. *Law and Justice in Buganda*. London: Butterworths, 1960.

Heidegger, Martin. *Being and Time*. Translated by John Macquarrie and Edward Robinson. New York: Harper and Row, 1962.

Hooker, Brad. *Ideal Code, Real World: A Rule-Consequentialist Theory of Morality*. Oxford: Clarendon, 2000.

Horsthemke, Kai. "African Communalism, Persons, and Animals." *Filosofia Theoretica* 7 (2018) 60–79.

Huebner, Bryce. "Minimal Minds." In *The Oxford Handbook of Animal Ethics*, edited by Tom L. Beauchamp and R. G. Frey, 441–68. Oxford Handbooks. New York: Oxford University Press, 2011.

Hull, David L. "A Matter of Individuality." *Philosophy of Science* 45 (1978) 335–60.

Hume, David. *Essays on Suicide and the Immortality of the Soul*. Munich: Decker, 1799.

———. "The Stoic." In *Essays, Moral, Political, and Literary*, edited by Eugene F. Miller, 146–54. Liberty Classics. Indianapolis: Liberty Fund, 1987.

———. *A Treatise of Human Nature*. Edited by David Fate Norton and Mary J. Norton. 2 vols. Clarendon Hume Edition Series. Oxford: Clarendon, 2007.

Hursthouse, Rosalind. "Virtue Ethics and the Treatment of Animals." In *The Oxford Handbook of Animal Ethics*, edited by Tom L. Beauchamp and R. G. Frey, 117–43. Oxford Handbooks. New York: Oxford University Press, 2011.

IBC. *On Consent*. UNESCO, 2008. http://unesdoc.unesco.org/images/0017/001781/178124e.pdf.

———. *On Social Responsibility and Health*. UNESCO, 2010. https://unesdoc.unesco.org/ark:/48223/pf0000187899.

———. *On the Principle of the Sharing of Benefits*. UNESCO, Oct. 2, 2015. http://unesdoc.unesco.org/images/0023/002332/233230E.pdf.

Igns, Thomas, and Lars Chittka. "Speed-Accuracy Tradeoffs and False Alarms in Bee Responses to Cryptic Predators." *Current Biology* 18 (2008) 1520–24.

Ijiomah, Chris. "An Excavation of Logic in African Worldview." *African Journal of Religion, Culture and Society* 1 (2006) 29–35.

———. *Harmonious Monism: A Philosophical Logic of Explanation for Ontological Issues in Supernaturalism in African Thought*. Bloomington, IN: Xlibris, 2016.

Ikuenobe, Polycarp. "Good and Beautiful: A Moral-Aesthetic View of Personhood in African Communal Traditions." *Essays in Philosophy* 17 (2016) 124–63.

———. *Philosophical Perspectives on Communalism and Morality in African Traditions*. Lanham, MD: Lexington, 2006.

Ilogu, Edmund Christopher Onyedum. *Christian Ethics in an African Background: A Study of the Interaction of Christianity and Ibo Culture*. Leiden: Brill, 1974.

IUCN et al. *World Conservation Strategy (WCS): Living Resource Conservation for Sustainable Development*. Grand, Switz.: International Union for Conservation of Nature and Natural Resources, 1980.

John Paul II, Pope. "Address to Representatives of Argentinian Culture." *Osservatore Romano*, Apr. 14, 1987.

———. "*Centesimus Annus*: On the Hundredth Anniversary of *Rerum Novarum*." Vatican, May 1, 1991. https://www.vatican.va/content/john-paul-ii/en/encyclicals/documents/hf_jp-ii_enc_01051991_centesimus-annus.html.

———. "*Ecclesia in Africa*: On the Church in Africa and Its Evangelizing Mission towards the Year 2000." Vatican, Sept. 14, 1995. https://www.vatican.va/content/john-paul-ii/en/apost_exhortations/documents/hf_jp-ii_exh_14091995_ecclesia-in-africa.html.

———. "*Laborem Exercens*: On the Ninetieth Anniversary of *Rerum Novarum*." Vatican, Sept. 14, 1981. https://www.vatican.va/content/john-paul-ii/en/encyclicals/documents/hf_jp-ii_enc_14091981_laborem-exercens.html.

———. "*Sacrae Disciplinae Leges*: For the Promulgation of the New Code of Canon Law." Vatican, [1983]. https://www.vatican.va/archive/cod-iuris-canonici/eng/documents/cic_introduction_en.html.

Jonsen, Albert R. "Casuistry: An Alternative or Complement to Principles?" *Kennedy Institute of Ethics Journal* 5 (1995) 237–51.

———. "Morally Appreciated Circumstances: A Theoretical Problem for Casuistry." In *Philosophical Perspectives on Bioethics*, edited by L. W. Sumner and Joseph Boyle, 37–49. 2nd ed. Toronto Studies in Philosophy. Toronto: University of Toronto Press, 1996.

Kabuga, C. E. S. "The Genealogy of Kabaka and the Early Bakabaka of Buganda." *Uganda Journal* 27 (1963) 205–16.

Kagabo, Liboire. "Alexis Kagame (1912–1981): Life and Thought." In *A Companion to African Philosophy*, edited by Kwasi Wiredu, 231–42. Blackwell Companions to Philosophy. Oxford: Blackwell, 2004.

Kagame, Alexis. "Le fondement ultime de la morale bantu." *Au Cœur de l'Afrique* 5 (1969) 231–36.

———. *La philosophie bântu-rwandaise de l'être*. Brussels: Académie Royale des Sciences Coloniales, 1956.

Kaggwa, Apolo. *Ekitabo kye Bika Buganda*. London: Macmillan, 1949.

Kalebic, Nereo, et al. "Human-Specific *ARHGAP11B* Induces Hallmarks of Neocortical Expansion in Developing Ferret Neocortex." eLife, Nov. 28, 2018. https://doi.org/10.7554/eLife.41241.

Kamm, F. M. *Intricate Ethics: Rights, Responsibilities, and Permissible Harm*. Oxford Ethics. New York: Oxford University Press, 2006.

Karlström, Mikael. "Imagining Democracy: Political Culture and Democratization in Buganda." *Africa: Journal of the International African Institute* 66 (1996) 485–505.

Kasenene, Peter. *Religious Ethics in Africa*. Kampala: Fountain, 1998.

Kasozi, Ferdinand Mutaawe. *Introduction to an African Philosophy: The Ntu'ology of the Baganda*. Munich: Alber, 2011.

Katongole, Emmanuel. *The Sacrifice of Africa: A Political Theology for Africa*. Grand Rapids: Eerdmans, 2012.

Kelbessa, Workineh. "Environmental Philosophy in African Traditions of Thought." *Environmental Ethics* 40 (2018) 309–23.

Kenward, Ben, et al. "Tool Manufacture by Naive Juvenile Crows." *Nature* 433 (2005). https://doi.org/10.1038/433121a.

Kessler, Hans. *Das Stöhnen der Natur: Plädoyer für eine Schöpfungsspiritualität und Schöpfungsethik*. Düsseldorf: Patmos, 1990.

Keurlatz, Jozef. "The Emergence of Enlightened Anthropocentrism in Ecological Restoration." *Nature and Culture* 7 (2012) 48–71.

Khoza, Amanda. "Our Lives Are Just as Important: Ramaphosa Criticizes Western Nations' Handling of Covid-19." *Sowetan*, Dec. 6, 2021.

Kiruki, Joseph Kahiga. "Polygamy: A Pastoral Challenge to the Church in Africa: Specific Challenges to Evangelization in Africa." *African Ecclesial Review* 49 (2007) 119–47.

Kisembo, Benezeri, et al. *African Christian Marriage*. London: Chapman, 1977.

Korsgaard, Christine M. "Fellow Creatures: Kantian Ethics and Our Duties to Animals." Tanner Lectures, Feb. 6, 2004. https://tannerlectures.utah.edu/_resources/documents/a-to-z/k/korsgaard_2005.pdf.

———. "Interacting with Animals: A Kantian Account." In *The Oxford Handbook of Animal Ethics*, edited by Tom L. Beauchamp and R. G. Frey, 91–118. Oxford Handbooks. New York: Oxford University Press, 2011.

Kyewalyanga, Francis-Xavier Sserufusa. *Traditional Religion, Customs and Christianity in Uganda: As Illustrated by the Ganda with Some References to Other African Cultures and Islam*. Freiburg im Breisgau: Renner, 1976.

Lafollette, Hugh. "Animal Experimentation in Biomedical Research." In *The Oxford Handbook of Animal Ethics*, edited by Tom L. Beauchamp and R. G. Frey, 798–825. Oxford Handbooks. New York: Oxford University Press, 2011.

Levinas, Emmanuel. *Autrement qu'être ou au-delà de l'essence*. The Hague: Nijhoff, 1974.

———. *Beyond the Verse: Talmudic Readings and Lectures*. Translated by Gary D. Mole. Bloomington: Indiana University Press, 1994.
———. *Difficile liberté: Essais sur le judaïsme*. Paris: Michel, 1976.
———. *Difficult Freedom: Essays on Judaism*. Translated by Sean Hand. Johns Hopkins Jewish Studies. Baltimore: Johns Hopkins University Press, 1990.
———. *Ethics and Infinity: Conversations with Philippe Nemo*. Translated by Richard A. Cohen. Pittsburgh: Duquesne University Press, 1985.
———. *Nine Talmudic Readings*. Translated by Annette Aronwicz. Bloomington: Indiana University Press, 1990.
———. *Otherwise than Being or Beyond Essence*. Translated by Alphonso Lingis. The Hague: Nijhoff, 1981.
———. *Totalité et infini: Essai sur l'extériorité*. The Hague: Nijhoff, 1961.
———. *Totality and Infinity: An Essay on Exteriority*. Translated by Alphonso Lingis. Pittsburgh: Duquesne University Press, 1969.
Lewes, George Henry. *Seaside Studies at Ilfracombe, Temby, the Sicily Isles, and Jersey*. Edinburgh: Blackwood and Sons, 1860.
Longman, Timothy. *Christianity and Genocide in Rwanda*. Cambridge: Cambridge University Press, 2010.
———. "Church, Politics and the Genocide in Rwanda." *Journal of Religion in Africa* 31 (2001) 163–86.
London, Leslie, et al. "Ethics in Occupational Health: Deliberations of an International Workgroup Addressing Challenges in an African Context." *BMC Medical Ethics* 15 (2014). https://doi.org/10.1186/1472-6939-15-48.
Lugira, A. M. *Ganda Art: A Study of the Ganda Mentality with Respect to Possibilities of Acculturation in Christian Art*. Kampala: Osasa, 1970.
Lynch, John. "Generational Chronotypes and Accounting for Unethical Medicine: Bill Clinton's Apologies for Radiation Research and the Tuskegee Syphilis Study." *Quarterly Journal of Speech* 107 (2021) 284–304.
Ma, Wenjun. "Swine Influenza Virus: Current Status and Challenge." *Virus Research* 288 (2020). https://doi.org/10.1016/j.virusres.2020.198118.
MacIntyre, Alasdair. *After Virtue: A Study in Moral Theory*. 2nd ed. Notre Dame, IN: University of Notre Dame Press, 1981.
MacLean, Paul. *The Triune Brain in Evolution*. New York: Plenum, 1990.
Magesa, Laurenti. *African Religion: The Moral Traditions of Abundant Life*. Nairobi: Paulines Africa, 1998.
———. *What Is Not Sacred? African Spirituality*. Maryknoll, NY: Orbis, 2013.
Mair, L. P. *An African People in the Twentieth Century: A Study of the Influence of European Civilization on the Structure of African Society and of the Practical Lessons to Be Learnt in the Shaping of Colonial Policy*. London: Routledge and Sons, 1934.
———. "Baganda Land Tenure." *Africa* 6 (1933) 187–89.
Mandeville, Bernard. *The Fable of the Bees, or Private Vices, Publick Benefits*. Edited by F. B. Kaye. 2 vols. Indianapolis: Liberty Fund, 1988.
Maquet, Jacques. *Africanity: The Cultural Unity of Black Africa*. Translated by Joan R. Rayfield. Oxford: Oxford University Press, 1972.
Matevia, Marilyn. "Justice for All: Revisiting the Prospects for a Biocommunitarian Theory of Interspecies Justice." *Journal of International Wildlife Law and Policy* 19 (2016) 189–202.

Mayr, Ernst. *Systematics and the Origin of Species from the Viewpoint of a Zoologist*. New York: Columbia University Press, 1942.

Mbeki, Thabo. "Statement of Deputy President Thabo Mbeki, on Behalf of the African National Congress, on the Occasion of the Adoption of the Constitutional Assembly of the 'The Republic of South Africa Constitution Bill 1996': Cape Town, May 8, 1996." Justice and Constitutional Government, Republic of South Africa, May 8, 1996. https://justice.gov.za/constitution/history/MEDIA/ANC.PDF.

Mbih, Jerome Tosam. "The Philosophical Foundation of Kom Proverbs." *Journal on African Philosophy* 9 (2014) 1–27.

Mbiti, S. John. *African Religions and Philosophy*. London: Heinemann, 1969.

———. *Introduction to African Religion*. New York: Praeger, 1975.

———. "Der Tod in der afrikanischen Religion und Kultur." In *Der Tod in den Weltkulturen und Weltreligionen*, edited by Constantin von Barloewen, 195–218. Munich: Diederichs/Hugendubel, 1996.

———. "Wenn es Gott und den Wolken gefällt: Die Vielfalt der Religionen." In *Der bunte Kontinent: Ein neuer Blick auf Afrika*, edited by Christoph Plate and Sommer Theo, 49–57. Munich: DVA, 2001.

McCarthy, Joan. "Principlism or Narrative Ethics: Must We Choose between Them?" *Medical Humanities* 29 (2003) 65–71.

Melanchthon, Phillip. "De Divortio Henrici VIII." In *Corpus Reformatorum*, 527–38. Berlin: N.p., 1834.

Menkiti, Ifeanyi. "Normative Conception of a Person." In *A Companion to African Philosophy*, edited by Kwasi Wiredu, 324–31. Blackwell Companions to Philosophy. Oxford: Blackwell, 2004.

Menzel, Randolf. "Searching for the Memory Trace in a Mini-Brain." *Learning and Memory* 8 (2000) 53–62.

Menzel, Randolf, and Martin Giurfa. "Dimensions of Cognition in an Insect, the Honeybee." *Behavioral and Cognitive Neuroscience Review* 5 (2006) 24–40.

Menzel, Randolf, et al. "Honey Bees Navigate According to a Map-Like Spatial Memory." *Proceedings of the National Academy of Sciences* 102 (2005) 3040–45.

Merkies, Hubertus Cornelis Gerardus. *Ganda Classification: An Ethno-Semantic Survey*. Nijmegen: Catholic University of Nijmegen Press, 1980.

Metz, Thaddeus. "African and Western Moral Theories in a Bioethical Context." *Developing World Bioethics* 10 (2010) 49–58.

———. "An African Theory of Moral Status: A Relational Alternative to Individualism and Holism." *Ethical Theory and Moral Practice: An International Forum* 14 (2012) 387–402.

———. "Human Dignity, Capital Punishment, and an African Moral Theory: Toward a New Philosophy of Human Rights." *Journal of Human Rights* 9 (2010) 81–99.

———. "Toward an African Moral Theory." *Journal of Political Philosophy* 15 (2007) 321–41.

Miller, Tyler, and Scott E. Spoolman. *Environmental Science*. 13th ed. Belmont, CA: Brooks/Cole, 2010.

Mkhize, Nhlanhla. "Ubuntu-Botho Approach to Ethics: An Invitation to Dialogue." In *African Perspectives on Ethics for Healthcare Professionals*, edited by Nico Nortjé et al., 25–48. Advancing Global Bioethics 13. Berlin: Springer, 2018.

Molefe, Motsamai. *An African Philosophy of Personhood, Morality, and Politics*. New York: Palgrave Macmillan, 2019. https://doi.org/10.1007/978-3-030-15561-2.

———. "A Rejection of Humanism in African Moral Tradition." *Theoria* 62 (2015) 59–77.

———. "Solving the Conundrum of African Philosophy through Personhood: The Individual or Community?" *Journal of Value Inquiry* 54 (2019) 41–57. https://doi.org/10.1007/s10790-019-09683-8.

———. "Ubuntu and Development: An African Conception of Development." *Africa Today* 66 (2019) 96–115.

Morris, Christopher W. "The Idea of Moral Standing." In *The Oxford Handbook of Animal Ethics*, edited by Tom L. Beauchamp and R. G. Frey, 255–75. Oxford Handbooks. New York: Oxford University Press, 2011.

Moss, Cynthia J. *Elephant Memories: Thirteen Years in the Life of an Elephant Family*. 2nd ed. Chicago: University of Chicago Press, 2000.

Mudimbe, Valentin-Yves. "An African Practice of Philosophy: A Personal Testimony." *African Journal of Philosophy/Revue Africaine de Philosophie* 19 (2005) 21–36.

Mudimbe, V. Y. *The Invention of Africa: Gnosis, Philosophy, and the Order of Knowledge*. African Systems of Thought. London: Currey, 1988.

Mulago, Vincent. "Die lebensnotwendige Teilhabe: Bantu Strukturprinzipien der Gemeinschaft." In *Theologie und Kirche in Afrika*, edited by Horst Bürkle, 66–72. Stuttgart: Evangelisch, 1968.

———. *La religion traditionnelle des Bantu et leur vision du monde*. 2nd ed. Bibliothèque du Centre d'Etudes des Religions Africaines 5. Kinshasa: Catholic Theological Faculty Press, 1980.

———. "Symbolisme dans les religions traditionnelles et sacramentelisme." *Revue du Clergé Africain* 27 (1972) 467–502.

———. "L'union vitale chez les Bashi, les Banyarwanda et les Barundi face à l'unité vitale ecclésiale." PhD diss., Pontifical Urban University, 1955.

———. *Un visage africain du christianisme: L'union vitale bantu face à l'unité vitale ecclésiale*. Paris: Présence africaine, 1965.

Murove, Munyaradzi Felix. "The Shona Ethic of Ukama with Reference to the Immortality of Values." *Mankind Quarterly* 48 (2007) 179–89.

Murphy, John D. *Luganda-English Dictionary*. Washington, DC: Catholic University of American Press, 1972.

Mvuanda, Jean de Dieu Mubaki. *Inculturer pour évangéliser en profondeur: Des initiations traditionnelles africaines à une initiation chrétienne engageante*. Studien zur interkulturellen Geschichte des Christentums 101. Frankfurt am Main: Lang, 1998.

Naess, Arne. "The Shallow and the Deep, Long-Range Ecology Movement." *Inquiry* 16 (1973) 95–100.

Nalwamba, Kuzipa M. B., and Johan Buitendag. "Vital Force as a Triangulated Concept of Nature and S(s)pirit." *HvTSt* 73 (2017). https://doi.org/10.4102/hts.v73i3.4506.

Narveson, Jan. "A Defense of Meat Eating." In *Animal Rights and Human Obligations*, edited by Tom Regan and Peter Singer, 192–96. Englewood Cliffs, NJ: Prentice Hall, 1976.

Nason, C. S. "Proverbs of the Baganda." *Uganda Journal* 3 (1936) 247–58.

Ndeti, Kivuto. "The Relevance of African Traditional Medicine in Modern Medical Training and Practice." In *Cultures of the Future*, edited by Magoroh Maruyama and Arthur M. Harkins, 179–94. World Anthropology. Berlin: De Gruyter Mouton, 1978.

Ndjimbi-Tshiende, Olivier. *Reciprocité-cooperation et le système palabrique africain.* Brussels: Ottilien, 1992.

Ndombe, Cesar Mawanzi. *Das symbolische Denken als Schlüssel zum Verständnis der negro-afrikanischen (Bantu-) Weltanschauung: Eine religionsphilosophische Deutung im Anschluss an die Kulturphilosophie Ernst Cassirers.* Europäische Hochschulschriften. Frankfurt am Main: Lang, 2008.

Nnabagereka Development Foundation, and Jimmy Spire Ssentongo. *Obuntubulamu: The Moral Concept and Way of Life.* Kampala: Uganda Martyrs University Press, 2022.

Norton, Bryan G., ed. *The Preservation of Species: The Value of Biological Diversity.* Princeton Legacy Library. Princeton, NJ: Princeton University Press, 1986.

Nsimbi, Michael B. *Olulimi Oluganda* [Ganda language]. Kampala: Eagle, 1955.

Nussbaum, Martha C. "The Capabilities Approach and Animal Entitlements." In *The Oxford Handbook of Animal Ethics,* edited by Tom L. Beauchamp and R. G. Frey, 228–51. Oxford Handbooks. New York: Oxford University Press, 2011.

———. *Frontiers of Justice: Disability, Nationality, Species Membership.* Cambridge, MA: Harvard University Press, 2006.

Nyamiti, Charles. *Christ as Our Ancestor: Christology from an African Perspective.* Gweru, Zimb.: Mambo, 1984.

———. "Christ as Our Ancestor: More Details on Christ's Ancestorship, Part II." *Pastoral Orientation Service* 4–6 (1982) 1–20.

———. "Christology from an African Perspective, Part I." *Pastoral Orientation Service* 5 (1981) 8–29.

———. "Comparison between African Brother-Ancestorship and Christ's Relationship to Men." *Voices from the Third World* 8 (1985) 16–19.

Odozor, Paulinus Ikechukwu, CSSp. "An African Moral Theology of Inculturation: Methodological Considerations." *TS* 69 (2008) 583–609.

———. *Morality Truly Christian, Truly African: Foundational, Methodological, and Theological Considerations.* Notre Dame: University of Notre Dame Press, 2014.

Office of the High Commissioner for Human Rights. "Universal Declaration of Human Rights at 70: 30 Articles on 30 Articles—Article 16." United Nations Human Rights Office of the High Commissioner, Nov. 25, 2018. https://www.ohchr.org/en/press-releases/2018/11/universal-declaration-human-rights-70-30-articles-30-articles-article-16.

Office of the President. "National Unity and Reconciliation Act of the Republic of South Africa." *Government Gazette,* July 26, 1995. https://www.gov.za/sites/default/files/gcis_document/201409/act34of1995.pdf.

Ogungbemi, Segun. "An African Perspective on the Environmental Crisis." In *Environmental Ethics: Readings in Theory and Application,* edited by Louis J. Pojman, 330–37. 2nd ed. Belmont, CA: Wadsworth, 1997.

Olsen, Christopher W. "The Emergence of Novel Swine Influenza Viruses in North America." *Virus Research* 85 (2002) 199–210.

Onwubiko, Alozie Oliver. "Re-Encountering African Culture in Living Christianity in My Father's Home." *African Journal of Philosophy/Revue Africaine de Philosophie* 19 (2005) 91–108.

Opongo, Elias, SJ. "'Fratelli Tutti' and 'Ubuntu' on Cosmological Friendship." *Civiltà Cattolica* 6 (2021) 85–95. https://laciviltacattolica.com/wp-content/uploads/2022/04/La-Civilta-vol.-5-no.-06.pdf.

Organization of African Unity. *African Charter on Human and People's Rights*. African Union, June 1981. https://au.int/sites/default/files/treaties/36390-treaty-0011_-_african_charter_on_human_and_peoples_rights_e.pdf.

Orobator, Agbonkhianmeghe E., SJ. "*Caritas in Veritate* and Africa's Burden of (Under) Development." *TS* 71 (2010) 320–34.

———. "'*Fratelli Tutti*' Is Ubuntu by Any Other Name." *National Catholic Reporter*, Oct. 6, 2020. https://www.ncronline.org/opinion/guest-voices/fratelli-tutti-ubuntu-any-other-name.

———. "Ethics of HIV/AIDS Prevention: Paradigms of a New Discourse from an African Perspective." In *Applied Ethics in a World Church: The Padua Conference*, edited by Linda Hogan, 147–54. New York: Maryknoll, 2008.

———. *Religion and Faith in Africa: Confessions of an Animist*. Maryknoll, NY: Orbis, 2018.

———. *Theology Brewed in an African Pot: An Introduction to Christian Doctrine from an African Perspective*. Paulines Africa, 2009.

Panikkar, Raimon. "Śatapathaprajñâ: Should We Speak of Philosophy in Classical India? A Case of Homeomorphic Equivalents." In *Contemporary Philosophy: A New Survey 7*, edited by Guttorm Fløistad, 11–67. Netherlands: Kluwer Academic, 1993.

Pankratz, Loren. "Fire Walking and the Persistence of Charlatans." *Perspectives in Biology and Medicine* 31 (1998) 291–98.

Passino, Kevin M., and Thomas D. Seeley. "Modeling and Analysis of Nest-Site Selection by Honey Swarms: The Speed and Accuracy Trade-Off." *Behavioral Ecology and Sociology* 59 (2006) 427–42.

Passmore, John. *Man's Responsibility for Nature: Ecological Problems and Western Traditions*. New York: Scribner's Sons, 1974.

Patterson, Francine, and Wendy Gordon. "The Case for the Personhood of Gorillas." In *The Great Ape Project: Equality beyond Humanity*, edited by Paolo Cavalieri and Peter Singer, 58–77. New York: St. Martin's, 1993.

Paul VI, Pope. "Eucharistic Celebration at the Conclusion of the Symposium Organized by the Bishops of Africa." Vatican, July 31, 1969. https://www.vatican.va/content/paul-vi/en/homilies/1969/documents/hf_p-vi_hom_19690731.html.

———. "*Humanae Vitae*: On the Regulation of Birth." Vatican, July 25, 1968. https://www.vatican.va/content/paul-vi/en/encyclicals/documents/hf_p-vi_enc_25071968_humanae-vitae.html.

———. "*Populorum Progressio*: On the Development of Peoples." Vatican, Mar. 26, 1967. https://www.vatican.va/content/paul-vi/en/encyclicals/documents/hf_p-vi_enc_26031967_populorum.html.

Payne, Katy. "Sources of Social Complexity in Three Elephant Species." In *Animal Social Complexity: Intelligence, Culture, and Individualized Societies*, edited by Frans B. M. de Waal and Peter L. Tyack, 57–86. Cambridge, MA: Harvard University Press, 2000.

P'Bitek, Okot. *Africa's Cultural Revolution*. Nairobi: Macmillan, 1973.

Pentin, Edward. "Pope's New Encyclical 'Fratelli Tutti' Outlines Vision for a Better World." *National Catholic Register*, Oct. 4, 2020. https://www.ncregister.com/news/pope-s-new-encyclical-fratelli-tutti-outlines-vision-for-a-better-world.

Phillips, Steven, et al. "What Do Transitive Inference and Class Inclusion Have in Common? Categorical (Co)Products and Cognitive Development." *PLOS*

Computational Biology 5 (2009) e1000599. https://doi.org/10.1371/journal.pcbi.1000599.

Phiri, Isabel A. "Why Does God Allow Our Husbands to Hurt Us? Overcoming Violence against Women." *Journal of Theology for Southern Africa* 114 (2020) 10–30.

Pimm, Stuart L., and Robert Leo Smith. "Ecology." *Britannica*, last updated Aug. 9, 2024. https://www.britannica.com/science/ecology.

Pius IX, Pope. *The Raccolta; or, Collection of Prayers and Good Works, to Which the Sovereign Pontiffs Have Attached Holy Indulgences*. Woodstock, MD: Woodstock College Press, 1878.

Plato. *Platonis Opera*. Edited by John Burnet. London: Oxford University Press, 1903.

Plotnik, Joshua M., et al. "Self-Recognition in [the] Asian Elephant." *Proceedings of the National Academy of Sciences of the United States of America* 103 (2006) 17053–57.

Pluhar, Evelyn B. *Beyond Prejudice: The Moral Significance of Human and Nonhuman Animals*. Durham, NC: Duke University Press, 1995.

Plutarch. "Beasts Are Rational." In *Moralia*, translated by Harold Cherniss and William C. Helmbold, 12:492–531. LCL. London: Heinemann, 1957.

———. "The Cleverness of Animals." In *Moralia*, translated by Harold Cherniss and William C. Helmbold, 12:309–491. LCL. London: Heinemann, 1957.

———. "On Affection for Offspring." In *Moralia*, translated by Frank Cole Babbitt, 6:328–57. LCL. London: Heinemann, 1939.

Pontifical Council for Justice and Peace. "Compendium of the Social Doctrine of the Church." Vatican, 2004. https://www.vatican.va/roman_curia/pontifical_councils/justpeace/documents/rc_pc_justpeace_doc_20060526_compendio-dott-soc_en.html.

Porphyry. *On Abstinence from Killing Animals*. Translated by Gillian Clark. Ancient Commentators on Aristotle. London: Duckworth, 2000.

Portuguese Bishops' Conference. "Responsabilidade solidária pelo bem comum." Conferencia Episcopal, Apr. 3, 2006. https://www.conferenciaepiscopal.pt/v1/responsabilidade-solidaria-pelo-bem-comum/.

Powell, Russell. "On the Nature of Species and the Moral Significance of Their Extinction." In *The Oxford Handbook of Animal Ethics*, edited by Tom L. Beauchamp and R. G. Frey, 603–27. Oxford Handbooks. New York: Oxford University Press, 2011.

Powers, Madison, and Ruth Faden. *Social Justice: The Moral Foundation of Public Health and Health Policy*. Issues in Biomedical Ethics. Oxford: Oxford University Press, 2006.

Raffaele, Paul. "Speaking Bonobo: Bonobos Have an Impressive Vocabulary, Especially When It Comes to Snacks." *Smithsonian*, Nov. 2006. https://www.smithsonianmag.com/science-nature/speaking-bonobo-134931541/.

Ramseyer, A., et al. "Accepting Loss: The Temporal Limits of Reciprocity in Brown Capuchin Monkeys." *Proceedings of the Royal Society B* 2731(2006) 179–84.

Rahner, Karl. *The Church and the Sacraments*. Translated by W. J. O'Hara. New York: Herder and Herder, 1963.

———. *Kleines Kirchenjahr: Ein Gang durch den Festkreis*. Freiburg: Herder, 1981.

———. *Meditations on the Sacraments*. New York: Seabury, 1977.

Randall, Alan. "Human Preferences, Economics, and the Preservation of Species." In *The Preservation of Species: The Value of Biological Diversity*, edited by Bryan G. Norton, 79–109. Princeton Legacy Library. Princeton, NJ: Princeton University Press, 1986.

Rawls, John. *Political Liberalism*. Columbia Classics in Philosophy. New York: Columbia University Press, 1993.
Raz, Joseph. *The Morality of Freedom*. Oxford: Oxford University Press, 1986.
Reagan, Donald H. "Duties of Preservation." In *The Preservation of Species: The Value of Biological Diversity*, edited by Bryan G. Norton, 195–220. Princeton Legacy Library. Princeton, NJ: Princeton University Press, 1986.
Regan, Tom. *The Case for Animal Rights*. Los Angeles: University of California Press, 1983.
Reiss, Diana, and Lori Marino. "Mirror Self-Recognition in the Bottlenose Dolphins: A Case of Cognitive Convergence." *Proceedings of the National Academy of Sciences of the United States of America* 98 (2001) 5937–42.
Rescorla, Michael. "Cognitive Maps and the Language of Thought." *British Journal for the Philosophy of Science* 60 (2009) 377–407.
Rheeder, Riaan. "Solidarity as a Global Bioethical Principle: Own Reasons for a Culture of Solidarity from a Protestant Perspective." *Verbum et Ecclesia* 39 (2018) a1816. https://doi.org/10.4102/ve.v39i1.1816.
Richards, Audrey I. *East African Chiefs: A Study of Political Development in Some Uganda and Tanganyika Tribes*. London: Faber & Faber for the East African Institute of Social Research, 1960.
Richardson, Henry. "Specifying, Balancing, and Interpreting Bioethical Principles." *Journal of Medicine and Philosophy* 25 (2000) 285–307.
Rickert, Heinrich. *Kulturwissenschaft und Naturwissenschaft*. Tübingen: Mohr, 1910.
Roberts, William. "Are Animals Stuck in Time?" *Psychological Bulletin* 128 (2002) 473–89.
Rolston, Holmes, III. *Environmental Ethics: Duties to and Values in the Natural World*. Philadelphia: Temple University Press, 1988.
———. "Is There an Ecological Ethic?" *Ethics* 85 (1975) 93–109.
———. "Values in Nature." *Environmental Ethics* 3 (1981) 113–28.
Romanes, George. *Animal Intelligence*. London: Kegan Paul, 1882.
———. *Mental Evolution in Animals*. London: Kegan Paul, 1885.
Roscoe, John. *The Baganda: An Account of Their Native Customs and Beliefs*. 2nd ed. London: Cass, 1965.
Rothman, David J. "Were Tuskegee and Willowbrook 'Studies in Nature'?" *Hastings Center Report* 12 (1982) 5–7.
Rowlands, Mark. *Animal Rights: A Philosophical Defence*. Basingstoke: Macmillan, 1998.
———. *Animals Like Us*. London: Verso, 2002.
———. "Animals That Act for Moral Reasons." In *The Oxford Handbook of Animal Ethics*, edited by Tom L. Beauchamp and R. G. Frey, 519–46. Oxford Handbooks. New York: Oxford University Press, 2011.
———. "Contractarianism and Animal Rights." *Journal of Applied Philosophy* 14 (1997) 235–47.
Ruch, Ernest Albert, and K. C. Anyanwu. *African Philosophy: An Introduction to the Main Philosophical Trends in Contemporary Africa*. Rome: Catholic, 1981.
Rwiza, Richard N. *Environmental Ethics in the African Context*. Nairobi: CUEA Press, 2021.

———. "Opportunities for Reconciliation in Africa." In *Practicing Reconciliation, Doing Justice, Building Peace: Conversation on Catholic Theological Ethics in Africa*, edited by Agbonkhianmeghe E. Orobator, 30–37. Nairobi: Paulines Africa, 2013.

Sakupapa, Teddy Chalwe. "Spirit and Ecology in the Context of African Theology." *Scriptura* 3 (2012) 422–30.

Sapontzis, S. F. *Morals, Reason, and Animals*. Philadelphia: Temple University Press, 1987.

Savage-Rumbaugh, Sue, and Roger Lewin. *Kanzi: The Ape at the Brink of the Human Mind*. New York: Wiley and Sons, 1994.

Schmidtz, David. "Are All Species Equal?" In *The Oxford Handbook of Animal Ethics*, edited by Tom L. Beauchamp and R. G. Frey, 628–40. Oxford Handbooks. New York: Oxford University Press, 2011.

Second Special Assembly for Africa of the Synod of Bishops. "Message to the People of God." Vatican, Oct. 23, 2009. https://www.vatican.va/roman_curia/synod/documents/rc_synod_doc_20091023_message-synod_en.html.

Second Vatican Council. "*Gaudium et Spes*: Pastoral Constitution on the Church in the Modern World." Vatican, Dec. 7, 1965. https://www.vatican.va/archive/hist_councils/ii_vatican_council/documents/vat-ii_cons_19651207_gaudium-et-spes_en.html.

Seeley, Thomas D. "Consensus Building during Nest-Site Selection in Honey Bee Swarms: The Expiration of Dissent." *Behavioral Ecology and Sociology* 53 (2003) 417–24.

———. "Division of Labour between Scouts and Recruits in Honeybee Foraging." *Behavioral Ecology and Sociobiology* 12 (1983) 253–59.

———. "Honey Bee Colonies Are Group-Level Adaptive Units." *American Naturalist* 150 (1997) 22–41.

———. "Social Foraging by Honeybees: How Colonies Allocate Foragers Among Patches of Flowers." *Behavioral Ecology and Sociobiology* 19 (1986) 343–54.

———. "The Tremble Dance of the Honey Bee: Message and Meanings." *Behavioral Ecology and Sociobiology* 31 (1992) 375–83.

———. *The Wisdom of the Hive: The Social Physiology of Honey Bee Colonies*. Cambridge, MA: Harvard University Press, 1995.

Seeley, Thomas D., and Susannah C. Buhrman. "Nest-Site Selection in Honey Bees: How Well Do Swarms Implement the 'Best-of-N' Decision Rule?" *Behavioral Ecology and Sociobiology* 49 (2001) 416–27.

Seeley, Thomas D., and William F. Towne. "Tactics of Dance Choice in Honey Bees: Do Foragers Compare Dances?" *Behavioral Ecology and Sociobiology* 30 (1992) 59–69.

Seeley, Thomas D., and P. Kirk Visscher. "Choosing a Home: How the Scouts in a Honey Bee Swarm Perceive the Completion of Their Group Decision Making." *Behavioral Ecology and Sociobiology* 54 (2003) 511–20.

Seeley, Thomas D., et al. "Collective Decision-Making in Honey Bees: How Colonies Choose among Nectar Sources." *Behavioral Ecology and Sociobiology* 28 (1991) 277–90.

Sekadde, Y. Ssaalongo, and Yosamu Semugoma. *Ndi-mugezi: Kitabo kya ngero za Luganda* (I am wise: Ganda proverbs). London: Macmillan, 1952.

Sempebwa, Joshua Wantate. *The Ontological and Normative Structure in the Social Reality of a Bantu Society: A Systematic Study of Ganda Ontology and Ethics.* Heidelberg: Ruprecht Karl University Press, 1978.

Setiloane, Gabriel M. "Towards a Biocentric Theology and Ethic—via Africa." In *Faith, Science, and African Culture: African Cosmology and Africa's Contribution to Science; Proceedings of the Fifth Seminar of the South African Science and Religion Forum (SASRF) of the Research Institute for Theology and Religion, Held at Unisa on 29 & 30 May 1997,* edited by C. W. du Toit, 73–84. Pretoria: Research Institute for Theology and Religion, 1998.

Sheets-Johnstone, Maxine. "Taking Evolution Seriously." *American Philosophical Quarterly* 29 (1992) 343–52.

Shutte, Augustine. *Ubuntu: An Ethic for the New South Africa.* Cape Town: Cluster, 2001.

Siegal, Gil, and Richard J. Bonnie. "Closing the Organ Gap: A Reciprocity-Based Social Contract Approach." *Journal of Law, Medicine, and Ethics* 34 (2006) 415–23.

Sindima, Harvey. "Community of Life." *Ecumenical Review* 41(1989) 537–51.

———. "Community of Life: Ecological Theology in African Perspective." In *Liberating Life: Contemporary Approaches in Ecological Theology,* edited by Charles Birch et al., 137–47. Maryknoll, NY: Orbis, 1990.

———. *Religious and Political Ethics in Africa: A Moral Inquiry.* London: Greenwood, 1998.

Singer, Peter. *Animal Liberation.* New York: Avon, 1975.

———. "Ethics." *Britannica,* last updated Aug. 5, 2024. https://www.britannica.com/topic/ethics-philosophy.

———. *Practical Ethics.* Cambridge: Cambridge University Press, 1993.

Singer, Peter, and Jim Mason. *The Ethics of What We Eat: Why Our Food Choices Matter.* Emmaus, PA: Rodale, 2006.

Smith, J. David. "The Study of Animal Metacognition." *Trends in Cognitive Science* 13 (2009) 389–90.

Sober, Elliot. "Comparative Psychology Meets Evolutionary Biology: Morgan's Canon and Cladistic Parsimony." In *Thinking with Animals: New Perspectives on Anthropomorphism,* edited by Lorraine Daston and Gregg Mitman, 85–99. New York: Columbia University Press, 2005.

Spiegelman, Willard. *Imaginative Transcripts: Selected Literary Essays.* London: Oxford University Press, 2009.

Ssejjoba, Eddie. "Ugandan Migrant Worker Loses Kidney in Jeddah, Saudi Arabia." *New Vision,* Kampala, Jan. 30, 2022. https://www.newvision.co.ug/category/news/ugandan-migrant-worker-loses-kidney-in-jeddah-NV_125732.

Ssemwogerere, Timony M., ed. *Katekismu ya Mapeera.* [Catechism of Rev. Fr. Lourdel Mourpel.] Kampala: N.p., 1983.

Stapleton, Timothy J. *A History of Genocide in Africa.* Santa Barbara, CA: Praeger Security International, 2017.

Steiner, Gary. *Animals and the Moral Community: Mental Life, Moral Status, and Kinship.* New York: Columbia University Press, 2008.

Stone, Christopher D. "Should Trees Have Standing? Toward Legal Rights for Natural Objects." *Southern California Law Review* 45 (1972) 450–501.

Strong, Carson. "Critiques of Casuistry and Why They Are Mistaken." *Theoretical Medicine and Bioethics* 20 (1999) 395–411.

———. "The Moral Status of Preembryos, Embryos, Fetuses, and Infants." *Journal of Medicine and Philosophy* 22 (1997) 457–78.
———. "Theoretical and Practical Problems with Wide Reflective Equilibrium in Bioethics." *Theoretical Medicine and Bioethics* 31 (2010) 123–40.
Sundermeier, Theo. *Nur gemeinsam können wir leben: Das Menschenbild Schwarz-Afrikanischer Religionen*. Munich: Mohn, 1990.
Tadjo, Véronique. "Lifting the Cloak of (In)visibility: A Writer's Perspective." *Research in African Literatures* 44 (2013) 1–7.
———. *The Shadow of Imana: Travels in the Heart of Rwanda*. Translated by Véronique Wakerley. Portsmouth, NH: Heinemann, 2002.
Takacs, David. *The Idea of Biodiversity: Philosophies of Paradise*. Baltimore, MD: John Hopkins University Press, 1996.
Tangwa, Godfrey B. *African Perspectives on Some Contemporary Bioethics Problems*. Newcastle upon Tyne, UK: Cambridge Scholars, 2019.
———. "Bioethics: An African Perspective." *Bioethics* 10 (1996) 183–200.
———. "Cameroon." In *Handbook of Global Bioethics*, edited by Henk A. M. J. ten Have and Bert Gordijn, 941–58. Springer Reference. Dordrecht: Springer, 2014.
———. *Elements of African Bioethics in a Western Frame*. Bamenda, Cmr.: Langaa, 2010.
———. "Ethical Principles in Health Research and Review Process." Supplement, *Acta Tropica* 112 (2009) S2–S7.
———. "Ethics Committees: Moral Agency, Moral Worth and the Question of Double Standards in Medical Research in Developing Countries." *Developing World Bioethics* 1 (2001) 156–62.
———. "Giving Voice to African Thought in Medical Research Ethics." *Theoretical Medicine and Bioethics* 38 (2017) 101–10.
———. "Global Health Inequalities and the Need for Solidarity: A View from the Global South." *Developing World Bioethics* 18 (2018) 241–49.
———. "The HIV/AIDS Pandemic, African Traditional Values and the Search for a Vaccine in Africa." *Journal of Medical Philosophy* 27 (2002) 217–30.
———. "How Not to Compare Western Scientific Medicine with African Traditional Medicine." *Developing World Bioethics* 7 (2007) 41–44.
———. "International Regulations and Medical Research in Developing Countries: Double Standards or Differing Standards?" *Notizie di Politeia* 18 (2002) 46–50.
———. "Leaders in Ethics Education: Godfrey B. Tangwa." *International Journal of Ethics Education* 1 (2016) 91–105.
———. "Moral Agency, Moral Worth and the Question of Double Standards in Medical Research in Developing Countries." *Developing World Bioethics* 1 (2001) 156–62. https://doi.org/10.1111/1471-8847.00022.
———. Review of *Global Bioethics: An Introduction*, by Henk ten Have. *Developing World Bioethics* 18 (2018) 268–70.
———. "Some African Reflections on Biomedical and Environmental Ethics." In *A Companion to African Philosophy*, edited by Kwasi Wiredu, 387–95. Blackwell Companions to Philosophy. Oxford: Blackwell, 2004.
———. "Third Party Assisted Conception: An African Perspective." *Theoretical Medicine and Bioethics* 29 (2008) 297–306.
———. "The Traditional African Perception of a Person: Some Implications for Bioethics." *Hastings Center Report* 30 (2000) 39–43.

———. "Vulnerable Human Beings." Supplement, *Acta Tropica* 112 (2009) S16–S20.
Taylor, Paul W. *Respect for Nature: A Theory of Environmental Ethics*. Studies in Moral, Political, and Legal Philosophy. Princeton, NJ: Princeton University Press, 1986.
———. "The Ethics of Respect for Nature." *Environmental Ethics* 5 (1981) 197–218.
Tempels, Placide Frans. *Bantu-Philosophie: Ontologie und Ethik*. Translated by Joseph Peters. Heidelberg: Rothe, 1956.
Ten Have, Henk. *Global Bioethics: An Introduction*. London: Routledge, 2016.
———. "Global Bioethics: Transnational Experiences and Islamic Bioethics." *Zygon* 48 (2013) 600–17.
Ten Have, Henk, and Michèle S. Jean. "Introduction." In *The UNESCO Universal Declaration on Bioethics and Human Rights: Background, Principles and Application*, edited by Henk ten Have and Michèle S. Jean, 17–57. Ethics. Paris: UNESCO, 2009.
Tham, Joseph. "Introduction: The Principle of Vulnerability; Meeting Ground of Six Religions." In *Religious Perspectives on Human Vulnerability in Bioethics*, edited by Joseph Tham et al., 1–7. Advancing Global Bioethics 2. Dordrecht: Springer, 2014.
Thelen, Esther, and Linda B. Smith. *A Dynamic Systems Approach to the Development of Cognition and Action*. Cognitive Psychology. Cambridge, MA: MIT Press, 1994.
Thom, Corinna, et al. "A Scientific Note on the Dynamics of Labor Devoted to Nectar Foraging in a Honey Bee Colony: Number of Foragers versus Individual Foraging Activity." *Apidologie* 31 (2000) 737–38.
Tiemessen, Erin Alana. "After Arusha: Gacaca Justice in Post-Genocide Rwanda." *African Studies Quarterly* 8 (2004) 57–76.
Tokumboh, Adeyemo. *Salvation in African Tradition*. Nairobi: Evangel, 1979.
Tomasello, Michael, and Josep Call. *Primate Cognition*. Oxford: Oxford University Press, 1997.
Tooley, Michael. "Are Nonhuman Animals Persons?" In *The Oxford Handbook of Animal Ethics*, edited by Tom L. Beauchamp and R. G. Frey, 332–70. Oxford Handbooks. New York: Oxford University Press, 2011.
Tossu, Kossi J. "Afrikanische Symbolwelt und Theologie." *Wirklichkeit und Theologie* 36 (1988) 41–59.
Toulmin, Stephen. "How Medicine Saved the Life of Ethics." *Perspectives in Biology and Medicine* 25 (1982) 736–50.
Tutu, Desmond. *No Future without Forgiveness*. London: Rider, 1999.
Tye, Michael. *Consciousness, Color, and Content*. Cambridge, MA: MIT Press, 2000.
UNC Research. "Nuremberg Code." UNC Research, n.d. https://research.unc.edu/human-research-ethics/resources/ccm3_019064/.
UNESCO. *Bioethics Core Curriculum, Section 1: Syllabus Ethics Education Programme*. Paris: UNESCO, 2008. http://unesdoc.unesco.org/images/0016/001636/163613e.pdf.
———. *Records of the General Conference: 33rd Session, Paris, 3–21 October 2005*. 2 vols. Paris: UNESCO, 2005. http://unesdoc.unesco.org/images/0014/001428/142825e.pdf.
———. *Universal Declaration on Bioethics and Human Rights*. Paris: UNESCO, 2006. https://unesdoc.unesco.org/ark:/48223/pf0000146180.
UNESCO Chair in Bioethics (Haifa). *Casebook on Bioethics for Judges*. Haifa: Israel National Commission for UNESCO, 2016. https://old.volgmed.ru/uploads/files/2017-4/68929-casebook_on_bioethics_for_judges.pdf.

United Nations. "The International Day of Human Fraternity." UNAOC, Feb. 4, 2022. https://www.unaoc.org/event/the-international-day-of-human-fraternity/.

United States Conference of Catholic Bishops. *Open Wide Our Hearts: The Enduring Call to Love; A Pastoral Letter against Racism.* Washington, DC: USCCB, 2018. https://www.usccb.org/issues-and-action/human-life-and-dignity/racism/upload/open-wide-our-hearts.pdf.

Van Binsbergen, Wim M. J. "The Roman Catholic Church, and the Hermeneutics of Race, as Two Contexts for African Philosophy." *African Journal of Philosophy/Revue Africaine de Philosophie* 19 (2005) 3–19.

Van Gelder, Tim. "What Might Cognition Be, If Not Computation?" *Journal of Philosophy* 92 (1995) 345–81.

Van Rinsum, Henk J., and Godfrey B. Tangwa. "Colony of Genes, Genes of the Colony: Diversity, Difference and Divide." *Third World Quarterly* 25 (2004) 1031–43.

Vatican. *Catechism of the Catholic Church.* Vatican, 1993. https://www.vatican.va/archive/ENG0015/_INDEX.HTM#fonte.

Vatican News Staff Writer. "UN Declares 4 February 'International Day of Human Fraternity.'" *Vatican News,* Dec. 24, 2020. https://www.vaticannews.va/en/world/news/2020-12/united-nations-institutes-international-day-human-fraternity.html.

Vicini, Andrea. "Bioethics: Basic Questions and Extraordinary Developments." *TS* 73 (2012) 169–87.

Virgil. *Aeneid.* Translated by Theodore C. Williams. Boston: Houghton Mifflin, 1910.

Wangari, Maathai. *Replenishing the Earth: Spiritual Values for Healing Ourselves and the World.* New York: Doubleday, 2010.

———. *Unbowed: One Woman's Story.* London: Heinemann, 2006.

Warren, Mary Anne. *Moral Status: Obligations to Persons and Other Living Things.* Issues in Biomedical Ethics. New York: Clarendon, 1997.

Watanabe, Shigeru, and Ludwig Huber. "Animal Logics: Decisions in the Absence of Human Language." *Animal Cognition* 9 (2006) 235–45.

Weir, Alex, A. S., and Alex Kacelnik. "Shaping of Hooks in New Caledonian Crow (*Corvus moneduloides*) Creatively Re-Designs Tools by Bending or Unbending Aluminum Strips." *Animal Cognition* 9 (2006) 317–34.

Wenders, Wim, dir. *Pope Francis: A Man of His Word.* Universal City, CA: Focus, 2018.

West, H. W. *The Mailo System in Buganda: A Preliminary Case Study in African Land Tenure.* Entebbe, Ug.: Government, 1964.

Wharton, David. "*Sunt Lacrimae Rerum*: An Exploration in Meaning." *Classical Journal* 103 (2008) 259–79.

White, Christopher. "'Synodal Spirit Is Alive in Africa,' Say Speakers at Major Theological Summit." *National Catholic Reporter,* Aug. 11, 2022. https://www.ncronline.org/news/synodal-spirit-alive-africa-say-speakers-major-theological-summit.

White, Lynn, Jr. "The Historical Roots of Our Ecologic Crisis." *Science* 155 (1967) 1203–7.

WHO. "H5N1 Highly Pathogenic Avian Influenza: Timeline of Major Events." WHO, Dec. 4, 2014. https://www.who.int/publications/m/item/influenza-a(h5n1)-highly-pathogenic-avian-influenza-timeline-of-major-events.

Winfield, Nicole. "What's in a Name? At the Vatican, a Debate on Inclusiveness." *Crux,* Sept. 17, 2020. https://cruxnow.com/vatican/2020/09/whats-in-a-name-at-the-vatican-a-debate-on-inclusiveness.

"Dr. Buyondo's deep explorations of the worldviews of his Black African ancestors yield a profoundly expansive vision. It offers both an invitation for creative dialogues between diverse cultural systems and potent challenges to the worldview we call 'modern.' His holistic bioethics may provide a therapeutic corrective to the deficiencies of our troubled world; in doing so, this work furthers the development of a truly global culture."

—NEIL THEISE,
professor of pathology, NYU Grossman School of Medicine

"This is a particularly important book for understanding the integrity of human beings and the ethical questions in the field of bioethics in a globalized world. It is about the comparison between African and European thinking. A holistic bioethical perspective. A very readable book."

—MATTHIAS BECK, MD,
professor of medical ethics, University of Vienna, Austria

"This is a wonderful book that will serve as a guide for understanding what ethics from a whole person perspective really means. It is easy to read, informative, and inspiring. I highly recommend the book to all those in the ethics field."

—HAROLD G. KOENIG, MD,
professor of psychiatry and behavioral sciences,
Duke University Medical Center

"Drawing from his roots in Africa, Dr. Buyondo invites us to envision a world shaped by deep bonds of solidarity, not only between human beings but also between humans and other nonhuman forms of life and realities. We badly need such a fresh vision of global solidarity and scholars, like Jude, who know how to articulate it."

—EMMANUEL KATONGOLE,
professor of theology and peace studies, University of Notre Dame

"Jude Buyondo presents a profound critique of Western principle-based ethics—not by neglecting its basic values but by broadening the perspective. He convincingly integrates the African experiences and value systems without giving up on the western concept of the dignity and the rights of the individual person. By presenting the relational interconnectedness of all living beings as fundamental basis for any ethic, this important theological study can serve as an eye opener for Western and African ethicists alike."

—GUNTER PRUELLER-JAGENTEUFEL,
associate professor of theological ethics, University of Vienna, Austria

"This fascinating book offers a fresh contribution to global bioethics from the perspective of African moral thought. Buyondo skillfully integrates the latest findings of modern science, Western ethical reflection, and African religious and moral life. The concept of the interconnectedness of life grounds his idea of holistic solidarity. Particularly remarkable is the extension of the moral community not only to other living and non-living creatures but also to human ancestors and future generations. A very inspiring and thought-provoking work."

—ROMAN GLOBOKAR,
associate professor of theological ethics,
University of Ljubljana, Slovenia

Wiredu, Kwasi. *Cultural Universals and Particulars: An African Perspective*. Indianapolis: Indiana University Press, 1996.

———. "Introduction: African Philosophy in Our Time." In *A Companion to African Philosophy*, edited by Kwasi Wiredu, 1–27. Blackwell Companions to Philosophy. Oxford: Blackwell, 2004.

———. "Moral Foundations of an African Culture." In *Person and Community*, edited by Kwasi Wiredu and Kwame Gyekye, 192–206. Vol. 1 of *Cultural Heritage and Contemporary Change*, 2nd ser., *Africa*. Ghanaian Philosophical Studies 1. Washington, DC: Council for Research in Values and Philosophy, 1992.

———. "An Oral Philosophy of Personhood: Comments on Philosophy and Orality." *Research In African Literatures* 40 (2009) 8–18.

———. "Reply to English/Hamme." *Journal of Social Philosophy* 27 (1996) 234–43.

———. "Social Philosophy in Postcolonial Africa: Some Preliminaries Concerning Communalism and Communitarianism." *South African Journal of Philosophy* 27 (2008) 332–39.

Wittgenstein, Ludwig. *Philosophical Investigations*. Translated by G. E. M. Anscombe. Oxford: Blackwell, 1953.

Wojtyła, Karol. *Love and Responsibility*. London: Collins, 1982.

World Commission on the Ethics of Scientific Knowledge and Technology [COMEST]. *The Precautionary Principle*. Paris: UNESCO, 2005. https://unesdoc.unesco.org/ark:/48223/pf0000139578.locale=en.

World Health Summit. "World Health Summit Regional Meeting 2021—Uganda, Kampala & Digital." World Health Summit, 2021. https://www.worldhealthsummit.org/regional-meeting/2021-uganda.html.

Xing, Lei, et al. "Expression of Human-Specific *ARHGAP11B* in Mice Leads to Neocortex Expansion and Increased Memory Flexibility." *European Molecular Biology Organization Journal* 40 (2021) e107093. https://doi.org/10.15252/embj.2020107093.

Yoder, P. Stanley, and Shane Khan. *Numbers of Women Circumcised in Africa: The Production of a Total*. DHS, 2008. Demographic and Health Research Working Paper 39. https://dhsprogram.com/pubs/pdf/WP39/WP39.pdf.

Zawidzki, Tadeus. "The Function of Folk Psychology: Mind Reading or Mind Shaping?" *Philosophical Explorations* 11 (2008) 193–210.

Zhang, S. W., et al. "Maze Learning by Honeybees." *Neurobiology Learning and Memory* 66 (1996) 267–82.

www.ingramcontent.com/pod-product-compliance
Lightning Source LLC
Chambersburg PA
CBHW050849230426
43667CB00012B/2218